# JAPAN: RESTLESS COMPETITOR

# Japan: Restless Competitor

## THE PURSUIT OF ECONOMIC NATIONALISM

Malcolm Trevor

JAPAN
LIBRARY

Japan: Restless Competitor

First published 2001 by
Japan Library

*Japan Library is an imprint of Curzon Press Ltd
Richmond, Surrey*

© Malcolm Trevor 2001

All rights reserved. No part of this publication
may be reproduced, stored in a retrieval system, or
transmitted in any form or by any means,
without prior permission from the Publishers in writing
except for the use of short extracts in criticism.

**British Library Cataloguing in Publication Data**
A CIP catalogue entry for this book is
available from the British Library

ISBN 1-903350-02-6

Typeset in Stone 9¼pt on 11 by Mark Heslington, Scarborough, North Yorkshire

# Contents

| | |
|---|---|
| *Preface by James Moorhouse MEP* | *vii* |
| *Introduction* | *ix* |
| 1. A Crisis of Confidence | 1 |
| 2. Myths and Realities | 42 |
| 3. A 'New' Japan? | 75 |
| 4. Power Holders – The Iron Triangle | |
|     i.  The bureaucrats: policy-makers and regulators | 137 |
|     ii.  Big business: work as national service | 161 |
|     iii.  The politicians: smoke-filled backrooms | 180 |
| 5. Will It Ever Change? | 210 |
| *Figure: Yen to the dollar 1949 to 2000* | *230* |
| *Japanese Terms* | *231* |
| *References* | *233* |
| *Bibliography* | *261* |
| *Index* | *269* |

# Preface

Dr Malcolm Trevor has had a long and distinguished career. I first met him when I was in Tokyo as a member of a European Parliament delegation and he was the European General Manager for the EU-Japan Centre for Industrial Cooperation. This was a post that gave him a close insight into the political and business outlook of our Japanese friends and I believe his comprehensive account deserves to be relayed to a much wider audience.

It carries a message which any wise foreign businessman seeking to win out in Japan would be wise to take on board. Inevitably, people from outside Japan will have a range of impressions. But there can be no getting away from the fact that the climate of opinion in Japan is very different from that in, say, Western Europe or North America. The Japanese have a large population for the size of their islands and their culture has remained largely unchanged over the years. At the same time, their politico-economic system is quite different from Adam Smith's concept and any foreigner who has had to make a living in Japan is made quickly aware of that. Efforts by outsiders to alter the equation have to a very large extent been resisted, though it is just possible that the current financial crisis is beginning to rock the previously solid state of Japan.

As a Member of the European Parliament from 1979 to 1999, and as the Rapporteur for the Parliament for most of that period on trade and economic relations between the EU and Japan, I warmly recommend this book which is a truly remarkable piece of work, reflecting as it does the personal experience of Dr Trevor, both in Europe and Japan, and his skilful comparison of the two systems which are not readily compatible.

*James Moorhouse, MEP 1979-1999*

# Introduction: Japan's Economic Nationalism

Soon after arriving in Japan for the first time in late 1962, I was introduced to an old English teacher and long-term resident in the country. For something to say, I remarked that he must have seen many changes. 'Nothing's changed', he replied. Obviously he found the question on the part of a newcomer naïve, though I was not in fact new to Asia.

To know whether or how far Japan has changed from its recent past, or even a more distant past, is something that anyone engaged in business or political relations and negotiations with the Japanese needs to know. Without such knowledge they will be easily misled and will risk making mistakes that will be hard to put right, with all that this implies for their organizations and themselves.

The problem concerns both the complex interrelations of political and business relations on the Japanese side and our own shortcomings in terms of awareness of what is at stake. Consequently this book concentrates on six main points:-

[1] That in talking about Japanese business activity, we are not simply dealing with a free market or private enterprise economic system but with a politico-economic system in which business and politics are inseparable. The building industry cartel, employing eleven per cent of all employees, which rigs bids among its members, funnels large sums of money to politicians and several of whose top managers are related by marriage with leading political figures, is one such example.[1] Most people had little difficulty in recognizing that in the former USSR trade, or business, was subservient to political aims but, while the Japanese system is not the same, despite certain similarities, a surprising number of people still believe that Japanese business and politics are quite separate.

[2] That Japan's problems after the bursting of the 'bubble economy' and the banking crisis are again leading people who should know better to underestimate its resilience and the other strengths it has. Japan will be back. Equally it should not be overestimated, as it was only a few years ago.

[3] That in Europe, USA and elsewhere there is still a dangerous ignorance of the realities of Japan's politico-economic system and how it operates, especially at the top decision making levels. This is despite the progressive penetration of European, American and world markets since the 1960s and the increase in overall Japanese economic control through their share of export markets and direct investment in manufacturing and services internationally.

[4] That images of Japan as a representative parliamentary democracy, with an 'internationalist' foreign policy, are considerably exaggerated – (how long does it take for parliamentary democracy to take root against a background of authoritarian rule stretching back over the centuries?) This particularly applies to images fostered by Japanese officials for foreign consumption and those with either a fleeting experience on short trips, or most likely no first-hand experience of living and working in Japan at all in situations in the business or political field where they would have to confront the hard realities behind the nice rhetoric. As Shigeru Yoshida, Japan's first post-war prime minister put it, 'History provides examples of winning by diplomacy after losing a war.'[2]

Naturally it is difficult for many people in more open liberal democracies to realize the means that Japanese officialdom has in terms of control over information, money for red-carpet trips to Japan etc., at its disposal for 'winning friends and influencing people'. While at home many people distrust what politicians and officials say, or what they read in the newspapers, some suspend their normal scepticism in regard to anything to do with Japan; which is a great help to those putting out the official 'party line'. In short, are we dealing with a 'new' Japan: or is it really the old Japan with a few cosmetic and superficial changes concealing what is underneath? Without a knowledge of Japan's past it is impossible to decide. Anyone who believes that 'history is bunk' in the case of such an old society as Japan's is seriously deluding themselves.

[5] That it is high time that corporate and government decision-makers outside Japan faced the fact that, as many Japanese themselves have been telling us, the world's second largest economy does not operate on the same lines as Anglo-Saxon capitalism.[3] Naturally this does not mean that the Anglo-Saxon and Japanese versions of capitalism are the only two in the world but most of the comparisons here will be between the two, rather than with Rhineland and other

Continental types. The simple reason is the overwhelming American engagement with Japan since the end of the Second World War in 1945 and that the Japanese themselves see the comparison very largely in terms of the contrasts between their own form of capitalism and the Anglo-Saxon, or more specifically the American, type.

This appeared clearly, for instance, in the presentations and statistics given by Japanese speakers to European managers at the EU-Japan Centre for Industrial Cooperation in Tokyo. Inevitably, producing statistics comparing Japan with all the member states of the EU has its own problems but it is hardly surprising that comparison with Japan's single major export market would be more significant to the Japanese; and that leaves out of account the US-Japan Security Treaty.

As far as alternatives to the Japanese system are concerned, in such areas as law, accounting and privatization for instance, it has been Anglo-Saxon models that have been discussed and when privatization became a popular topic it was the policies of the Thatcher government that were a major talking point.

[6] That the first necessity in dealing with the 'Japan problem' is to recognize that it exists, instead of pretending that there is only one type of capitalism in the world or of indulging in the wish fulfilment of dreaming that it will one day (when?) conform to Anglo-Saxon models.[4]

The second necessity is to see that the problem has interconnected politico-economic aspects in the broad sense – or wheels within wheels to put it in everyday language – and that in consequence any attempt to deal with it by just looking at a single aspect, whether it be financial, social, psychological or whatever is insufficient to grasp it in its complex entirety. Thus 'bean counters' who look at sets of figures without realizing how they have arisen and what they actually mean in the Japanese context are being simplistic in trying to apply the criteria that they are familiar with from their own background to a different environment where different criteria apply.

Once it is accepted that Japanese capitalism differs from Anglo-Saxon capitalism – and that the Japanese élites who control it intend to keep it that way in their own interests, even if some compromises at the edges might be needed – then it is clear that Japanese capitalism must be tackled holistically as a different system, not just in odd bits here and there. From this it also follows that the EU, US and others need to follow different policies towards Japan compared to the ones that would fit a trading partner whose own policies and practices were based on Anglo-Saxon capitalism. As a former American Commerce Secretary, Maurice Stans, remarked to Nixon and Kissinger about American policy towards Japan. 'Overriding weight has been given . . . to geopolitical and military factors to the subordination of economic and financial factors.'[5]

This shows a different type of relationship between politics and business, based on a world geopolitical view very different from that of Japan's.

## JAPAN'S POLITICO-ECONOMIC SYSTEM

'The real problem in Japan is political', was the comment of a foreign diplomat in Tokyo at the time of the banking crisis and Upper House elections in July 1998.[6] Anyone who has not understood this in relation to, for example, how to deal with the banks' huge amounts of bad loans, has not penetrated below the surface.

Information is a competitive weapon in any business system and none more so than the Japanese, with its collusive and mutually supportive links between the three dominant élites consisting of the leaders of big business, the political kingmakers and heads of the political factions, and the senior permanent bureaucrats at, for example, vice-minister level, the real heads of the ministries despite the politically appointed ministers.[7]

Popularly known with good reason as 'the Iron Triangle', these groups may have their differences and will naturally defend and try to extend their power but linked as they are by money, information and influence, they are the people acting together to a greater or lesser degree in concert who decide which way the Japanese politico-economy shall go. Currently, the politicians are trying to increase their power and influence at the expense of the Ministry of Finance, which has lost prestige because of the financial crisis, but how far they have the expertise to do this, particularly if the bureaucrats are deliberately unhelpful, it will be interesting to see. Politicians in Japan are extremely poorly regarded.

The classic *Art of War* by Sun Tzu, the Chinese Clausewitz of antiquity, is a text recommended to Japanese managers and to others in competitive situations, like politics for instance, and has much to say on the camouflaging of intentions so as to disorientate the enemy or competitor. Western managers should read it too. Misinformation is the equivalent of camouflage and in Japan's politicized economy to write about it at all is a political act.[8]

This explains why the Japanese authorities, which throughout this book means all who represent the orthodox or 'official' line of the Iron Triangle, are so sensitive about anything they regard as foreign criticism, since to reveal the inner workings of the Japanese politico-economic system might cause others to raise questions about things like trade policy and non-tariff barriers for instance. Meanwhile, the authorities welcome foreign comment that fits in with their agenda, no matter how ill informed or exaggeratedly fulsome it may be.

Much of the information the authorities themselves put out is quite literally propaganda and not to be taken at face value. The technique relies on the blatant use of the difference between the two most important words in the Japanese language: *tatemae*, facade, and *honne*, the real intention, meaning, fact etc. This distinction, bound up with avoiding disagreements and either losing 'face' oneself or causing another to lose it, is something taken for granted in Japan. It leads either to the use of euphemism or in more extreme cases to the assertion of the exact opposite.

Thus, in a talk for senior European managers on one of the EU-Japan Centre's courses in Tokyo the speaker on Japanese society stated that Japan had no minority problems. As an educated man, who had studied abroad and was the head of an international organization in Tokyo, he was aware that there are minorities in Japan who are discriminated against. He would also have known that because these minorities, such as Koreans, outcastes and Okinawans are indistinguishable from ordinary Japanese in the eyes of new arrivals from Europe, no one would have disbelieved him. He also knew that he should not admit that such discrimination existed. So he used *tatemae*, or how things are supposed to be, instead of how in reality they are.

This was not an isolated instance with the speakers selected by the Ministry of International Trade and Industry – the famous or notorious MITI, depending on one's point of view – though some were more objective than others. The official facade of *tatemae* is something that anyone staying longer in such circumstances has to get used to, while remaining alert for clues as to what is really going on. *Tatemae* is often quite simply too good to be true.

KNOW THE COMPETITOR

At home, many companies follow the basic business principle of knowing the competition. Unfortunately, many have neglected Japan, seeing it as remote, expensive and inscrutable; as if even a far-off competitor could safely be ignored.[9] This shortsightedness has had well publicized impacts on such important sections of the economy as cars, motorcycles and consumer electronics in Europe and America and even on such previously impregnable and prestigious sectors as the Swiss watch industry, which failed to take the Japanese advance into the new quartz technology seriously enough.

Starting in 1868 as a late developer with the government behind a policy of full-scale industrialization, Japan was first underestimated as 'backward'. The same mistake of not taking Japan seriously enough was then made not once but twice more: during the Second World War and during the period of postwar recovery and development.

Now many seem to be making the same mistake a third time, despite Japan's having overtaken European states to become the world's second largest economy, with all that this implies for world prosperity in an era of globalization, and despite Japan's being the world's largest creditor and a leader in industries whose products are in such great demand as motor vehicles and electronics. For a country not significantly larger than Britain, though admittedly with a little more than twice the population, or comparable in size to the State of California, this is an amazing achievement; especially when one remembers the low point from which it started out again after 1945.

To explain away this achievement, which is another way of not taking a competitor seriously, some people ascribe it to so-called secrets of success, often said to be related to special Japanese characteristics: an idea bordering on racialism which some Japanese commentators are happy to encourage. Once Japanese products had overcome their pre-Second World War reputation for being 'cheap and nasty' and, as with cars for instance, had achieved internationally recognized high standards of reliability and quality, the Quality Circle movement was a case in point.

Japanese lecturers on the subject, as at the EU-Japan Centre, like to stress Quality Circles in terms of the groupish nature of Japanese workers and their devotion to their work, etc. They seldom stress the degree of management control over Circles, that work discipline in Japan is extremely strict – comparable to Britain in the 1930s or earlier? – and that the power of the employer under the Japanese industrial relations system is infinitely greater that that in the EU or US.

This is not to disparage what the Quality movement in Japan achieved but to emphasize that it has to be understood against the background of a national need after 1945 to earn hard currency to pay for imports of food, equipment and raw materials. To make this possible, management had to introduce measures to improve quality at what was a time of crisis and hardship in order to make their products attractive to foreign buyers.

To believe that Circles exist as a result of some sort of ideally harmonious world of human relations, rather than such more rational factors as management quality policy and the organization and training of employees is to fall for the propaganda. The latter has generally less to say about the actual results achieved and the efforts that are needed to keep the momentum going.

Some companies like to show visitors the huge numbers of suggestions they get from their employees, as if numbers alone were more significant than the quality of the suggestions and how many had led to real improvements. Some visitors are undoubtedly impressed but, as with Quality Circles, they may be unaware of the element of compulsion involved. Employees who do not make suggestions, whatever they are worth, are unlikely to get on as well in the company as those who do, while in some companies employees must make a certain number of suggestions within a given period. The show, or *tatemae*, put on for foreign visitors can make it harder to see what is really going on by making a mystery out of allegedly 'unique' Japanese features. Who would want to speak out of turn?

Meanwhile, some go away believing that what they have seen is a technique that can be applied rather like a patent medicine; while others conclude that 'it's alright for them but it wouldn't work for us'. Neither is the right way to form an accurate evaluation of the competitor; and if that is lacking, how can companies or governments implement effective competitive strategies of their own?

JAPANESE CAPITALISM

Japan ran trade deficits with the US up to 1965,[10] although the first trade disputes in certain sectors had started ten years earlier. As part of its Cold War policy to keep Japan out of the Communist camp and to assist in its economic recovery, the American government had opened its markets to Japanese goods. This provided Japan's mercantilistic leaders with an opportunity that they were only too happy to exploit. Now the US is Japan's biggest debtor, giving Japan leverage to exploit.

From the beginning of government policy in 1868 to follow the path of full-scale industrialization, Japan's leaders have never believed in Adam Smith and the theory of the free market, or in the theory of comparative advantage, according to which the different economies of the world should produce those things they are best endowed for. Instead, their inspiration has come from the theory of the national economy of Friedrich List: an economic philosopher, whose name is largely unknown in Britain, who was not just in an ivory tower of academe but who was extremely influential at the time of Bismarck and in the US.[11]

List (1789–1846) was a friend of Presidents Jackson and Madison and in his 'Outlines of American Political Economy' attacked free trade and advocated the protection of American industry. That was in 1827. The following year the American government introduced a general tariff, in line with his ideas.

His economic philosophy was likewise welcomed in France, where he claimed that he had been inspired by Louis XIV's finance minister, Colbert, whose policy was to stimulate French manufacturing and to prohibit imports.

It is a pity List is not better known in Britain: familiarity with his ideas would help people to understand Japanese capitalism so much better. The idea of the mercantilist national economy as a zero-sum game, in which the mobilization and coordination of the economy directed towards national policy goals, even if not always perfect, and resembling what more free market economies only know in wartime, is not difficult to grasp. Whether one likes it or not is of course another matter especially, as the actual evidence shows, it implies a high degree of government control in other areas.

TRADE FRICTIONS

It was already mentioned that trade frictions with the US, Japan's most important market for its exports, began as long ago as 1955, in industries such as textiles. The EU, and other countries, have also had continuing trade deficits with Japan, contributing to its status as the world's largest creditor. Following List's principles of the national economy and in line with their own interests, Japan's ruling élites have always sought to export their way out of a recession, as the current [2000] trade figures show, while avoiding internal restructuring or reform as much as possible. Those people who think that Japan is 'finished' because of recession and that because of its, undoubtedly serious, domestic financial problems, Japanese competition will somehow wither away, should ask themselves whose cars, cameras, audio and video products, office automation and computer equipment, watches and even beer etc. people continue to buy.

Continuing trade deficits with Japan have irritated many governments, aware of unemployment figures and the charge that Japan is exporting unemployment while keeping its own markets closed. To soothe these irritations, the Japanese authorities have periodically published 'market opening measures', despatched missions like the Maekawa Mission of 1986 to listen to complaints and to publish reports for future action, and have established a Manufactured Imports Promotion Organization, within MITI, and a JETRO (Japan External Trade Organization) business centre in Tokyo with the ostensible aim of helping foreign business. By such techniques, the authorities have continued to finesse the demands of the EU, US etc. for open markets.

Businessmen and officials who are insufficiently experienced in Japanese affairs may think that the market liberalization measures that have been announced necessarily mean what they say but only familiarity with the realities of the competitive situation, the ability of domestic producers to bring pressure to bear on politicians and bureaucrats, and the ability of bureaucrats to obstruct free market access can enable foreign business to assess its prospects in Japan accurately. And these are only some of the possible problems. Others include delays in getting licences under the complicated system of official regulation, the unwillingness to accept international standards, and, from the point of view of people used to dealing within the framework of something like an Anglo-Saxon legal system, the relative absence and unhelpfulness of the law.

For years anyone wanting to open a shop, chain store or department store with a floor area above a certain size had to apply to MITI for permission under the notorious Large Scale Store Law, the purpose of which was to protect the thousands of small family-owned and retail shops to be found everywhere in Japan. These small shopkeepers are an important constituency for the governing party, the Liberal Democratic Party (LDP), which has been in power since 1945, except for ten months in 1947–48, though more recently it has been forced into a brief coalition before returning to power again. The political connection matters because it is generally only the larger stores that handle imports.

Under the Law, a businessman or company was forced to obtain the agreement of the small shopkeepers who would be affected i.e., the agreement of his direct competitors, who might well fear that their livelihoods would be harmed. What this meant in practice was that they would have to be financially compensated. In 1995 the authorities announced that the Law was to be eased, making it look as if it would be less restrictive and therefore better for foreign imports: a good piece of public relations, or in this case *tatemae*. In reality, what happened was that instead of the central government i.e., MITI, the local governments took control: the very people most likely to be close to the local shopkeepers and in collusion with them. As the Japan Times put it, the apparent easing of restrictions was 'being undermined by obstacles put in place by local governments'.[12]

Following the dramatic bankruptcy of Yamaichi Securities in 1997, which attracted worldwide attention, and the authorities' realization that Tokyo would not develop as a world financial centre while it was so limited in its appeal to foreign institutions, there was much discussion of a Japanese Big Bang. The theory was that this would make Japanese financial markets 'free, fair and international' but it soon became apparent that because of certain problems and practices to be discussed later this might lead to the so-called 'Wimbledon effect', where the host country supplies the site for the competition but it is the foreigners that win it. Partly also because of the customary vagueness of official pronouncements, suspicions soon surfaced that the Big Bang would turn out to be more of a damp squib; especially if the Japanese securities companies, whose public credibility in Japan had been severely damaged, were likely to lose out to the foreigners.

Big Bang had been trumpeted as a major instance of deregulation, a slogan or buzzword that had largely replaced the undefined but agreeable sounding 'internationalization', which almost certainly meant different things to the Japanese authorities who propagated it and those it was directed towards. Attracted by the huge pool of Japanese household savings, said to amount to ¥1,200 billion, foreign brokerage houses made major advances into the Japanese market on the basis of the initial market openings.

Then in June 1998 the government proposed to set up an investor protection fund, ostensibly to protect small investors who would have lost money in, for example, Yamaichi Securities – and other Japanese brokerages that would be unlikely to survive subsequent deregulation. Especially since there have been so many scandals of undeclared losses, not only by the Japanese securities companies but also by the banks, this would mean that foreign brokers, who were not involved in Yamaichi's and others' problems, before deregulation took place, would be expected to write blank cheques for whatever the real sums that eventually were brought to light might be: a novel interpretation of a Big Bang in which the foreigners would be expected to clear up the mess of their Japanese competitors, with unlimited liability.

It can be assumed that this was not quite what they had expected when they entered the market; but then in Japan things are frequently not quite what they appear because of the 'wheels within wheels' and the discrepancies between *tatemae* and *honne*. A typical official view was that quoted in the *Financial Times*: 'Foreign companies cannot come into Japan for free';[13] something of an understatement in the circumstances. As the same newspaper observed not long afterwards, 'Japan may have no Wimbledon at all'[14] if it went on with such blatantly discriminatory measures.

The list of imports that either have been or are the subjects of trade disputes is practically endless: cars, car parts and accessories, skis, whisky and brandy, cellular phones, microchips, bulbs and cut flowers, financial services etc. In other words, in any type of sector the local producers are being protected. Even Japanese researchers have calculated how much the cost is to Japanese consumers.[15]

Some individual items become the focus of a dispute, as Motorola's cellular phones did for example, in 1994. Previously, the Japanese firm NTT had been the market monopolist but in 1985 the Ministry of Posts and Telecommunications had decided to introduce some competition. The problem was that the company responsible for the infrastructure, IDO, was already using NTT technology and had little inclination to invest in the different system used by Motorola. By dragging its feet, this meant that Motorola could not compete on an equal basis in the main urban areas of Tokyo and Nagoya.

The affair was taken up at the highest government level of the US Trade Representative, at that time Mickey Kantor.[16] A Japanese official threatened someone I knew at Motorola that, 'If you persist with this complaint your company may suffer serious damage.' With tongue in cheek, my friend replied, 'And I thought this was a free market system.' The official laughed and put the phone down.

Under the US-Japan Semiconductor Agreement the American government succeeded in getting a figure for a specific percentage of the Japanese market, bearing in mind that simply an agreement to accept an increased figure for imports might not have much value. The Japanese authorities swore that they would never do this again and used the argument against 'managed trade' in an ironic turning of the tables.

Sometimes the arguments used are plainly ridiculous and can only be interpreted as showing that the authorities do not care what others think. Probably the most celebrated case is that of the argument that 'Japanese snow is different', to protect the Japanese ski-makers against French and Italian imports. What had happened was that the Consumer Product Safety Association (CPSA) had passed a new standard for skis, knowing that the foreign products would not meet it. This standard had then been approved by senior officials in the relevant ministry, MITI. When asked to justify this, an official replied that it was an industry matter and that MITI had 'no influence' on the CPSA, which was an industry association, and therefore independent.[17] This was as disingenuous as the argument against 'managed trade' just referred to.

For years the Dutch government had pressed for market opening for bulbs and cut flowers, in which the country is something of a market leader. Previously the regulation was that bulbs had to be planted in the soil in Japan, which meant that by the time the prescribed period was up they were no good for sale. After tedious negotiations the problem was eased but for the cut flowers the problem of bureaucratic delays during which they may be spoilt remains.

Dutch apples were similarly unwelcome because of the alleged discovery of a 'Mediterranean Fruit Fly' in Rotterdam Harbour. Meanwhile, Tokyo consumers were paying as much for two apples as an entire sackful would cost in New Zealand; as I discovered on holiday there with a Japanese party, who were visibly surprised and only wished they could have taken them home.

In 1995 Sir Leon Brittan, then Vice President of the EU, wrote to the Japanese Foreign Minister to complain that of 160 measures for deregulation requested by the EU only 21 had been included in the latest Japanese government deregulation plan; and this in a plan to be spread out over five years.[18] In Tokyo the head of the European Business Community, an umbrella organization with some 1,000 members equivalent to a Europe-wide Chamber of Commerce, Alain Coine, president of Rhône Poulenc Japan and a respected figure in the European business world with considerable experience in Japan, described the government's 1,091 item five-year deregulation plan as 'meaningless'.[19] Expressing the 'great frustration' of EBC members he criticized its use of such phrases as 'will be considered' and 'to be reviewed', asserting that, 'We are afraid that things under consideration will remain under consideration for many years.' These are of course classic delaying tactics.

Something like a deregulation plan is drafted by bureaucrats, though officially it comes from the government. A former bureaucrat said that during his training one of his superiors told him that, 'The reason why bureaucrats have such power is because of their ability to control information.' This means that Members of the Diet, or parliament, depend on what the bureaucrats, who draft the laws and even speak in the Diet for ministers, are inclined or not to give them. Members of the Opposition parties naturally get the least.[20] In bureaucratspeak such phrases as 'we'll study it', *kento shimasu*, are one of the *tatemae* ways of saying no: hence the irritation expressed by Alain Coine on behalf of the European Business Community in Japan.

In Britain it is customary to talk of Civil servants, despite the old joke that they were no longer Servants, as much as masters, and no longer civil i.e. polite. The highly amusing television series *Yes, Minister* portrayed them as Machiavellian manipulators of naïve politicians but some of them might have envied the power, influence and status in society at large that Japanese bureaucrats have at their disposal.

An old Japanese saying is 'revere the officials, despise the people' *kanson mimpi*, and at least until 1945 the officials were the servants of the emperor, not the people. Thus to call them Civil Servants would have the wrong connotation. They are privileged people with the power, as one of the three élites making up the Iron Triangle, to exercise a major role over the economy, based on vaguely worded rules that they themselves draft which allow them maximum freedom of action.

In licensing a business, for example, they can make it easy or difficult for a company, depending on how 'cooperative' the company has been. In regard to trade frictions they should be seen as major actors, not just as people who write down what ministers tell them. Real 'deregulation', which they know is a word that has a pleasing sound to foreign governments, would be a threat to their power.

For many years foreign policy-makers and business executives have clung to the simplistic notion based on the crude application of free market theory that the reason they could not sell in Japan was that the exchange rate was against them. Unfortunately, the much discussed appreciation of the Yen after the Plaza Agreement of 1985 which had made the dollar and other European currencies cheaper did not automatically lead to lower import prices for Japanese consumers, as many had assumed would be the automatic result. This showed that other factors relating to Japan's political economy were at work: for example, the distribution system, where the intermediate layers of Japanese middlemen were only too happy to take increased profits while not cutting prices to consumers.

Simultaneously, the authorities used the issue of the appreciation of the Yen, *endaka*, to tell people that they must work harder to become more competitive to make up for the threat posed to exports. A mood of national crisis was whipped up through the press but it was a Japanese research institute that found that many electronics companies could still make a profit if the exchange rate was ¥100 to the dollar. When a journalist on a major Japanese newspaper was asked by an American who had heard this why his paper did not print this interesting piece of news he replied, 'It would be contrary to the national interest to print such a story!'

The answer did not surprise the questioner, a former director for Japanese affairs with the Office of the US Trade Representative, later an executive with a major US multinational in Japan and one of the most knowledgeable people in the field.[21] What it says about the press in Japan will be dealt with later.

It is true that after the speculative 'bubble economy' had burst there was a new search by consumers for economically priced goods around 1995–96, for which someone invented the catchy slogan 'price destruction', *kakaku hakai*, when some European motor manufacturers for instance were able to increase their sales, though mostly from a minuscule share of the market. But when the recession began to bite and most consumers felt that the thing to do was to keep whatever money they had, these exports declined again. Throughout all this: the oil crisis of 1973, which some people thought would seriously affect Japan's export ability because of its dependence on oil imports: the upward revaluation of the Yen after the Plaza Agreement of 1985: the bursting of the 'bubble economy', the Asian crisis and the recession: the American trade deficit with Japan continued to grow.

This matters not only when core industrial and technological competencies are lost, not to mention direct competitors, but also has political implications that tend to get overlooked because of free market thinking that separates politics and economics in a way that is inapplicable to the Japanese politico-economic system. Having a huge trade surplus with the US gives Japan's policy-makers political leverage. Perhaps that is largely the idea. A later example suggests that one cannot afford to upset one's principal creditor too much.

That the appreciation of the Yen after the Plaza Agreement did not lead to a surge of competitively priced imports as free market economic theory would have dictated, does not of course mean that Japan is somehow above the laws of economics, even though some in Japan appeared to think so. Like any other system, the Japanese system has its costs, as the housing association, *jusen*, scandals, the banks' bad debts and the huge debts left behind by the privatized Japan National Railways (JNR) show. Indeed, in July 1998 these debts, outstanding since privatization in 1987, were on the agenda for the new government of Keizo Obuchi to deal with along with the banking crisis.[22] These costs, along with those of the constant financial scandals and inadequate standards of accounting or reporting that crop up all the time in the Japanese press, are passed on to the Japanese consumer or taxpayer.

For a variety of reasons that will become clearer later, Japan is a society where the majority close their eyes to its defects and where it may incur work-related or social risks to do anything different. For people living in more open societies where it is taken for granted that opinions will be frankly expressed in daily life or in the media, it may be hard to grasp how stereotyped the picture of Japan presented to them by many Japanese people is and how closely it conforms to the official view, and its hidden agenda.

So far, for instance, there has been no consumers' movement as it would be understood in Europe or America and no Ralph Nader. The head of the Housewives' Association was once asked if she liked paying seven times the world market price for rice, due as elsewhere to the importance of the agricultural lobby in politics. The answer was that she did not, 'But we have to support the Japanese farmer': a reply that would have pleased the ministry responsible for regulating agriculture. Though Japan is not the old USSR, consumers play an insignificant role compared to national policy aims. The Japanese economy has often been described as producer-dominated instead.

This has important implications for trade relations in, for instance, the smaller proportion of manufactured goods that Japan imports compared to other major industrial economies, which continues to be a cause of international friction. Japanese often say that they are not rich, only the companies are rich. To others it sometimes seems that Japan, having been poor as recently as the period of recovery after 1945, still behaves as if it were poor by following a policy of 'exports good, imports bad', to paraphrase George Orwell.

The point here is not what the Japanese 'should' do, which is for them to decide, but what the EU or the US should do if they want to pursue policies based on the realities of how Japan works rather than on how they would like it to work or hope that it would work one day.

How Japan's Iron Triangle would like others to behave was nicely summed up by a MITI official during a discussion at the Royal Institute of International Affairs in London: 'In this country you have the great tradition of Adam Smith and the philosophy of the free market. We very much hope that you will keep to this tradition.' Of course he did! Judging by their expressions, one could see that some of the audience unfortunately found this piece of flattery to their liking.

JAPAN AS COMPETITOR

The starting point for evaluating Japan as a competitor is the crisis of confidence of the present time: something for which the potential weaknesses such as the rackety financial system and its penetration by organized criminal groups had been an open secret in Japan, if not elsewhere. Some writers had indeed prophesied a coming crisis[23] but, as with the collapse of the Berlin Wall, it was still possible to be surprised when it actually happened. For the outside world at least, a positive result of the crisis has been the forcing into the open, for a wider public to become aware of, of aspects of Japanese business, politics and society that are normally hidden.

Some may still believe that this is just a problem for the Japanese in the sense that it is their banks etc. and not ours that are in trouble but what happens in the world's second largest economy affects, first, Asian countries, where Japan has invested and which need to export to Japan and, second, the world as a whole, few corners of which remain untouched by Japan's economic expansion.

Friedrich List's philosophy of the 'national economy' – and by extension Japan's politico-economic philosophy – are not hard to grasp, though the latter has often been obscured, whether deliberately so as not to alarm competitors, or by unfamiliarity on the part of outsiders. What are complex, however, are the relations between the different parts, such as those among the organizations and individuals that make up the Iron Triangle; some of which may even seem outlandish to those people used to societies inspired by Adam Smith. So the necessary references are to be found at the end of the book. Following the practice in Japan's English-language newspapers, names are put in what would be the normal order in English i.e. personal name first, family name second, and not the other way round, as in Japanese, which for something written in English might seem a bit affected.

☐

What follows is based on an involvement with Japan dating back to late 1962, including fifteen years working in the country; first in the 1960s and again in the 1990s. What changes, if any, took place during those thirty years is a question that has often been discussed but the answer is not to be expressed by yet another stereotype.

The involvement with Japan included research on Japanese companies both in Japan and the UK and culminated in a five-year contract as European General Manager of the EU-Japan Centre for Industrial Cooperation in Tokyo from 1991 to 1996. The Centre was established as a 'common venture', to use the official terminology, between the European Commission's Directorate-General III (Industry) and MITI.

'Industrial cooperation' was a slight misnomer, since the actual job of the Centre was to run training courses lasting several months or weeks for European managers with a minimum age of thirty-five and solid professional experience; together with an information service. Managers from the EU member states came to Japan, in most cases for the first time in their lives, to follow these programmes of lectures and visits to factories, offices and other organizations, in order to learn about the realities of Japanese business.

Some wanted to sell to Japan, others wanted to learn about Japanese manufacturing methods, while for a smaller number it was a valuable experience of direct familiarization before they started working in their company's Japanese branch. A major aim on the European side was to get to know the competitor: something that the Japanese themselves generally know very well.

Most of the managers who came on the courses got a great deal out of them and anyone being assigned to Japan had a head start over managers in those European or American companies that still send people out without such a familiarization period: a recipe for disaster in terms of mistakes in approaching clients etc. and the time it takes most managers to begin to be able to function effectively in a business and social environment very different from that at home. Even now not enough corporations, or official organizations, have people at the top level with Japan experience who can appreciate the situation of the man on the ground. This leads to the 'head office problem' that was regularly discussed at the final panel discussion on the course.

Getting to know Japan's politico-economic system has been compared to peeling an onion: when you peel back one layer, there is another one underneath, and though the Centre's courses offered a valuable introduction they were not the same thing as the degree of penetration below the surface to be found among managers and others who had already spent many years working at the sharp end in Japan. Fortunately, working at the Centre provided plenty of opportunities for contact with managers of many different nationalities in companies covering a wide spectrum of manufacturing, sales and service organizations: with the European Business Council and the national Chambers of Commerce: with the commercial and science and technology attachés at the European embassies with the EU delegation in Tokyo, headed by the EU ambassador: and of course with my masters in Brussels.

The fact that the Centre was a government-to-government organization, involving one of the two key Japanese ministries, MITI – the other being the Ministry of Finance – and its relations with the European Commission, meant that there were highly political overtones and daily exposure to the policies, attitudes and some of the personalities within MITI. The experiences both of my German predecessor and my French successor have been similar. Having returned to Europe after the conclusion of the contract, the views expressed here are of course my own, not an official EU statement.

The years 1989 to 1996 spent in Japan, including the years at the Centre, which was probably the most fruitful learning experience out of fifteen years in the country, coincided with a number of significant events. The 'bubble economy' burst. There were the housing and loan, *jusen*, scandals: the Great Hanshin, or Kobe, Earthquake killed over 5,300 people, injured almost 27,000 and left 300,000 homeless, exposing the government and bureaucracy to criticism over their ineffectual response:[24] the attack by the criminal and outlandish sect, Aum Shinrikyo, with sarin nerve gas at Underground stations in the central Tokyo ministry area during the rush hour aimed at knocking out the government, that killed 12 people and injured nearly 5,500[25] – which some of the Centre's course participants missed by half an hour: the rise of the Yen to its highest point of less than ¥90 to the dollar: and the death of Emperor Hirohito, now called the Showa Emperor, and the ensuing discussions over his reign, including the period of the Second World War, and the form and meaning of the ceremonies associated with the accession of his successor – a weighing up of the past and questions about the future of a controversial nature.

Last, but by no means least, I want to express what really cannot be expressed, the immense debt I owe to the tolerance of my family and the support of my wife, Chieko, to whom this work is affectionately dedicated.

■ CHAPTER 1

# A Crisis of Confidence

The startling top news on British television, in the financial press and also the mainline quality newspapers, which are not normally especially concerned with Japanese affairs, was the bankruptcy of Yamaichi Securities, one of Japan's Big Four securities or stockbroking companies, in November 1997. Viewers watched in astonishment as Yamaichi's senior manager, Shohei Nozawa, bowing deeply and apparently weeping tears of shame at a press conference in Tokyo, implored other financial institutions to give Yamaichi's redundant employees a job.

In rapid succession there followed, as the *Financial Times* reported, further bankruptcies and daily rumours that major Japanese banks, insurance and other companies were in a critical situation; and all this at a time when Thailand, Korea, Malaysia and Indonesia, where Japanese banks were heavily exposed and which would normally be major export destinations for Japanese machinery and equipment, manufactured products and investment, were themselves in serious trouble.

The shock was all the greater because it was so unexpected, since most people outside Japan had been led to believe in the strength of Japanese industry, the unswerving dedication of its workers, famously described by a former EU Commissioner, Sir Roy Denman, as 'workaholics living in rabbit hutches', the might of its commercial and financial power and the apparent infallibility of its managers, who had masterminded the country's dramatic economic advance since 1945. Yet here before their very eyes was one of the Big Four stockbroking companies publicly confessing its failure.[1] Whether people should have been so surprised is another matter. Yamaichi had already been bailed out once before by the Bank of Japan as long ago as 1965: something I personally remember hearing discussed in Japan at the time.

Yamaichi was then the largest of the Big Four and there was anxiety about the effect on confidence in the Japanese economy if the government had not rescued it; particularly as another of the Big Four, Nikko Securities, was also about to fail. An interesting sidelight on the affair was that stockbroking in the 1960s, and to some extent today, was not officially seen as respectable: rather perhaps in the way that moneylending was not seen as respectable in medieval Europe, though with the difference that the Stock Exchange played a smaller role in comparison with European and American systems and that most company finance was provided by the banks, with whom they had long-standing ties, often in their own group of companies, or *keiretsu*.

In theory, the Bank of Japan was not allowed to make loans to the stockbroking companies, though it had a four-man Securities Bureau to keep an eye on them. Already, in 1963, the head of the Bureau had warned the Ministry of Finance, as the body with jurisdiction over the Bank of Japan, that the stockbroking firms were in an unhealthy state but the Ministry had done nothing. Because of their low status as manipulators of other people's money rather than providers of proper goods or services, the stockbrokers had never been welcome at the Bank of Japan but now they were summoned to the Bank by the head of its Securities Bureau and told to explain their position. No other bank would have been likely to shore them up.

Although officially not allowed to do so, he provided loans to all of the Big Four in February 1965; but neither wrote the figures down, nor informed the Board of his own Bank! The sums were not inconsiderable. At the exchange rate of the time, they were: Nikko Securities US $37.5 million (¥13.5 billion): Daiwa Securities US $23.8 million (¥8.6 billion): Yamaichi Securities US $22.7 million (¥8.2 billion); and Nomura Securities US $14.5 million (¥5.2 billion). Nomura did not in fact need such a low interest loan but on the basis of the 'convoy system' of keeping companies at the same level in the same industry together it was official policy to treat them in the same way. In the crisis of the 1990s, whether to allow banks to fail or whether to try and somehow keep them together was a similar manifestation thirty years later of the 'convoy system'; though allowing banks to fail has of course the most serious implications for any economy.

By the middle of 1965 the seven main daily newspapers and NHK, the public corporation broadcasting organization, were aware that frightened customers were getting rid of Yamaichi bonds but had agreed to keep the news quiet. The Japan Socialist Party, the main opposition, had also agreed to keep quiet until the crisis, which was an open secret in financial circles, had been brought under control.[2]

Once again, this collusion among bureaucrats, politicians, businessmen, journalists and politicians, including the opposition, aimed at keeping the Japanese population in the dark about what was really going on, gives a good idea of how things are done behind the screen and why it is correspondingly more difficult for the outside world to grasp: foreigners, or *gaijin*, quite literally 'outside people', being the furthest removed from the centre. As the Introduction pointed out, all that outsiders are likely to get, if indeed they get anything at all, will be *tatemae* or misinformation.

In the Yamaichi case of 1965, however, something exceptional did happen. In normal circumstances, journalists on so-called serious newspapers, as opposed to the weekly magazines, the notorious *shukanshi* comparable with the tabloid press and scandal sheets in other countries, are organized into 'press clubs', *kisha kurabu*, whose members are bound by the rules to agree to release a common version of the news at the same time and not to scoop one another: yet another cartel![3] Hence the quotation in the Introduction about '. . . not printing stories that would be contrary to the national interest'.

But a journalist on a regional paper, which for some reason was not part of the agreement to keep quiet about Yamaichi, had heard that the company was to be reorganized. The effect of publishing this information on a panicky public was electric, forcing the Minister of Finance to make a statement. The Bank of Japan then had to lend a further ¥28 billion to Yamaichi, this time publicly, plus ¥5.3 billion to another firm called Oi Securities. As again with the housing and loan scandals, the banking crisis and the huge debts of the former Japan National Railways thirty years later in the 1990s, Japanese taxpayers were not happy that they were being forced to pay the bills. What they had still not been told – is there no end to the wheels within wheels? – was that billions more were being lent to other firms.

The headline that had forced the Minister of Finance to speak was, 'Yamaichi ready for reconstruction': traumatic because Yamaichi was then Number One, as many Japanese like to put it, of the Big Four. Yamaichi lost its position to Nomura, never to regain it, and the presidents of all the Big Four except Nomura had to resign. The Finance Minister was Kakuei Tanaka, a tough character with a strong construction industry (!) background, criticized by some for not having been to university. Later prime minister, he was forced out of office in 1974 over land deals related to public works that would have been highly profitable for him. Because of testimony given in the US Senate, not in Japan, about the business practices of American multinationals, it then came to light two years later that while prime minister he had accepted a bribe of ¥500 million to persuade the private All Nippon Airways to buy 21 Lockheed jet airliners. In 1983 he was sentenced in Tokyo to four years in prison and a fine of ¥500 million. The Lockheed scandal, as it was called, was one of the biggest but not the biggest in postwar Japan.[4]

Except for not having been to university, Tanaka was not an untypical politician or faction leader in the world of Japanese money politics and yet again the whole affair, which most people learning about Yamaichi's failure in 1997 were unlikely to have been aware of, shows the danger of trying to understand it in the light of free-market thinking. Britain, for instance has been a major recipient of Japanese investment, with a large number of Japanese financial institutions and their European regional headquarters in the City of London, and is also of course characterized by the sort of belief in the free market that can only make it harder to appreciate how closely entwined business, politics and bureaucracy in Japan are. This is a practical rather than a philosophical argument, since other countries trading with Japan need to do so on the basis of recognizing what these interconnections within Japan mean for them, and is not intended as an attack on free-market thinking in itself.

Economics inevitably affects other sides of life and, as one of the British managers put it at the end of an EU-Japan Centre course, 'The Japanese system very much hangs together as a piece. You can't have bits of it without all the rest.' Those in the Western world – Asians generally seem to have fewer illusions – who are attracted by Japan's postwar economic achievements and its 'harmonious' industrial relations etc., which may appear to make the job of a manager easier, though managers themselves are just as much locked into the system, need to ask themselves whether they would really like to live in the sort of society that 'the rest' implies. This is one of the points to be discussed in what follows here and in other chapters.

In fact, even the Yamaichi crisis of 1965 was not the first financial crisis. Before that there had been the Showa bank crash of 1927; even before the better known Wall Street crash of 1929. Eurocentric or Americacentric views need to be corrected.[5]

With the second Yamaichi crisis of 1997 and what followed it some of the shine was taken off the Japanese economy in foreign eyes. Those who had come to believe in the frequent pronouncements that Japan and the 'tiger' economies that had followed it were the wave of the future, and a wave that would engulf not only Europe but the US as well, were perplexed. There had been many prophecies that the future belonged to Asia and the evidence of its penetration of European and American markets and its factories spreading out there was already visible.

To judge from some of the media, it seemed that the continuing revelations from Japan and other Asian countries had put the notion of Asia as the wave of the future into question; though it is to be hoped that this will lead to a more balanced judgement and not just a publicity-induced swing from one exaggeration to its opposite. It is a positive sign, for instance, that theories of 'Asian values', advanced by some Asian political leaders and commentators in Europe and America to explain high economic growth rates and social stability, and by some apologists to justify authoritarian or collectivist political systems, are being reexamined.

To many outside Asia, the notion of 'Asian values' is probably more of a stereotyped mixture of Confucian or pseudo-Confucian values emanating from East Asian economies that have succeeded in industrializing than an accurate reflection of the variety found among Asian states. The notion attracted attention because the prominence given to statements by, in particular, Lee Kuan Yew of Singapore[6] and Mahathir Mohamad of Malaysia: two rather different states themselves. Of the two, the latter was more extreme, going so far as to claim that, 'Asian values are universal values. European values are European values.' In other words, that European values had become characterized by too much emphasis on individualism.

The story goes that a leading British politician was received by Lee Kuan Yew and listened to his, in many respects reasonable, criticism of anti-social behaviour, drug-taking and irresponsibility in present-day Britain, prompting the reply, 'You know, Mr. Lee, you are the last true Englishman!' He had seen the similarity between the 'Asian' values he had just heard outlined and the former 'Victorian values' or, to go back further, Max Weber's 'Protestant Ethic', which Weber saw as the origin of the 'Spirit of Capitalism'.

Scholars have long debated what Confucius meant and the connections that undoubtedly exist between what people believe or what values they hold on the one side and their economic and political systems on the other.[7] Those who have claimed that Japan's economic achievements, for example, were due to innate Japanese characteristics, as one often hears in Japan, must now face the problem of Japan's current economic and political difficulties: how do they explain them? – assuming of course that their original claims were based on fact. What is certain is that Japanese employers put great emphasis on 'attitude' in job interviews and how they evaluate their employees, while the Japanese Ministry of Education aims to inculcate a certain outlook in school pupils, specifically in the teaching of ethics. Thus Japanese education propagates an official ideology, comparable to the 'ethics', *shushin*, taught up to 1945.

The Yamaichi case of 1965 was an example of problem-solving by bureaucrats and politicians acting outside what were supposed to be the rules and concealing information. 'Administrative guidance', *gyosei shido*, what some might call 'an offer you can't refuse', is the bureaucrats' preferred means of enforcing their will, giving favours to companies that comply and making life difficult for those that are recalcitrant. It has been described as a system 'based on relationships, as in feudalism, not rules', largely relying on face-to-face meetings and the bureaucrats' avoidance of putting anything down on paper.[8]

Following the collapse of Yamaichi in 1997 the *Financial Times* turned the spotlight on common practices in company accounting and Japan's financial sector, which must have been news to many outside the country, though once again open secrets within it. These practices include the dressing up of accounts by *tobashi*, literally meaning the 'putting aside' and concealment of losses[9]: the lack of proper independent auditing procedures: the inadequate scrutiny of investment proposals within the closed circles of interconnected banks and companies: the statements for public consumption of, for example, the amount of the banks' bad debts, believed in by no one, least of all the officials responsible for regulating the banking sector at the Ministry of Finance (MOF), who could be expected to know the real position because of the close connections between them and ex-officials who had 'parachuted', *amakudari*, 'descent from heaven' into comfortable posts in the private sector, a regular means of ensuring their continued employment, where their personal connections and knowledge of their former ministry would be useful: the general lack of transparency throughout the financial system; and the penetration of organized crime syndicates, the *boryokudan*, (literally 'violent groups') into the financial world, as notably seen in the housing and loan, *jusen*, scandals and a significant reason for why so many bank debts became uncollectable. At first sight such practices might appear to be a domestic matter only but the banking crisis and its effect on the international economy showed many for the first time that they have international ramifications.

Although the roles of the Stock Exchange and shareholders in Japan do not have the prominence that they have in Anglo-Saxon systems, companies are obliged to hold an annual shareholders' meeting. The important part played by organized crime syndicates and the lesser place of law in Japan's political economy will be discussed later. Regarding company affairs there are gangsters, *sokaiya*, who become specialists in this field, using a mixture of blackmail and violence.[10] If they can discover a discreditable secret about a company, they will threaten to expose it, which they can easily do by buying one share in the company that will give them the right to attend the shareholders' meeting. Rather than face the acute embarrassment, and perhaps prosecution, companies pay up, putting themselves in the blackmailers' hands.

Their other related activity is to prevent shareholders from asking questions that are inconvenient for the management, by verbally and if need be physically intimidating awkward questioners. They are of course paid by the company. In recent years the police strategy has been to persuade companies to hold their shareholders' meetings on the same day, on the principle that it will be more difficult for the *sokaiya*, 'shareholders' meeting men to cover all of them. Some meetings have been reduced to a farce lasting no more than ten minutes thanks to the control over them exercised by the *sokaiya* at the management's behest.

Anyone believing that it is only dubious, hole-in-the-wall companies that are deeply involved with the *sokaiya* might be shocked to discover that their clients include blue chip companies of the highest rank. In 1985 Japan Air Lines, for instance, at that time 35 per cent owned by the government, hired a 'corporate research team' of thugs from a well known *sokaiya* organization to control their annual meeting. There had been a crash that year and they were worried that their inability to pay a dividend would lead to problems.[11] This and other cases are mentioned in the book by a former Nomura Securities employee, that Nomura were keen to prevent being published.

Some see Japanese accounting practices as further removed from international accounting practices than those of any other major industrialized state. The American-inspired Certified Public Accountancy Law of 1948 was supposed to promote the truthfulness of information disclosed in financial statements by the use of CPAs (Certified Public Accountants) but the Sanyo Special Steel case of 1964, which I remember causing a stir in Japan at the time, revealed that the system was not working as originally intended by the Occupation authorities. Company money had been misappropriated on a large scale, including for such egregious purposes as large decorative rocks to beautify executives' gardens, and Sanyo Special Steel filed for bankruptcy, admitting losses of ¥50 billion, the equivalent of US $463 million in October 1966. But, as the recurrent failures to admit much more serious losses in the 1990s kept on showing, it was later found that the company 'had been window dressing its financial statements to a gross extent'.[12]

In 1996, some thirty years later, the Law was amended but this does not seem to have had any effect on the figures announced for the banks' bad debts, which are generally believed to be only a third of the true figure. Even bank officials themselves, speaking anonymously, admitted that the figures were dressed up by *tobashi*, or shifting losses around so as to hide them in the accounts of affiliated firms or subsidiaries, and by tactics such as the repayment by debtors of purely nominal amounts of interest. According to the Federation of Bankers' guidelines, companies who make such purely nominal repayments or who are somehow being excused from making any repayments at all are treated as 'healthy borrowers' for accounting purposes. Even so, the country's twenty-one leading banks wrote off ¥1.47 trillion of bad loans in the year ending March 1993: not an inconsiderable sum.[13] In the circumstances, it is not surprising that the *Financial Times*, normally known for its restrained language, commented on Japanese end-of-the-year financial results in its issue of 1 April 1998 under the blunt headline, 'No one fooled by end-of-the-year window dressing'.

A risk for people who constantly fool others is that they end up by fooling themselves, by pretending that the real figures do not matter for instance and that they can always be manipulated; but eventually the bills become due. This is one aspect of the crisis of the 1990s.

In addition to the manipulation of accounts, a Japanese journalist further alleged that insider trading is common both on the main Tokyo Stock Exchange and others such as Osaka. With the usual Japanese emphasis on personal relations and the trading of favours within a highly structured, or collusive, business system, this would not be surprising. The *tatemae* or facade, especially for outsiders, would be a business system based on open dealing, which is now the professed aim of the Big Bang, while the reality would be based on the significance of those with inside information. The risk of corruption exists of course in any system but is increased in one where the emphasis on personal connections, accompanied by flimsy accountability and close, and sometimes surprisingly open relations, between business and organized crime, is prevalent.

A case that received considerable publicity was that of a pharmaceutical company, Nippon Shoji, listed on the second section of the Osaka Stock Exchange, in which 43 per cent of the employees were at the same time shareholders in their own company. On 20 September 1993 it discovered that its new anti-viral drug, Usevir, had killed more than a dozen patients who were also on anti-cancer drugs. One week later, on 27 September, it reported this to the supervising ministry, the Ministry of Health and Welfare (MHW), and one week after that it informed two hundred of its own representatives in 4 October. The Ministry did not however make a public announcement until 12 October.

On the back of the news about Nippon Shoji's apparently successful new drug, the company's shares had been rising but between the time that the company knew that the drug was not safe and the Ministry's public announcement, 175 company employees, including 82 senior managers, had sold 360,000 shares, knowing of course that they would seriously lose their value. Another 44 company members even managed to get rid of their shares on the very morning of the day when the Ministry's announcement was made. Nippon Shoji's lawyer then announced that in the circumstances it was difficult to decide whether insider trading within the meaning of the Securities and Exchange Act had taken place.

His view was reflected by the country's leading drug maker, Takeda, in a similar statement.[14] It was perhaps another instance of the Alice in Wonderland principle that, 'A word means what I want it to mean'. Yet Japanese speakers, at the EU-Japan Centre for instance and elsewhere, who explain the Japanese business system for foreigners frequently characterize it as a 'high trust system', to the detriment of allegedly 'low trust' systems in other parts of the world. Nippon Shoji's, and other companies', view of business ethics was, to say the least, interesting.

Exchange-listed companies should be properly scrutinized by the Exchanges where they are listed but the requirements for firms dealing on an over-the-counter basis are more lax. A company called Ipec had run up debts totaling ¥9.4 billion and had extremely poor standards of accounting but in June 1994 Daiwa Securities, one of the Big Four, and the Japan Securities' Dealers Association were cleared of negligence in the affair. Another firm, called Hanix Industry, finished with debts of ¥130 billion and the suicide of its president, who had been accused of tax evasion, on the premises of the National Tax Administration Agency.[15]

These serious problems in accounting and the sort of regulation which would mean more than the exercise of power by bureaucrats allow companies to avoid disclosing anything like the true state of the business: something commonly referred to as a lack of transparency, though one might think that this itself was an understatement.[16] In the 1990s it has led some foreign financial institutions to be very wary of ventures with their Japanese counterparts for fear of skeletons in the cupboard.

A Japanese speaker was twice invited to address the Japan Statutory Auditors Association and upset many of the audience by openly criticizing the auditing practices of such internationally renowned first class companies as Toyota and Matsushita. The Association's custom was to print a guest speaker's address in its magazine but his was not included on either occasion.[17] One of his points was that if all the auditors except one were themselves members of the company being audited, the outsider would be under strong pressure to conform and would soon turn into an inside auditor: so how could auditing be independent or objective?

For what it is worth, a small number of strong companies had introduced full consolidated accounting by April 1998, which was due to become compulsory in April 1999.[18] For others that were profitable the problem was to avoid paying tax as far as possible and it was an open secret that many that reported 'losses' were in fact doing well. This was the explanation for the apparently large number of firms that were loss-making: the opposite case from the banks, for instance, who were also shuffling figures around and using dubious criteria to claim that debts were being repaid when they really were in deep trouble.

The same critic was also invited to comment on a proposed amendment to the Commercial Code before the House of Councillors, i.e. upper house, Judicial Affairs Committee. Twelve years previously the Code had been amended in an attempt to suppress the *sokaiya* by laying down that a company manager who paid for their services of intimidating shareholders or closing down meetings quickly should be arrested and charged.

This happened to the heads of the general affairs departments at leading companies, such as Kirin Beer, then the market leader, and a member of the Mitsubishi Group *keiretsu*, Sumitomo Marine and Fire Insurance, Isetan, the major department store, Konica, the well known camera maker and many others. The farcical nature of the proceedings was that, although the managers were prosecuted as if they had been acting independently, everyone was aware that they had been acting on company instructions and that the company would make up for any penalties that might be imposed.[19]

Many companies do not open their shareholders' meetings either to the public or to the media and, although new rules may be announced, it will not be easy to change the underlying reality; if one assumes that that is the genuine intention and not just another piece of *tatemae*. Here it is not the intention to argue whether these ways of conducting business should be changed or not, which the Japanese themselves must decide. It is simply a question of being realistic about the system as it is, which is of great concern to European, American or other firms doing business with Japan and to anyone who needs to understand that Japanese business rests on accounting, auditing and presentation techniques that make it look very different from what it is. This helps to explain why the crisis of the 1990s, initially brought home to people by Yamaichi's bankruptcy, but which follows others in the past, is not as surprising as it at first appears. Sometimes, as Stalin put it, the truth is so important – to competitors for instance – that it must be protected by a bodyguard of lies.

That there are Japanese critics of accounting practices etc. shows that the present system does not command universal support and in this and other instances to be discussed there are even people prepared to incur the risk of physical violence from the *yakuza*, the gangster members of the organized crime syndicates, sometimes known as the Japanese Mafia. Since false accounting, rigged shareholders' meetings and disclosure of information that may well not give a full and fair picture of a company's situation produces losers as well as winners, some readers may now be wondering why the losers apparently do little about it.

In a postscript to the Yamaichi affair, though hardly likely to be the end of it, the *Financial Times* reported that forty shareholders were actually suing the Yamaichi management and their auditors: 'The suit is the first fully-fledged legal action taken against an auditing firm in Japan!' This led the new head of the accountancy association to comment that, 'This is new in Japan. It will force the accountancy profession to act more rigorously in the future'[20], though how likely this is remains to be seen.

The paper also reported that several of the Big Six international accountancy firms had been worried about their network partners and had been trying, with what degree of success was not clear, to press them to improve standards. In the Yamaichi case, the auditors had passed accounts, which were later revealed to be concealing ¥260 billion of hidden losses. Even so the Ministry of Finance had tried to insist that the company was still solvent. Then in June 1998 Yamaichi had admitted that its liabilities exceeded its assets by ¥22.5 billion, or £100 million at current rates, and that it could not repay ¥43 million in subordinated loans from insurance companies. The auditors refused to comment and the Ministry denied knowing about the losses: to which one might reply that they would do – of course.

As of June 1998 the *Financial Times* reported that, 'Cozy relations between companies and auditors impugn the veracity of audited figures. Consolidated accounting is still scarce and cashflow statements are unaudited'. The way in which the first suit in Japan against a firm of auditors was described as an epoch-making event gave an idea of how revolutionary it appeared.

The role of law, rather than rule of law, in Japan will be discussed later but it can briefly be said here that it is not usually much help and even slower than in a country like Britain, where it has never been famous for speed. Recourse to law is said to represent a breakdown in relations and a failure to solve problems that should be settled by negotiation, often involving a go-between. In the light of what was said earlier about the importance in Japan of 'relationships, as in feudalism, not rules', it should be clear that Japan does not have what Max Weber termed a 'legal-rational' order and that it would be a mistake for a foreign business to proceed as if it did. Because they have power, bureaucrats can insist on a highly legalistic application of rules as they interpret them but that is not the same thing as the notion of equality before the law. The move 'from status to contract', to use the famous phrase of Sir Henry Maine, in other words from subjective, personalized, patron-client relationships to objective, statute-based relations, frequently defined in writing, as in everything from job descriptions, equal opportunities law and supplier contracts to codes of rights and duties, does not characterize Japan. An old joke is that it is only when the contract has been signed that the hard bargaining begins.

The important point is to recognize that a way of operating based on 'status' in Maine's sense and another based on 'contract', to put it briefly, are very different. Japanese lecturers at the EU-Japan Centre and elsewhere liked to compare a system where recourse to the law is less frequent with those where it is more common. Naturally, their main comparison was with the US, criticized elsewhere for being too litigious and, unless one happens to be a lawyer, it can seem attractive to settle matters more informally by negotiation. This sounds fine until one asks who is likely to win in a negotiation: the strong or the weak? Without a more objective basis, the answer is obvious, making basically a lawless system less attractive. It is part of the explanation why the suit brought by disgruntled shareholders who had lost money against Yamaichi and its auditors was so startling.

In these circumstances, where much business depends on the famous 'trust' between individuals who may have known each other for a considerable time, and who are careful not to inform others or to put down too much on paper, so that things can easily be denied, it is not surprising that the world's so far biggest commercial scandal since the Second World War and another major international financial scandal in which the supposed regulatory body, the Ministry of Finance, colluded with the offending company in suppressing information, both involved Japanese corporations. And not just any old corporation but companies of the first rank and household names in Japan. The world's so far biggest fraud was the Sumitomo Corporation copper trading scandal, while the international financial scandal involved Daiwa Bank, New York.

In 1995 the old-established British merchant bank Barings had gone bankrupt as a result of losses of £869 million run up in unauthorized deals by an inadequately supervised derivatives trader on the Singapore Exchange.[21] Barings was not bailed out by the John Major government in Britain and was taken over by the Dutch concern ING.

In July of the same year, 1995, Toshihide Iguchi, executive vice-president of Daiwa Bank, New York, confessed in a letter to headquarters in Japan that he had lost US $ one billion, at that time £710 million, in unauthorized dealings in US Treasury securities: a straightforward business compared to derivatives. These undetected losses had been hidden for no less than eleven years, despite the fact that they represented just over a ninth of the total assets of Daiwa Bank in New York. Nevertheless, the bank filed a regular quarterly report to the American authorities in which they did not disclose the losses and stated that they still held the US Treasury bonds that they knew Iguchi had already sold to cover his losses. Doubtless by coincidence, the bank disposed of 1,500 boxes of documents in July, denying of course that this had anything to do with a cover-up. Iguchi was arrested and Masahiro Tsuda, the New York manager, was charged with complicity,[22] attempting to hide the losses from the American authorities by using an intermediary in the Cayman Islands.[23]

What infuriated the Americans was that, on their own admission, the Japanese Ministry of Finance regulators did not inform them of the Daiwa fraud for six whole weeks. Inevitably there were questions about what had been going on between Daiwa and the Ministry in the meantime; but the Ministry announced that they were not prepared to testify in New York, as the American authorities had requested.

It should be emphasized that Japanese banks abroad are still subject to the guidance of the Ministry of Finance (MOF) and that their head offices in Japan would not want them to do anything that would upset their relations with this key ministry. Japanese banks have people who are responsible for their relations with MOF known as 'MOFtan': a compound word made up of the English initials for the Ministry plus 'tan', the abbreviated form of the common Japanese term *tantosha*, meaning 'person responsible'. MOF officials may periodically visit Japanese banks overseas, especially in financial centres like London or New York.

Unlike Barings, Daiwa did not go bankrupt and was able to absorb its losses: a source of satisfaction to some MOF bureaucrats, who saw this as proof of the strength of Japan's banking system. But in a deal reached at the Manhattan Federal Court, Daiwa was banned from operating in the US and fined US $340 million. This was a considerable loss of face, although Daiwa's American operations were taken over by the Sumitomo Bank; to some extent 'keeping it in the family'.

In its leading article of 7 November 1995 the *Japan Times* commented that Daiwa was unlikely to be an isolated case because its way of doing business was characteristic of the 'cooperative' Japanese style; or as some might say, collusive. If that is so, and what has happened since the Daiwa affair would appear to bear out the *Japan Times's* contention, how many other companies may there be that with the connivance of the auditors and ministries concerned present a sound-looking facade to the outside world while being a great deal less solid in reality?[24]

How difficult it is for anyone not on the inside to get the real picture is shown by the wildly different figures given at different times for the bad debts of the leading financial institutions. In November 1995 for instance the American banking research company Veribanc Inc. gave the figure of ¥140 trillion for the bad debts of 150 leading Japanese financial institutions: the Ministry of Finance gave the figure of ¥38 trillion.[25] Whether Veribanc's figure is accurate, one can be pretty certain that MOF's was understated, not merely because MOF would not want to suggest that the banking system was shaky, but also because an admission that this was the case would lead to accusations that MOF itself as the ministry responsible was not making a proper job of ensuring its soundness.

Rightly or wrongly, many Japanese blame MOF, as the main creator of the country's economic policy, for the recession and MOF has undoubtedly lost face.[26] This is a serious matter in Japan and one that will not easily be forgotten or repaired. It might be compared to the Major government's loss of the Conservative Party's reputation for competent economic management over the ERM, the European exchange rate mechanism; with the difference of course that governments in Britain can be voted out, while the Japanese bureaucracy goes marching on.

MOF's reputation has not been helped by the allegations of bribery and corruption against some of its officials and the sight of investigators from the prosecutor's office descending on its premises. A common allegation was that officials had passed on confidential information after being 'wined and dined', and perhaps more. Since, to follow the *Japan Times's* comment on the 'cooperative' style of business in Japan, everyone knew that 'wining and dining' had been going on for years, and is indeed common throughout the Japanese business world, which has most generous entertainment allowances, the question is why MOF was attacked at that particular time: it could not just be coincidence when the law has left such practices alone for so long. Nature abhors a vacuum, in this case of power, and MOF's relative loss of face and credibility was seen by some politicians as a chance for them to increase their influence on policy-making at MOF's expense.

The worth of statistics depends on the criteria on which they are based and on their interpretation. Japanese accounting and auditing practice can easily avoid presenting a full and fair picture of a company's position. The unemployment statistics that attract so much admiration outside Japan are easily massaged. According to the criteria used, people who work only a very small number of hours a week are included among the employed. Women who become unemployed are classified as working at home and therefore drop out of the unemployment figures. It takes longer to be registered as unemployed in Japan than it does in Britain for example.

Particularly in international comparisons, it is important to be sure that one is comparing like with like: and not making comparisons of apples with pears, as so often happens with information on Japan put out by Japanese officials and others, including some foreign supporters, that show the Japanese politico-economic system in a flattering light at others' expense. Information is a competitive weapon, as Sun Tzu showed.

In the case of the banks' bad loans, one needs to look first at the criteria on which the figures released to the outside world are based. There are four categories:-

1. Loans considered recoverable.
2. Loans requiring a warning to the debtor.
3. Loans that may not be recovered.
4. Loans judged to be unrecoverable.

It requires little imagination to see how the banks or the Ministry, or both cooperating behind the screen, can classify or reclassify the status of loans according to their convenience.

The demerit system operating in the Japanese bureaucracy means that if problems are caused by what a bureaucrat has said outside his career will suffer. So it is safer to give away as little as possible.[27] Those in Britain who complain about official secrecy should consider themselves fortunate by comparison. The US, of course, has the Freedom of Information Act.

Japan's leading economic newspaper wrote that many loans in the second category, requiring a warning to the debtor, were likely to find their way into the bottom, or unrecoverable, category after a few years. The paper stated that in 1997 MOF and the Bank of Japan had announced that the amount of doubtful loans held by the major banks was ¥79 trillion, then US $612.4 billion: a figure 3.1 times higher than the official figure for 1996. The major banks accounted for ¥57.3 trillion and the regional and second tier banks for ¥21.7 trillion. The total represented 14 per cent of all money loaned: an immense sum.[28]

Under international pressure, MOF admitted subsequently that the amount of risky loans was indeed larger than anything that had previously been revealed, if a wider definition of what was risky was used. The banks were also said to have ¥65,300 billions worth of risky loans that they had not provided for. MOF claimed that most would be repaid, although a Bank of Japan survey had shown that 13 per cent of such loans had become uncollectable after three years.[29] As the developing crisis showed, these official expressions of optimism were likely to have the opposite effect on the outside world, simply producing greater scepticism.

In April 1998 a new estimate of problematic bad loans was put at ¥77 trillion, or US $595 billion. Foreign investors such as Goldman Sachs were buying them, unaware in some cases that they were *yakuza* related loans with special recovery problems. The house occupied by an executive of the American firm Cargill was set on fire, presumably as a warning. Japanese banks naturally denied that they had deliberately sold *yakuza*-related loans to foreigners but one foreign investment banker remarked that, 'Some people have been very naïve.'[30] There could not be a clearer example of the need to know the nature of Japanese business before getting into things.

The Yamaichi affair was significant not only because it was a major disaster for one of the four top rank stockbroking firms but also because of the impact it had outside Japan as an unexpected surprise and because of what it revealed for the first time to an unsuspecting international public of the real position of the firm. The same thing can be said about the banking crisis, the Daiwa Bank, New York, affair and the Sumitomo Corporation copper trading scandal.

This last speculative fraud, the biggest anywhere since the end of the Second World War in 1945, involved Yasuo Hamanaka of Sumitomo Corporation, known and feared as 'Mr Copper' or 'Mr Five Per Cent', who traded on the London Metal Exchange, the global centre of copper trading. Sumitomo Corporation is the trading arm of the Sumitomo Group, or *keiretsu*, one of Japan's most venerable firms dating back to the seventeenth century, with a long history in the copper business. It is proud of the two business precepts handed down from the founder dating from about 1650. The first stresses 'integrity and sound management'. The second commits its employees not to 'pursue easy gains or act imprudently'.[31]

Sumitomo Corporation is the world's biggest copper trader and

Hamanaka's superiors supported him in his drive to keep prices up, though this was denied. In 1991 they devoted two pages of the Corporation's report in praise of him but in the same year the London Metal Exchange (LME) had been investigating fluctuations in the copper price which suggested that it was being rigged. They had also investigated an allegation by another trader on the LME that Hamanaka had asked him to confirm trades that had not taken place, stating that a false invoice was needed by Sumitomo in Japan 'for tax reasons'.

Then in 1996 the position that Hamanaka had built up in the market collapsed. He informed Sumitomo of the losses totalling US $2.6 billion, or £1.6 billion, that he had been making, was fired and disappeared.

Turning up in Japan, he admitted fraud and forgery. A week later the president of Sumitomo Corporation resigned, to 'take responsibility' as they say in such cases in Japan, although the Corporation claimed that what had happened was solely the work of one person. But would Hamanaka have received the president's commendation without adequate proof of his value to the company? He had also been working in a head office environment close to other colleagues and staff. Japanese authorities who explain the basis of personnel management in Japan emphasize the importance of relationships at work, expressed in such terms as teamwork, information sharing and cooperation:[32] the opposite of keeping information to oneself and something that in a typical Japanese open plan office would not be easy in any case.

From personal experience of organizations in Japan, one of the things that strikes one when one gets to know them is that, behind an outward impression of harmoniousness, there is considerable watchfulness of what other people are doing. There is gossip and even what someone would like to keep secret has a habit of leaking out. The well known novel *Shoshaman* i.e., trading company man, written by a Sumitomo Corporation manager, though not one connected with the copper business, and other Japanese business stories give the flavour of the company atmosphere.[33] In the wider society it is common to be curious about neighbours and to watch out for even small things about them. In some people it develops a sixth sense about what they are really up to. As a male manager of Sumitomo's 'permanent staff', Hamanaka was very much a company insider, which would imply close relations with colleagues. Loners in such a traditional company would not be the style.

The involvement of the Ministry of Finance in covering up the Daiwa Bank, New York, affair was already mentioned. In the Sumitomo Corporation copper scandal one might also wonder what the role of the supervising ministry, the Ministry of International Trade and Industry (MITI), was. They would certainly have had an interest in seeing that there were adequate supplies of such a strategic metal as copper for Japanese industry and they could hardly have been ignorant of the fact that Sumitomo was the world's biggest copper trader. The Sumitomo Group, or *keiretsu*, was one of the four pre-war *zaibatsu* at the heart of the Japanese economy and continued to play a role in the power structure of the Iron Triangle of big business, bureaucracy and political fixers commensurate with the weight and scope of its score or so member companies making up its nucleus, plus many more in which it has shareholdings and interlocking directorships.[34] It is hardly the sort of group of companies that MITI would not take a keen interest in.

Investigations into Hamanaka's activities had started in London at the LME and the case had American connections through others engaged in the copper business and the LME copper warehouse at Long Beach, California. But with his trial being held in Japan under Japanese jurisdiction, neither the Serious Fraud Office in London nor the American authorities were able to make much progress.[35] In February 1998 Sumitomo Corporation claimed damages of ¥736 million, or £3.4 million against Hamanaka, his former superior Saburo Shimizu and a company set up by the latter called Scat: a word defined in the Oxford Dictionary as 'to depart quickly' or 'a wordless jazz song'! The grand total of Hamanaka's frauds was said to be US $2.6 billion, or £1.5 billion: a rather different sum from the one that Sumitomo was claiming.

Hamanaka had made his first confession to Sumitomo in June 1996 but as late as March 1998 – a year and three-quarters later – investigators in Britain were still trying to discover how the copper price on international markets had been manipulated. In the US, Sumitomo and some American companies were being sued for alleged manipulation of copper futures contracts.

At his trial, Hamanaka pleaded guilty but was not permitted to comment on what had happened. Prosecutors demanded a ten-year prison sentence but this was reduced to eight. The two charges raised referred only to a sum of US $770 defrauded from a Sumitomo subsidiary in Hong Kong: not, for example, to Hamanaka's role in influencing world copper prices over more than a decade. The judge criticized Sumitomo for its lax management and for being too oriented towards sheer profit. He accepted the view that Hamanaka's main motive had been to prevent losses for his company and to hide them in order to save his face at work: remarks that do not suggest great awareness of what has been frequently claimed to be the 'internationalization' of Japan.

Two years after Hamanaka's original confession, in May 1998, the US Commodity Futures Trading Commission (CFTC) announced that Sumitomo had agreed to pay the biggest fine in the agency's history of US $150 million, or £92 million, to settle charges of illegal copper trades. This brought the investigations by the CFTC and by the Financial Services Authority (FSA) in London to an end as far as Sumitomo was concerned, although investigations into other companies involved were proceeding with Sumitomo's help. The CFTC explained that the high level of the fine reflected the profits made by Hamanaka, Sumitomo and those acting with it that had artificially forced up the price. Three months later it was announced that Sumitomo had taken 'another big step towards wiping the slate clean' by agreeing to pay US $99 million to settle six class actions brought in New York: while continuing to negotiate in other class actions brought in California. The fine imposed by the FSA in London was US $8 million. As with the American CFTC, this was a record amount.

The Daiwa Bank, New York, and the Sumitomo Corporation copper speculations may have been gambles and frauds on a large scale but much of Japanese business and industry as a whole launched into a binge of over-investment and speculation during the 'bubble economy' of the 1980s. Perhaps it will become as famous in time as the Dutch tulip mania of the seventeenth century or the South Sea Company bubble of the eighteenth century. In Britain, in the 1970s, there was the Barber Boom, named after the Chancellor of the Exchequer of the Heath government, in which real estate and the building of offices for which there were then no tenants, as subsequently in Japan, played a large role; but Japan's 'bubble economy' was on a vaster scale.

The Finance Minister of the time was Kiichi Miyazawa, who was forced to resign because of the Recruit scandal, Japan's largest postwar scandal, involving gifts of shares in return for political favours: not, be it noted, for whatever he may have done about controlling the 'bubble', although there were criticisms of him later for not having done more. He then reappeared as prime minister from November 1991 to August 1993, being succeeded in rapid succession by two prime ministers on whom people had pinned hopes of reform. Finally, in August 1998, he was invited by the new prime minister, Keizo Obuchi, in the midst of the banking crisis to become Finance Minister again. If this sounds strange to some people, it should be borne in mind that Miyazawa occupied an important place in what it is convenient to refer to as the party of government, virtually without interruption since 1945, the Liberal Democratic Party (LDP), as a powerful faction leader. Indeed, the new prime minister himself, Obuchi, who took over after the policy of his predecessor, Ryutaro Hashimoto, was generally agreed to have been a disaster, and which lost the LDP its control over the Upper House, was the least popular of the three candidates for the post with the public. But such is the power of the LDP factions and the deals carved up in the smoke-filled backrooms of Japanese politics, to be discussed later.

To understand how the 'bubble' – the Japanese use the English term – occurred, one has to go back to Occupation policy in the late 1940s, which first fixed the ¥-dollar exchange rate after the war. An emissary of the US Federal Reserve had recommended a rate of between ¥270 to ¥300 to the dollar but the Occupation authorities had decided on ¥360 to the dollar instead. Due to the comparatively rapid postwar recovery and in particular the development of competitive export industries, backed by the need to save and industrial banking at home, the Yen became undervalued, though by 1971 it had appreciated to ¥270 to the dollar, as Mr. Young of the Federal Reserve had suggested in the first place.[36]

Japanese exporters had liked the old rate of ¥360 to the dollar – and in 1962 the rate had been ¥1,000 to the pound – since it helped them sell to price-sensitive consumers in their principal overseas market, the US, where there was little of the 'imports bad, exports good' philosophy that was being assiduously followed in Japan and where few people cared where the goods they bought came from. As already mentioned, part of America's Cold War policy was to provide access to its markets for Japanese exporters.

By the 1980s the situation had changed and while the Yen had fluctuated between ¥275 and ¥200 to the dollar, the reasoning was that an undervalued Yen was giving Japanese exporters too much of an edge. As the American trade deficit with Japan rose from US $1.2 billion to US $33.6 billion it was increasingly felt that the policy of the late 1940s had become too much of a good thing.[37]

An international meeting was therefore convened at the Plaza Hotel, New York, in September 1985 to revalue the Yen upwards at a more realistic rate,[38] beginning the *endaka*, or appreciation of the Yen, that was used by the authorities in Japan to stimulate a mood of crisis and get everyone to work harder and make industries more competitive still by cost cutting. Quality management, not just applied to quality but to ways of making manufacturing more efficient and cost effective, and such famous techniques as JIT (Just in Time) systems, largely getting rid of buffer stocks and keeping the workforce on its toes, contributed to increased competitiveness to offset the effects of the high Yen. Indeed everything that is nowadays associated with 'lean management' can be seen in the same context of the relentless drive towards increasing competitiveness and cost reduction, or 'cost down' as it is termed in Japan.

After the Plaza Agreement of 1985, further pressure was added, resulting in the Louvre Agreement of February 1987. The following year the Yen rose sharply and between then and 1992 it fluctuated around ¥150 to ¥125 to the dollar. Each time it appreciated there were howls of anguish from Japanese manufacturers, although it suited those who were buying companies and property abroad, especially when the Yen reached its peak of ¥86 to the dollar in 1995. At that point it made some Japanese feel that they had after all won the

Second World War and were now the greatest. Some had already felt that earlier on, like the business leader who publicly stated that, 'In the twenty-first century Japan will use Australia as a mining concession and the US as a grain silo.' On being asked by a British journalist how Europe would 'fit into your plans', he replied that, 'I suppose we could use Europe as a boutique.'[39]

Like the US, the EU has had constant trade deficits with Japan, ranging from ECU 16 billion in 1984, ECU 31 billion in 1992 and ECU 22 billion in 1994. After the collapse of the 'bubble' Japanese exports again increased, while imports declined, with the inevitable effect on the balance of payments.[40] The Japanese manufacturers' howls of anguish at the high Yen and the officially orchestrated campaign to work harder for internal consumption may also have had the effect of lulling competitors into a false sense of security and of encouraging all those who, on the basis of a crude application of free market theory, were once again prophesying the imminent collapse of the Japanese economy. What they had not reckoned with was how exaggerated the handwringing over the high Yen was and how effective the measures that Japan's leaders would adopt to make the Plaza and Louvre Agreements largely a dead letter would be.

Anyone who was in Japan at the time will remember the feverish discussion of the threat that the high Yen posed to national competitiveness: a discussion fanned by management pronouncements and a compliant media that, as other topics do from time to time, became the fashionable talking point. In a more free market system, the objective basis for the anxiety would be understandable, but as late as 1998, well after the bubble had burst and when Japan was facing the serious problems that this had caused, the chairman of Mitsubishi Heavy Industries, the country's largest maker of heavy machinery, could still say that, 'Profit maximization is inappropriate for manufacturing industry'; meaning that increasing market share and maintaining employment were more important.[41] In the light of the number of car makers, including the Mitsubishi Group's own Mitsubishi Motors, and Nissan and Mazda, as well as firms in other such strategic sectors as steel, that stood in great need of improved profitability, it was an amazing statement.

It would have been quite natural, however, thirteen years earlier, the time of the Plaza Agreement of 1985 and the decision by the Ministry of Finance to offset the effects of the Agreement by making it cheap for companies to borrow the money that they needed to re-equip themselves and to encourage them to do so. The Ministry's decision then opened the way for the speculative bubble, the bills for which were to become due in the late 1990s.

At home, many Japanese, supposedly sober savers and investors, were persuaded to invest in stocks and land by promises of speculative gains. Organized crime piled into 'housing and loan' schemes, supposedly set up to provide housing for the ordinary person, but in fact leading to the *jusen* scandals and unrecoverable loans. Abroad, the high Yen meant that Japanese companies went on a spending spree. Such all-American icons as New York's Rockefeller Centre, Columbia Pictures and MCA Studios in Hollywood, were bought by Mitsubishi Real Estate, Sony and Matsushita Electric respectively. Japanese purchases of property, hotels and golf clubs in Hawaii reached the point where they caused serious local friction, not least because part of it was alleged to represent the laundering of drug money by the *yakuza*, the Japanese Mafia.[42] A famous piece of 'conspicuous consumption' was the purchase of one of Van Gogh's 'Sunflower' paintings for US $85 million. Where was the belief in long-term strategies rather than in speculation that Japanese lecturers and books liked to tell their foreign audiences was one of the hallmarks of Japanese management and a principal reason for its success?

Many investments, like Rockefeller Centre etc. turned out badly. Previously it was Japanese manufactured products and how they had penetrated world markets that had attracted attention. Now it was the power of financial institutions that caused a stir. By 1990 Japanese banks controlled a quarter of California's banking: California alone being the world's sixth largest economy.[43] In 1989 Japanese banks' loans for property in Britain shot up by 56 per cent from £2.3 billion to £3.7 billion: a figure in excess of one tenth of all property loans in the UK.[44]

With the exchange in their favour, Japanese tourists flooded abroad, benefiting the producers of sought after high status luxury goods like Burberry, Dunhill, Gucci, Hermes and Louis Vuitton, whose goods were heavily marked up in Japan due to the layers of middlemen in the distribution system, each taking his commission. Some visitors would buy these products in Europe for resale in Japan, so that shops like Hermes had to 'ration' 'individual Japanese customers to a certain number of scarves for example.

The paradox was that, because of the difference between the exchange value of the Yen in Europe or America and its real purchasing power in Japan, tourists could enjoy an illusion of wealth overseas, staying in expensive hotels and buying luxury goods, that high prices at home made impossible. But unless they were familiar with living conditions in Japan, most people in the countries they visited were unlikely to know that and imagined instead that Japan must be an extremely rich country. Few Japanese wanted to lose face or spoil their holidays by disillusioning them.

Speculation in land, by the big general trading companies among others, drove prices up to absurd levels, where Japan's land value was theoretically four times that of the US: a country twenty-five times larger. The nominal value of the Imperial Palace grounds in Tokyo was supposed to be greater than that of California. This land price inflation was good for those who owned property, and correspondingly bad for anyone hoping to buy some land and build a house on it in their lifetime; unless perhaps they accepted the banks' latest wheeze, which was a hundred year mortgage.[45] Landowners, however, could use their property as collateral: some using the same collateral several times over with different banks and recycling shares and money in the bank to borrow even more to speculate on the Stock Exchange or in land, the banks being only too happy at that time to lend as much as possible. The imprudence of the speculative lending spree was to come back to haunt them in the late 1990s when the English term 'credit crunch' came into use; but then the banks did not check how many times the same collateral was being used.

The devastatingly simple point about the price of land in Japan was that it obviously did not depend on international market forces. Instead, its price was what Japanese financial institutions, which really meant the Ministry of Finance, abetted by speculators and landowners, said it was. In the bubble, the inflated price they said it was worth, as collateral, enormously increased the total amount of money that banks could lend, either for speculation or investment.[46] Where was the traditional Japanese frugality that we used to hear so much about? It was only later, in the ensuing banking crisis, that the resemblance of this bubble to other classic bubbles of the past became clear and for a great many people in Japan the resulting hangover after the orgy was equally painful.

In the meantime, the stockbroking companies used such tricks as ramping up prices, deliberately giving investors misleading advice and 'churning' i.e. making an excessive number of trades for the same investor, profiting each time on commissions and margin interest. A notorious incident was the case of Wakabayashi Real Estate Co., who had lost large sums because of 'churning' and who sued New Japan Securities, a firm in which the Industrial Bank of Japan had a share, although not in excess of the statutory five per cent.

Nomura Securities, not merely Japan's but the world's biggest stockbroking company, and Nikko Securities, another of the Big Four, were caught openly dealing with gangsters from organized crime syndicates: whereas the accepted method was to do so through a middleman. The services of these *yakuza*, with their own considerable property interests, could be called upon: both for settling debts and for persuading the occupants of property desired by more powerful interests for speculative development to move out. Gangsters who specialize in this work, by such means as noise, dogs and threats of violence, are known as *jiageya*.

To discuss all the (known) scandals that occurred would take too long but a good example of how the Stock Market was rigged against the small investor and how business was done behind the screen with the powerful was revealed in the compensation scandals of

1989-1990. In 1989 Daiwa Securities and Yamaichi admitted that they had compensated certain large and important clients for losses on the Stock Market: an interesting sidelight on what was in theory a free market institution. They had then tried to declare the sum of ¥18 billion paid in compensation as tax-free business expenses! This had been rejected by the National Tax Authority, who made them pay. Nomura at that time denied that it had been compensating important clients but was not generally believed. The company was famous for training and driving its salesmen hard and for clearly distinguishing between clients according to how much they invested.[47]

A further problem for investors who were not grand enough to be able to hope for compensation was the absence of independent credit rating agencies, since the official agencies that did exist were under government influence, especially as regarded disclosing information. Ironically, it was an ex-Nomura man who had been in America who founded his own independent agency in 1975 and who had been warning that the profit levels of the bubble era were unsustainable. The belief that companies could not fail, because the web of relations between their creditors, customers and partners supported them was deeply ingrained, leaving little room for credit agencies, except perhaps among foreigners. But after the collapse of the bubble, this form of cooperation – or cronyism? – came under increasing pressure and the new independent credit rating agency began to attract more Japanese clients.[48]

At one stage during the recession the foreign agencies that had downgraded the credit ratings of Japanese companies were attacked by the Ministry of Finance 'for causing the slump': a classic instance of shooting the messenger who brings bad news. Since the agencies were American, it was also a good chance to scapegoat the foreigners.

The Nikkei Stock Market index reached its peak at the end of 1989 but by October 1990 it had lost 48 per cent of its value. The resulting client dismay can be imagined and when Nomura and Nikko were found in June 1990 to have been compensating their biggest clients after all it created yet another scandal. By way of the customary ritual apology, the two presidents resigned 'to take responsibility', as the stock phrase has it – and were moved up to the higher position of vice chairman – but smaller clients did not get their money back.

The technique was the same as that in other instances, for example, when the president of a dubious private university in Kyoto had been caught out in another case of financial manipulation, he resigned as president in the *tatemae* act of apology – and moved into an even grander office as chairman of the Board of Governors, from which he continued to run things as before. Cases where politicians caught taking bribes and then 'purifying' themselves by, for example, going to a Shinto shrine are too numerous to mention. An intriguing rumour at the time of the compensation scandal was that

Nomura, Nikko and others did not want to continue paying back such large sums to clients after the market had collapsed but could not actually say this to them directly and so used the device of being 'caught' by the tax authorities as a way out of their difficulty. Whether true or not, the fact that no one saw anything unlikely about the use of such a Machiavellian, or perhaps one should say Sun Tzu-like, subterfuge is suggestive of how business is conducted in a system where connexions, *konne*, are more important than rules i.e. in a basically lawless environment.

The then Minister of Finance, Ryutaro Hashimoto, later to become prime minister but forced to resign in 1998 over the mishandling of the recession, took a pay cut along with several senior MOF bureaucrats. This was to 'take responsibility' for the Ministry's role in the affair. Allegedly, the Ministry had first given 'administrative guidance' to the securities companies to pay compensation and then changed its mind: without leaving written evidence of course. Such affairs remind one of Sir Winston Churchill's remarks about the Soviet Union: a riddle wrapped in a mystery inside an enigma. This deliberate obfuscation serves to keep the man in the street in ignorance of what is going on behind the screen and to mystify foreigners and their prying eyes.

In Nomura's case, the president who resigned, Yoshihisa Tabuchi – nicknamed 'Little Tabuchi' to distinguish him from Setsuya, or 'Big Tabuchi', who was no relation but an ex-chairman of Nomura – did not fade out of the picture either.[49] People could hardly forget that Yoshihisa Tabuchi had been president in 1987, the year when Nomura had been Japan's most profitable company, and it is not uncommon for a manager with such a reputation to exercise power behind the screen through a protégé or puppet. This is common in politics, where the real power is wielded by *kuromaku*, the men behind the scenes, such as the late Shin Kanemaru and ex-prime minister Noboru Takeshita, whether they are formally leaders of an LDP faction or not. The same thing happened at the EU-Japan Centre after a theoretical change in the top management in 1990, where it quickly became apparent that the new incumbent was 'his master's voice' and dependent on the guidance of his predecessor, who sometimes worked openly at the Centre when the European general manager was away in Brussels or with the trainees. At Nomura, it was said that Tabuchi wanted to get back his old power after the situation had quietened down at the expense of Hideo Sakamaki, the new chairman.[50]

Then on 25 March 1997 the prosecutor's office sent no fewer then 180 investigators into Nomura's office in the sort of ritual and highly telegenic show for public consumption put on by the media in such cases of business or political corruption:[51] something I saw many times over a period of fifteen years. In this instance the media had been tipped off in advance and their announcement of the raid before it took place had led to an anticipatory drop in Nomura's share price.

The allegations were that Nomura had been paying billions of Yen to a property company called Kojin Building, that was connected with gangsters, and that it had been funding these payoffs by trading with Kojin's name without getting its permission: something that had just been forbidden in the same year.

In several quite notorious cases involving political leaders and government ministers the big initial show of the accused being hauled off by the police in the full glare of television reporting has been followed by the tapering off of the affair into insignificance, when the accused is admitted to hospital, spins things out with the lawyers or is fined a small sum. This is what the Japanese refer to as *ryuto-dabi*, 'the head of a dragon and the tail of a snake', or a bright beginning and a dull finish' as the dictionary puts it. It helps to explain the weary cynicism felt by so many Japanese about their political system.

This time, however, Nomura's stockbroking business was suspended for a week and dealing on its own account was closed down for five months; though of course it still had huge assets. President Sakamaki, two directors, 'Big' Tabuchi and 'Little' Tabuchi all resigned – for the second time in the latter case.[52] The new president, Junichi Ujiie, stated at a press conference that Nomura would now 'do its best' to abide by rules and regulations but did this lukewarm expression inspire confidence and, although the players might change, would the game?

Nomura had more than once promised not to have any more dealings with gangsters but in 1991, for instance, it had been involved with one of the most notorious gang leaders: Susumu Ishii, head of the second largest crime syndicate, the Inagawa-kai. Nomura's involvement included, among other things, ramping up the stock of Tokyu Corporation, the well known blue chip railway and department store group with an annual revenue of over ¥430 billion, to benefit Ishii: lending him ¥36 billion through affiliated companies; and buying, together with other companies, bogus private membership amounting to ¥38 billion in a golf club that Ishii was building that was in reality a public course, not private at all. Because golf in Japan is the high status game and because private membership, mostly paid by companies for business-related reasons, costs sums beyond the reach of most individuals, the construction of golf courses and their associated country clubs is a lucrative business and one that has led to quite a few scandals.

The heads of Nomura and also Nikko were obliged to apologize to the Diet, or parliament, although MOF's Securities Bureau stated that they could find no evidence of the ramping up of Tokyu shares. This time the Minister of Finance, Ryutaro Hashimoto, subsequently prime minister of course, also resigned.

The size of the sums involved and the nature of the dubious practices were an indication of the difficulties that were likely to be encountered during the changes that would be required over a period of four years starting in April 1998 to complete the so-called Big Bang. No wonder some people were sceptical that everything would be as above board as the publicity claimed.

The prosecutors' raid on Nomura in March 1997 uncovered the list of important clients due for special consideration. The list included the names of politicians needing large sums for election purposes and of bureaucrats who could be expected to return favours. It was further evidence, if this were needed, of the wide ramifications of this moneyspinning business and of the difficulty of clearing it up, if this was the intention, to ensure the transparency that would gain the confidence of investors: especially of the international institutions that the Big Bang was supposed to appeal to, in order to realize the aim of making Tokyo an international financial market on the scale of London or New York.

The compensation scheme that foreign brokers would have to contribute to, and about which they were of course only told *after* they had entered the market, was but one example of how what was advertised never quite lives up to expectations: like the repeated official statements of how seriously the government was taking the situation and how this time they really would take the serious and urgent steps necessary to deal with it etc. etc. Foreign diplomats saw the idea of the scheme as a device to hold back the influx of foreign brokers into the ranks of the top Japanese firms: something they would be sure to protest about as unfair if they were to receive similar treatment in New York or London. As one diplomat said, 'Let's face it. Foreign groups have the capital, the clean accounts and the effective management systems – and in a deregulated market, you can expect them to be the main beneficiaries'[53] – assuming that it really is deregulated.

The same report in the *Financial Times* mentioned that Japan's was the only developed market in which brokers were not legally required to separate their own assets from those of their clients. The government had apparently said that this would be changed but, yet again, had 'not confirmed a timetable': not exactly a sign of a serious commitment to the sort of change that would inspire confidence. It would be interesting to know what action foreign governments were taking to protect their firms against discrimination.

Nomura admitted that the penalties imposed upon it as a result of the compensation scandal of 1997 had halved its profits for that month, while some of its clients had decided to go elsewhere. Shikoku Electric Power Co., for instance, which had intended to raise ¥30 billions' worth of bonds, or US $240 millions' worth, with Nomura decided to take its business elsewhere. But how far will Japan's politico-economy, which revolves around the policy of keeping the foreigners at arm's length, really be willing to move outside its cozy and exclusive charmed circle?

Five Yamaichi executives had been arrested over payoffs to gangsters in September 1997. At Daiwa Securities the chairman, president and six executives resigned for the same reason. A high official at MOF was arrested on 18 January 1998 and charged with taking bribes from Nomura in return for favours i.e. inside information and other senior bureaucrats were being investigated.[54]

All these events help to explain the collusion, manipulation and speculation that drove up the prices of land and shares in the bubble but they were in a sense incidental to the main concern of manufacturing industry: how to continue to be competitive after the upward revaluation of the Yen following the Plaza Agreement, which was seen as a threat to their competitiveness. The idea was that using the cheap and plentiful credit available they would be able to re-equip themselves and become more efficient, thus avoiding the need to raise export prices.

At the lower end of the market they were already facing increased competition in steel, electronics, cars and ships from Taiwan, Korea and South East Asia and would have to watch China in the future. Whereas in the 1960s all Japanese domestic electrical products had been made in Japan, in the 1990s products such as telephones, radios and televisions were increasingly made elsewhere and, although they had the names of the big Japanese manufacturers on them, they contained a declining number of Japanese parts.

This move of production abroad out of Japan was, like the high Yen, discussed in apocalyptic terms by managers and in the media as the 'hollowing out', *kudoka*, of the Japanese economy, as if there would finally be nothing left to support Japan's large, and ageing, population. Fingers were pointed at the American example, where corporations had moved radio and electronics manufacturing off shore when it was no longer cost effective at home, losing their competence in these technologies and therefore their future potential as well.

But this handwringing was once again disingenuous. Firstly, it was a characteristic move to create a mood of crisis and to play on the latent feelings of insecurity that are seldom far from the surface in Japan, with the transparent aim of encouraging people to still greater efforts. Secondly, it glossed over the fact that, from the viewpoint of global competition, these moves of production offshore extended Japanese economic control and the formation of Japanese-style vertical relations between manufacturers and suppliers, tying the overseas sub-contractors to the main Japanese customer companies in dependent relationships.

The popular board game in Japan is not chess but *go*. Both games rely on strategy and thinking ahead but, whereas chess relies on the destruction of the enemy and the checkmating of the king, the essence of *go* is the invasion of territory and the securing of one's own position by keeping out the enemy. Shown weekly on Japanese television, it is a game that Japan's competitors should study. It is a good analogy for the penetration and conquest of markets previously held by others and which they had come to regard as their own out of force of habit.

Brazil, sometimes referred to as being in America's 'back yard', is a case in point where, starting out from a low position, Japanese firms, working together with the help of the information networks of their banks, general trading companies and official organizations such as JETRO (Japan External Trade Organization) made increasing inroads into the market, displacing their American competitors. It could be considered as a prototypical case study.[55]

The spread of Japanese companies and production abroad had of course started before the bubble economy but the increased gap in labour costs and the growing ability of firms in South East Asia etc. to produce to the standards required by their Japanese customers accelerated the process.[56] But many companies in Japan visited by the EU-Japan Centre in 1991–96 stated that their firm aim was to keep the core technology at home, without which they believed they would have no future: an aim that the authorities surely approved. To critics on the political Left, it seemed, however, that this overseas spread was Japan's 1940s 'Greater East Asia Co-Prosperity Sphere' – a nicely Orwellian expression – dressed up in new clothes.[57]

The high Yen made it possible for Japanese companies to buy up relatively cheaply not just physical assets but also knowledge-based technology in such fields generally agreed to have a bright future as biotechnology. At a company visit in 1995, for example, Kirin, Japan's leading brewer of the time, stated that they were buying one British and one Dutch company in this field, for their expertise in regard to plants.

A member of the European visitors' group felt that this was 'unfair' but instead of philosophizing it would be more to the point if the governments of the EU, US etc. did something about an uncompetitive situation where Japanese companies can buy up European or American etc. firms but where foreign firms cannot buy up Japanese firms except in rare cases, including those where, as with the hi-fi maker Sansui several years ago, the company was in such a state that no Japanese company would have wanted it. But what are the governments of the EU, US etc. doing? To ignore the potential for sharpening Japanese competitiveness that takeovers of firms with new, leading-edge technology give is extremely shortsighted. In the Japanese context, it is the kind of crowding out the competition from a field on which future competitiveness and prosperity depend that a good *go* player would appreciate. It is a question of seed corn.

Since Japan began its major industrialization under official guidance in 1868 and again, with a fresh impetus, after 1945, the purpose of the financial system has been to channel money to industry through the savings deposited in the banking system. Interest rates for individual savers have not been high but the need to save to build a house, to educate children, for emergencies and retirement has been a powerful motivation, reinforced by the ideology of thrift as a traditional virtue although, despite the propaganda, the Italians have consistently had higher savings rates than the Japanese.

This policy of channelling savings to industry, or of industrial banking for short,[58] placed the companies in an enviable position because of the close links between the banks and themselves; especially in the case of the large industrial groups, the *keiretsu*, such as Mitsui, Mitsubishi and Sumitomo, with their own bank at the heart of the group and sympathetic to their plans of long-term business expansion. This system of financing by the banks, and not by the Stock Exchange as in the Anglo-Saxon system, meant among other things that the companies did not have to worry overmuch about shareholders concerned with short-term company performance. They could also use the *sokaiya* to keep them quiet if necessary. At least until the bubble, when the methods of artificially creating huge amounts of money with which to speculate, that have already been outlined, most Japanese shareholders looked for modest but stable returns on their investments, rather than a killing.

The industrial banking policy was undoubtedly successful in building up Japan's industrial and commercial strength during its progress as what has aptly been described as a 'capitalist developmental state'[59] Through measures such as the crossholding of shares by companies in one another and the web of relatively stable business relations, seen most clearly in the motor and electronics industries for example, the aims of Friedrich List and his 'national economy strategy' were fulfilled. Foreign control through mergers and acquisitions was almost totally excluded and for many years the foreign share of a joint venture was limited to a minority shareholding of 49 per cent. Indeed, even having 51 per cent or more may not make a significant difference in practice. Japanese staff seconded to a joint venture with a foreign company continue to owe their loyalty and their fortune to their Japanese employer and the fact of being under the jurisdiction of Japan's particularistic system of regulation means that foreign managers, unless they have considerable experience, will always be at a disadvantage. A foreign manager at one joint venture on a tour around the office asked one of the Japanese staff what he was doing and was most surprised to be told, 'Oh, I'm making a report for the Ministry of Finance.' It was the first he had heard of it.

As recently as 1980 laws relating to foreign exchange and the control of foreign trade made direct investment by foreigners in

Japanese companies impossible. After that date structural barriers, such as crossholdings of shares and membership of one of the large industrial groups – which has become an issue in US-Japan trade negotiations – continue to act as powerful barriers. It is not difficult to see the principles of the game of *go* in operation.

The most famous example of an attempt by a foreign shareholder to increase its control over a company in Japan was the Koito case. This company, a major producer of car parts, is a member of the Toyota Group in which Toyota naturally holds shares. An American merchant bank, Boone Co., controlled by the colourful financier T. Boone Pickens, had bought a 26.4 per cent stake in the company at a cost of ¥145 billion, at that time US $1.2 billion. Toyota, with a stake of 20.2 per cent had three Board members and Pickens wanted a seat or seats on the Board too. After various delays, Pickens got a court order to see Koito's books, though after what was already said about Japanese accounting practices this might not have been much help to him. At all events, no Japanese accountant would explain them. Concluding it was a waste of time, Pickens gave up. It has been estimated that 70 per cent of all Japanese company shares are crossholdings, held by other companies or financial institutions, who in normal circumstances will not trade them.[60]

The absorption of one Japanese company by another is certainly not unknown but is usually the result of one company having got into trouble and having to be rescued by the other. A famous case was the takeover by the general trading company C. Itoh of Ataka & Co., another general trading company that had got into trouble over an overseas oil contract, back in 1975. After the bursting of the bubble in the 1990s, there was much discussion of similar rescues in the seriously troubled banking sector. But until then most mergers had been between smaller firms, with a company like Ataka, formerly 'number ten' among the big general trading companies, being the exception.[61]

The rarity of M & A (mergers and acquisitions) by foreign firms in Japan can be understood from the fact that over a period of nearly thirty years, from 1955 to 1984, there were only 32 cases: a drop in the ocean by prevailing standards elsewhere. Between 1984 and 1991 there were just eleven cases where American companies bought the majority interest in Japanese firms. The British company Glaxo, after over four decades in a joint venture and a considerable period of negotiation, was finally able to buy out its Japanese partner, who had apparently been reluctant to make significant investments in the venture. Glaxo had approximately five per cent of the world pharmaceutical market but even after more than forty years only two per cent of the Japanese market, which was described in the press as 'notoriously closed'. Taking full control in 1996 (sic) was intended to improve its market position.[62]

As noted above, 70 per cent of all Japanese shares are crossholdings that are not traded in normal circumstances. Until Nissan, the most interesting case of a major manufacturing company that had got into trouble and been forced to compromise was Mazda.

Back in the 1970s at the time of the oil crisis the new gas-guzzling rotary engines that the company had introduced from NSU nearly finished the company off and the main creditor, the Sumitomo Bank, sent in its people to turn the company round. Then in 1979 Ford entered into a collaborative agreement with Mazda and took a stake of 24.5 per cent, profiting from Mazda's skills in production engineering and product development. But this was not all sweetness and light and in 1992 Ford brought an anti-dumping suit against several Japanese motor manufacturers, including Mazda. There was tension and rivalry between the two, despite the cooperative agreement.

While an innovative company with an excellent state-of-the-art factory at Hofu in Western Japan, Mazda's strategy to expand in order to challenge its rivals higher up the Japanese ranking order was a failure and in 1994 it ran up losses of US $294.4 million in six months in Japan alone: almost twice as much as in the preceding year. This time the Sumitomo Bank asked Ford to take over Mazda's management – an epoch-making event – while Mazda's plant in the US had also been mismanaged and lost money. Some 320 out of 400 Japanese expatriates were sent home and Sumitomo was worried about Mazda's debts of nearly US $8 billion. In an unusually frank remark, the chairman of the Sumitomo Bank plainly stated that, 'I wanted Ford, which is profitable in the US, to come and teach Mazda.' Ironically, in view of the problems that have plagued the British motor industry since 1945 and the fact that it is now virtually entirely in foreign hands itself, it was a British manager who was chosen to repair Mazda. Ford's chairman, Alex Trotman, was also British.

Ford's intervention was described as, 'A major event in world economic history: a major US company taking over a major Japanese company', by James P. Womack, one of the authors of the book about Japanese lean management techniques in the motor industry, *The Machine that changed the World*. Whether this is so remains to be seen and Ford's stake of just under a quarter of the shares was not exactly a takeover in the usual sense.

When Ford did increase its stake to 33.3 per cent in 1996, the Japanese press saw Mazda's rescue by Ford as a national disgrace. Previously the Mazda union's leader had said that they did not like being helped by Sumitomo 'and they are Japanese. If Ford takes over Mazda, we would like it even less'[63]. These comments may be compared with those in Britain, where the government offered investment incentives worth £4 million to Nissan for example and where comment in the media and the unions is normally expressed in terms of how many jobs foreign investors will create and what a good thing this is. At Mazda, in 1997, it was reported that there was still 'resentment about being under the control of Ford and having a "foreign" leader'.[64]

Some predicted that in the 1990s Anglo-Saxon styles of M & A would become more usual in Japan but, as the incomplete Ford-Mazda case shows, it would seem more likely that it will be resisted or diluted and only even partially adopted out of the most bitter necessity.[65] Ford's annual sales in 1994 were almost five and a half times Mazda's but despite this disparity it was not a takeover in the accepted sense.

From all this, it should be clear that the Japanese system and the Anglo-Saxon system are incompatible. The latter is a threat to the former and to all those vested interests who would stand to lose in the unlikely event of a change that was more than just on the surface: not merely vested interests in the business world but vested interests reaching into the heart of relations within Japan's politico-economic system.

Of course no discussion of M & A would be complete without taking account of the stereotyped arguments against it commonly heard in Japan. A typical statement would be along the lines that buying and selling companies like any other commodity is immoral because companies are made up of people and human relations that are not to be treated as things. So 'human trafficking', or 'hijacking' a company, unless it has to be rescued from bankruptcy, are disreputable and show only a concern for profit, not people. But, as one Japanese consultant asked, 'If M & A is truly immoral, why do Japanese companies pursue it in other countries?'[66]

Quite simply, therefore, it is a matter of double standards: one for Japanese and another for foreigners, meaning that as in other instances this is a one-way street? What is incredible is that foreign governments, whose firms compete with Japanese firms, either do not have a clear insight into this simple fact or are indifferent to their own companies having to compete with one arm tied behind their backs.

Meanwhile, Japanese companies are free to buy up foreign companies like the biotechnology companies previously referred to which will give them the lead. They can also buy companies as a means of entering the market and then expanding market share in a way that is denied to foreign companies in Japan, with its informal but highly effective barriers against newcomers. The foreigners may than have to rely on less than whole-hearted joint ventures, or establish their own distribution networks at huge cost, as firms like BMW have done. They certainly do not enjoy the same advantages of ease of access that Japanese firms in free market systems abroad do. The late Akio Morita of Sony wrote that, 'The US is the most open market in the world, overall',[67] and both Sony and Honda in particular have done well there.

During the bubble Japanese manufacturers began to go in for

securities and property trading, as well as using the plentiful credit available to re-equip themselves to become more competitive. The new word *zaiteku*, meaning 'financial technology' was coined to express this new departure: greatly at variance with the philosophy of Akio Morita for instance, who spoke critically of dealers whose time horizon was ten minutes, while his as a manufacturer was ten years.

Some of the results, while they lasted, were nevertheless remarkable. In 1986-87 Nissan, the 'number two' in the motor industry, would have made a loss if it had not been for the profits it earned on securities trading. The following year profits from securities trading added up to well over half the pre-tax profits of such well known manufacturers as Matsushita, Nissan, JVC and Sharp. *Zaiteku* profits at Sanyo were over twice those from its real business of manufacturing electrical and electronic products, while at another vehicle manufacturer, Isuzu, they were over twenty times.[68] It provided an interesting contrast with some of the things that have been said about the primacy of the 'real economy', or manufacturing, in Japan, the importance of focusing on the core business and not being distracted by speculation.

The enthusiasm of such mainline manufacturers for *zaiteku*, not to mention the scandals of Daiwa Bank, New York, the Sumitomo Corporation copper speculation affair, the housing association or *jusen* loan speculations, and the leading stockbroking firms and their association with organized crime syndicates etc. showed that old established firms and others were no different from anyone else when the opportunity to speculate that the bubble presented arose.

Also, much discussed since the bursting of the bubble, is how much of the investment made in the bubble years was justified. Some have compared the long-term investment perspective, which served Japan well during its catching up period after 1868 and again after 1945, with the short-term perspective said to characterize Anglo-Saxon capitalism. In doing so, they sometimes point to the strategy of aiming for increased market share rather than profit per se, which was said to typify Japanese companies, although only the major corporations could afford it. It has further been argued that expanding market share at the expense of competitors, rather like invading territory in the game of *go*, would in the end lead to greater and more sustained profit in any case.

This claim should not be taken out of context, which is that in almost any field in Japan, whether banking, trading, insurance, machinery, motor manufacturing, electronics or building etc. there are a number of established major competitors. Many small companies go bankrupt[69] and it is extremely difficult for new entrants to compete at anything like the same level with the established companies that dominate the industry but the latter go on competing amongst themselves for increases in market share. That is quite rational in view of their need to maintain their position and of the way in which contracts are 'carved up', for example, in the building industry according to the power of the companies based on their market share. Motor manufacturers, for example, also allocate contracts among the different steel makers on the same principle. It all makes for cozy, cartel-like arrangements, which are technically illegal.

Since the bursting of the bubble and with the succeeding credit crunch, it is now being asked for the first time whether the policy of funneling people's savings into the banks and from there into industry has not in fact led to over-investment; specifically the wrong sort of investment in plant and projects that has not been subjected to strict enough evaluation. The recession following the bubble, with company profits down, consumers frightened to spend money and unemployment rising, suggested that Japanese managers had not been thinking enough about profitability after all.

Some are being forced to do so. Tomen, for instance, Japan's seventh largest general trading company, was reported to be divesting itself of affiliated companies and to be 'focusing on profitability'. In the old days, the general trading companies prided themselves on being able to handle any kind of business 'from a pin to an elephant' but this philosophy was now said to belong to the past. A Tomen managing director stated that because the company had to compete internationally, 'The creation of long-term shareholder value is the only assurance of continued success.'[70] It is very different from what was said before.

Yet, before leaping to the conclusion that 'Japan is really changing now', it should be remembered that the chairman of Mitsubishi Heavy Industries had said as late as 1998 that, 'Profit maximization is inappropriate for manufacturing industry', as already quoted above. On top of the distortions caused by insufficiently evaluated company investments is the open secret that huge amounts of public works spending, involved in measures to stimulate the economy during the recession, literally consisted of 'bridges to nowhere', that could not be justified on economic grounds and were political measures instead. They benefited the building industry, the country's biggest single employer and a major contributor to the funds of the LDP, the governing party.[71]

Peter Drucker long ago stressed the need for companies to achieve a proper balance between long-term and short-term aims but, following the tactics of the game of *go*, in an industry where over-capacity already exists, companies that do not have to worry so much about profitability in the short term could force out competitors that do. European motor manufacturers, for instance, face such pressures.

They already have the capacity to produce twenty million cars a year, while sales are only thirteen million.[72] Under EU-Japan agreements,

Japanese exports to the EU were limited to a market share of eleven per cent until the end of 1999, after which they were to be free. Indeed, already in 1998 the quota was increased by 53,000 over the previous year to 1,167,000 as a result of MITI's claim that sales of cars in the EU would be expected to increase:[73] an example of punctiliousness that one would not expect to be applied in the other direction. At a time of poor sales in Japan due to the recession, it is easy to see why the Japanese manufacturers would want to export their way out of it by increasing market share and increasing their grip on the European market,[74] including in at least one case by adding further capacity.

These were some of the results that the bursting of the bubble were having on Europe and other regions. Imports into Japan had fallen by 17 per cent in the year ending April 1998 compared with the previous year. Japan's current account surplus had almost doubled.[75] MOF reported in February 1998 that the trade surplus had risen by a staggering 68 per cent; though it added that it did not expect this to continue. Even exports to Asian countries that had their own problems to deal with after their bubbles had burst still rose by 2.1 per cent. The *Financial Times* considered that the situation was bound to lead to demands from the EU and the US that the Japanese government stimulate domestic demand, instead of trying to export its way out of the recession at the expense of its trading partners: deregulation and tax cuts were usually what was mentioned. Meanwhile, in the absence of real deregulation, which was even less likely than usual at a time when it might entail job losses on top of already rising unemployment, exporters to Japan continued to face the non-tariff barriers that the EU and US had so often complained about.[76] Sales of European cars were down and the producers of the high status luxury goods like Scotch malt whisky, French perfumes and Italian fashions were suffering.

Writing in 1992 after the bubble had already burst, a respected authority referred to the 'purge of the economy' as 'the most difficult stage ahead'. This meant getting rid of the after-effects of the orgy of speculation, such as bankruptcies and bad debts; which had been the price of the cheap loan policy that industry had enjoyed.[77] The prophecy that the purge would be painful was more than adequately fulfilled, though at the time there seemed to be more than a few people in Japan who believed that they were not subject to the laws of economics, as demonstrated by previous bubbles in history, and that they could escape the consequences.

The two key economic ministries, MOF and MITI, had frequently basked in the credit for managing Japan's spectacular economic advance since the Second World War; even if the benefits had not always trickled down to consumers and those whose hard work had brought this advance about. After the bubble burst, it was a case of hubris, or pride going before a fall, especially in regard to MOF, whose offices had to be protected by extra police guards. Many blamed the ministry for being unable to put the economy back on the right track and it became unpopular for the first time in the postwar period. In a situation where middle aged managers and 'office ladies', or secretaries, were being made redundant, companies were going bankrupt and there was a mood of gloom after the previous euphoria, many people felt that MOF should now take the blame for allowing the bubble to get out of hand: after all, it resulted from their policy after the Plaza Agreement that had pushed the Yen up.

For other countries, the big question was whether Japan, as the world's second largest economy, together with a large part of Asia, would drag the world into recession? Economic interdependence, or globalization, means that what happens in Japan affects the EU and the US and for the EU, with high levels of unemployment already, the prospect of further deterioration was not pleasant. The government's Economic Planning Agency (EPA) calculated that Japanese companies were going to cut their overseas direct investments in nearly all regions, with the exception of China, by no less that 57 per cent in 1998: a move likely to have severe consequences for South East Asian economies already struggling the their own problems. Some Japanese banks and companies were heading home.[78]

Mitsubishi Electric, a company that like the car company was in trouble, closed its television factory at Haddington in Scotland, with a loss of 500 jobs, and the staff at Yamaichi's London branch found themselves in the street the day after the announcement of its bankruptcy. At some companies previously Japanese managers had assured local staff that they were there to stay and that they did not believe in the 'hire and fire' policies of some other multinationals: an obvious dig at American companies, who were alleged to abandon overseas investments and local workforces with speed if they were unprofitable.

Though there may have been an element of special pleading, two of Japan's leading industrialists spoke up with what in Japan was quite exceptional bluntness. Norio Ohga, chairman of Sony, criticized the disastrous policies of the then prime minister, Ryutaro Hashimoto, comparing him to Herbert Hoover, the American president at the time of the Wall Street Crash of 1929. He warned that, 'If Japan falls into a deflationary spiral, it would affect the Asian economies. In that case, not even the US economy would be able to maintain its healthy state.'[79] Hiroshi Okuda, the Toyota president, warned in similar terms that, 'There is a possibility of Japan triggering a worldwide financial crisis, such as a steep stock market plunge involving Europe and the US. To avoid that, solving the bad loan problem is an urgent task.'[80]

These were staggering statements, when for years people had been used to the apparently relentless march of Japanese companies into every corner of the world, supported by their banks, trading companies and official organizations in what seemed an unstoppable combination. For years the invincible competitiveness of Japanese companies, supposedly based on the particularities of their management style, had been promoted by officials and managers and had dented the self-confidence of competitors.

What people were now hearing from some of Japan's top business leaders was something many would not have imagined: perhaps the system that they had so often heard praised, and which had produced – from a low starting point – such incontrovertible achievements as high growth rates over the years, actually was built on foundations of sand after all? Otherwise, how had it got into such a mess? Furthermore, were the Asian 'tigers' who, following Japan, had also been achieving high growth rates, likewise from a low starting point, not destined to be the wave of the future after all?

Once one gets away from the propaganda and the stereotyped images, unless one really does believe that the Japanese politico-economic system can flout economic rationality without paying the price, rather as the now generally discredited Communist system pretended was possible, there is no need to make a mystery out of the speculative bubble and the purging of its disastrous after-effects. The bankruptcy of Yamaichi and of other banks and financial institutions might be mistaken for a purely technical problem of accounting but its causes are rooted in the nature of Japan's political economy. 'Bean counters' who are tempted to evaluate it solely by the – frequently incomplete and misleading! – numbers will be unable to draw the right conclusions. Japan's economy does not work according to the principles of Adam Smith and neo-classical economics, even if it is convenient for the authorities to convey this impression for foreign, especially American, consumption.

Indeed, a former US trade negotiator warned that, 'Economic orthodoxy to the contrary, Japan is different from the US in its political economy, more so than any other advanced industrialized country.' This being the case, he then went on to warn anyone that still harboured illusions that the two systems were on the way towards convergence by quoting Akio Morita, the former Sony president, who asserted that Japanese companies expanded market share through cut-throat pricing, underpaid and overworked their employees, paid meagre dividends to shareholders, neglected the environment and made insufficient philanthropic contributions. 'Clearly "convergence" between Japan and the West is unlikely soon.'[81]

What is meant here by flouting economic rationality refers to the costs of the Japanese system and those who have to pay them: costs which officialdom may try to sweep under the carpet but which are real enough. Akio Morita spoke of Japanese companies underpaying and overworking their employees and another major item is the use of taxpayers' or public money. ¥685 billion of public money was used, for instance, to bail out the *jusen*, building societies in British parlance, or savings and loans in American.[82] A revealing sidelight on the collusive relationships between the bureaucracy and the *jusen* was that five out of the seven companies concerned were headed by former MOF officials who had parachuted, *amakudari*, into their private sector positions after retiring from the Ministry. They did very well out of the affair, to the annoyance of taxpayers. Even the government's Economic Planning Agency (EPA) warned that the use of taxpayers' money for write-offs could lead to executives taking unjustifiable risks[83] but in the light of continuing practice it is hard to say how seriously this was meant.

The involvement of organized crime in business, which seems to be an ineradicable part of the Japanese system, was a principal reason for the vast amount of irredeemable debt. Gangsters intimidated bank officials, especially at the Sumitomo Bank, which had pursued a highly aggressive lending policy during the bubble. Two of its managers were murdered and one more at the Hanwa Bank.[84]

The privatization of the former Japan National Railways, a bureaucratic organization that with the exception of the high speed lines lost large amounts of money, left behind a mountain of debt. During the bubble when land prices rose, it would have been possible to reduce this by selling surplus land that the railways had been sitting on but bureaucrats foolishly would not authorize it. Land prices fell and the bubble collapsed and it was reported in 1996 that the accumulated debt to be settled by the taxpayer amounted to ¥28 trillion.[85]

The six fiscal packages announced by the government between April 1993 and August 1998 that were supposed to stimulate the economy and get it out of recession amounted to a total of ¥71,600 billion, or US $651 billion. A commentator writing in the *Financial Times* observed that this was greater than President Roosevelt's 'New Deal' of the 1930s and greater than the total spent on the Vietnam War of the 1960s.[86]

Taxpayers grew restless at the time of the *jusen* bail-out, particularly because of the scandalous profiteering of senior executives, and politicians knew that the use of public money to bail out all and sundry was a sensitive issue. It was said that the strategy therefore was to soft pedal the issue for the time being, judging that when things began to get serious, as they did in the recession, the public would even prefer the use of taxpayers' money to the threat of the uncertainty surrounding a possible financial collapse; playing once again on people's fear of insecurity.

Thus by the time of the Long Term Credit Bank (LTCB) crisis, one of the three major long term banks designed to finance industrial ventures, the government could announce that it would inject ¥500 billion to ¥1,000 billion of public money into the LTCB to rescue it, equivalent at prevailing rates to £2.1 billion to £4.2 billion.[87] Interestingly, Sumitomo Trust which was under official pressure to accept a merger from LTCB, had already decided to hire a foreign accountancy firm, Arthur Andersen, to audit LTCB's assets, despite the fact that Japan's own Financial Supervisory Agency (FSA) was doing so. A banker expressed the opinion that if the results of these two audits were found to differ or if they were concealed, the credibility of the FSA would be undermined. The Swiss bank UBS also removed any reference to LTCB from the brand name of its joint venture.[88] These signs of a lack of confidence once again threw the rackety nature of the affair into relief. Indeed the *Financial Times* commented in a leading article that Sumitomo Trust's action in hiring an independent – and foreign – auditor was 'unprecedented behaviour in Japan' and that it showed 'just how far Sumitomo trusts the government'.[89] Need one say more?

At the same time, in spite of the propaganda about making the Tokyo financial market 'free, fair and international', the government was behaving in the opposite way by the prime minister's announcement to the Diet that he would refuse to publish the results of an audit into the country's largest banks, on the pretext that it would be likely to undermine 'market order'.[90] This followed an earlier move when the prosecutor's team investigating financial corruption was cut from 70 to about 30 people and the news that the prosecutor himself would be transferred to a remote rural district in Toyama Prefecture, well away from Tokyo: a good example of the lack of independence from the government of the judiciary and the dependence of its members' careers on the goodwill of the government, earlier referred to as the role of law in Japan, in contrast to the rule of law.

The seriousness of this decision can be gauged from its results: six suicides, three large securities companies suspended from trading (again!), sixty resignations among banking and securities executives, ten among bureaucrats and a further loss of credibility among the institutions investigated, including the Bank of Japan and MOF. The main points of the investigation were the payment of 'hush money' to gangsters by some of the country's biggest banks and securities companies and the bribing of government officials by 'lavish entertainment' in return for favours.[91]

Thus, it appears that the Japanese taxpayer will have to go on paying for what looks like a bottomless pit of bad loans. At the time of the Hashimoto government in January 1998, for example, a new figure for 'potentially risky loans' was given as ¥76,710 billion, or £361 billion, a figure 'higher than anything previously revealed' as the Tokyo correspondents of the *Financial Times* put it. But how could anyone now believe that this was the ultimate reality? At an EU-Japan summit, the EU trade commissioner, Sir Leon Brittan, warned the Japanese government, 'That the EU would not tolerate a further rise in Japanese exports to Europe unless Tokyo clearly tackled its economic problems'; though such things are easier said than done.[92]

No system of political economy is perfect and, as Sir Winston Churchill was fond of saying, 'Democracy is the worst system – except for all the others.' The Introduction stated that Japan's political economy was not that of Anglo-Saxon democracy and free markets, though it contains a skilful blend of competitive elements, yet it is uncanny how it illustrates points made by the proponents of the free market system. The cooperative, or collusive, Japanese system illustrates Adam Smith's dictum in 'The Wealth of Nations' that, 'People of the same trade seldom meet together even for merriment and diversion – (including "wining and dining", *karaoke* etc.?) – but the conversation ends in a conspiracy against the public, or on some contrivance to raise prices.'

Japan's export offensive since the Second World War, from the base of a home market protected by an exclusive system of inter-company and ministry-company relations, manipulated through a network of informal or personal contacts, within the framework of a national economic strategy following the ideas of Friedrich List, is reminiscent of Smith's remark that, 'Consumption . . . is the sole end and purpose of all production. . . . But in the mercantile system, the interest of the consumer is almost constantly sacrificed to that of the producer and it seems to consider production and not consumption as the ultimate end and object of all industry and commerce.'

While it is obvious that Japanese standards of living have improved over their low pre-Second World War levels, has the ordinary person benefited from the country's impressive industrial advance to a commensurate extent, especially now that the Yen no longer has an artificially high exchange value? Japan is often referred to as a producer-dominated economy, and not necessarily only by people who have been reading Adam Smith.

The author of one of the best known books on Japan's political economy and society indeed sees it as a productive juggernaut out of control, racking up trade surpluses without end – and for what?[93] Hardly to improve the life of the ordinary person.

Obviously the Japanese system 'works', in the sense that in the years after 1945 it became a highly competitive industrial and commercial machine; rather as the old Soviet system became an alarming military machine. As has become increasingly clear over time, both systems contained a considerable measure of inefficiency and neither was as monolithic as the face they presented to the outside world appeared to show: Japan's faction-ridden politics and university departments, the jockeying for power among the government ministries and the struggles for market share and influence among industrial and commercial rivals are examples. It is not simply a case of 'we Japanese', *wareware Nihonjin*, though this is often presented either spontaneously or intentionally for foreign consumption and the 'national economic' outlook does encourage a sense of a common identity of interest; in its extreme form as the paranoia of 'Japan against the world'.

The Soviet machine, based on the projection of military power, could easily be understood as having a political aim but, because the Japanese machine is based instead on economic power, its political nature has often been misunderstood outside Japan. This is frequently the case in societies where the 'business is business' philosophy prevails, especially the USA. Policy-makers are trapped in a circular logic that as Japan since 1945 has succeeded, at any rate until the recession of the 1990s, and as only the free market can lead to success, therefore Japan must be a free market system QED. It is to be hoped that the other aspects of Japan's political economy to be dealt with here and what they mean for the ways in which business in Japan is actually run will demonstrate the falsity of such pseudo-logic. One also hears occasionally that, 'They've beaten us at our own game' but a coordinated economy and one in which firms are largely on their own, without a web of relationships and understandings of the Japanese type to support them, are not the same game!

Thinkers like Friedrich Hayek have discussed the relation between economic freedom and political freedom and governments that seek to regulate and coordinate economic activity are more likely than others to seek to control the lives of their populations outside the economic sphere as well. Some indeed might think that the corporatist and collectivist aspects of the Japanese system resemble what Mussolini was trying to do; and in Japan the trains notoriously run to time, as they were supposed to in Mussolini's Italy. Already in the nineteenth century, a Japanese politician could state that national socialism was the Japanese way; in other words, a mixture of collectivism and nationalism.

Why the political rationale of Japan's economic behaviour is so often hidden and why it can be difficult to get beyond surface appearances must next be discussed. In this context, the statements of Professor Jun Eto of the Tokyo Institute of Technology to *Newsweek* magazine on 2 April 1990 should be borne in mind: 'We are not that frank even speaking among ourselves. Sometimes the *honne* (genuinely felt) element could emerge, like the Morita-Ishihara book *The Japan that can say No*. But when we speak to foreigners, often we still speak *tatemae* (false front). Sometimes, we feel relatively relaxed, free to make any kind of comment or speech. But in the face of criticism we suddenly shrink and begin hiding ourselves.'

■ CHAPTER 2
# Myths and Realities

In spite of the advance of Japanese business into Europe, America and the world at large, Japan and what makes it work are still widely regarded as mysterious – though not in Asia – and in some undefined way 'different': a land of myths and stereotypes. Because of the distance, the cost and other problems, few people from Europe and America even travel to what is the second largest economy in the world; let alone become familiar with the realities of the situation by working there long enough in the sorts of jobs that reveal what is going on behind the facade presented to tourists – and sometimes to the senior executives from a European or American head office, who spend thirty-six hours at a swanky Western-style hotel in Tokyo, enjoying red-carpet treatment and think everything is wonderful, before jetting off again, to the frustration of those at the sharp end who have to grapple with the difficulties.

Comparing the 1990s with the 1960s, there are more European and American businessmen in Japan than before and both the EU and the US have training schemes for managers and engineers but they are still a small proportion of the numbers of Japanese businessmen stationed in the EU and USA. If one believes that the first law of business is to know the competitor, this is a serious deficiency. Unfortunately, many companies still send out managers virtually unprepared, exposing them to their own misconceptions as well as local misinformation, while those who stay longer must worry about their career paths and whether their familiarity with Japanese conditions will be put to good use by the company when they eventually return home.

From what they say and do, many Japanese people do not understand Europe or America, in regard to the basis of democracy for instance, as well as they imagine but the fact is that we need to do much more about the deficits of information and awareness on our own side. Without such awareness it is not possible to deal adequately with Japan, as the world's second largest economy, as a competitor. How can we deal with the problem, of trade imbalances for example, if we cannot first identify what the politico-economic nature of the problem is? Thus the lack of awareness is primarily of our own making, compounded as we shall see by the propaganda put out by the Japanese authorities, who are usually quite good at exploiting foreign ignorance, and by officials, managers and others in Japan's conformist society. What it is convenient to refer to as the Japanese Establishment, in other words the holders of power in Japan and those who either support them or are working to join them, are the source of the propaganda and hence what is put out for foreign consumption but, as a friend with many years experience in a Japanese company in the UK put it, the extent to which many ordinary Japanese people appear to believe this propaganda, and certainly repeat it, should not be underestimated. The point is commented on below by a well-known Japanese business consultant.

To anyone born in the 1930s the way that the stereotypes of Japan as an industrial power have been reversed is striking and ironic. Before and again just after the Second World War the common stereotype was that Japanese products were cheap and nasty: inferior copies of Western goods resulting from a copycat mentality and lack of creativity. After 1945 such long since defunct companies as the Austin Motor Company and the Rootes Group were content to sell their technology of the Austin A40 and then the Austin Cambridge, which ironically became the basis for the Nissan Bluebird, and the Hillman Minx respectively to Japanese motor manufacturers; not taking them seriously as potential competitive threats. Austin transferred this technology in 1952 and just four years later the cars were entirely made from components manufactured in Japan.[1]

The Japanese themselves were so worried about their weakness that in the early 1950s they concluded an agreement with the Italian government to limit the import of Italian cars into Japan and the export of Japanese cars to Italy to two thousand a year. In the 1990s, when most people had either forgotten or simply did not know that it was the Japanese government itself, fearing a flood of Fiats into Japan if the market were open, that had taken the initiative in pressing for this agreement, it was commonly cited by Japanese officials and others as an example of anti-Japanese EU discrimination: a nice instance of black propaganda.[2]

Looking back in 1980, an offshoot of MITI, JETRO (Japan External Trade Organization) – itself modelled on the British Export Trade Organization disbanded in the early postwar period – was realistic in admitting that in the past, before the introduction of proper industrial standards and Quality Control, the words 'Made in Japan' had meant poor quality products.[3] What industrial products indeed did Japan export to Europe or the USA before the Second World War? As a child, I remember a few cheap toys; like the seed of an artificial flower that when dropped into a glass of water sank to the bottom, sending up petals that opened out on the surface – something quaint and insubstantial. Books and films of the time reinforced the same image. In Graham Greene's novel *The Power and the Glory*, published in 1940, for instance, a seedy dentist scraping a living in a South American backwater uses second-rate 'Japanese drills': an intentional symbol of failure.

In those days the expression 'Japanese management' was never heard, or if it was it was synonymous with backwardness. A visit to YKK's museum, for example, at its main factory by the Japan Sea shows how what is now not only Japan's but the world's largest maker of zip fasteners was a cottage industry until the introduction of modern American machinery after the Second World War. Up to that time the idea that people in the most developed industrial states would one day be driving around in Japanese cars and listening to Japanese hi-fis or 'Walkmen' was laughable. It was an attitude that led to a dangerous underestimation of Japan on no fewer than three occasions: before the Second World War, during the war and, for which there is less excuse, again after the war. With the collapse of Yamaichi, and the banking crisis etc., there are again signs that some people have gone back to the old way of thinking that Japan can be safely written off.

From the 1960s onwards the common stereotype changed. There was the illusion that almost overnight Japanese companies had changed from producers of cheap junk to indefatigable producers aggressively churning out and marketing high quality, sophisticated products, ranging from cars that consistently obtained the highest ratings for reliability to the latest, innovative electronic goods. Japanese companies appeared to be unstoppable and after they took off in the 1960s there was a boom in books on Japanese management and a search for the 'secrets' of their success, which were sometimes recommended to others like patent medicines without too much regard for differences in legal, industrial relations and political systems.

With the publication of *Japan as Number One: Lessons for America*, by a Harvard professor, the wheel seemed to have come full circle; Japan receiving something like an official commendation that it had overtaken its postwar mentor. It was just the sort of message that the Japanese Establishment was only too pleased to get and to use, showing that its way was right and able to appeal to feelings of narcissism. But by the time of the Yamaichi Securities collapse it was a fact that Japan had achieved a worldwide commercial empire[4] and leading positions in key product areas in the modern age such as cars, electronic devices, machine tools, computers, office automation (though not using so much itself!), photocopiers, cameras, clocks, watches etc.

Then people began to wonder whether Japan's great advance in commerce and industry was not built on sand after all. Indeed, a Japanese friend wondered if there was not a parallel with Japan's seizure of large parts of Asia during the Second World War which had proved to be an unsustainable over-extension of power, followed by a crushing collapse. Such an apocalyptic view reflects the latent feelings of insecurity that, as already mentioned, are never far from the surface in Japan but, although business may be treated as war, there are obvious differences and the analogy should not be taken too far.

For companies and countries on the receiving end of Japanese competition there is a strong element of wishful thinking in the idea that Japan is finished and that Japanese competition will just go away. But the effects of defeat in 1945, the oil crises of the 1970s and no doubt the crisis of confidence of the 1990s have always been to spur the country to ever greater competitive efforts. Only if Japan were 'burnt out' would this change; and what signs are there of that?

What both the old stereotype of pre-Second World War backwardness and the post-1960s stereotype of unstoppability have in common is ignorance, together with a feeling that there is little need to bother oneself further. If people are seen to represent no economic threat, they can be ignored. Equally, if it is impossible to compete with them and they are on the other side of the world, with different sorts of systems that work for them but not for us, then they can also be put out of mind; even if high unemployment in the EU and the competitiveness needed to support living standards remain a problem.

The view here is that Japanese penetration of and investment in European, American and world markets – visible every day on the roads, in the shops and in the home – shows that this ostrich-like attitude is a mistake and that Japan as competitor is still not being taken seriously enough. What is required is increased awareness of the workings of Japan's political economy as a reality not as a matter of either praise or blame. But while it is not our business to tell the Japanese how they should run their affairs, which they would be unlikely to listen to in any case, it becomes very much our business when it is a question of our own living standards and the competitiveness on which they depend.

The obvious barriers to familiarization include not only cost, time and distance but also the language and social differences and it has to be emphasized that there is a gulf between visiting a country as a tourist and working there over time in a situation exposed to the workings of the local power structures, or for example bureaucracy. This applies to some countries in Europe, which may be delightful to visit on holiday but which would be rather different to work in. It is especially true of Japan because of the big differences between substance and reality that are likely to be encountered, the importance of not losing face, which means that many Japanese will be keen to impress on the foreigner that Japan is the best of all possible worlds, and the consequent use of obfuscation and euphemism. A classic case is what in English is called the Emperor's surrender broadcast of 1945 by which Japan capitulated. It did not include the word 'surrender' and included the memorable phrase that the war 'had not necessarily developed to Japan's advantage'. The Allied occupation forces were similarly referred to as an 'advance army'.

Nor does awareness start out from a neutral point. A Frenchman, for instance, may find the networks in Japan between government bureaucrats and private sector industrialists reminiscent of the ties in France between graduates of the ENA (Ecole Nationale d'Administration) and of the Grandes Ecoles in the two sectors. An Italian may not find Japanese politics so hard to understand in the light of how things are done at home. In neither country, despite some recent moves in the direction of privatization, would the idea of the considerable involvement of the state in business seem particularly strange.

But those from Britain, the USA and countries that follow what can be called for short Anglo-Saxon capitalism will go dangerously wrong in interpreting what they find in Japan if they try and impose their preconceived ideas of how an economy works, or should work, on it. In their preoccupation with the free market, anti-monopoly law, the separation of business and Civil Service, company governance as it affects, for example, the significance of the stock exchange and the attention that has to be paid to shareholders, accounting by independently qualified professionals working to objective standards, access to legal professionals and the courts in cases of commercial and other disputes etc., they are likely to overlook entirely the all-embracing political, indeed national political context within which Japanese business operates, abroad as well as at home. That is why the discussion must be about political economy not just economy.

It is a historical fact that it is the United States, the leading exponent of Anglo-Saxon capitalism, that has had the greatest political and economic involvement with Japan since the end of the Second World War in 1945. At least until the outbreak of the Korean War in 1950, which followed the Cold War attempt by the USSR to force the Western Allies out of Berlin at the time of the airlift of 1948, a major aim behind Occupation policy had been to remake Japan as a democratic society in the image of America. It is said, for instance, that by the end of his time in Japan as Occupation supreme commander, General MacArthur really believed that the Japanese had 'changed into a new people', with even a great sense of war guilt[5]: if true, a remarkable change in a mere five years of a society with centuries of history, not to mention authoritarian rule, behind it.

To be fair to General MacArthur, he had also said that Japan seemed to him to have a 'brooding, ominous quality', while his most famous remark, which was not appreciated in Japan was that, 'Measured by the standards of modern civilization, the Japanese would be like a boy of twelve as compared with our development of forty-five years.'[6]

That the results of the Occupation policy to democratize Japan were, to say the least, mixed and that governments frequently prefer to indulge in wishful thinking, help to explain the persistent blindness in believing, or pretending, that Japanese capitalism operates according to the principles of Adam Smith and the free market. Under the Occupation, for example, the famous *zaibatsu* nucleus company Mitsui Bussan, or trading company, had been split up into no fewer than two hundred separate companies. When the Occupation ended, they were put together again. In the political arena a staff of no more than twenty Americans had to deal with two-and-a-half million cases of people associated with the wartime regime to decide whether they should be purged or not. The Americans were 'helped' by Japanese officials.

In the name of continuity, people were kept in office who should not have been and, ironically in view of subsequent American complaints about Japanese trading practices, the banker Joseph Dodge recommended the strategy of a government-guided export-driven economy. 'Later described as a "capitalist developmental state" or less charitably as "Japan Inc." (this) was nurtured by American directives.' During the Occupation, trade had been under the control of the American authorities. When they left, they handed this power to the Japanese bureaucracy, who could hardly believe their luck. Apart from their past dubious history connected with the war, their vested interests were sharply at variance with the working of the free market. Following the end of the Occupation, 200,000 ex-military officers were 'depurged' and the wartime head of the Ministry of Munitions, a forerunner of MITI, Nobosuke Kishi, who had sat for three years as a suspected Class A war criminal in Sugamo Prison, but who subsequently became prime minister, was treated likewise. By October 1952 no fewer than 42 per cent of the members of the Diet, or parliament, were 'ex-purgees'.[7]

One could go on giving examples to show just how little had changed either in the political sphere or in the economic sphere in Japan either during and particularly after the Occupation. The most trenchant comment comes from Leon Hollerman, who himself worked in the overseas trade branch of SCAP (Supreme Commander Allied Powers) headquarters during the Occupation. 'In liquidating the Occupation by "handing back" operational control to the Japanese, SCAP naïvely presided not only over the transfer of its own authority but also over the institutionalization of the most restrictive foreign trade and foreign exchange control system ever devised by a major free nation.'[8]

The desire to see Japan in the image of America and the belief or hope that it will one day 'converge' as part of a natural process is a grotesque illusion that has damaged the ability of the USA, as the principal interlocutor with Japan, to adopt realistic policies towards it. On its side, the Japanese bureaucracy generally knows how to play up to such erroneous wishful thinking, using 'front men' to say things they know the foreigners would like to hear and to encourage them in their illusions. A good example at the highest level was Saburo Okita, a former official of MITI's Economic Planning Agency (EPA) and former foreign minister, who was made minister in charge of external economic relations. As such, he had high status and some of those he met abroad may actually have thought that he represented the Japanese government, not knowing that he and others like him had no power to negotiate and were only there to listen and to deflect complaints by making sympathetic noises. Many officials at a lower level do exactly the same thing.[9]

The basic stance of Japan's economic policy-making bureaucrats – note for British readers, not Civil Servants – in one of the two economic ministries, MITI, will be discussed later. Here it is enough to say that it is not based on the thinking of Adam Smith and the 'invisible hand' of the free market. Instead it follows the thinking of the 'theory of the national economy' of Friedrich List: a grossly neglected figure in Britain. List lived from 1789 to 1846 and helped provide the intellectual support for Bismarck's national economic policies at the time when the German Empire of the nineteenth century was being founded. As professor of political economy, and the 'political' needs emphasizing, List attacked free market economics, pointing out that such a regime favoured the strongest trading nation, at that time Britain, to the disadvantage of competitors who were trying to build up their industrial strength, and that even Britain had not attained its position by free market means alone, since it had used restrictive measures such as the Navigation Acts to ensure that goods were carried in British ships. When Britain then preached the virtues of free trade to others, List saw this as a device for maintaining its own superiority.[10] For Japan, starting with a national economic policy to develop as an industrial state in 1868, in other words having to catch up, the rationality of List's analysis was clear. It was only after Japan itself had become a major industrial power over a hundred years later that any virtue was discovered in free market economics – and then only for countries trading with Japan, not for Japan itself.

Another problem in Anglo-Saxon economic contexts is the tendency to look at business in an excessively abstract way, putting too much emphasis on a mechanical reading of 'the numbers' without reference to their background. It is a criticism levelled at companies dominated by 'bean counters' who do not know about the product and sometimes at business schools. Understanding this form of exaggeration, which is not the same thing as having proper financial controls over investment for example, where Japanese companies in the 1990s have revealed severe shortcomings, may help to explain the behaviour of British and even more American businesses; and Japanese companies who send their budding managers to the Harvard or London Business Schools to find out how the competitor thinks evidently agree. But just looking at 'the numbers' will not help those from the Anglo-Saxon business world to get to grips with the Japanese competition operating within its own overarching framework of national policy.

For the USA, which remains the key player in relations with Japan not only in business terms but especially in geopolitical or strategic defence-related policy, there is the further difficulty that the two aspects of the relationship do not necessarily coincide. Initial Occupation policy after 1945 had been to prevent the Japanese from starving and to get the country back on its feet again, both on humanitarian grounds and to avoid excessive burdens on the US taxpayer. Then from the time of the Cold War onwards the priority became keeping Japan out of the Communist camp. Some far-sighted American officials warned of the risk of Japan coming back later as a strong competitor but it seemed as if no cost was considered too high in pursuing the geopolitical strategy of the State Department, even if it meant ignoring the activities of Japan as a competitor and the threat it came to pose to America's own competitive position, jobs and markets.

The overweening strategic aim was famously expressed by the former Ambassador Mike Mansfield in his mantra that the US-Japan relationship was the most important in the world, bar none. The consequent ability of the Japanese government to play 'the security card' when trade frictions looked as if they might get out of hand has frustrated the Department of Commerce and in particular the US Trade Representatives who have to negotiate with the Japanese government on behalf of American commerce and industry. One, with a wealth of direct experience in Japan, has called for the US to reformulate its policy towards Japan[11] but since, as with some other countries, maintaining 'good relations' with the Japanese authorities continues to be more important than supporting its own business and industry it is hardly surprising that the constantly simmering trade frictions are not played up more.

On their side the Japanese authorities have displayed nothing of the same hesitancy when it comes to the promotion of a strategic industry, such as machine tools for example. In 1970 Yamazaki Machine Works, now considerably expanded as Mazak, had entered into a ten-year licencing agreement with the American company Houdaille, under which it had agreed to sell the resulting products only in Japan and East Asia. To Houdaille's surprise it had then imported products into the US and when challenged claimed that they were not the same thing, though investigators could find little beyond the maker's name that was different. Houdaille's petition was brought to the attention of President Reagan's cabinet but a Japanese trade diplomat had learned of the meeting and immediately telephoned Tokyo.

Two messages then came from Prime Minister Nakasone, with whom Reagan was supposed to have a close relationship, reminding him that Nakasone was facing elections in the Upper House and that he had spoken about increasing Japan's defence capabilities, as President Reagan had requested. Consequently, he suggested that the President might like to consider the broader i.e. defence-related issues when deciding about the Houdaille case. Development of the machine tool industry was seen by MITI as a strategic aim and was supported by hidden subsidies from the profits from gambling on bicycle racing that MITI had at its disposal.[12]

This source was the Japan Bicycle Association, an organization said to produce annual revenues of no less than £106 billion, or US $170 billion, with the top riders earning up to US $ three million annually. At the EU-Japan Centre for Industrial Cooperation where I worked its sponsorship was acknowledged in the Centre's Newsletter.

The Ministry of Transport had at its disposal funds from gambling from motorboat racing, which had materially contributed to the fortune of the controversial Ryoichi Sasakawa, also a Class A war criminal incarcerated but released without trial who was to set himself up as a well known philanthropist. In Japan there was nothing odd about such funds at the disposal of the various ministries. Sasakawa will appear again later.

Some have criticized the quality of foreign, especially American, reporting of Japanese business for its naïvete and failure to grasp how the cozy nexus of big business, which dominates the smaller firms in top-down relationships, the bureaucracy and the influential political figures and faction leaders works. It is a failure that 'blindsides' much media comment that results from an inability or unwillingness to see that the mind set of Japanese business has Friedrich List's 'national economy' and not Adam Smith's free market as its basis.[13]

Those like Ambassador Reischauer in the 1960s and Ambassador Mansfield in the 1980s, seen as too indulgent towards the Japanese authorities at the expense of American business interests, also have their critics in America. Part of the criticism is that they still represented the paternalistic wishfulness of seeing Japan in the image of America, as if nothing had changed in the balance of the relations between the two countries in the years since the Occupation ended in 1951: an illusion that it naturally suited the Japanese government to play up to.[14]

Foreign visitors to Japan, in particular those on officially sponsored tours, face a further difficulty in distinguishing between myth and reality. Those from open societies, accustomed for instance to a free press and uninhibited discussion, will not be prepared for the all-pervading official line on Japan, the Japanese (*sic*) and in consequence Japanese business, which misrepresents all three in a stereotyped manner as a seamless whole. Industrial societies consist of different groupings of people, frequently in competition with one another, and even if the official view is of 'we Japanese', *wareware Nihonjin*, without distinction, as one so often hears, the distinction between the power holding élites that rule Japan and the ordinary man or woman cannot be overstressed.

Foreign visitors to an overtly totalitarian state, as under the Communist system for instance, would know in advance to discount the 'party line' and to try and find out for themselves what the realities were. Because Japan appears to be open and 'modern', with institutions whose names are familiar to them, such as political parties, elections, a prime minister, a supreme court, newspapers, universities and stock exchanges, they all too easily assume that these labels really do mean the same things as the political and economic institutions that they are familiar with at home. Once again, those likely to make the greatest mistakes are those from Anglo-Saxon backgrounds, who are supposed to follow the principle of 'say what you mean and mean what you say' and who may easily believe that being prime minister in Japan is much the same as being prime minister in Britain or that there is little fundamental difference between the stock exchange in New York or the one in Tokyo.

When the official 'party line' is put over with such aplomb, and when the reddest of red carpets is rolled out for officially sponsored visitors, it can be easy to be deluded by the appearances that disguise the substance. Outsiders need to be clear that in the Japanese political economy information is used as a competitive weapon. In open societies, companies and other bodies seek to persuade people to buy their products, or that they are fulfilling their functions, by their own advertising or public relations but there is a great difference between these individual efforts and the consistently national line constantly repeated in Japan.

Being national and uniform, it resembles government information in wartime rather than normal commercial advertising or, for example, party political broadcasts in Britain where different viewpoints are advocated. The tradition of analysis and a search, however imperfect, for objectivity, such as grew up over the centuries in Europe is not, for reasons that will become apparent, part of the Japanese tradition. The official line leaves no room for other views.

It is a commonplace that information is power and what is meant here by the official line are the views constantly propagated by the holders of power in Japan, such as officials and managers and, to an extent that may surprise outsiders more used to people's individual opinions, a great many ordinary employees, housewives and others.

The use, or manipulation, of information as a competitive weapon to serve national economic aims and to preserve the status quo comes naturally because of the contrast between *tatemae*, the facade, and *honne*, the real intention, fact etc. These are the two most important words in the Japanese language.

They represent a distinction that children learn as they grow up and that therefore appears perfectly natural. *Tatemae* is the appearance, which in Japanese life is usually all-important. It expresses how things should be, or how they might be in an ideal world. It is about what it is politic or advantageous to say, even if the speaker knows it is not true, and perhaps especially then. It is 'the right thing to say'. It is the face-saving white lie to prevent embarrassment and the euphemism. *Honne* can be said to be the substance, the reality, how things actually are: things which it may impolitic or impolite to say, in a system where, apart from being careful to behave towards superiors, formal politeness is more highly valued than truthfulness.

It is unlikely that representatives of the Japanese Establishment would use *honne* to foreigners because that would be giving valuable information to the competition, which no sane person would do. The real weaknesses and imperfections of Japan's economy and society should be hidden and face should not be lost.

What is more acceptable is to talk about Japan being a poor country, with few natural resources except people, threatened by competitors and facing severe crises etc. For foreign consumption this has the advantage of encouraging the view that Japan is finished, while for domestic consumption it reminds those coming out of schools and universities that jobs are scarce and that they had better toe the line. For all employees it serves as a stimulus to renewed efforts. So much for Japan being finished!

Despite the economic problems that Japan can be objectively seen to face, such as slow economic growth compared to preceding years and the effects of the rackety financial system, the official line strongly implies that Japan has a superior social order. Usually without being overtly rude, many official speakers have developed a nice line in demonstrating this by comparing the *tatemae* of Japanese society, for example, that Japan is a crime-free society, the safest in the world etc., with the *honne* of a 'Western' society, most likely the USA, to the effect that America is riddled with crime, you cannot go out safely etc. Or in explaining Quality Circles it is asserted that Japanese workers are naturally 'cooperative', while 'Western' workers are naturally 'individualistic'; which reflects badly on them for being 'selfish', seen as a major moral fault in 'Western culture'.

While the whole quality movement in Japan has had an immense effect on improving both product quality and manufacturing processes, it has also become something of a mystique abroad and thrown up stereotyped explanations such as those just quoted, which are unlikely to be of much practical help. Just as it is wrong to talk about 'the Japanese', so it is wrong to make comparisons between 'Japan' on the one side and an undifferentiated mass called 'the West' on the other. Some may also remember that the notorious case of a society claiming to be 'crime-free' was the USSR, where crime allegedly did not exist because it was uniquely one of the 'contradictions of capitalist society'. The reality both in the USSR and in Japan was very different.

Here it may be objected that *tatemae* and *honne* are not unique to Japan, even if some Japanese clearly think so, and that something like them exist in, for instance, European countries; though in some more than others, again showing how oversimplified the common Japanese comparison of Japan and the 'West' is. We also use euphemisms to disguise unpleasant facts and so as not to upset people but the difference is in the extreme degree the distinction so often has in Japan, where it frequently appears that appearance is more important then reality and where people act out elaborate charades to avoid the truth of which they are all well aware. Such acting becomes second nature and makes it easy for officials to tell foreigners what is expedient while maintaining their polished aplomb.

A Japanese ex-bureaucrat and critic who, almost inevitably one would say, has spent a considerable time abroad, has compared this behaviour to what George Orwell called 'doublethinking'; in other words holding two contradictory views at the same time and accepting them both.[15] It is not a coincidence that George Orwell had hit upon this expression as a result of his direct experience with Communist totalitarianism, in whose manipulation of information and people 'doublethinking' was conspicuous.

The *tatemae-honne* distinction requires the constant use of euphemism, indirect or unclear language and the evasion of controversial points, making discussion difficult. It is frequently more important to create a good 'mood' than to speak factually, which might upset listeners. Reading between the lines may be important but it can be difficult to pick up the right cues. For Japanese people the reverse can be true with English understatement or irony.

For all these reasons, it can be said that words by themselves are taken less seriously than they would be in English. It has often, though to judge by the mistakes that have been made, not often enough said that 'yes' simply means 'I hear you' and not 'I agree with you', while one is not supposed to say a blunt 'no', to a request for example. So the usual way round the difficulty is to say *muzukashii*, 'it's difficult', i.e. out of the question. This is taken as a great sign of how polite people are. The favourite of the bureaucrats is *kento shimasu* i.e., 'we'll study it', in other words 'forget it'.

The *tatemae-honne* dichotomy may seem a great strain to those from intellectual traditions where analytical thinking and clarity of meaning and expression are valued and certainly does not help to disentangle myth and reality. However, for outsiders, and the word is used intentionally, it makes it easy to grasp why things in Japan are seldom what they appear and why, at any level, appearances can be deceptive. That particularly applies to anything for foreign consumption.

In the Japanese company world a common instance of *tatemae* is an assertion such as, 'Lifetime employment is the Japanese way'; normally followed by the explanation that this accounts for happy and dedicated workers, in contrast to those in Europe or the US. This is misleading for several reasons but often impresses even foreign managers who, as they are intended to, think how wonderful a system that guarantees job security must be. As competitors, they should know better.

The first reason why such *tatemae* is misleading is that the majority of Japanese employees work in small and medium-sized companies who cannot afford to provide employment until retirement, even if they might like to.[16] Nor do they offer the fringe benefits that the biggest firms provide, that have also attracted media attention elsewhere. Instead, they pay lower wages.

The second reason is that the sweeping assertion glosses over the fact that even the giants of Japanese commerce and industry, the Toyotas, Matsushitas and Hitachis of this world divide their workforces into three categories:-regular, i.e. permanent staff: temporary; and part-time. Only the first group has, in principle, job security. Temporary and part-time staff can be laid off at any time, for example, in a recession. They are not eligible for union membership and do not enjoy the fringe benefits of the permanent staff. They are also paid less.

To determine how many employees are 'permanent', therefore, with the presumption of job security, is difficult because the companies decide the categories and can ease out employees to lower status subsidiaries at will. Do they then count as 'permanent'? General estimates are that at most not more than twenty per cent of all Japanese employees enjoy the sort of job security that has been claimed and it could be less. So where does that leave the alleged claim of the link between long-term employment and motivation?

In fact, in the recession of the 90s, many Japanese, including managers, have been shocked to discover that what they thought was a job for life when they entered the company was a promise that not all companies have kept and that they have been forced into early retirement. The question of what employees have to pay for job security in other ways will be discussed later. Here again the trick of implying the superiority of the Japanese system by making a comparison between the Japanese ideal and the European or American reality is clear but in fact the comparison is so inaccurate that it is like comparing apples and pears. But to appear superior is to gain face and to demoralize the competition, as the effect on European managers attending courses at the EU-Japan Centre often showed.

Japanese officials and officially approved speakers are both sufficiently intelligent and well informed to know that the myth that all or even the majority of Japanese employees have the security of so-called 'lifetime' employment is contradicted by the facts. Yet they continue to trot it out for unsuspecting foreigners, rather as if it were an article of faith as well as a good piece of propaganda: a good instance both of *tatemae* and doublethinking.

But why is it that this has become one of the most pernicious and enduring myths about Japanese working life? To understand that one has to go back to as long ago as 1958, when the first book by a foreign researcher, and indeed the first book in English, resulting from research in the field of large-scale industrial companies in Japan was published.[17] This ground-breaking work used the expression 'lifetime employment' and suggested that this was part of a special reciprocal agreement between company and employee, whereby the former made an implicit pledge of job security, until the retiring age of sixty in those days, later raised in most large companies to sixty-five, only to fall under the severe pressure of the recession of the 1990s, and whereby the employee pledged loyalty to the company. 'Loyalty' was of course an emotive, but again ill-defined term, not necessarily meaning the same thing as it would in the UK or US, that was contrasted with employment relations in countries where it was implied that a job was just a job and that there was not the same warm kind of mutual pledge between employer and employee.

This idealized view was highly flattering and, in a way that the researcher himself could not have foreseen, was seized upon by those putting out the orthodox Japanese line. As in the later case of *Japan as Number One. Lessons for America* by a Harvard professor, no less, the 'lifetime' myth and its implications in terms of 'loyalty' etc. had to be true because it was an American expert that had explained it! What could be more persuasive for foreigners? As such, the theory came to play a major part in explaining the reasons for Japan's unexpected industrial success after 1945.

That was not, however, the end of the story as far as the researcher, later to become a successful business consultant in Japan, was concerned. His book *Kaisha* (Company) of 1985 showed by its subtitle how his views had changed over the intervening years: *How marketing, money and manpower strategy, not management style, make the Japanese world pace-setters.*[18] At an EU-Japan Centre seminar in Tokyo in 1995 he regretted having used the expression 'lifetime employment' in his original research of 1958, because of how it had later been misused, saying frankly that he had 'got carried away'. It had become what in a soccer game would be called an 'own goal'.

He also regretted having used another slogan-like term that had been similarly popularized and which he found misleading: 'Japan Inc.', which suggested that the country was a homogeneous monolith, rather than a collection of ministries, political factions and companies competing for the upper hand, managers within the same company competing for the top posts, and children at school being pushed, mostly by their mothers, to pass exams and get on the career escalator.

But in 1958 it was an achievement to have taken an interest in company management in Japan, before Japanese products began to make a strong international impact or gain any real reputation, even if others later pointed out that conditions in the far larger numbers of small and medium-sized enterprises were very different from those in the top corporations and that employees themselves might not see the system as so benevolent as management informants had claimed.[19]

As is clear in the 'lifetime' employment myth, the orthodox views about Japan and how it works involve the use of stereotypes of the 'we Japanese' type, which portray the Japanese population as an undifferentiated mass and make it easy for an image like 'Japan Inc.' to become widely accepted. In reverse, it underlines the degree to which foreigners of whatever nationality are stereotyped in Japan and seen as representatives of whichever country they come from and not as individuals, for which there are also other reasons to be discussed later.

It should be stressed that the repetition of orthodox stereotypes and views is by no means restricted to officials and others whose job it is to spread them. As Japan's best known management consultant, Kenichi Ohmae, has remarked, anyone who has been in Japan any time at all will have been struck by how often ordinary people repeat not merely the same views but how they express them in practically the same order with the same words and phrases.[20]

An example he refers to originates in postwar textbooks, which in a few lines sum up the official view of Japan's economic situation and explain what everyone has to do to deal with it. The mantra is that Japan is a small country, most of which is mountainous and with few natural resources, in which a large population must live crowded together. To survive, it must manufacture value-added products and export them in order to buy food and raw materials. No one else will do this for us.

Ohmae refers to this as a 'litany of economic necessity'. In a few simple, highly concrete words it sets out a situation that anyone can grasp, which is one reason, apart from constant repetition and a play on what will happen if it is not followed, why it has been so effective.

It could be contrasted with the efforts of British politicians and others to put over messages about the economy that are too abstract and therefore without a similarly immediate effect. Virtually the identical mantra was repeated to an American writer in Japan by a lady who told him that Japan had to 'mobilize the energy of our people'[21] The word 'mobilize' normally refers to military effort and while the economies of European countries and the USA were mobilized in wartime it is back to 'business as usual' once the war is over. For a country whose economy was largely destroyed by war, as happened for instance with Germany, where the expression 'economic miracle' originated, it is natural to make extra efforts to rebuild the economy. What is unusual is to continue long after the war with the same fervour.

The 'we Japanese' syndrome can be banal in phrases like, 'We Japanese enjoy raw fish but foreigners cannot eat it', and others which may or may not be true, or disquieting in the images it conjures up of a homogenized, mobilized population being inexorably impelled towards economic domination. It is an exaggerated image of a totally unified population, designed to show Japan's strengths and to hide the conflicts that exist within it, as they do anywhere else. In more open societies, where greater value is put on thinking for oneself and the public expression of different viewpoints, it smacks of totalitarianism.

In Asian countries that experienced Japanese behaviour before and during the Second World War it conjures up feelings of distrust. In France, Jacques Calvet, former head of Peugeot Citroen, stated that Japan had an in-built drive to dominate, while the former French prime minister and later EU Commissioner, Edith Cresson described Japan as an ant-like society similarly geared towards economic domination. In Japan, her remarks were judged to be unfriendly but can those who propagate the official line of an entire disciplined population working single-mindedly towards national economic goals be surprised?

In reaction to the persistent trade deficits against the EU, the EU-Japan Centre for Industrial Cooperation was set up in May 1987 to provide training courses in Japan for managers coming from Europe and a business information service, despite reluctance on the part of the Japanese authorities. The idea was that European managers and businessmen could familiarize themselves with business and production practices in Japan by means of a programme of lectures and visits to factories and offices in different parts of the country over periods of approximately eleven to sixteen weeks. They would also learn many things by their direct experience of life and living conditions in Japan that they could never learn at second hand. The Centre's establishment followed that of the previous Executive Training Programme for younger managers lasting a year and a half and was followed by other programmes such as the Manufacturing Training Fellowship. Altogether there seemed to be more programmes devoted to Japan than to any other country: a fact that some might find more than just a coincidence in itself.

Many managers found their stay in Japan valuable, even if it could not be compared with the experience of longer-staying European or American businessmen over the years, and one must hope that they communicated their findings to colleagues and decision-makers at home afterwards, but calling it a Centre for Industrial Cooperation when its main function was management training was misleading. Industrial cooperation would rather have implied actual business deals, such as the introduction of buyers and sellers, the establishment of joint company projects and the promotion of European direct investment in Japan: another area where there was a persistent and glaring imbalance in favour of Japan and against the EU of the order of nine to one. These were all points that would have to be tackled if the trade imbalance, the *raison d'être* for the Centre's existence, were to be dealt with.

To set up such a Centre is the easy part. Officially it was a 'common venture' between the European Commission's Directorate for Industry and MITI, in which the two partners were supposed to have an equal voice. In the normal circumstances of a common venture, reciprocity might have been expected, but the Japanese authorities were nervous about the European managers on the courses getting what they would have considered a 'wrong view', in other words anything that deviated from the official line. Thus, for the authorities, the control of the course content became a competitive issue, with the post of Japanese general manager reserved for a MITI official.

Ministries such as MITI have wide powers to dispense or withhold favours. These cover membership in their advisory committees, which are attractive to many academics, and help or hindrance in their sphere of competence, not merely limited to granting or denying official permission for a business venture. Under the system of unwritten 'administrative guidance', *gyosei shido*, it is the bureaucrats in the ministries who decide on a case by case basis how the rules are to be interpreted and applied – which they normally frame in a sufficiently elastic way to give themselves the maximum of power – and it seldom pays to be 'uncooperative'. It was easy, therefore, to select 'safe' speakers who could be relied upon not to deviate too far from the official line from among ministry officials, senior company managers and academics. A few consultants and foreigners completed the list.

Normally it would be natural to want to listen to speakers from the country concerned, not foreigners, but one has to remember the analogy with Communist party officials, whose job it is to control whatever information is put out and who can be relied upon to make things sound rosier than they really are. At the first briefing for a group of European managers straight off the plane, almost none of whom had ever been in Japan before, the Centre's Japanese general manager informed them that, 'Our way of business is the same as yours, apart from some differences because of our culture.' If so, some might have wondered why they had had to come all the way to Japan just to hear this bland statement.

This and following remarks gave the impression that Japanese markets were open and could have implied that foreign direct investment and mergers and acquisitions were welcome; all of which would have been news to Japan's long-serving foreign business community. It represented what people would like to hear but as the official line for foreign consumption it was disingenuous, as will be made clear later. The line was even repeated by an official speaker at the lunch of one of the European Chambers of Commerce in Tokyo. Predictably, the response was one of tired disbelief, with one or two pointed questions.

In 1995, when the Yen was riding high against the dollar, the Centre's course participants were told by a bullish official that the reason more European companies did not succeed in Japan or could not sell more of their products was because 'they did not try hard enough'. This was a good ploy since the participants had to admit that there was a grain of truth in it – the principle on which Dr Goebbels had based his propaganda – whereas the reality was the exclusive nature of Japan's political economy, with its web of internal interests between companies and between companies, ministries and politicians to satisfy, based on the economic nationalism of List's 'national economy'.

A friend of mine, for instance, was the head of a major European bank in Tokyo. Knowing the rate of interest at which a certain Japanese company was obtaining loans, he approached the company with the offer of future loans at a lower rate. The answer was 'thanks, but no thanks' on the grounds that the company already had long-standing relations with the Japanese bank that was providing loans and that, although the company would like to obtain loans more cheaply, it would not like to damage this connection.

My friend had been many years in Japan and there could be no doubt about the soundness of his bank, which was a household name at home, but it was obvious that no matter how hard he 'tried' he would not be able to enter the charmed circle. In excluding him, the Japanese company was doing nothing legally improper and could be claimed to be acting rationally within the Japanese context but it would be disingenuous to pretend that this was not one of many instances of the difference between being a Japanese insider and a foreign outsider.

Informally, I urged European course participants to talk to people in Tokyo's foreign business community, many of whom had a wealth of experience and could give informed guidance. In the past there had been a few visits to European firms but for some reason they had been discontinued and the only meeting with European businessmen, excluding consultants, on the programme was at the panel discussion at the very end of the course. Having contacted a well known European multinational, I therefore instigated a day's visit to the factory in which it had made a large investment, where there were presentations on the operation in Japan as a whole, ranging from manufacturing, marketing, distribution and personnel issues to Japanese consumer behaviour. Rather than the stereotyped 'party line' of the officially sanctioned 'safe' speakers, this gave an idea of the realities faced by foreign companies in Japan and direct investors in particular.

The Centre's main programmes included sessions on business, financial and social topics, as well as production-related topics like Quality Control: in short, sessions on a comprehensive range of subjects to help managers in Japanese environments, not forgetting Japan's historical background, for example. The subject that was conspicuously missing from the programme was politics. Not perhaps realizing its sensitivity, participants asked why it had been left out.

I passed this request on to the Japanese colleagues, mentioning the name of a possible speaker, who was the head of a British academic organization in Tokyo and one of the rare specialists in the field who had connections with an LDP political faction: ironically in view of his own political outlook. To my surprise, the idea met with agreement, although in other cases my Japanese opposite number was quite open about wanting a speaker of his choice. Normally, he did not attend presentations but this time he sat there taking notes, while my friend described the nature of 'money politics', *kinkin seiji*, factional rivalry and corruption that are endemic in Japan. At a debriefing session at the end of the course, he announced that the talk had been 'misleading' because what had been described might have been the case a few years ago but 'had now all changed'. My friend was not invited back as a speaker and did not receive an invitation to the formal farewell reception for the course, held at one of Tokyo's best hotels, with the EU paying half the cost, to which all speakers and others who had helped the course by, for example, arranging company visits, were invited. But I ensured that he received an invitation all the same.

As the course speaker on politics, he was replaced by a Japanese journalist. Despite the presence again of the Japanese general manager, he was fortunately relatively open. Perhaps this was partly because he had worked abroad, partly because what he said to some extent expressed his own views and partly because he must have realized that censorship would be futile when the participants could read in the English-language press about the continual scandals in

Japanese political life and would be likely to ask questions about them.

Presentations on Japanese society stressed such expected points as 'harmony', *wa*, 'consensus', *konsensasu*, and the homogeneity of the Japanese population, without any awareness that this might be tantamount to what would nowadays be termed 'racism'. The image projected was that of a population that worked together for the common cause and intuitively understood one another and cooperated because of their homogeneity and because, as one speaker put it, they were 'all in the same boat'. More or less implicitly, this was contrasted with the individualism, equated with selfishness, of 'Western' societies that could not unite to compete cohesively, giving Japan morally as well as materially the upper hand. Some of the course participants, mindful of Japan's postwar industrial advance and its objective achievements in fields such as product quality and reliability, found this a demoralizing message, implying that Japanese competitiveness was invincible.

If they had been able to remain in Japan, working there for a longer period, they would have been more likely to question some of the broad, not to say stereotyped, explanations of the sort just quoted and would have discovered that some were simply distortions of the facts: hence the reluctance to have a session on politics, or for that matter journalism, in the programme, which might have led to probing questions on the emotionally-tinged use of the term 'harmony' for example.

To take one of the most frequently used key words, 'homogeneity', it was asserted by one of the speakers referred to earlier on Japanese society and what Japanese people (*sic*) believed that, 'Japan was fortunate not to have any minority problem, since the Japanese population is homogeneous.' Whereas it as an open secret in Japan and a taboo subject that the opposite is the case. But the speaker was safe in using this spurious claim, or *tatemae*, knowing that his recently arrived audience would not be able to recognize any physical difference in Japan's between one and three million outcastes if they saw them.[22] Nor would they have been likely to know about the equally invisible Korean minority,[23] whom no good Japanese company would employ, and others such as the Ainu, the surviving original inhabitants of the northern island of Hokkaido, and the more numerous Okinawans, who are also not considered 'real' Japanese.[24]

What is to be emphasized is that the speaker was a highly educated man, partly educated in America and a fluent English speaker; head of an organization aimed at bringing Japanese and foreigners together. Like the man in the street, he knew that Koreans and outcastes are discriminated against but he also knew that it would have been a loss of face to have admitted this to his foreign audience and so he used *tatemae*, or what was supposed to be instead of what was. This allowed another implied contrast with less obviously homogeneous or less well regulated societies, adding to the impression of a unified competitive force, however misleading this might have been to his audience. Saving face and giving the impression that the Japanese form of society is perfect took precedence over speaking the truth. It was not an isolated instance but a constant problem throughout the course.

One foreign consultant mentioned during the training that for managers being assigned to Japan there is often a 'honeymoon' period. Because outward appearances are so important and because discreditable or disagreeable features must be hidden or not even mentioned, the surface of life may well seem more pleasant than elsewhere. The problem then is what to do when it turns out that all that glitters is not gold.

Some who stay for shorter periods, unless of course they are engaged in hard bargaining with officials or businessmen for permits or contracts, become curiously naïve. At home they are naturally suspicious of politicians, officials and what they hear through the news media but in Japan they fall into a suspension of disbelief, making them susceptible to official propaganda. Perhaps they feel that Japan, in spite of being a formidable industrial competitor and the world's second largest economy, is still somehow exotic and should be given the benefit of the doubt, even when they hear things that do not seem to fit the facts. They do not want to appear prejudiced, which would be inadmissible in this politically correct age; although the Japanese authorities themselves, with their own national ethos, would have no qualms. Businessmen, who like to think of themselves as hard-headed and not easily taken in, can be no different from anyone else in this respect. Officials may find that it makes for an easier life if they go along with what they would like to hear or to believe, even if something tells them it is not true. As far as the participants on the Centre's courses were concerned, most would realize after a while that there was a certain official line and that they would need to get beyond the idealized picture, or *tatemae*, being presented.

Japanese business as a whole has entertainment allowances well in excess of those in the US or UK and oiling the wheels is regarded as an essential part of doing business. Visitors to Japan likewise may not know how much the ministries can lavish on what is identified as the key task of 'winning friends and influencing people', when they roll out the red carpet for missions that come to enjoy their hospitality for ten days or a fortnight.

These missions consist of targeted groups of foreign opinion formers, such as journalists, academics and others in the media or with useful connections who are judged to be worth cultivating for the favourable climate of opinion towards Japan that they can spread. Or they may be those who can be expected to occupy positions of influence in the future, such as European university graduates who have recently completed a five- or six-month internship in the European Commission in Brussels and can be seen as an élite on the way up; or graduates from Asian countries with which the Japanese ministries want to cement political and economic relations. Attendance at receptions for such groups gives an insight both into how they are composed and the lavish hospitality provided in terms of smart hotels, luxurious catering, first class travel by super express and attentive staff. Their time in Japan is too short and too supervised to do more than scratch the surface rather like tourists, although when they travel into Tokyo from Narita Airport they cannot avoid seeing the poor, cramped housing in which so many of the population live and the lack of parks and greenery.

At one reception for opinion formers from Europe and America the twenty or so visitors were able to meet the head of the ministry responsible; something that they might not have been able to do at home and which underlined the importance attached to this official public relations campaign. In the welcoming speech he assured them that, contrary to what they might have heard, the Japanese market was completely open, and that he was completely at the disposal of anyone who might have problems with it. This expression of personal concern and willingness to help evidently impressed some of the audience, though they were opinion formers rather than businessmen, and a European journalist who was not in Japan for the first time dismissed it as *tatemae*, a façade.

The head of the ministry was homing in on the sensitive subject of the large and persistent trade imbalances with the two regions represented by the targeted audience, the EU and the US. The mission and the speech were part of the ministry's national economic effort, comprising a 'soft sell' to a non-business audience, in contrast to the more aggressive stance of the ministry towards the European managers on the Centre's courses, who were told that the reason they were not more successful in Japan was that they 'did not try hard enough'.

Apart from these missions directly organized by the ministries, there are also organizations and publications which may give an impression of independence but which are actually under their control. The Journal of Japanese Trade and Industry, for instance, claims to be independent and gives no outward sign of putting forward official views, while its publisher, the Japan Economic Foundation, sounds a foundation like any other: until one learns that the Foundation's presidents have included a famous MITI vice-minister i.e. the operative head of the ministry, Naohiro Amaya, along with previous heads of JETRO, a MITI offshoot, like Shoichi Akazawa and Minoru Masuda. In these circumstances, it is to all intents and purposes an official organ, even if it may not look it. In Japanese business, as in war, propaganda and disinformation to confuse and disorientate the opponent or competitor are all part of the struggle, following the widely studied principles of the 500 BC Chinese strategist, Sun Tzu, in his *Art of War*. The importance of Sun Tzu and the influence he has had as the Asian Clausewitz cannot be overstated and anyone dealing with politics and business in Japan would be well advised to read him. Fortunately, recent editions of his classic indicate that more notice is now being taken of the *Art of War* in Europe and America.[26]

Sun Tzu has much to say on the importance of both camouflage and of espionage, with the best outcome being so to put the enemy off-balance that the best general wins the war without having to fight it. Disinformation, and in our case our own ignorance and consequent failure to adopt adequate measures to deal with Japanese competition, has an important role to play. During the Cold War the prevalence of Soviet disinformation and espionage were taken for granted but it is not only in war that the thinking of Sun Tzu is applied. He should be paid more attention in Europe and America.

During a discussion at the Royal Institute of International Affairs previously referred to, a MITI official remarked that, 'In England you have the great tradition of Adam Smith and the free market. We hope that you will always follow this tradition.' Of course he hoped so! Directed at a predominantly non-business audience, this flattery was aimed at distracting attention from trade imbalances and non-tariff barriers, which in reality mean that the free market operates as a one-way street. Unfortunately some of the audience, to judge by their expressions, found the flattery gratifying. It was a good example of the effectiveness of telling people what they would like to hear.

Of course, this does not always work. A senior European executive commented that, 'Even after twenty years, I can't get used to the way they tell you these blatant lies and expect you to behave as if you believed them.' A senior American diplomat from a political background joked that, 'I've been in the bull ... business for forty years but I've never met anything like this before!' European graduates at a joint reception with a similar group of Asian graduates were amazed to find how distrustful of the Japanese authorities the Asians were. But then they do not find Japan exotic and do not indulge in the sort of overblown theorizing found in Europe and America.

This theorizing plays into the hands of those who propagate the official self-image of Japan according to the *Nihonjinron*,[27] *Nihonjin* meaning 'Japanese people' and *ron* meaning 'theory': best described as a theory of Japaneseness, of the essence of Japan and the Japanese (*sic*) etc, based on an assumption of 'uniqueness'; along with 'different' a much loved word, of being unlike any other people or country, and hence uniquely difficult, or rather impossible, to understand. The theory is usually presented in the manner of an abstract Platonic 'idea', without an awareness of when and how it arose as an ideology with a political purpose or consciousness of its exclusive, 'racist' nature. It is taken with great seriousness, except by the usual minority of deviants, and is recognized by the repetitiveness of the stereotyped assertions and circular logic that it gives rise to. As a major component of official ideology, we shall return to it later in more detail.

A popular joke among foreign residents in Japan gives the flavour of this way of thinking; or perhaps it would be better to say feeling, since it is not strong on analysis but is mostly emotional. A Japanese professor was once asked to explain a certain aspect of behaviour in Japan to a foreigner. Having done so, he asked the foreigner if he had understood. The latter tells him he now understands completely; whereupon the professor looks sad, saying, 'Then I didn't explain it properly because if I had you would not have understood.' In other words, only a Japanese born and bred in Japan could have done so.

People like the professor are seldom conscious of how ethnocentric, or parochial, this attitude is and of how it is inconsistent with another popular self-image of being 'international'; let alone all the propaganda about 'internationalization', *kokusaika*. But then, as a popular British philosopher used to say, it all depends what you mean by 'internationalization'. Does it, for instance, apply as much to foreign investment in Japan as to Japanese investment overseas?

An American chemical company wanted to set up a plant in Japan and had found a suitable site. The Japanese chemical manufacturers' association naturally heard about this and persuaded the local landowners not to sell to the foreigners, forcing the American company to drop its plans. Meanwhile, the imbalance between Japanese investment in the EU and EU investment in Japan is about nine to one; suggesting that 'internationalization', like open markets, is a one-way street.

The case of the American company could stand for a great many others and the well known and frequently repeated complaints about the informal or hidden barriers that serve to keep the foreigners at arm's length under the 'national economy' policy. Thus it is clear that to talk about 'internationalization', which to many outside Japan would imply a two-way not a one-way process, is a trick of words, though following Sun Tzu, it makes good propaganda for foreign consumption.[28]

Paraphrasing George Orwell, it can be said that while all countries are different some feel they are more different than others, with Japan, in the *Nihonjinron* view, being 'different' in a special way that puts it and its people outside the scheme of things. Anyone who has compared different types of society as a student of anthropology would regard this with scepticism but Japanese schoolchildren are still taught about the divine descent of the land and its monarch[29] and the

*Nihonjinron* leads to a great deal of deliberate obscurity, which is necessary to protect its myths, which does not make it easier for non-Japanese to uncover the realities. This failing, as just noted, applies in particular to the 'Western' world rather than to Asia, where more similar myths but also greater realism about Japan are to be found.

Just as the meaning of 'internationalization' depends on the interpretation that certain people give it and cannot be taken for granted, so the word 'understand' in the context of the *Nihonjinron* and in 'understanding Japan' etc. is loaded. In English, too, it can either mean to understand in a factual and objective sense, for example, what makes an aeroplane fly, or in a subjective and judgmental sense, for example, why a person feels the way they do, why a political leader did or should (not) have embarked on a certain course of action etc. In this second meaning, 'understand' means quite plainly to agree, to be 'one of us'.

A nice example of the tricks that words can play was at a discussion among British personnel managers working for Japanese companies in the City of London. One lamented that the problems between local and expatriate staff were because, 'They do not understand each other.' This evoked the reply from a more experienced local manager that, 'On the contrary, they understand each other only too well!' At issue were things like job responsibility and promotion prospects, involving career competition between local staff and expatriates, against the background of the two separate employment systems being operated for local staff and Japanese expatriates respectively. The same manager compared this to 'a colonial situation'[30] and local staff dissatisfaction with promotion prospects has led to law suits in the US under employment discrimination legislation, showing that the problems are not only about 'understanding' one another.

In the context of orthodox *Nihonjinron* types of thinking, frequently found in Japanese explanations for foreigners, including at the EU-Japan Centre for instance, it is naturally the second or 'agreeing' meaning of 'understand' that is in use, though this is not made plain. Thus, to the extent that foreigners accept the official line and do not challenge it by wanting to analyze, let alone criticize, it, they may be said to show some 'understanding', even though of course they can never really 'understand' in the end. Some may become apologists and may be useful in helping the authorities' public relations efforts abroad but although the authorities find them useful they do not respect them.[31] Their attitude is that of Lenin when he spoke sarcastically of 'tools and fools'.

On the other hand, the idea that foreigners are not qualified by birth to 'understand Japan etc' provides great scope for one-upmanship and anyone who is sceptical about the orthodox 'line' can be cast into outer darkness by just saying that they do not 'understand'. It is a wonderful way out. The really surprising thing is not that this self-serving line is so often used but that so many people in the EU and US, where the nature of Japanese competition and its results should have become clear, are apparently content to accept it.

A further minor difficulty for Europeans is that, due to the great impact of the US on Japan since 1945 and the preoccupation of Japanese policy-makers with their trade and defence relationships with America, they tend to get explanations through the Japanese-American contrast that the Japanese have constructed, since they look the same and are politically less important. Most of the statistics presented by Japanese speakers at the EU-Japan Centre, for example, were Japan-US comparisons – the difference in the number of lawyers was a favourite – and this influenced some of the discussion, for example, about the possession of firearms, even though the Japanese gang members of organized crime syndicates, the *yakuza*, are themselves increasingly well armed. Some of course might blame the foreigners by saying that the guns were Russian or had been sold to them by dealers in the Philippines.

So with all these difficulties, what tools are there for disentangling the realities from the myths and getting to grips with Japan's politico-economic structure and what makes Japan as competitor tick? Put briefly, people can act in two sorts of ways and frequently out of a mixture of the two. The first is to do what is expedient to get, for example, power, money, influence etc. and to avoid poverty, punishment by others etc. The second is to act out of beliefs that are held of an ethical, religious, artistic or philosophical etc. nature. Both ways are rational when judged by their own standards and mixtures of the two are the stuff of everyday life. Psychopaths and sociopaths could be said to be acting out of an absence of beliefs. Another way of looking at it is to be clear that some actions are 'instrumental', in other words aimed like expedient actions at goals like those just mentioned; while others are 'affective' or motivated by human feelings and emotions, ranging from those to which strong emotions are attached to things we just feel like doing at a particular time.

In these respects, Japan is no different from anywhere else, although the official ideology would deny this, claiming instead that anything Japanese is *sui generis* or 'a thing in itself – *ein Ding an sich*', and therefore beyond analysis or criticism. This particularly applies to the question of power: who in Japan has it, how they use it and who does not have it, both in the political and economic arena as a whole and in its sub-units, such as political factions, government ministries and business organizations.

Rather as one of the myths of the former Soviet Union was that there were no classes and that the population, under the benevolent leadership of the Communist party, were building socialism and creating an ideal society, so in Japan the ideology of 'we Japanese' and the claim to be operating an ideally 'harmonious' society seek to gloss over power relations. The idea is not markedly dissimilar from the wartime ideology of the entire population's hearts 'beating as one'.

Naturally, people in Japan, such as company employees for instance, are keenly aware in their daily lives who has the power but it would be impolite to ask those who control the ideology about such discrepancies. During the years of the 'bubble economy', when absurd rises in the price of land were making it impossible for so many to settle down in their own home after a lifetime of work, I suggested to a Japanese professor of business studies that there was a crucial difference between those who had land and could use it as collateral to make more money and those who could not even afford their own home. He became quite upset – but it was of course my own 'misunderstanding', *gokai*.

The ideological need to distract people's attention from who has power and what they do with it requires the use of an alternative explanation or alibi. The Communist solution was to use the technique of the big lie, as recommended by Dr Goebbels, to claim that it was only in societies suffering under 'the contradictions of capitalism' that exploitation based on unequal power relations existed. In the Japanese case it is the alternative explanation of 'culture'; as the large number of books using the word in their titles to explain Japan to foreigners published in foreign languages show.

The advantages of using this word are that there is no definition of what it might mean, which makes it an ideal way of making things deliberately mysterious, as in the case of the *Nihonjinron*. As well as mystifying foreigners, which can put them at a disadvantage when negotiating with the Japanese authorities, for instance, the constant harping on 'culture' directed at Japan's own people serves to reinforce feelings of being 'unique' and exclusive: at variance, as already pointed out, with 'internationalization' understood as a two-way process.

Because the term 'culture', especially 'Japanese culture', is so frequently used by Japanese people in explanations for foreigners and is so loosely used to cover just about anything, it must be stated why it is objectionable. In the limited case of management writing, the expression 'company culture' may be almost acceptable as a shorthand way of explaining 'how we do things here in this company', though as one critic put it, this may be more of a mixture of 'fantasy and management propaganda' than anything else: comparable to the popular use of words like 'philosophy' to characterize a 'manufacturing philosophy' for instance.[32]

But the vagueness of the term is more serious when applied to entire countries and their peoples; especially when it seems that it dominates every single member of a particular society as something up in the clouds that is unchanging and unchangeable. Such is the claim of the *Nihonjinron*, while excluding the possibility of change clearly reflects the interests of those who hold power. Those who promote the official ideology bear the heaviest responsibility for stereotyping their own population as 'the Japanese' as an indeterminate mass: an expression better avoided.

Apart from its general use to refer to books, music etc, what many people assume 'culture' to mean was expressed in the phrase of the American anthropologist Lewis White as 'the sum total of learned behaviour'. But if what one really means by this are, for example, the dominant values of a society, what is considered to be accepted behaviour, and characteristic patterns of thought etc. being specific about them will be a greater aid to comprehension than using a vague term like 'culture'. As someone once said, it means either too much or too little.

The statement by the Japanese general manager of the EU-Japan Centre to a newly-arrived group of European managers in Tokyo to the effect that business in Japan was 'the same as yours, apart from some differences because of our culture', that was already quoted, gave an idea of the usefulness in the hard world of trade and other negotiations of the key terms 'difference' and 'culture'. For many years, for instance, discriminatory rates were levied on imported spirits such as whisky and brandy that were four to six times higher than the rate levied on domestically produced *shochu*, a spirit, like vodka, produced from potatoes. In 1987 the EU won the case against the Japanese government when it took the issue to the GATT (General Agreement on Trade and Tariffs), the predecessor of the WTO (World Trade Organization) but then had to go again to the WTO for the same thing eight years later. Also complaining were the US and Canada. One of the reasons adduced for the differential rates, which clearly benefited domestic producers against imports, were 'cultural differences'.[33]

In another instance 'culture' and research were cited by the Japanese government as pretexts for its policy to support the whaling industry. Whale meat used to be a regular item of school meals and is still eaten in some restaurants. A Japanese professor wrote to the *Financial Times* to explain that this was part of Japanese culture but was this an independent view outside official efforts to continue with whaling? The power of the bureaucracy to co-opt academics on to its advisory committees, enhancing their status and influence, has already been mentioned. There were public protests at the time of the International Whaling Convention meetings but the Japanese authorities argued that the ban on commercial whaling should be lifted and permitted Japanese whalers to hunt in a whale sanctuary in spite of international appeals to cut quotas.[34]

Persuading others that one is 'different' can therefore be a good way of getting 'different' i.e. more favourable, treatment; but to draw attention to such stratagems, or to other things that one is not supposed to mention in Japan's case, such as power relations and scandals, is to run the risk of being attacked for not 'understanding' Japan or even for being 'anti-Japanese', as if it were alright to point out the underside of every other society except Japan's.[35] As a long-term foreign resident put it during my early days in Japan, 'You never have been able to get away with criticism of Japan and you never will'.

For reasons that will now be obvious, this applies to Japanese people themselves. Back in 1969, a former Japanese ambassador published a book in English that made quite a stir at the time entitled *Japan Unmasked*, in which he spoke frankly about some of the things one is not supposed to mention.[36] When asked for a comment, the Japanese Foreign Ministry replied that they 'had not had time to read it'. The author then wittily referred to himself as 'the extinguished ambassador'.

In 1973 an account of how hard life on assembly line in a car factory was appeared, making quite specific points.[37] When asked for a comment, the company did not refer to the points made, simply stating that the author was not a regular employee but a journalist and therefore did not 'understand' the company.

In 1994 an English translation of *An insider's irreverent view of bureaucratic Japan* gave a trenchant view of life inside one of the ministries by a qualified doctor who was at the time in the bureaucracy. At a talk to one of the European Chambers of Commerce in Tokyo he later described his superiors' reaction to his revelations of what went on behind the screen, though many colleagues at his own level recognized it as all too accurate.

Apart from having life made uncomfortable the technique, as in the car assembly line example above, was not to answer the specific points raised but to do everything to destroy his reputation by, as he said, character assassination. While he was talking, there was a whooshing noise outside and two faces suddenly appeared at the window. 'Look out, Dr Miyamoto, they're watching you!' joked the quick-witted chairman of the Chamber. They were of course window cleaners. Dr Miyamoto is no longer in the ministry but anyone who has to deal with the Japanese authorities or who wants to understand how the bureaucracy works and the power that it wields should read his book.[38]

All this is consistent with the use of information and comment as a competitive weapon, as recommended by Sun Tzu in *The Art of War*, in the struggle for political and economic power. What is sometimes comic, if it did not have such serious consequences for this struggle, is the attitude of well-meaning but insufficiently informed people in the 'Western' world.

A long-serving chief executive of the German Chamber of Commerce in Tokyo told me about a talk he had given in Hamburg on the realities of doing business in Japan, at which some Japanese people were present. None of the latter disputed the points he had raised afterwards but some of his fellow-countrymen told him that he should have been 'more polite to the Japanese'. One wonders if a similar comment would have been made if the talk had concerned another country.

After retiring from the EU-Japan Centre, I spoke about some of the same issues at an international conference in Europe and was accused by one person of talking nonsense. It turned out that he had never been in Japan at all. Of course, for anyone wanting access to government organizations and information, or to companies and other sources, it would not be a good idea to be known to be too critical, if one wants to do research. About funding, it is hardly necessary to say anything, as people who have worked on subjects like Japan's outcastes have discovered.

More useful than what is often little more than the *tatemae* of 'culture' is to look at how far Japanese business or society functions on a universalist or particularist basis. Universalism here means treating everyone on the same basis, so that all banks or financial institutions for instance that meet the same officially laid down requirements can trade in the market on an equal footing. Particularism would mean that only banks etc. of one's own society would receive the same treatment, while others would be treated less favourably. According to the writer on international management Geert Hofstede, particularistic treatment is characteristic of collectivistically organized societies.[39]

The 'we Japanese' syndrome, which equates individualism with nothing more than selfishness, is a collectivist ethic and many Japanese as well as foreign commentators have commented on the groupish nature of Japanese society, which results in many cases where members of that society who are for some reason separated from the group literally feel like fish out of water.[40] Added to that is the Listian emphasis on the national economy, in which the Japanese collective as a whole is seen to be engaged in a struggle with its competitors; of which the particularistic industrial policy that has been so much discussed outside Japan is one manifestation, while it goes without saying that the *Nihonjinron* with its insistence on being 'different' or 'unique' is the particularistic ideology par excellence.

The analogy should not be taken too far but more than one commentator has been struck by the resemblances between the Japanese and the Communist systems, most clearly expressed in a book with the catchy title of *Where Communism Works*. Both systems have a collectivist ideology that denigrates the individual, privileged political and bureaucratic classes, strong state control over what is taught to children at a young age and both national or state policy before economic activity as it would be understood by followers of Adam Smith. The obvious difference between, for example, the old

USSR and Japan, is that the former aimed to spread its power using a military machine, while the latter aims to spread its power using a commercial and industrial machine.

In fact Japan also has strong military forces but they remain largely invisible and it is rare to see a uniform but, since the concept of the Japanese national economy is of one economy, not split into separate civilian and military parts but cross-fertilizing each other, it is this technonationalism and its overall contribution to technological, industrial and commercial advance that is the most significant point.[41]

At the level of ideology, the current arguments about 'Asian values' and whether they are 'universal' or particularistic' show the force of these two concepts and why it can help to untangle myths and realities by looking at, for example, how the Japanese economy is managed, in this light. It is suggested here that there is still too much of a trend in 'the West' to see it as something exotic, which is not matched by other Asian observers.

Sometimes the reason is the difference between what people say they are doing, for example, in relation to 'loyalty to the company', and what they are really doing, making it essential to go beyond the spoken words to consider how far they are motivated by expediency and how far it is a matter of a genuinely held value. In public, *tatemae* or 'saying the right thing', 'not letting the side down' and 'not washing dirty linen in public', especially to foreigners, may create an impression of harmoniousness greater than actually exists. What people say they are doing is certainly interesting and can provide clues as to how a work group or a society is supposed to function but it is not as crucial as what they really are doing. In a society like Japan's, where it so important not to lose face, to preserve the exterior appearance, often at great cost to the underlying substance, and not to be different from other (Japanese) people – 'the nail that sticks out gets hammered down', as they say – these are things to bear in mind, whether one is engaged in negotiations with Japanese businessmen or officials or whether one is looking more generally at the situation.

What is certain is that people are capable of holding sincere and perhaps quite emotional beliefs, such as those about the value of the group in Japan, or about the value of the individual in the US or Europe for instance. They can also believe, or bring themselves to believe, what suits their interests and, as already mentioned, hold two opposed beliefs at the same time if the situation requires what George Orwell called 'doublethinking'. There also seems to be no limit to what people can believe that is dangerous or outrageous, as was proved in Japan in March 1995 by Aum Shinrikyo's sarin gas attack on the Tokyo Underground.

With the decline of the traditional religions in Japan, as in other industrial societies, cults like Aum Shinrikyo, dominated by clever but unscrupulous leaders, have seen their chance to exploit gullible – and preferably rich – followers who feel their lives are empty. Yet even after the arrest of the ringleader, Shoko Asahara, and the revelations of the murders, kidnappings, extortion and ill-treatment of followers there were still followers who remained loyal, maintaining that Asahara was the great guru and that he had been framed by the authorities etc. etc. It can be misleading to interpret behaviour, including in a business environment, as being more guided by reason than it really is.

Many have commented on the conformist nature of Japanese society, which is what the education system aims to produce, and compared, for example, to contemporary Britain this is undoubtedly the case but it is still better to keep an open mind and to be prepared for surprises. In the 1960s I used to do some work for one of the large general trading companies: a very conservative firm with a very 'Japanese' management style. It made one very aware of its management ideology enshrined in the statement of the company's principles, which we spent a long time trying to translate into English, and of features of the traditional management system in a large company such as decision-making by consensus, whether actually followed in practice or not as much as some of the books say.

With this memory of a very traditional large trading company in mind, I later met a senior Japanese manager in one of the company's large competitors overseas. To my astonishment, he began by talking about decision-making by consensus as a waste of time, though he remarked that some of his colleagues found it 'therapeutic'. He said he would prefer a system of delegated authority and individual decision-making responsibility on European or American lines: a highly unorthodox statement for a senior manager in such a company to make and probably not the sort of view to endear him to the top management. But it was a useful reminder to be ready for the unexpected.

For us, the problem remains that we have devoted far less effort to familiarizing ourselves with the workings of Japan's political economy than Japan's ruling circles, ministries, trading companies, banks, manufacturers, sales organizations etc. have with us. Some of what has been done is unfocused and uncoordinated, so that the feeling of competing against an opponent that is powerful yet hard to pin down adds to our feelings of being confused and of responding inadequately.[42] Yet if we understand the problem for what it is by disentangling the realities from the myths and by taking it more seriously, we would be quite able to respond to it.

Finally, there is the problem of those in the 'Western' world who hanker after a perfect society. For years, many intellectuals and others believed and wrote that it was to be found under Communism and, in spite of the evidence of the crimes it produced and the collapse of the Soviet Union, believers still remain. In a similar way, there are those, again especially intellectuals, who see Japanese society through rose-tinted spectacles; even if it has taken a bit of a knock in the crisis of the 1990s.

Apart from out-and-out apologists who have their own reasons, some are attracted by a strong collectivist ethic, state guidance of the economy at the macro level and the promise of powerful governing élites. An analogy would be with what is now called 'Old Labour', in contrast to the 'New Labour' Party, in Britain and with comparable movements on the Continent such as the German Green Party, which seems to represent old wine in new bottles.

Others who feel the problems of modern industrial societies such as crime, disorder and a general feeling of emptiness – the 'alienation' or 'anomie' of the sociologists – want to believe that the grass must be greener on the other side of the hill, particularly when they hear the stories of how happy the workers are, how little crime there is etc. Yet what has been revealed since the collapse of Yamaichi Securities and the crisis in Japan's banking system, in which politicians and bureaucrats are deeply embroiled, looks less like a perfect society than one in which corruption and cronyism are rampant.

This should not of course deter research into Japan's undoubted achievements in the industrial field and other areas in which there may be something to be learned: indeed, it is essential to study them in order to know the competition but to overestimate the quality of Japanese society as a whole is an insidious distortion. Books like *Japan as Number One* may have pleased the Japanese authorities but to many ordinary Japanese it was an irritating distortion of the realities they have to live with.[43]

Shortly after arriving in Japan for the first time in late 1962, the brother of a manager in a large industrial company told me that they were looking for someone to teach English. Although I had never met him before, he astonished me by his unprompted remarks that his brother had had a nervous breakdown and was not yet back at work. He then went on to explain that his brother could not see any point in his job in the company and that it would make no difference if anyone else did it. In spite of all I had heard about how different things in Japan were said to be, it did not sound as if there was so much difference between alienated company men in Japan and the US or Europe after all.[44]

# ■ CHAPTER 3
# A 'New' Japan?

'Who controls the past, controls the future; who controls the present, controls the past', as George Orwell put it in '1984', his acute portrayal of totalitarian social control. Thus the past does not automatically determine the present but can be a powerful means of moulding people's emotions to justify and support the ideology that suits the interests of those who hold power.

In Japan this is done through the school system, especially through the teaching of history under the rigid control of the reactionary Ministry of Education, and by such means as the time, effort and seriousness devoted to the propagation of the *Nihonjinron*, the 'theory of the essence of Japaneseness etc.',[1] which in other countries might be laughed out of court as ethnocentric, lacking in any scientific basis or as 'politically incorrect'. Appealing to the emotions rather than to reason, the results are an unashamedly strong national ethos and national consciousness, as expressed, for instance, in the constantly repeated expression 'we Japanese' and a feeling of 'separateness' from the rest of the world. When this ideology, which reflects the interests of the governing party, the LDP, which has been in almost continuous power since 1945, is backed up by the group social controls within Japanese society, it produces strong national cohesion, comparable to what would only be found in 'Western' societies in wartime.

Indeed, a recent writer on the authorities' involvement in 'moulding Japanese minds' considers that Japan both at the beginning and the end of the twentieth century remains 'a nation at war in peace'.[2] Anyone who does not understand this mobilization of Japan in the business field, for instance, can have no real idea of the nature of Japanese competition.

Outwardly, Japan's big cities, though not rural areas where conditions can be quite primitive, may appear modern and visitors who only know the country from brief visits may make the mistake of concluding that it is 'Western'. But material objects such as smart and expensive hotels, air-conditioned taxis (necessary in Japan's hot and sticky summers) and the latest electronic gadgetry do not by themselves make a country 'Western' or mean that how it is run does not hark back to considerably earlier. It was the late US Ambassador Reischauer, born in Japan of missionary parents, married to a Japanese lady, who spent his entire career as an academic at Harvard and then Ambassador closely involved with Japan – and who could not possibly be described as being 'anti-Japanese' – who expressed the same idea. He wrote that Japan appeared international 'on the surface' but that underneath it was 'an isolated, inward-looking country'. His question was whether it was 'destined always to be an international odd man out?'[3]

Of course it is the 'international, democratic etc.' image that the Japanese authorities want to promote abroad but no one doing business with or conducting foreign relations can afford to ignore the question raised by former Ambassador Reischauer and others to which it gives rise. These include such basic issues as whether Japan has a tradition of democratic or authoritarian rule and how and why Japan developed as a major industrial state. Are the ultranationalism of the 1930s and 1940s – a period that is not all that long ago if one thinks about the rise of comparable fascist movements in Europe – really as dead and buried as we are told, though it often seems as if they have been airbrushed out of history altogether? Are the attitudes and behaviour of Japan's ruling élites significantly different from those of their predecessors, even if their goals are now commercial and industrial?

These are living issues for businessmen and government organizations that have to negotiate with their Japanese counterparts: not just 'ancient history'. In particular, they are problems for the 'Western' world, because of such naïve 'universalist' beliefs that 'business is business' all over the world and that the need or motivation to make a profit explains how managers behave in any politico-economic system.

Apart from doing more to grasp the realities of how the world's second largest economy works and what it aims at, we should stop for a moment to think why this is our problem and not a problem for other Asians. These are the people who directly experienced Japanese hegemony and who do not find Japan mysterious or elusive. Their attitude is frequently that of 'deep-seated wariness, cynicism' (towards the control mechanisms used by the authorities to keep foreign ideas out and their own ideology in) and a 'sense of *déjà vu*'.[4] Some of their remarks will be quoted later.

References in Japanese life to what happened in some cases a very long time ago are not uncommon. In 1281, for instance, a Mongol invasion fleet that had come to attack Japan was dispersed by a typhoon, or 'divine wind', the *kamikaze*: the same name given to the suicide pilots who attacked American aircraft carriers during the

Second World War in 1945. Between 1637 and 1868 the Shogun's regime enforced a 'closed country' policy, *sakoku jidai*, reducing contact with the outside world to an absolute minimum. In 1994 during a television discussion, Kenichi Ohmae, former head of McKinsey Japan and unsuccessful candidate in an election for Tokyo Governor, remarked that Japan might be going into another period of 'new seclusion,' *shin sakoku*. His fellow panellists nodded, though in Japan where, as they say, 'you should never take yes for an answer', whether this meant that they really agreed, whether they just wanted to show that they had heard his view, or whether they simply wanted to be polite is not clear; but as a leading commentator and business guru with international experience it can be taken that his remarks were not lightly made.

In 1703 there occurred the Incident of the Forty-Seven Ronin, masterless samurai, who avenged the insult to their former feudal lord but who were ordered to commit suicide by the Shogun. Made into a play celebrating the virtues of loyalty, duty and revenge, *Chushingura*, it was 'the most popular of all the Kabuki plays', as Professor Reischauer noted.[5] It was not, unsurprisingly, banned under the Occupation. Even now many Japanese visit the graves of the Forty-Seven, strewing them with their visiting cards.

In 1853 Commodore Perry's force of 'Black Ships' sailed into Tokyo Bay, obliging the Japanese authorities to accept a letter from the President. In the 1960s when there was a big, but of course groundless, scare about an invasion of foreign capital into Japan, the newspapers whipped up emotions about the new 'Black Ships'. Apart from this, many Japanese seem to have a sketchy view of their own history beyond certain stereotyped remarks, which brings us back once again to the rigid, centralized policies of the Ministry of Education.

Concerning the more recent history of the Second World War, the nationalistic utterances of LDP government ministers and politicians which keep on cropping up, causing offence and distrust elsewhere in Asia in particular, again show that the past is not dead. In an irony of history, it was a supremely practical man who himself changed the history of how work is organized in industrial society with his new concepts of mass marketing and mass production on the assembly line – Henry Ford – who made the notorious remark that, 'History is bunk'. But getting away from the idea of academic history as an irrelevant pastime, and remembering Ambassador Reischauer's earlier remark about Japan being an odd man out, it will be found that an understanding of Japan's experience over the centuries during which the 'Western' world underwent the Industrial Revolution and the long process of developing democratic forms of government is very relevant at the present time, even if some of the outward labels may have changed.

Indeed, even the most ancient past, before records existed, has an influence on the feelings of being 'different' or 'unique' and the determination to remain so found in present-day Japan. This refers to the national myth of origin and to the sensitive subject of the Emperor's antecedents.

Japan is still popularly known as the 'Land of the Rising Sun' and the Rising Sun name appears in many places, such as the Asahi Newspaper, Asahi Glass Co. and Asahi Beer. The flag with the red globe of the sun on a white background, flown far more frequently and at more places than generally found, for example, in Western Europe, reinforces the image. Japanese naval vessels fly the version of the flag in which the rays of the sun radiate out to all four edges; more widely seen in the years before 1945, with its expansionist overtones. During the Second World War the suicide pilots took off wearing a white headband with the red globe of the sun in the middle: a symbol with powerful emotional reverberations. Under the LDP's educational reforms of 1984, aimed at giving a more nationalistic and conformist element to the curriculum, schools were ordered to fly the flag and to sing the national anthem at all events such as entrance or graduation ceremonies, with the threat of punishment for school principals who disobeyed.

Numerous examples show how faithfully the censorship of school history textbooks follows earlier nationalistic teachings and how correct George Orwell was to emphasize the importance of the control of the past as a means of moulding the minds of succeeding generations under a political system like that of Japan's.

Lafcadio Hearn had been the first European writer to make an impact with his romantic writings on Japan in the latter half of the nineteenth century, had taken a Japanese wife and even Japanese nationality: a highly unusual step at that time. Shortly before his death in 1904, he gave his considered view of the country in his *Japan: an attempt at interpretation*. In it he quotes the nineteenth-century scholar Hirata (1776-1843) who asserted that, 'There exists no hard-and-fast line between the Age of the Gods (*sic*) and the present age' and that since the Japanese (*sic*) were of divine origin they were superior to all other peoples.[6]

Compare this with what the Ministry of Education insisted be included in a textbook – in 1986! The Ministry insisted that the ancient legends of the *Kojiki* and the *Nihon Shoki* be referred to as 'books of history' and that the birth of Japan be included. Censorship, therefore, means not only suppressing material that the Ministry, or rather government, does not like but also including material not in the author's draft at official insistence. The 1986 textbook consequently had to include the lines that, 'According to these books (i.e. the *Kojiki* etc.), the Imperial family's ancestral deity is Amaterasu-O-Mikami, the goddess of the sun, and at her order, the Emperor started to rule the nation.'[7]

These myths of divine origin and hence racial superiority were openly propagated during the Second World War, with the talk of 'spreading the Imperial Way' etc. as an ideology of expansion, while the whole flavour of the 1986 textbook's assertion about the Emperor's 'ancestral deity' contradicts the post-war Constitution of 1947. This states that the Emperor is, 'The symbol of the state and of the unity of the people, deriving his position from the will of the people with whom resides sovereign power',[8] though many would say that this type of American-inspired 'We, the people' sentiment is a pious hope rather than a reality: or to put it in Japanese terms, more *tatemae* than *honne*, when one considers the circumstances in which the post-war Constitution arose.

Different sorts of myths of origin will be familiar to people who have studied anthropology, while in other countries one can believe that God made the world, or that there is a scientific explanation, or that it is uncertain. What is striking about the Japanese national myth of origin is that it is just that: national. The legend tells how the one country, Japan, was created: not the whole world, in contrast to the other explanations just mentioned. Thus the Japanese are the 'children of the sun' or rather, paradoxically in the light of the position of women in Japanese society, of the sun goddess Amaterasu-O-Mikami. The rest of the world undoubtedly exists but perhaps at a lower level of reality than the 'land of the gods' proclaimed by ideologists like Hirata and those who follow in his footsteps?

In another throwback to a mythical past of no less than 2,600 years ago, the Japanese authorities organized a commemoration in 1940 of the foundation of their empire by Emperor Jimmu, supposedly in 660 BC. This was just over a year before their attack on the American fleet at Pearl Harbor in December 1941 during the militarist, *gunkokushugi* and ultra-nationalistic period, and after their attack on China in 1937. No historical evidence for the existence of Emperor Jimmu exists[9] but in the supposedly enlightened post-war world this did not stop the economic boom between November 1954 and June 1957 being given the name of 'Jimmu boom' after this mythical figure.

Nor was this an isolated instance. Again connected with ancient Japanese mythology, there was the 'Iwato boom' of 1958-61 and the 'Izanagi boom' of 1966-70, closely connected with the national myth of origin. In what other countries does one find such contemporary and down-to-earth events as economic booms referred to by such ancient, mythological names?

In the 1930s and 1940s, as just alluded to, it was dangerous to question the existence of Emperor Jimmu and the other mythical Emperors. A prominent scholar of Tokyo University, Professor Minobe, lost his job for proposing the theory that the Emperor was 'an organ of the state' and may have been lucky not to lose anything more. According to the ideology of State Shinto, the official state version of Japan's indigenous religion, the Emperor was a *kami*, or god, though not to be confused with the one God of Christianity or Islam. State Shinto was officially abolished in 1945 and there is supposed to be the separation of religion and state but, because of State Shinto's close connection with the totalitarian period, many Japanese are nervous of any sign of government backsliding, particularly in relation to ceremonies at Yasukuni Shrine in Tokyo, where the war dead, including those executed as war criminals, are enshrined. On the other hand, many Japanese, and naturally the supporters of what it is convenient to call the Establishment view, are extremely proud of the antiquity of the Imperial line, whether entirely historical or not.

Since ideas of 'uniqueness' are so important in the official ideology, the *Nihonjinron* and Japanese self-images at large, it is not surprising that modern research techniques of archaeological excavation and carbon dating are not encouraged, although some Japanese scholars are in favour. Since 1995 some Japanese and foreign researchers have been using DNA to study present-day Japanese and their remote ancestors, which could throw light on who the Japanese are, and in 1980 a sixth-century tomb which was somehow outside the control of the Imperial Household Agency, the ultra-traditional bureaucracy in charge of Imperial affairs, revealed evidence of contacts with Korea and China. The Agency, however, will not authorize other tomb excavations.[10]

Ironically, it was Japanese anthropologists themselves who believed some years ago that the first Emperor had been a Korean conqueror: ironic because of the contentious relations between the two countries over the centuries and the mutual images that they have of one another, not to mention the weight put on the Japanese theory of the origin of the Imperial line. Though the theory was not supported by adequate evidence, DNA research suggests that Korean immigrants between 400 BC and 250 AD greatly contributed to the modern Japanese gene pool. About the Korean connection in terms of Buddhism and pottery, for instance, there is no doubt.

The origins of the Japanese population may still be unclear but it is generally considered that there have been the northern streams from China and Korea and perhaps southern streams from the Pacific area. Some see the traditional Japanese wooden house with its mat floors as southern, while Professor Reischauer sees the Japanese myths of origin as similar to those in Polynesia and, in his view, 'naïvely crude by modern standards'[11] The original inhabitants of Japan's northern island of Hokkaido, now greatly reduced in number, were of Caucasian origin and similar to the inhabitants of Siberia. But an important item in the modern official myth is that 'Japan has a homogeneous population'.

To determine at the present time how far people believe in the national myth of origin would be very difficult and the 'Emperor system', *Tenno seido*, is generally a taboo subject. A parallel might be made with European countries where few people are formally religious and do not go to church but still have a belief in God at a subliminal level. Thus, in the Japanese case, where there is not the same tradition of intellectual inquiry, the lack of a formal belief in the myth of how Japan was created would not stop people from believing that Japan was somehow special and 'different' from others and destined to remain so, or that the Emperor should not be put on the more workaday level of European constitutional monarchs. It is often said outside Japan that it is mostly older people who think like this – a version of the 'becoming more like us' wishfulness – but with the resurgent self-confidence accompanying Japan's status as a major economic power, it is by no means necessarily the case. Younger people who follow a revived nationalism are little different.

Politically, the first Japanese that are known about were organized into clans, of which the Yamato clan, the presumed forbears of the present Imperial house, became the most powerful in the year 0-400 AD, although there are no reliable written accounts. The first written accounts of Japan were compiled by Chinese writers around 300 AD.[12] The name 'Yamato' is still popular among firms and in place names, while in yet another reference to the distant past the expression '*Yamato damashii*', meaning 'the spirit of Japan' in the sense of strength of purpose, strong willpower, backbone etc. has strong nationalist reverberations as qualities specific to Japan and the Japanese.

The first of several Japanese attacks on Korea was made by Empress Jingo in the fourth century: again paradoxical in view of the prevalence subsequently of male heads of the Imperial house and the fading of the Empresses into the background, continuing up to the present time. The next attacks were made in 1592 and again 1597 by one of the warlords, Hideyoshi, who first succeeded in uniting Japan. Then, after defeating Russia in 1905 and extending its influence over its neighbouring territory, Japan made Korea its colony in 1910, later forcing the Korean population to adopt Japanese names and to speak Japanese.

Yet, in 1995, the former Japanese Foreign Minister and prominent LDP politician Michio Watanabe stated that Korea had 'harmoniously' agreed to Japanese occupation and had not been under the threat of force in signing away its independence by the treaty of 1910; although the takeover had involved the murder of the Korean queen.

Proving once again that the past is far from dead, his remarks caused uproar in Seoul, where students petrol-bombed a Japanese cultural centre. A Japanese Foreign Ministry spokesman requested the Korean government to prevent such 'regrettable' attacks in future but did not comment on the remarks that had caused them.[13] The *Korea*

*Herald* criticized, 'A growing number of Japanese who are becoming once again belligerent, patronizing and self-righteous, just as they were in the war years':[14] the sort of remark that most of the European or American press would be too inhibited to make, even if it expressed what they really felt. Like others both before and after him, Watanabe was forced to withdraw what he had said and to apologize but by then the harm had been done.

Despite, or perhaps because of, the repeated claims of Japanese 'uniqueness', the records of the past show the strong Chinese and Korean influence on Japan. The Chinese origin of the ideograms or written characters is as obvious as is the architecture of the Buddhist temples, even if the Japanese have modified some of the characters and introduced their own auxiliary syllabic writing. There was a population of 100,000 Chinese and Koreans in Japan in the sixth century, including scribes at court, Buddhist teachers and potters; the art of calligraphy being a characteristic Chinese import. Japan formerly paid tribute to China – the 'Middle Kingdom' – and was looked upon, if not down upon, as an outlying Chinese vassal. The Chinese authorities sometimes remind the Japanese government of this, and of more recent events of course, during political negotiations at the present day.

Indeed, the ultra-nationalistic Japanese Foreign Minister of the 1930s and 1940s, Matsuoka, acknowledged this relationship when he compared China to an elder brother that had become corrupted and had to be given a sharp shock by its younger brother, Japan, to bring it to its senses. Today, many Japanese tacitly accept that Japan should not have attacked China, while not feeling the same scruples about other Asian countries, or for that matter the USA.

At the same time there were important political differences between China and Japan in the matter of the Emperor. The Chinese Emperor could lose 'the mandate of heaven' if he was not a capable ruler, in other words his legitimacy, but in Japan the Emperor always had 'the lasting virtues of divine descent', which is an ideology that has persisted into the modern period. In the Second World War, for instance, soldiers were taught that an order that in reality came from a superior was an order from the Emperor.

Indeed, a dualistic view of the Emperor had already emerged as early as the sixth century. The Emperor was still considered divine but he was by no means necessarily the most powerful figure. The real rulers were the clan leaders of, for example, the Fujiwara clan in the eighth century – a name still remembered today – or the Minamoto clan in the twelfth. Japan was unified by the warlords and the Shoguns, the 'great generals', ruled from 1600 up to 1868, although they had to defer in a purely formal sense to their ritual superior, the Emperor. It was an example of *tatemae*, the triumph of form over substance, since everyone knew that the Shogun held the real power, having originally gained it in war.

Thus, when Commodore Perry in 1853 wanted to present a letter from the President of the US to the person presumed to be in charge, the Emperor, he was in fact delivering it to the wrong address. At least Perry knew that he should be firm and called himself 'Admiral' as a way of insisting on dealing with senior officials but the Shogun's officials tricked him all the same with empty ceremonial shows and, as continues to happen right up to the present, the implementation of the agreements that he and the first American envoy to Japan, Townsend Harris, thought they had made required hard bargaining all over again. It was again the old Japanese joke that it is only after the agreement has been signed that the real bargaining begins, while many foreign businessmen continue to experience difficulty in finding out just who it is that they are negotiating with and what, if anything, their interlocutors are authorized to agree.

The contrast between the numinous or symbolic power of the Emperors' 'virtues of divine descent' over the centuries and their political weakness can be compared with those kings and queens of, for instance, England and France who were politically strong rulers until the Civil War in England in the seventeenth century challenged the notion of the Divine Right of Kings and the French Revolution overthrew the monarchy altogether. The Emperors of the time were not powerful rulers like Queen Elizabeth I or Louis Quatorze, the Sun King. When the new capital at Kyoto, whose layout was copied from that of the Chinese Emperors' capital at Peking, was inaugurated in 794 AD it was the lords, comparable to European barons, not the Emperor, to whom taxes were paid. The first Shogun, or military ruler, from the Minamoto clan took power as early as 1192, underlining the political weakness of the Emperor, who remained a ritual figure, within the confines of the court. But it was this numinous or divine character of the Emperor that was to become a powerful instrument in the hands of the real rulers of Japan, from the oligarchy that made up the new regime in 1868 and the militarists from the 1930s at least until 1945.

It is an example of how the past finds strong resonances in the present: not just as an archaic survival but as a political and emotional underpinning of Japan's social and political order.

It applies in the same way to one of the key values of Japanese society: 'harmony', *wa*, as promoted by Prince Shotoku, whose portrait is found on post-Second World War banknotes, although it was his famous Confucian constitution of 604 AD that promoted the value of 'harmony'. This meant something to the effect that if all members of society fulfilled their roles correctly and did not disturb the social order there would be nothing that could not be achieved.

Indeed, the company principles of many Japanese firms, to be treated with reverence whether *tatemae* or not, reflect the values proclaimed by Prince Shotoku; such as harmony, virtue, diligence and public service. In the aftermath of the Second World War, the company song of one of the largest corporations, Matsushita Electric, proclaimed not only the 'building (of) a new Japan' but 'harmony and sincerity'; though 'sincerity' here did not mean what it would mean in English-speaking countries but something like 'doing things in the accepted Japanese way'.

The *kamikaze*, or suicide, pilots of the Second World War and the emotional associations surrounding the ancient name 'Yamato' have already been referred to and it goes without saying that this was a period in which the myths of the past were pressed into service to the maximum extent. *'Yamato damashii'* Japanese spirit, for instance, was proclaimed as superior to Western materialism and therefore as the means to victory. The 'Yamato' was also one of the largest battleships.

Whatever the feelings of the *kamikaze* pilots may have been, it is not surprising that they are commemorated in the war museum within the precincts of the Yasukuni Shrine in Tokyo, though there are no translations of the Japanese labels that accompany the exhibits. The past connected with the special quality of the Emperor and therefore the special loyalty owed to him is present in the form of the Imperial Rescript for Soldiers and Sailors, which contained the well known phrase that, 'Duty is weightier than a mountain, while death is lighter than a feather.' It was written in 1882, though not of course by the Emperor and was a prominent part of the military ethos during the Second World War.[15]

At another level, it fitted in with a popular belief that to die for something was the sign of ultimate commitment that no one could question. When this something was a war that was clearly being waged against overwhelming odds, whatever the official propaganda machine might be saying, it had the added poignancy of what is known in Japan as 'heroic failure', in the quasi-religious context of the State Shinto cult of the Emperor.

State Shinto was officially abolished in 1945 but deep, emotional beliefs and attitudes cannot be legislated so quickly out of existence. They are found among the 'Rightist' groups, whose noisy convoys with loudspeaker vans frequent areas around the Imperial Palace and Shibuya in Tokyo, and among the more reactionary supporters of the LDP.

An event that anyone who was in Japan at the time will remember sent a shock through the population was when the well known writer Yukio Mishima committed ritual suicide after his appeal to soldiers at the Eastern Regional Headquarters in Tokyo to rise up and restore the Emperor and to rewrite the post-war Constitution fell on deaf ears. That was in 1970.

Although Mishima and his 'private army' had trained with soldiers and had been allowed to use military facilities, which some might find odd, he had misjudged the situation. The present-day forces do not have a good image and it is rare to see a uniform. In 1992 a soldier in an infantry regiment told a reporter that sixty per cent, including himself, of his comrades had 'a negative attitude' and that he had only joined because he had failed to get into the police but had heard that military service would improve his chances next time. An official spokesman admitted that forty per cent of new recruits left the service after two years – and collecting a bonus at that time of ¥600,000. Another forty per cent left after four years – and collecting a bonus of ¥1.2 million. They evidently had quite pragmatic ideas about joining up even if, like other armies, the force had its share of those who were more nationalistically inclined. The soldier interviewed particularly mentioned that they did not like civilians to discover what they were when they went out, which says something about civilian attitudes.[16]

Mishima's death may have shown the ultimate commitment although even LDP politicians like the then prime minister, Eisaku Sato,[17] thought it was the act of a madman, but this commitment tends to overshadow the object that it was being committed to. One of the worst examples involved a group at the other end of the political spectrum, the so-called Red Army, a group that had hijacked a domestic flight and forced it to fly to North Korea in 1970 and carried out the massacre at Lod airport, Israel, in 1972. The same year they 'purified' their movement by torturing eleven of their number to death and killed a policeman.

After a siege by police, they gave up without a fight, but it was the press comment that was significant. The *Mainichi* newspaper, which did not support whatever it was that the Red Army was supposed to be fighting for, passed over the fact that the five who had surrendered had murdered eleven of their comrades and a policeman. Instead it expressed its disillusion at the conspirators' 'pampered spirit' and that they had shown they were not to be taken seriously by failing to die for their cause.

In other words, the newspaper editorial was not interested in what the cause was or whether it was worth dying for, not to mention killing others, but only in the gang's own 'commitment'.[18] They did not have 'the spirit of Japan': in this case a dangerous mixture of frustration and extremism. But just how genuine was Mishima's commitment? At his army medical examination during the Second World War he exhibited the symptoms of tuberculosis – a pronounced cough – falsely claiming that he coughed blood. Thus he avoided serving the Emperor.

Since the 1960s the expression '*kamikaze* taxi' became a popular way of referring to wild young drivers who worked for taxi companies and drove cars that did not belong to them. A popular song, to the tune of the real *kamikaze* song, was performed on television.

Obviously, Japan has a long, and proud history, but the impression fostered by some official speakers that it has been a united, homogeneous nation since time immemorial or the mythical period of the earliest chronicles is misleading. Japan as a nation state in the modern sense has only existed since 1868 and for over two hundred years, from 1339 to 1573, it was the scene of constant civil wars, the so-called *Sengoku Jidai*; comparable perhaps to the struggles for supremacy between the barons in Europe.

Into this chaotic situation of constant warfare, the first Europeans arrived by accident: the Portuguese, who had been blown off course while sailing to their trading post at Macau on the Chinese coast in 1542. They brought two important things with them: one, a technology, that the Japanese soon learned to make their own; and another, a belief, which was in the end rejected. It was a situation to be paralleled much later in the nineteenth century when the new regime of 1868 embarked on full-scale industrialization. The technology was that of the musket, which the Japanese were quick to adopt in the armies of the feudal lords: the belief was that of Catholicism, which proved to be politically controversial.

Francis Xavier, the famous Jesuit missionary, arrived in 1549 and at least, initially, had more success than his fellows in present-day Japan but his success was compromised by the arrival of Spanish Franciscans and Dominicans from the Philippines. The Jesuit strategy had been to target the feudal lords, in the knowledge that their followers would have to follow if their lord was converted to Christianity, while the Spanish Franciscans spread their message among the downtrodden peasantry: a potentially subversive policy. Matters were made worse when a Spanish ship's captain boasted of the Spanish king's power and the role of the missionaries in extending it.

This boast infuriated one of the most powerful warlords, Hideyoshi, who became paranoid about foreign conspiracies and the potentially politically subversive threat of foreign ideas, in this case Christianity: something that it would not be far-fetched to compare with the atmosphere in Japan in the 1930s and the campaign to root out 'dangerous thoughts', *kiken shiso*. While balancing the advantages of trading with the Portuguese and Spaniards, he later ordered the expulsion of the missionaries and confiscated their land at Nagasaki, but the order was not strictly adhered to for another ten years. Then six Spanish Franciscans, three Portuguese Jesuits and seventeen Japanese converts were crucified at Nagasaki in 1597: the site of the atomic bomb in 1945.

How far being a Christian is compatible with being a member or of being considered a normal member of Japanese society is still an interesting question. According to the well known social anthropologist Chie Nakane, obedience in Japan means 'total submission', while the saying that 'no man can serve two masters' is one that is 'wholeheartedly subscribed to'.[19]

Finally, at a time contemporaneous with that of Elizabeth I of

England, Japan was politically united for the first time under the three warlords Nobunaga, Hideyoshi and Tokugawa between 1578 and 1590; although that was not the end of the scheming and fighting. Even today television series and books on the times and strategies of these warlords are popular, not least with business leaders, who see the parallels with their own campaigns and for whom the code of loyalty to superiors on the part of their own subordinates has obvious attractions. There may not be as many samurai dramas, *chambara*, on television now as there were in the 1960s but the social order and behaviour that they present continue to have a strong appeal, rather as if viewers had a longing for pre-industrial Japanese life, in its idealized form.

The figure who is most admired and quoted today, the great warlord who not only won the decisive battle in 1600 but who succeeded in gaining the ultimate power for himself and his descendants right up to 1868, was Ieyasu Tokugawa, who persuaded the Emperor to give him the title of Shogun. This will be familiar to those who have watched the television series 'Shogun' or read the book.

Tokugawa policy was to entrench its power by rigid social control, backed up by the force that its victory in war had given it, which also kept the peace. Leaving the Emperor behind in his palace in Kyoto, the Shogun demonstrated his power by building his large castle at Edo, present-day Tokyo, which is now the Emperor's main residence. That the Shogun's centralized system of social and political control was able to last for over two-and-a-half centuries gives an idea of how carefully it had been thought out and how thoroughly it was put into practice. Even forty years after the end of the Tokugawa regime, Lafcadio Hearn could write that the regulations had existed in 'ferocious detail'.

Control over the lords was enforced by the hostage system, which compelled them to leave wives and children at the Shogun's capital, Edo, and by the 'attendance in turn' system, *sankin kotai*, by which half the lords at any one time had to be in attendance at the Shogun's court. These proved to be effective measures in preventing rebellion. The lords' ceremonial duties, the extent and quality of their retinues as they travelled up to Edo from their domains were prescribed in detail. The *tatemae*, or pretence, was that both the hostage system and the attendance system were entirely voluntary; but what better way of keeping an eye on the lords and tying them down with onerous duties?

The old Tokaido road between Kyoto and Edo, made famous in Hiroshige's woodblock prints, for instance, of the '53 stations', was equipped with barriers where the Shogun's agents or spies checked up on travellers. They watched for women leaving Edo or guns going into the city: signs that a plot might be afoot. A system of censorship kept watch on books and pictures, with special emphasis on new ideas or anything out of the ordinary.[20]

This system of repression and regulation reached down from the Shogun to the lords and from the lords to the common people. On the pretence that metal was needed for a great Buddha hall in Kyoto, Hideyoshi had instituted a 'sword hunt', which had disarmed the peasantry, leaving them at the mercy of the samurai. The latter were the only class allowed to carry arms and they had the right to 'cut down and leave', *kirisute,* any commoner whom they considered showed them insufficient respect. It encouraged people to be polite; at least on the surface.

Regulations, in 'ferocious detail' as Hearn noted, applied to all aspects of life, such as what degree of wedding ceremonies and even children's toys were allowed. For example, if a farmer offered the guests at a funeral saké, he was not allowed to serve it in saké cups but only in soup cups. At the Boys' Festival, a male child could only receive one paper flag and two toy spears from the whole family including grandparents.

In an attempt to buttress the Shogun's power still further by preventing the population from moving up in society and threatening those above, the Tokugawa regime divided it into four hereditary classes, plus outcastes. Beneath the Shogun, the hierarchy was headed by the samurai, the only class allowed to bear arms, though to draw a sword in the grounds of the Shogun's castle was a capital crime. As the Tokugawa peace was established, the samurai gradually became administrators of the lords', *daimyo,* estates rather than warriors but the place they still occupy today in terms of popular appeal in television series, films and of course the Kabuki plays is remarkable.

Next, but far below the samurai, came the farmers who, in almost Marxist style were seen as the producers: rice being a major measure of wealth. Most were miserably poor and when they from time to time revolted, in spite of all the regime's preventive measures, they were suppressed with great savagery. Third were the craftsmen, who produced the high grade steel swords for the samurai and the objects nowadays sought by collectors, such as lacquerware, pottery and small carvings, *netsuke.* Though preceding the industrial age, their work showed great concern with detail and attained high technical standards. Production of objects such as paper lanterns and paper fans of the traditional type still continues.

Last among the four classes were the merchants who, again rather in Marxist fashion, were regarded as unproductive parasites and as a possible threat to the social or political order, since money brings power and merchants who could become richer than samurai could undermine the hierarchy. Underneath the four official classes listed in most accounts were the outcastes, who were relegated to what were considered unclean jobs, such as tanning leather, handling dead bodies, disposing of night soil etc. Today, they do not officially exist but they still run butcher's shops and shoe shops and live in particular districts, *buraku*, especially in Western Japan. They continue to be discriminated against in marriage and employment and remain a taboo subject.

Under the Tokugawa regime, marriage between the classes was strictly forbidden but even the Shogun could not entirely legislate for human nature, which led to hopeless matches ending in double suicides: a sentimental theme in Kabuki plays and part of the nexus of ideas about suicide being the way out of an insoluble problem, for example, the theme of 'love versus duty', which still finds an emotional resonance today. The idea was to prevent social mobility or the blurring of class distinctions that could upset the hierarchy and to tie people to their superiors, particularly their lord, and to control them by organizing them by groups.

An effective method of doing this was by the 'five-man group', *gonin gumi*, system, a collective system under which the whole group would be punished for the offence of one of its members. Not surprisingly, this encouraged the formation of group consciousness, which continues to be a conspicuous feature of Japanese social organization today. Collective punishments were used in the Japanese forces at the time of the Second World War.

In addition to the strict hierarchy of the Tokugawa regime – which lasted right up to 1868! – and its methods of censorship, regulation and repression, which seem comparable to those of modern totalitarian states, there was one other key factor that many see as still having an influence today. This was the decision in 1637, with the earlier experience of the disruptive influence of the foreigners and their un-Japanese ideas in mind, to turn Japan into a 'closed country' and to seal it off from these unwanted and politically subversive intrusions.

This policy also continued up to 1868, though it ended in defeat for the Shogun. Its results are reflected today in what Professor Reischauer described as the 'isolated' and 'inward-looking' nature of the country and by what is expressed in the Japanese term *shimaguni konjo*, or 'island country complex'. Thus for over two-and-a-half centuries Japan was both a state that was very strictly regulated internally and virtually cut off from the rest of the world and the changes taking place there externally; and this up to the modern industrial age.

The Tokugawa Period is often loosely referred to as 'feudal' but one of the regime's most significant characteristics was its highly centralized system of government, more like a modern totalitarian state than the feudalism that existed in Europe. Today the word 'feudalistic' is commonly used in Japan to criticize anything the speaker does not like because he thinks it is old-fashioned or reactionary: not in any precise sense.

As Chie Nakane and many others have pointed out, ranking and hierarchy remain of great concern in Japanese society[21] and are extended internationally to who has, for example, the Number One, Number Two etc. airline, motor manufacturer and so on. The stamp left by the long period of authoritarian Tokugawa rule to have a place for everyone and everyone in their place prompted Professor Reischauer to comment that, 'The rigidity and formalism of Tokugawa ethics may be responsible for a tendency to sacrifice moral principles and true courtesy to a punctilious observance of form and etiquette. The burdensome sense of obligation in the Tokugawa code of ethics and its strict limitations on the freedom of the individual also seem to have produced a certain tenseness of personality among the Japanese.'[22] But Tokugawa ethics were essentially social or political with, like today, a system of concrete social sanctions for any transgression, rather than ethics in a transcendental sense outside social relations, such as a belief that certain actions are morally good or bad in themselves.

Ieyasu Tokugawa was already fifty-seven when he came to power and the regime which he established represented a long-term strategy to keep himself and his descendants in power. Even today his patience and foresight are celebrated in the popular story of a caged bird that its captors wanted to sing. Other warlords wanted to force the bird to sing, or even to kill it if it refused, but Ieyasu's policy was to 'wait until it sings'.

He showed his patience, and guile as a political strategist, in dealing with the most serious threat to his power: the son of the warlord Hideyoshi, with whom he had originally united the country. After fourteen years consolidating his power, he used a transparent pretext – the inscription on a bell in a monastery! – to force his opponent to fight. The enemy forces consisted mainly of lords who had been dispossessed and masterless samurai, *ronin*, but no other important lords dared join them.

Failing to take Osaka castle, Ieyasu persuaded his opponent to agree to a compromise peace, by which Ieyasu's forces were permitted to fill in the outer moat and dismantle the outer battlements. The following summer Ieyasu broke the agreement, attacked the castle now minus its outer defences and was victorious in a few days. His victory, due to his patience in building up his strength, concentrating his forces and concealing his real intentions, was very much in line with the teachings of Sun Tzu's much earlier *Art of War*[23] – still studied by those in business and politics today – which might be compared with some aspects of Machiavelli's *Prince*.

Only five years after winning the battle that brought him to power, Ieyasu technically resigned as Shogun but that was again *tatemae* and he remained the real power in the land until his death. In the meantime, he had appointed not his first son as successor but his third son, whom he judged to have the necessary steadiness of character – and who had to carry out all the formal duties at the Shogun's castle in

Edo. In modern Japan, companies that have been established by strong entrepreneurial leaders, such as Konosuke Matsushita of Matsushita Electric, have also had an indelible stamp left on them by the founder, no matter what formal title he may eventually hold. This is quite natural and easily understood, even if it does not square with the formal organization charts favoured by some management theorists.

Like Hideyoshi before him, Ieyasu was not against trade with the Europeans but, like him again, he was on his guard against the potentially subversive influences they might bring: a policy echoed by Japan's nineteenth century modernizers and again after the Second World War. To paraphrase George Orwell, 'foreign trade good (up to a point): foreign ideas bad'.

Then it seemed that trade and the risk of subversion could be separated. Will Adams, the English pilot of a Dutch ship stranded in Japan, and not interested in missionary work, made himself so useful to the Shogun as an adviser on trade and shipbuilding that he was not allowed to leave. Later, Dutch and English ships came to Japan for purely business purposes.

But a number of factors eventually convinced Ieyasu that Christianity was a threat to the system of social control that he had so carefully built up and he banned it in 1612. Any of his retainers who had been converted were made to give up Christianity on pain of death, churches were closed and an attempt made to expel all missionaries, though some managed to smuggle themselves in on trading ships. There was a fear that Spain, using Christians as a fifth column, might invade, which led to a general persecution. A revolt in South-Western Japan turned into a Christian rebellion but after it had been crushed, Christianity ceased to exist except in a few remote areas.

With amazing persistence, these groups carried on until they could come out into the open in the nineteenth century when, by an irony of history, they felt that they were the true believers rather than the Catholic Church of the day. In the post-war world after 1945, Christianity has a lower proportion of followers in relation to the size of the population than it did in the first heyday of Francis Xavier, though it has included some important personalities.

Prior to the 'closed country' policy, Chinese traders had been coming to Japan and Japanese traders had been sailing to Chinese and South-East Asian ports but now the policy meant that Japanese were entirely forbidden to leave the country on pain of death while foreigners, with two exceptions, were not allowed to enter Japan. Chinese merchants were restricted to Nagasaki, while the Dutch were kept at further arm's length on Deshima, a small artificial island in Nagasaki harbour.

Each year their senior representative also had to attend the

Shogun's court and right up to the end of the Tokogawa regime they had to wear the same seventeenth-century clothes. They were not allowed out of Deshima and contact with them was kept to a bare minimum. The model of Deshima in one of Amsterdam's museums gives an idea of their isolation. In the 1990s the Dutch made a huge investment in 'Oranda Mura', Holland Village, at Nagasaki, complete with replicas of bridges, canals, hotels and of course windmills, to promote trade and other relations. Other smaller ventures have been 'Canada Village', 'Shakespeare Village' etc., which have a similar appeal.

There has been some argument about just how closed Japan was during its two-and-a-half centuries of enforced isolation and about its level of technological development. Obviously, it missed the full force of the Industrial Revolution but the technologies of steel making for swords, bronze casting for large Buddhist images and the construction of earthquake proof temple pagodas were advanced, as were the techniques employed by the craftsmen. Through the Dutch, some modern learning, in for example medicine, did enter Japan, where it was known as *Rangaku*, or 'Dutch learning'. Education in reading, writing, arithmetic, abacus and calligraphy was provided by some 140,000 'temple schools' *terakoya*. Poor people paid in kind, such as farm produce, while the merchants were keen to have their children taught. These skills were useful advantages when the new regime of 1868 embarked on full-scale industrialization.

Even with all their repressive measures, the Tokugawa could not succeed in keeping the merchants in their place and firms that are well known today, like Mitsui and Sumitomo, were founded during their rule. The Kabuki theatre was one of the pleasures enjoyed by the merchants, who created a vibrant life of their own very different from the duty-bound and formal life of the samurai.

By missing the Industrial Revolution and closing the country off, the Tokugawa regime in the end exposed Japan and themselves to precisely the commercial and political pressures from outside that it had been their express purpose to avoid. Psychologically, Japan was a country turned in on itself, which as a result of the Tokuagawa policies was hardly surprising, and scarcely in a position to avoid the difficulties in coming to terms with the outside world and its inhabitants, with all that that implies. It was indeed in the world but not of it. Ieyasu's only overseas venture had been his conquest of the Kingdom of the Ryukus, the present-day Okinawa, in 1609, whose inhabitants and way of speaking are still not regarded as quite Japanese.

For it was not only the Industrial Revolution that Japan under the Tokugawa had missed. It had also remained apart from the intellectual traditions of independent thought and inquiry and the developments in political philosophy of the countries that after 1868 it sought to compete with on equal terms: developments that had taken several hundred years to come about. Did its experience of Tokugawa authoritarianism provide a suitable basis for some form of democratic order? – always assuming of course that this was what any of its subsequent rulers wanted.

Weighing up the legacy of the Tokugawa Period, Lafcadio Hearn thought at the beginning of the twentieth century that, 'Those who write today about the extraordinary capacity of the Japanese for organization, and the "democratic spirit" of the people as natural proof of their fitness for representative government in the Western sense, mistake appearances for realities. The truth is that the extraordinary capacity of the Japanese for communal organization, is the strongest possible evidence of their unfitness for any modern democratic form of government.' Hearn went on to assert that the difference between the two forms of government was, 'Fundamental, prodigious – measurable only by thousands of years', and that the Japanese form was 'the most despotic form of Communism.[24] It bears repeating that Hearn's writing, like Reischauer's, is highly sympathetic towards Japan: too much so in the view of some. Others may object that Hearn was writing at the beginning of the twentieth century and that of course 'it has all changed now' but the collectivist and groupish character of how society in Japan is organized, which many Japanese lecturers are keen to show as a positive advantage compared to the 'individualistic' and less cohesively motivated 'West', is still one of the most striking features and well after the Second World War people are still writing books with titles like *Where Communism Works*.

Though incarcerated on Deshima Island off Nagasaki, about as far from the capital as it was possible to keep them, the Dutch had tried to warn the Shogun's government of the risks of the exclusion policy but little was done. Consequently when the American 'Black Ships' of Perry's squadron, which were to become a deeply etched folk memory that could be recalled when necessary, sailed into Tokyo Bay in 1853 the Shogun badly lost face by being seen to be unable to oppose them and the demands of the foreign powers for port facilities and trade. Apart from the usual tactics of obfuscation and delay, one of the few advantages the Shogun had was a Japanese castaway who had picked up English and could provide a better grasp of Perry's intentions than he suspected. In a far-sighted report home, Perry stated that the skills he saw among the Japanese could well lead to the creation of the type of state that would one day have to be taken seriously.

The first Japan-US Treaty was signed in 1854, followed by others and the arrival of the first foreign merchants in Japan three years later. These strange and threatening people and the powers behind them were not liked and the slogan for domestic consumption was 'expel the barbarians', though the reality was that the Shogun was incapable of doing so.

The so-called 'unequal treaties', still sometimes referred to as another example of foreign high-handedness imposed on a weak Japan, that were signed in 1858 provided for the trial of foreigners in their own courts. In our politically correct and 'anti-imperialist' etc. age, they may seem like blatant discrimination but the traditional system of justice in Japan at the time, and for that matter China, has to be taken into account. The idea was that justice was only complete when the accused had confessed and, that if he or she was unwilling to do so, then they had to be tortured until they did. As late as 1880, Emile Boissonade, a French legal expert who had drafted Japan's first post-Tokugawa legal code, had to protest against the torture of suspects in the same compound where he had been given an office.[25] Even today, confession is regarded as 'the king of evidence', however obtained.

Seeing the Shogun's weakness, powerful clans in Western Japan saw their chance to advance themselves by urging anti-foreign action and by involving sympathizers at the Emperor's court. The Emperor himself was persuaded to order the Shogun to expel the foreigners in 1862: a way of claiming the Emperor's authority for their own aims that was to become conspicuous right up to 1945. Merchant ships were fired on, a number of foreigners were murdered and European and American warships bombarded shore gun emplacements and towns, such as Kagoshima in western Japan. Nevertheless, the foreign envoys were given verbal assurances that nothing had changed, though the people plotting against the Shogun could see that it was the foreign warships and not the Shogun that were enforcing the treaties he had been forced to make.

The Shogun of the time was not a personality with the strength and political skills of an Ieyasu Tokugawa and the clans plotted and manoeuvred for power, arming themselves with modern weapons as they did so. Civil war broke out in 1868 under the rousing slogan 'Revere the Emperor, expel the barbarians!' and the new groupings around the legitimacy of the Emperor were victorious though they knew perfectly well that they could not literally expel the 'barbarians', whose technology and skill they needed in order to build up Japan into a country that could compete on the same basis. They knew that even if the whole of China was too vast to have been physically colonized it was largely under the economic and political domination of the Western powers and they were determined that the same thing would not happen to them. This did not stop them from joining the international military force that crushed the Boxer Rebellion in China in 1900 and from penetrating China economically.

As already noted, the new era when Japan was to modernize and industrialize was given the name of the Meiji Period, after the name of the Emperor. Some people continue to think that modernization automatically means the same as 'Westernization' but whether this is a fact should become clearer by the end of this book. What is significant is that what is referred to as the Meiji 'Restoration' in English is called *Meiji Isshin*, literally 'Meiji Revolution', in Japanese; but this is misleading because it was neither a 'bottom up' middle class revolution like the French nor a popular revolution like the American. It was, on the contrary, a 'top down' imposition of rule by a new oligarchy, using the Emperor to legitimize and proclaim its policies and as a new focus of national consciousness in an era of aggressively competing imperial rivalries.

In a word, Japan went from one form of authoritarian rule to another. Loyalty under the Tokugawa had always meant the active fulfilment of the superior's wishes, not just a passive state of mind, and the oligarchs made the restored Emperor the powerful symbol of the national effort that had to be mobilized in order, as one of the oligarchs put it, to enable Japan to 'take her stand as the equal of all the other countries'.[26]

The oligarchs themselves were powerful autocratic figures like Hirobumi Ito, or Marquess Ito as he was now termed in the European style, who had studied in England, although significantly he had joined in an attack on the British Legation as a young man. Later, he became Governor-General of Korea, where he was assassinated by a Korean patriot. After the Second World War, his portrait appeared on the ¥500 banknote.

The oligarchs knew that Japan urgently needed to 'catch up' if it was to avoid China's fate and this meant using the foreigners for the industrial, commercial and military skills they could transfer but this did not mean that they should be made more welcome than absolutely necessary. The Japanese ideal is the bamboo, which bends with the storm and then snaps back upright once it has passed.

The oligarchs issued their orders in the form of Imperial commands or Rescripts and of slogans which the population could easily understand. In liberal democracies, slogans are normally associated with advertising and might seem comic in politics, but elsewhere such commands from the rulers to the ruled are part of the natural order. The best known slogans of Meiji Japan were:-

- Japanese spirit, Western technology
- Rich country, strong army
- Develop industry, promote enterprise

The first of these clearly indicated that although Western technology was welcome, it was 'Japanese spirit' and not, for instance, Western ideas, such as parliamentary democracy, that was required. The new regime underlined the point in the words of the Emperor's Restoration Rescript, which asserted, 'A return . . . to the government used at the time of Emperor Jimmu, the founder of Japan and the first Emperor of the Japanese people.' [27] There could be no clearer statement that this was a 'return' and not a revolution in the normal sense of the word. As was to happen again in the period up to 1945, the mythological past was being pressed into service to provide emotional support or legitimacy for the actions of the current rulers.

'Catching up' by the transfer of Western technology and the national purpose for which it was to be achieved were made plain right from the beginning of the new regime in its first year: 1868, the year of the Charter Oath. With the Emperor behind it, it commanded that, 'Knowledge shall be sought throughout the world so as to strengthen the foundations of Imperial rule.' It referred to an economic policy for national ends: not to one based on following Adam Smith. Something of the official view of the period can be gained from the contents of the Meiji Memorial Picture Gallery in Tokyo.[28]

The knowledge to be transferred to Japan mainly concerned technical matters, such as the navy, the railways, medicine etc. but in one important instance it concerned matters of high state policy. Though not prominent today, Social Darwinism, meaning the 'survival of the fittest' and 'the struggle for existence', was a current philosophical trend and one of its leading exponents was the English thinker Herbert Spencer, who still seems to have a following in Japan. Spencer advised the oligarchs that their policy should be one of keeping Americans and Europeans at arm's length as much as possible. 'In the presence of the more powerful races your position is one of chronic danger, and you should take every precaution to give as little foothold as possible to the foreigners'.[29] This advice to the Japanese Prime Minister was repeated again later in the letter. If Spencer were able to look back now, he should be gratified to see how well successive Japanese regimes have taken his advice to heart.

Initially, there had been some discussion over whether to introduce a British-style or a Prussian-style Constitution but admiration for Bismarck and what his policies had achieved first in Prussia and then in the new German Empire of 1871 inclined the oligarchs to follow his example. A later comment was that, 'Liberalism . . . was a movement with no roots in the Japanese tradition . . . Japan's first political parties . . . were more a reflection of the divisions within the élite than meaningful parties.'[30] Lafcadio Hearn wrote that the struggles of the early elections and parliamentary sessions were, 'Between clan interests, or party interests; and the devoted followers . . . understood the new politics only as . . . a war of loyalty to be fought for the leader's sake, a war not to be interfered with by any abstract notions of right or justice.'[31] His remarks may be compared with the factional nature of Japanese politics today and the all-important patron-client relations between the faction leaders and their followers, in which 'money politics' rather than abstract principles play a major part.

So the Meiji Prussian-style Constitution, which was only replaced by the American-inspired post-war Constitution of 1947, was presented as the Emperor's 'gift to the people' on 11 February 1889: a date heavy with overtones as the anniversary of the mythological founding of Japan by Emperor Jimmu in 660 BC, and known during the militarist years as *Kigensetsu*. It was abolished as a public holiday, or as they say in Japan a national holiday, under the Occupation but was reinstated amid severe misgivings about its nationalistic overtones in the 1960s, when the name was changed to *Kenkoku-no-hi*, or National Foundation Day. The date of course remained the same.

Under the Meiji Constitution, the upper House of Peers and the lower House of Representatives were theoretically equal; but the Peers could veto the Representatives. If the Diet i.e. parliament, rejected the budget, the government was automatically entitled to use the one from the preceding year. The Emperor's subjects were allowed freedom of religious belief 'within limits not prejudicial to peace and order and not antagonistic to their duties as subjects' a catch-all piece of wording that would allow the authorities the maximum freedom of interpretation.

In fact the 'gift to the people ' of the Constitution was less generous than the expression implied. The right to vote was restricted to Japanese males aged over twenty-five and paying more than ¥15 in tax, which was a considerable sum before the age of inflation, that meant that only 453,474 people out of a population in the first year of the Constitution, 1889, of 40,072,000 had the vote.[32] The tax qualification was progressively reduced and was finally abolished in 1925, when all Japanese males aged twenty-five and over were entitled to vote. By such means as the restrictions on the right to vote, the power of veto of the House of Peers and the power of the government to use the preceding year's budget in the event that the Diet were to vote against a new one, the oligarchs made sure that the Constitution threatened them as little as possible.

As early as 1900 the government issued an Imperial Ordinance stating that only serving generals and admirals could sit in the cabinet as Ministers of War and the Navy respectively. In the 1930s,when militarism was in the ascendant this was to have serious consequences, as the forces could get their way by refusing to appoint their cabinet members until the civilians accommodated their views. The Imperial Rescript to Soldiers and Sailors of 1881 had already made it clear in any case that the supreme command of the forces was in the Emperor's, or rather the oligarchs', hands and would not be delegated to others; such as an elected civilian authority for example. In the light of this tradition, it is hardly surprising that many in Japan are nervous about civilian control of the military, especially after the army's behaviour in China in the 1930s.

The ideological underpinning of the Meiji Constitution was the notion of the *kokutai*, or 'polity', an unusual word in English that had both a strong mythological and a practical political meaning at the same time. Its significance can be judged from the fact of its appearance in the first sentence of the Meiji Constitution in the form of words stating that Japan 'shall be reigned over and governed by a line of Emperors unbroken for ages eternal': that is the political reality of what is also referred to in the bland translation of *kokutai* as 'the structure of the state'.

This political reality was naturally very important to the Meiji oligarchs and the historian Richard Storry, writing in 1960, thought that it was still the essence of the 'national polity' that 'conservative Japanese' supported.[33] A Japanese historian, mindful of the connection with Shinto myth, called it 'Japan's myth of the twentieth century',[34] and to oppose or cast doubt on it in the 1930s and 1940s was a police matter. The Ministry of Education propagated it throughout schools and colleges and right up to the end of the Second World War in 1945, with destruction and defeat staring them in the face, the preservation of 'the structure of the state', with the Emperor, remained an overriding concern of the regime. In Storry's view, they feared revolution more than defeat.

In fact, the only major revolt that the oligarchs faced was Saigo Takamori's rebellion of dissatisfied former samurai in 1877, though there were again peasant uprisings in the 1880s and some political agitation. As under the Tokugawa before them, these uprisings were ruthlessly suppressed and the first of the series of Public Peace Preservation Laws, bringing the police under greater central control, was brought in in 1887. How sensitive the authorities were about anything that looked as if it might be a threat to the established order, or 'national polity', was shown when the Japan Socialist Party was founded in 1901. It was immediately banned.

Ten years later an 'anarchist plot' was discovered, allegedly aiming to overthrow the 'Emperor system' or 'structure of the state', providing an opportunity for further suppression of the socialists and the execution of those involved. The first section of the Special Higher Police, the *Tokko*, also known as the thought police, was established in the same year, 1911, though they only really came into their own from the 1930s onwards.[35]

In 1937, for instance, the director of the National Police Training School stated that, 'The most urgent need is for police officials to . . . become protectors of the *kokutai*' – the 'structure of the state' etc. Stressing the 'uniqueness' – that word again! – of the Japanese police he strongly implied that they should not be the servants of the public, as they were said to be in some European countries. In the militarist period the *Tokko*, along with the *Kempeitai*, the military police but more the equivalent of the Nazi Gestapo,[36] became one of the most feared instruments of state repression. But although the past does not necessarily determine the present in some mechanical fashion, the creation of an overtly political police was not inconsistent with the totalitarian nature of the social and political control imposed under the Tokugawa and the authoritarian nature of the Meiji oligarchy.

To build up modern military forces, the oligarchs introduced conscription in 1873, consisting of three years service and four years in the reserves: a considerable economic burden for a nation that was industrializing, modernizing and anxious to compete with the existing powers all at once. It was at first resisted by farmers, who wanted their sons' labour and five years later, in spite of the loyalty to the Emperor and the need for obedience that were being emphasized in service manuals, there was a mutiny, leading to the execution of 53 soldiers and the punishment of 218.[37] To stiffen morale, the Imperial Rescript expressed the idea that the soldier who died for the Emperor was like the briefly flowering cherry blossom that fell while it was still perfect and it was this new, largely peasant army that defeated Russia in the face of heavy losses in 1905. Even though it is a myth that no Japanese soldiers surrendered voluntarily in the Second World War, the fresh emphasis on this old code hardly needs mentioning.

Japan's defeat of China in a war over influence in Korea in 1894, as a result of which Japan had received a considerable indemnity and possession of Formosa, or Taiwan, had not gone unnoticed among the powers. Korea had been, in the words of one of the German officers training the Japanese army, 'a dagger pointed at the heart of Japan',[38] while the British government judged that Britain and Japan had a common interest in containing Russian expansion in Asia. Under the Anglo-Japanese Alliance of 1902, Japan equipped itself with British warships and trained its navy with British help, leading to its decisive victory over the Russian fleet in 1905. Thus the oligarchs realized the second half of their 'rich country, strong army' policy by turning to the powers they believed to be the best to suit their needs: Germany for the army and Britain for the navy. By taking on China, they also showed how far they had come out of the 'closed country' policy of the Tokugawa and how they could play the game of realpolitik like anyone else.[39]

To realize the aim of 'developing industry, and promoting enterprise' using 'Western technology' without compromising 'Japanese spirit', as their slogans expressed it, the new regime, after a few unsuccessful attempts with state-owned shipyards, for instance, had decided that the best way forward for industrial progress was through the giant combines known as the *zaibatsu*. These were the most powerful industrial and commercial groupings, such as Mitsui, Mitsubishi, Sumitomo and Yasuda, that had banks and companies over a wide spread of business fields, with a holding company at the centre. They exercised top-down control over the small companies under them and as the dominant forces in the economy, whose leaders were in close touch with government figures, were an ideal instrument for putting the aims of the oligarchy into practice. They became deeply involved in politics and indeed government and though the holding companies and family interests were removed in 1945, with the purge of senior managers, they were to re-emerge after the Occupation in the form of the *keiretsu*. Unfortunately, both terms are translated into English as 'industrial groupings'.

The success of the Meiji policy of 'catching up', unlike quite a few countries that have tried to do the same thing later, coupled with the economic gains that Japan was able to make during the First World War, fought on the Allied side, meant that by 1918 Japan had no foreign debts, a trade balance in its favour and twice the gold reserves as before the war: a considerable achievement.[40]

People outside Japan tend to forget that while the country has a long history, which successive authorities have found it useful to tap into for their own purposes, Japan as a nation state in the modern sense has only existed since 1868; even if it did have over two-and-a-half centuries of centralized control under the Tokugawa Shoguns. This was why the new, oligarchic rulers from 1868 onwards felt it so necessary to indoctrinate the population with a strong national consciousness and to promote the idea that Japan was like one large family, with the Emperor as its head. How well they succeeded in their aim of promoting 'Japanese spirit, Western technology' is still reflected today in the way in which foreign technology continues to be separated from its social and intellectual origins, though the 'strong army' of the oligarchy's slogan preceded the 'rich country' by a long way.

In the international arena, where the oligarchs' policy was to see that Japan could 'take her stand as the equal of all the other countries', results, too, were not slow in coming, though they were at first disputed by the other powers. After Japan's defeat of China in 1894 – a mere twenty-six years after modernization, but not Westernization, had begun – Russia, France and Germany had 'advised' the Japanese government to give up its gains on land, apart from Formosa. This provoked violent anti-foreign feeling in Japan, lasting many years.[41] Commenting a century later on the war with China, the *Japan Times* saw it as a 'watershed' marking military control of foreign policy and a 'shift ... towards territorial expansion in Asia':[42] something that many people both inside and outside Japan today continue to regard with great anxiety after the subsequent experiences of the 1930s and 1940s.

The pattern continued with the murder, with the connivance of the Japanese agent in Korea, General Miura, and the Japanese army of Queen Min of Korea in the following year, 1895.[43] Evidence of this connivance was not uncovered until a hundred years later by a Japanese scholar from documents in the Fukushima Prefectural Library.

The murder was followed by the Japanese 'protectorate' of Korea in

1905, the disbanding of the Korean army and the installation of Japanese officials, provoking a nationwide rebellion, suppressed by the Japanese burning villages and killing 12,000 people in one year. Ultranationalist Japanese groups, such as the Black Dragon Society founded in 1901 and later active during the militarist period, favoured annexing Korea as a colony and when Korea did become a Japanese colony in 1910 it was 'generally approved by Japanese opinion, liberal and otherwise.[44] Japan had defeated China, to whom Korea had historically paid tribute, so the idea of Korea as a subject state seemed natural, while the defeat of the other big power in the region, Russia, made the Japanese government increasingly confident. Indeed, this was the first time that a 'Western' nation had been defeated by a non-Western one: a fact still commented on with pride by some people in Japan.

Russia's defeat led to the Japanese occupation of Southern Sakhalin, a large island off the coast of Siberia, with climate to match, north of Japan's northernmost island of Hokkaido in 1905. With the Russian Revolution, Japan intervened again against its old enemy, and still one of the least popular foreign countries according to Japanese public opinion surveys. Japanese troops stayed in Siberia until 1922 and in Northern Sakhalin until 1925. In the run-up to the Second World War in 1938-39 there were two battles in Outer Mongolia between Japan and Russia over disputed territory, with the Japanese army getting the worst of the second battle due to the Russian use of tanks and aircraft.[45]

On 8 August, 1945 – one week (!) before the end of the Second World War – Stalin, with whom the Japanese government thought they had a mutual non-aggression pact, launched his armies down through Manchuria, with the aim of taking part in the post-war occupation of Japan and using this as a means of adding another satellite to his empire, as he had in Germany. His 'treachery' in Japanese eyes and the fact that many of the large number of prisoners his forces took did not survive the Siberian labour camps added to anti-Russian feeling: an ironical piece of moral self-righteousness in the light of the behaviour of Japan's own forces. Some prisoners who had been brain-washed under the Stalinist system were also used to try and spread the Soviet doctrine when they eventually returned to Japan.

The reason why this is not 'ancient history' is the continued occupation by Russia since 1945 of Southern Sakhalin and the Kuriles, a group of small islands off the northeast coast of Hokkaido, creating what is known in Japan as the 'Northern Islands Problem'. As a result, there has been no peace treaty with Russia, so that technically Japan and Russia are still at war more than half a century after the end of actual fighting! Economically, the islands are of little value and the entire Japanese population of Southern Sakhalin was expelled in 1945 but for both sides prestige is an overriding factor.

Successive Japanese governments have tried to dangle incentives for the return of the islands in front of Russian negotiators but have been stonewalled. In the meantime, incidents involving Russian patrol boats and Japanese fishing vessels accused, as in some other places, of fishing where they have no right have not made for a more congenial climate.

Under Japanese colonial rule, Koreans were forced to learn Japanese and after 1940 to adopt Japanese names. A Shinto shrine was built on a prominent site in Seoul and palace buildings were demolished to make way for the Japanese government building. During the Great Tokyo Earthquake of 1923, Koreans who had come to Japan in search of work were rumoured to have deliberately started fires and to have plotted with Japanese Communists to set up a revolutionary government. Many, identified by their accent, were murdered by the mob.[46] In the 1990s, Korean requests for an apology or a memorial were rejected by the Japanese authorities.[47]

Large numbers of Koreans were brought to Japan during the Second World War, both as forced labour in mines and factories and as unwilling recruits in the Japanese forces but were not sent to fight, being considered inferior or unreliable. Many became prison camp guards, where they had a bad reputation. One former British POW who worked in Japan after the war considered that they had 'all the bad characteristics of the Japanese and none of the good'.[48]

Up to the present the relations between Japan and Korea continue to be bedevilled by recent history, by continued discrimination against Korean residents in Japan and by the tactless remarks of people like the prominent LDP politician Michio Watanabe that were previously quoted. Even the Socialist Prime Minister Tomiichi Murayama at the time of the coalition in 1995 remarked that the annexation of Korea in 1910 had been 'legally valid' and then, after the inevitable storm of protest, had been forced to admit that the instrument of annexation had been signed under duress.[49]

Matters have not been helped by a territorial dispute over an uninhabited island, or rather a small rock, lying between the two countries: Tok-to in Korean, or Takeshima in Japanese; and the violence of official and popular reaction in Korea to the Japanese government's claim shows the resentment that has built up. It is part of a continuing problem, not just something that belongs to the past, that gives an edge to Korean ambitions to beat the Japanese in business and to shake off the humiliations of the past.

Japan entered the First World War on the Allied side and was able to obtain German possessions in East Asia and the Pacific as part of the peace settlement but failed to have a declaration of racial equality accepted as part of the Covenant of the League of Nations in 1919, though how far Japanese attitudes and actions have been consistent with racial equality people must judge for themselves.

During the War, the Japanese government had taken advantage of the situation to try and expand its influence in China by presenting the Chinese government with the so-called 21 Demands, which would have made China a Japanese satellite. The Demands aroused American opposition but a new agreement enabled Japan to extend its rights in Manchuria: a huge territory for which it was to put more ambitious plans into operation in the 1930s and which could be compared with what the Nazis referred to as Lebensraum, or living space. It was to become a major part of Japan's wartime empire. In 1994 Shin Sakurai, the LDP director-general of the Environment Agency, stated that Japan had had no intention of waging an aggressive war in the 1930s and 1940s. Once again there were storms of protest. Japanese officials in Beijing and Seoul had to apologize and Sakurai was forced to resign.[50] The unrepentant attitude of such leading LDP figures was all too obvious.

The economic boom caused by the First World War ended with the peace. The rice price doubled, leading to riots and arson, in which over a hundred people were killed and thousands arrested. As elsewhere, war profiteers, specifically big business became detested and in the view of a respected historian, 'The seeds were sown, to shoot up a decade later, of Japanese military fascism.'[51]

In other countries, the 1920s were a time of frantically trying to enjoy life after the horrors of the war and the fashionable Japanese *'moga'*, or 'modern girl', was the equivalent of the flapper. Since the democracies had won the war, this seemed to show that there must be something in democracy after all, which encouraged what became known as the brief interlude of 'Taisho democracy', named after the reign of the current Emperor. But it fell apart in disillusion with the corruption of political life and the continual scandals: a problem little different from what exists today.

At American and other prompting, the Anglo-Japanese Alliance was wound up in 1921 and replaced by another, but empty, international treaty, which represented a loss of face for the Japanese government. Like other losses of face, real or imagined, it was strongly resented, especially by those of a nationalist turn of mind. In the same year the Washington Naval Conference agreed that the capital warship tonnage of the US, Britain and Japan should be fixed on the ratio of 5:5:3 and that no major naval bases would be built at either Hong Kong or in the Philippines – that could be seen as a potential threat from the Japanese point of view. In practical terms, especially as the bulk of the British fleet, for example, would not be in the Pacific in any case, this was a good agreement for Japan but nationalists saw it as an insult and murdered the prime minister, Hara. It was one of a considerable number of political assassinations, continuing up to the present day.

Nine years later, the next prime minister to die at the hands of an ultranationalist assassin and basically for the same reason was Yuko Hamaguchi, shot at almost exactly the same place: Tokyo Station. He had also been accused of not standing up for a larger warship tonnage for Japan and, which in the eyes of some was worse, daring as a mere civilian to oppose the will of the head of the naval general staff; but he did have the agreement of the Emperor. It was to be one of the last attempts to exert civilian control over the military, at the London Naval Conference of 1930.

The third prime minister to be murdered in the inter-war period was Tsuyoshi Inukai, assassinated along with a former finance minister and a senior director of the Mitsui *zaibatsu* holding company, by ultranationalists belonging to a group calling itself the 'League of Blood'. None was sentenced to death and most were released from prison well before Japan entered the Second World War in December 1941.

On the extreme Left, the Japan Communist Party was set up in 1922: to be answered by the State two years later with a new public order law providing for up to ten years imprisonment for advocating change in the 'national polity'; in other words the 'Emperor system' and the established political order. In 1931 the law was to provide for the death sentence for advocating such change.

Even before the Wall Street Crash of 1929, there was the Showa Bank Crash of 1927, which some in Japan were to remember during the financial crises of the 1990s. Also in 1927 a book began to circulate that, while supporting the Emperor system, was strongly opposed to the existing capitalist system. Its author, one Ikki Kita, proclaimed a corporatist, fascistic message.

In addition to the economic crisis of the 1930s, politics was widely regarded with contempt, what with fights in the Diet, corruption and scandals, and junior army officers plotted their first attempt at a *coup d'état*. If many Japanese today are extremely frightened of any sign suggesting a revival of militarism, it is not surprising, given the absence of tradition of civilian control of the military and the precedent of what happened not so long ago when the military, seeing that there was nothing to stop them, did indeed get out of control.

New plots followed in March and again in October 1931. The former was known to at least one of the generals, who advised against it, but no one was disciplined in spite of the original orders dating from the Meiji Period to the military to keep out of politics. Many of the plotters were young officers from the country who knew the sufferings of the rural population in the depression and sympathized with them. They were strongly anti-big business, anti-politician and anti-foreign.

Away from Japan, the army found its opportunity. Fabricating what became known as the 'Manchurian Incident' as a pretext, it seized the main town and strategic communications centre, Mukden, leading to the establishment of the puppet state of Manchukuo in 1932. In the 1990s this was to become the basis for Bertolucci's famous film *The Last Emperor*; though this had to be cut for showing in Japan, so sensitive were some of the incidents even sixty years later. There was heavy bombing of Shanghai.

The League of Nations, forerunner of the UN, condemned the Japanese army's invasion of Manchuria and its incorporation as the puppet state of Manchukuo, whereupon the Japanese Foreign Minister walked out, clearly demonstrating his determination to go his own way. In an unusually self-critical piece nearly sixty years later, a Japanese newspaper commentator wrote of Saddam Hussein's invasion of Kuwait in 1991 that, 'Iraq is like pre-war Japan'.[52] By fabricating another incident near Shanghai in 1937, the Japanese army then sought to expand its control over China in what became known as the 'China Incident': a euphemism used in Japan even today, in contrast to other wars such as, for example, the Vietnam War. What had happened in effect was that the army had carried out a *coup d'état* in Manchuria and was pursuing an agenda of its own.

The *coup d'état* that was attempted by junior officers in Tokyo, with at least the tacit support of one of the main army factions, is still well remembered today and has been the subject of more than one film. Known as the '2-2-6 Incident', because it took place on 2 February 1936, it failed but not before the ringleaders had issued a proclamation saying that Japan's problems were due to the politicians, the big industrial combines and elder statesmen who represented the past. They proclaimed their loyalty to the Emperor, a characteristic way of laying claim to legitimacy, but on this occasion the Emperor acted with particular decisiveness, insisting that the ringleaders be tried in secret. Thirteen were executed, plus another radical colonel who had assassinated a general and Ikki Kita, whose book on 'A plan for the reorganization of Japan on state socialist lines' was deemed to have been an important influence.[53]

The Emperor's decisive intervention in 1936 has since led to considerable comment. Some have argued that, as a constitutional monarch, the Emperor had virtually nothing to do with the Second World War, while others have argued the opposite, pointing out that at a symbolic level it was fought in his name and claiming that he was in favour of the war so long as it was going well. Another view is that the Emperor, although the Meiji Constitution had given him sole authority over the military, had become over-cautious about using this authority after Prince Saionji had told him in 1928 that he had mistakenly interfered in affairs of state.[54]

In view of the sensitive, controversial nature of the Emperor's role during the 'China Incident' and the Second World War, most Japanese people would probably be unwilling or unable to discuss it with anyone else; and perhaps not among themselves. But two points may be made here. First, the attempted coup of 1936 was a potential threat to the Emperor's position and even his own safety. While swearing loyalty, there was a tradition of criticizing or worse those seen as 'bad advisers' and, as a Japanese informant once told me, the militarists would have let no one stand in their way. Secondly, the Emperor's casting vote in 1945 to end the war was made when the war was clearly lost; but even then ultranationalistic officers tried to get hold of the discs of his broadcast so as to destroy them.

Under the Shoguns the Emperor had been a virtual prisoner, in spite of the ritual respect due to him, and now the imperial institution, along with such notions as the 'national polity' etc., were used as a symbolic focus and justification for the war aims of Japan's military and political leaders, just as the Meiji oligarchs had used the myth of divine origin to legitimize their power and their policies. As late as 1937, the Social Mass Party, a miscellaneous collection of socialistic elements, could use the following sort of words to pass a motion to 'positively support the holy war (*sic*) for the fulfilment of the historical mission of the Japanese people'.[55]

These questions of the Emperor and his role in the war were opened up again on his death in 1989, posing the problem for the representatives of the countries that had fought against Japan of how they should conduct themselves at the funeral. In Britain, for instance, there was a good deal of press discussion beforehand as to what the Duke of Edinburgh, himself a former Naval officer with service in the East would do. In the event, he managed a brief nod. But the wider questions remain part of the unfinished business from the war that Japanese officialdom passes over if it can.

Thus, the Japanese army in attacking China was at least theoretically acting in the Emperor's name and 'spreading the imperial way' etc. in, for example, its atrocious assault on Nanking and the Nanking Massacre of some 200,000 Chinese: the first of a series of major war crimes. Two years later, Japanese bombers attacked Chungking with fire bombs for three days; sowing the whirlwind that was later to engulf Japanese cities.

Having seized a large part of China, first by a gradual extension of influence and then by outright annexation under the fiction of the 'independent' state of Manchukuo, followed by the neighbouring region of Jehol, Japan's leaders were increasingly confident and, following Hitler's victories in Continental Europe joined the Tripartite Pact with him and Mussolini in 1940. It seemed obvious to them that Hitler was bound to win the war and reports from their attachés in London that Hitler had no means of mounting a cross-Channel invasion were ignored. This then was an ideal situation in which to create the 'Greater East Asia Co-Prosperity Sphere', or new Japanese empire. The prime minister, Prince Konoe, reported to the Upper House on 21 January 1941 that the chance was too good to miss[56] and with startling candour, Japanese politicians, journalists and intellectuals in 1940 spoke about the need not to 'miss the bus'.[57] Their opportunism was obvious, in contrast to some of the rationalizations that have since been heard.

To knock out the American fleet at Pearl Harbor in a single devastating blow, what was at the time the largest and best equipped carrier-borne force of torpedo planes and bombers was assembled: obviously not a defensive force. Ironically, it was British thinking that had provided the inspiration: the writings earlier in the century of the naval journalist Hector Bywater who had first considered the possibility of naval warfare between the USA and Japan, and the severe losses inflicted on Mussolini's fleet at Taranto by a smaller force of British torpedo planes. Admiral Yamamoto, who had nevertheless warned that a long war could not be sustained, had personally met Bywater and a colleague and the plan that he used bore a marked resemblance to the one sketched out in Bywater's book. Bywater, who was later officially advised to carry a pistol, died in mysterious circumstances before the attack on Pearl Harbor in December 1941.[58]

A tragi-comic footnote to the Japanese attack without a declaration of war, while the envoys Nomura and Kurusu were still negotiating, was that it took over fifty years for the Japanese Foreign Ministry to admit this 'mistake'. According to the Ministry, documents released in 1994 showed that there had been 'a lack of a sense of urgency' at the time. But no one had been reprimanded.[59] In 1991, the fiftieth anniversary of Pearl Harbor, there were striking examples of how the use – and as George Orwell emphasized, the misuse – of history can play a significant role in forming national consciousness and influencing public opinion, particularly in a society like Japan's, with its background of authoritarian government, discouragement of open debate and emphasis on the conformist acceptance of the 'right view'.

Watching the nightly television programmes, some of which were more open than others, one could not fail to be struck by the comments of members of the post-war generation to the effect that, 'We were never told about that at school', or probably anywhere else for that matter. Post-war generation Japanese travellers to China, Korea, Singapore, Manila etc have often been shocked at what they have seen or heard, which suggests that their surprise is genuine, particularly when the way the Japanese Ministry of Education has glossed over or ignored Japanese wartime behaviour is realized.

The opportunistic nature of the attempt by Japan's leaders to become the masters of Asia and to dominate the 'Greater East Asia Co-Prosperity Sphere' needs to be remembered when considering what has often been said since to justify it. There is, for example, the argument that Japan was being encircled by the ABCD powers: American, British, Chinese and Dutch. Or that economic rivalry between USA and Japan in China led to the war. Or that Japan's aim was to free the

Asian peoples from the yoke of Western imperialism – though not Japanese of course.

What is missing from all these economic or political arguments is the propaganda promoting the Japanese conviction of themselves as superior, comparable to the Nazi idea of the *Herrenvolk*, the master race, and the superiority of the divinely descended imperial house and 'national polity' etc, which would in themselves justify the 'holy war'. The author of a book on the very different treatment of the war in Japan and Germany in the post-war period has elsewhere described the common 'racial hierarchy' found in Japan, with South East Asians, for instance, low down the list and treated accordingly in present-day Japan.[60] Naturally, this does not mean that everyone in Japan thought in the same way as the ultra-nationalists and militarists of the wartime period and those who were appalled by it refer to the time as the 'dark valley'. But with the post-war growth of Japanese economic and therefore political power, no one should think that the old ideas have simply disappeared.

In many cases the Japanese authorities have succeeded in portraying Japan as the 'victim' of the war because of the atomic bombing of Hiroshima and Nagasaki, though not to those in China, Korea and other parts of Asia who were the real victims of Japanese militarism and not to those in Japan who see this as an attempt to shuffle off the responsibility of the wartime leaders who misled them, telling them up to the time of the collapse that they were winning if they would make one more effort. It has also enabled them to claim a moral equivalence and to help cover up their own actions and, given the fear of atomic weapons that any normal person feels, to use moral blackmail to persuade some well-meaning but naïve people in Western – but not Asian – countries to swallow the official line of Japan as war victim. This fits in with the line of Japan as 'poor', which many of the ordinary people undoubtedly are, in spite of the size of Japan's GNP and the richness of some of its firms. What is surprising is that now that so much more information about what actually happened is available, as has also been the case in the US and Europe, levels of awareness both outside and inside Japan are not higher.

Even after the dropping of the two atomic bombs, the Imperial Conference on whether to continue with the war or not was split. Half the war leaders wanted to arm the population with bamboo spears and fight on, not knowing at that time that only two atomic bombs had been produced; which does not suggest a very great concern for their own people.[61] No notes were taken at the Conference and although the Emperor gave the casting vote to end the war it is uncertain whether he joined the 'peace camp' before June 1945. He apparently insisted on the need to preserve the imperial line and to safeguard the 'three sacred treasures' of mirror, sword and jewel, which might be endangered if the Shinto shrines at Ise, with its continuing imperial connection today, and Atsuta were to fall into enemy hands if the war continued. An official later 'managed to get the false official version of the Emperor's role in the war inserted into *The Reports of General MacArthur* under the Occupation.[62] With defeat staring them in the face, Japan's leaders succeeded in securing the continuance of the 'polity' and the Emperor continued on the throne, despite the fact that Australia, Britain, China and New Zealand wanted to have him tried as a war criminal and that the US was also talking in these terms after the surrender as late as 6 October 1945.

Deciding what to do with the Emperor in 1945 was a difficult decision, especially for those who were not well informed about likely reactions, but another myth of the Emperor as a 'man of peace' was promoted, according to which the Emperor had told MacArthur that he was prepared to accept responsibility for the war by abdicating. If true, it might have been a good solution. Unfortunately, the most reliable record of the famous meeting on 27 September 1945, made by the interpreter, does not mention such an offer, which would have been too important to overlook: not surprisingly, most of the talking was done by MacArthur.[63]

There is a tradition in Japan, as there used to be among ministers in the British government, that the senior person, at least formally, should resign to 'take responsibility' for a serious mistake or failure. Quite a number of Japanese who fought in the war think this would have been the right course and one, writing in the Asahi newspaper, said that the Emperor could have entered a temple to pray for the souls of the soldiers who had died. He also stated that he refused to sing the national anthem 'with its prayers that the imperial family will flourish'.[64]

The result of keeping the Emperor, whatever his precise involvement in the war might have been, and preserving the 'polity' has been that Japan's post-war leaders of the older generation who had unreconstructed views were able to claim that since the wartime Emperor was retained Japan's cause in it was justified; for surely the Allies would have replaced him if they had not thought so? Under the Occupation, the Emperor announced that he was not a god but he did not say that he was not divinely descended; and in any case it was something that the foreigners wanted him to say . . . so what force did it really have?

Thus, the failure to draw a clean line under the war lends a spurious justification to the unreconstructed views and antics of ultra-nationalists and provides a continuity with the past in which economic rather than military aims are the dominant force. This is to say nothing of the distrust to which it contributes abroad and what occurred, for instance, in London in 1998 when the successor to the wartime Emperor encountered protesters from war prisoners' and civilian internees' groups demanding that the Japanese government face up to Japan's wartime history instead of sweeping it under the carpet. This followed considerable press exposure.

The Japanese authorities seem to have been largely successful, thanks to the degree of control that they exercise over education and the media, in concealing the existence of Japan's own atomic bomb programme; something that again has a connection with how the war continues to be seen, not least in the context of the promotion of the idea of Japan as war 'victim'. In fifteen years in Japan I never heard or saw the programme referred to, until in 1995 it was mentioned in four issues of the *Japan Times*.

Japanese journalists, however, had obtained a copy of classified records from the Japanese National Institute for Defence Studies, showing that General Tojo, at that time prime minister, army minister and home minister, and seen by some historians as the man most responsible for leading Japan into the war,[65] had ordered the formation of a team of scientists under Professor Yoshio Nishino to work on an atomic bomb. Tojo had stated that the USA and Germany were both working on the bomb and after the war these facts were reported to the Japan Defence Agency. Professor Nishino's laboratory was destroyed in an American air raid on Tokyo in the spring of 1945.[66]

To produce a bomb, the Japanese made efforts to obtain uranium oxide from two sources: from Hungnam in present-day North Korea(!) and by submarine from German-occupied Czechoslovakia. 560 kg, enough for one bomb, was sent by submarine U-234 but fell into American hands – and may have been used in the bomb dropped on Hiroshima. The two Japanese colonels on the U-boat committed suicide.[67]

Journalists also interviewed Tetsusaburo Suzuki, a member of Nishino's team, who told them that the team's documents had been destroyed at the end of the war, enabling this like other wartime programmes to be kept secret, but he was obviously proud of his work. 'I was confident at the time we could have built a bomb if we had had better equipment. . . . We had no doubt about using it if we could', though he said he had changed his mind after seeing Hiroshima and Nagasaki.

Members, unspecified, of the Imperial family had visited the laboratory to encourage the team in their work and his colleagues had not been troubled by the mass destruction of human life that the bomb could cause, unlike other scientists such as the American Robert Oppenheimer, who had agonized over the morality of using it.[68] Suzuki apparently believed that they would be able to make a bomb within a year, if they had had sufficient resources but compared to the Manhattan Project what they had was very little.

In fact, there had been a magazine interview with Professor Nishino as early as 1949[69] but this seems to have had little effect on the promotion of Japan as war 'victim' and on the high moral tone used in attacking the Americans in particular for dropping the bombs. That so many well-intentioned Westerners have been taken in can only be ascribed to their ignorance of what the Japanese themselves were doing and what they would have done if only they had had the chance.

The Japanese forces in China used chemical and bacteriological weapons and in 1942 President Roosevelt warned that America would retaliate in kind if necessary. Kokura, which was to have been the atomic bomb target if it had not been for bad weather, was a major production site and produced 1.6 million poison gas shells between 1937 and 1945.[70] Okunoshima Island just opposite Hiroshima produced 3,400 tons of toxic gases between 1931 and 1941. Workers there were sworn to secrecy and the site was removed from maps. In 1995 some 6,300 former employees were suffering from gas-related disorders but, fifty years after the war, some were prepared to speak. 'We should admit what we did', was how one ex-employee and now the curator of the museum put it.[71] Clearing up at Okunoshima and in China became major jobs after the war. Kokura was also the site where balloon bombs to be launched across the Pacific at the West Coast of the US were produced but few reached the area, though it was rumoured that they might contain bacteriological substances.

Some have claimed that the war could have been ended without the atomic bomb or by dropping it on open country but, as is well known, Japanese soldiers were taught to fight to the bitter end. They were ordered, in the Field Service Code of 1941, for example, 'never (to) give up a position but rather die',[72] and that 'Japanese spirit' would overcome 'Western materialism', or perhaps compensate for the greater industrial power of the US which they finally came to see as a major factor in their defeat.

But how do those who fought on the Japanese side see it? Colonel Saburo Sakai, a well known fighter pilot and author of his reminiscences, stated that, 'If they had not dropped the bomb, many more would have died. There was no chance of Japan winning. It was utterly absurd to take on the Americans – and the stupid men running our navy and army should have surrendered much earlier.' In his view, the Emperor should have taken responsibility either by abdicating or by committing suicide.[73] In spite of all the propaganda, it is probably a view held by more people than would care to express it publicly, or than people in other countries might imagine.

A Japanese historian, and wartime battalion commander, interviewed in 1995 was scathing about those, such as kind-hearted souls in the 'West', who believe that Japan was on the point of surrender anyway: 'Anyone who makes such a claim has no concept of the wartime Japanese leadership, or the Japanese people in those days. We lived under a rigid Imperial system. Absolute obedience to authority was the only acceptable pattern of behaviour.' General Umezu, the chief of staff, had told the Supreme War Leadership Council that the word 'capitulation' was not in the Japanese military dictionary[74] and these remarks give something of the flavour of Japan's wartime psychology. Would there have been an end to the war in 1945 if it had been known that the US did not have more than two of the bombs?

Another fact that tends to be overlooked is that orders had been issued to Japanese commanders that in the event of an Allied landing on the main Japanese islands all prisoners of war and civilian internees were to be killed. This is attested by the accounts of those who, thanks to the dropping of the atomic bombs survived, including a copy of the Japanese order to 'kill them all and leave no traces' now in the US National Archives in Washington. Civilian internees included citizens of neutral states and even some from Japan's Axis allies:[75] the copy of the order to kill all prisoners is found in the personal account of a former British POW, used with others as slave labour in extremely dangerous mining work, whose book was translated into Japanese.[76] In 1991 the Japanese translator, whose pacifist views were well known through his journalistic work, died a violent death in unexplained circumstances.

The seeds of the Japan as 'victim' syndrome can be traced back to the Emperor's broadcast of 1945 announcing the end of the war. Sometimes referred to erroneously as the 'surrender broadcast', it does not mention the word 'surrender' anywhere. Instead, it stated that 'the enemy has begun to employ a new and cruel weapon', as if Japan's own conduct had not been. The Emperor exhorted the population to 'bear the unbearable': the same phrase that had been used in 1894 when Russia, France and Germany had 'advised' Japan to give up its territorial gains after the war with China. It was an uncanny throwback from the past or, if one prefers it, another sign of continuity.

Referring again to the atomic bombs, it stated that, 'Should we continue to fight, it would ... result in obliteration of the Japanese nation', while in a face-saving euphemism it explained that, 'The war situation has developed not necessarily to Japan's advantage'. The broadcast ended by calling on 'the entire nation (to) continue as one family ... ever firm in its faith of the imperishableness of its divine land',[77] a characteristic repetition of the State ideology dating from the Meiji Period from 1868 onwards. Did this look like the beginning of a 'new' Japan?

While referring to the possibility that continuing the war 'would lead to the total extinction of human civilization', the self-justifying tone of the broadcast helped 'victim consciousness', *higaisha isshiki*. to perceive the war, as one foreign historian put it, 'as fundamentally a Japanese tragedy', not an international disaster. Hiroshima and Nagasaki 'became icons of Japanese suffering – perverse national treasures of a sort', that both fixed themselves in the national memory and served to obliterate memories of how Japan had treated others when it looked as if it was winning.[78]

Such an introverted and self-pitying attitude remains common and can be used for political purposes by both the Right and the Left for whom, as George Orwell showed, the control of the past is important for their present political agenda. Even such an educated and 'international' person as Mrs Sadako Ogata, the UN Commissioner for Refugees, referred in a television broadcast on the refugee problem created by war to Japan, too, being a 'victim of war'; but in a reference to the treatment of Japan's wartime past by Japanese officialdom, another writer asked whether it was a case of 'amnesia or concealment?'[79] This has not stopped Japanese governments from seizing the propaganda advantage, thus further deflecting criticism of wartime behaviour, by playing on feelings of guilt and fear to be strong in condemning nations such as France, China, India and Pakistan that have carried out tests of nuclear weapons.

Because the Second World War is not just 'ancient history' in Japan but remains a live and emotional political issue, how it has been treated since by official bodies is one of the clues in judging the 'new' Japan in comparison with the 'old'. Ten years after the end of the war in 1955 the Memorial Peace Museum and a Peace Park were set up at Hiroshima and every year the ceremonies held there, broadcast on television and attended by official dignitaries, are the centre of national attention: a controversial mixture of the painful personal memories of the sufferers and their relatives and the agenda of the politicians and ideologues using the strong emotions that such an anniversary naturally gives rise to for their own purposes.

To start with, the Museum was criticized for showing the horrific results of the bomb without any reference to the events that had led up to it being dropped as foreign visitors pointed out in the visitors' book. As a result, inscriptions were added some years later admitting that 'Japan, too, inflicted great damage', 'Japan's colonization policies inflicted incalculable harm on the peoples of many countries' and that 'In Nanking, Chinese were being massacred by the Japanese army.' Subsequently, a new wing, popularly known as the 'aggression wing' was added to explain what had led up to the use of the bomb.[80] Other new war museums at Osaka, Kawasaki, Okinawa and Kyoto's Ritsumeikan University, famous or notorious for the Leftist political stance of many of its professors, were opened showing the aggressive actions of the militarists. This was less surprising in Okinawa, where people feel that they were sacrificed to protect the main islands and where part of the problem of the American bases is resentment at the faraway central government in Tokyo.

But how far other museums are prepared to go in revealing the actions of the militarists from the time of the 'Manchurian Incident', or earlier, is a controversial political issue. Under the heading 'Still struggling with history' the *Japan Times* published a cartoon of the proposed War Dead Peace Memorial Hall planned for Tokyo, a modern s-shaped building with a shape resembling the 'S' of the notorious Nazi SS insignia. The obvious implication was that the Hall would follow the nationalist interpretation of history.[81]

Among the casualties at Hiroshima were an estimated five to eight thousand Koreans, brought to Japan as forced labour for the war industries in the area. They suffered discrimination in medical treatment and burial, being excluded from any memorial. In the 1970s, when Japan's diplomatic recognition of China's Communist regime led to increased attention being put on Japanese behaviour in China between 1931 and 1945, the question of a Korean memorial was also raised. Eventually, one was put up; but not in the central ground. Japanese atomic bomb victims, *hibakusha*, were also discriminated against, partly because they were disagreeable reminders of the past and partly because of the tradition of hiding family members with physical or mental ailments that would reflect badly on the family and make them unattractive as marriage prospects, or reduce the prospects of brothers and sisters.[82]

Inevitably, the invention of atomic weapons, which people realized could not be 'disinvented', and the horrific effects that the use of just one produced became a focus of attention but this has distracted attention from the effects of the use of conventional weapons, which needs to be put into context. Tokyo, for instance, reported 97,031 civilian deaths in air raids, compared to 70,000 at Nagasaki. 63 other cities reported altogether 86,336, though the largest total of 140,000 was at Hiroshima: the point focused upon by Japanese propagandists to support the 'victim' syndrome, while ignoring the casualties caused by the Japanese bombing of Shanghai, Chungking and what would have been caused if they had succeeded in producing atomic weapons first.[83]

The site chosen for the new War Dead Peace Memorial Hall, destined to stir up fresh controversy within Japan because of the 'unfinished business' of the war and the constant fear of anything that might indicate a return to militarism, was next to Yasukuni Shrine in central Tokyo: the Shinto shrine where all the war dead, including General Tojo and others executed as war criminals in 1945, have been commemorated since the war with China in 1894. It is a magnet for ultra-nationalists and a repeated source of controversy over whether, for instance, the prime minister and cabinet members should make an annual visit to the shrine in an official or a private capacity and whether the LDP is trying to lend official support to this politically most sensitive shrine and Shintoism, which would go against the separation of religion and state under the post-war Constitution. The anxiety is explained by the role of State Shintoism and the Imperial cult during the war.

Responsibility for the new Hall was given to the Ministry of Health and Welfare, the Ministry that pays the benefits to the families of war veterans, which might sound innocuous if it was not realized that this makes it susceptible to the views of the War-Bereaved Families Association. At the time it was headed by a politician known for his nationalistic attitude, Ryutaro Hashimoto, who was also prime minister from 1996 to 1998. His remark that it was, 'Difficult to assert the characteristic and aim of the war', caused fresh offence in Korea and one of the newspapers quoting it on the fiftieth anniversary of the end of the war commented that, 'The anniversary year left the war almost as much of a taboo topic as ever.'[84]

And a taboo topic of informed discussion, as opposed to propaganda put out by the authorities or favoured by them, is what it largely remains. The police do nothing about the deafening noise made by the convoys of 'Rightist' loudspeaker vans when they drive through Tokyo haranguing the crowds, or stop them when they go through a red light, and the connections between these groups and organized crime syndicates, the *yakuza*, are an open secret. People like the writer Yukio Mishima, whose suicide was already referred to, and the late Ryoichi Sasakawa, correctly referred to in the obituary of the London *Times* as 'a rabid nationalist', find no difficulty in forming their own uniformed 'private armies'.

They may represent a minority but Sasakawa was an admirer of Mussolini and a member of Tojo's wartime government. Arrested as a Class A war crimes suspect, he was not brought to trial and successfully re-emerged as an influential political figure behind the scenes at the time of the LDP prime ministers Sato and Tanaka in 1964-74. Having acquired a large post-war fortune in motorboat racing and other business interests, he spread large sums of money around in a new career of philanthropist and was said to be trying to be awarded a Nobel Prize. He was photographed jogging with President Jimmy Carter.[85]

The point here is how the authorities continue to use history for their own ends, specifically by means of the system for censoring school history textbooks: something that would be normal under a Communist regime but not in the case of a system claiming to be democratic. This system was started by the Ministry of Education in 1880 and, after the interruption of the Occupation, is still a live political issue.[86]

The way in which it was reinstated after the Occupation gives an interesting insight into how the Japanese style of democracy works. In 1955 the governing party, the LDP, began to attack the 'bias' in textbooks it did not like and introduced a bill for the tighter regulation of their contents into the Diet in the following year. Because of the strong opposition of those in education, the bill could not be enacted but the then Minister of Education took the law into his own hands anyway and ordered the Ministry to appoint textbook examiners to carry out the government's wishes. From then on, only textbooks centrally approved by the Ministry, not the local boards of education, or books for which the Ministry had the copyright could be used in schools. The Ministry also determines the course of study, so that the formal possibility of using other materials is just *tatemae*.

For textbook publishers the risks of having a book rejected or even delayed are costs to be avoided and so it is easy for the Ministry to censor what is taught, following the system of 'controlled education', *kanri kyoiku*, which has a political aim similar to what was officially laid down as the purpose of education in the late nineteenth century by Arinori Mori, the first Minister of Education. Mori made it clear that, 'In the administration of all schools, it must be kept in mind, what is to be done is not for the sake of the pupils, but for the sake of the country.'[87]

Like Ryoichi Sasakawa, Prime Minister Kishi (1957-60) was another Class A war criminal suspect who was arrested but not brought to trial and his Education Minister, To Matsunaga, promoted what was called 'racial reconstruction', *minzoku saiken*, and reintroduced 'ethics' into the curriculum. This might sound harmless enough but 'ethics' in the Japanese context has the connotation of the nationalistic teaching of *shushin* that existed until 1945. Kishi had been Minister of Commerce and Industry, one of the key posts, in Tojo's wartime cabinet and had played an important role in the exploitation of Manchuria. His political views may be imagined.

The upshot of all this was 'the gradual reappearance of nationalistic tendencies and the slanting of history even to the extent of misrepresenting events'. In a rewriting of history, normally associated with the Communist system that George Orwell had so pointedly attacked, events that had been well documented were simply excluded. These included, for example, the Nanking massacre, the Korean rebellion of 1919 and the bringing of Koreans to Japan for forced labour in war industries. The result was strong protests from China and Korea. In other cases euphemisms were used, such as describing Japan's attack on China as an 'advance'. To their credit, the three leading newspapers attacked the reactionary trend of the policy of censorship, with the Asahi commenting that there was 'a further move back to "pre-war" authority over textbooks'.

On Emperor Akihito's visit to the US in 1994 the Chinese Alliance for Memorial and Justice and its sponsoring Chinese and Korean organizations accused the Japanese government of passing off 'atrocities as the "liberation" of Asian countries from Western colonial powers – a lie that is propagated daily in Japanese classrooms and press' and called on Asian Americans to demonstrate outside the White House and the UN.[88]

Sometimes even the Ministry's textbook censors are not the most reactionary force. In 1988 an English textbook for high schools was to be published by a well known firm, Sanseido, which mentioned wartime atrocities. Under pressure from a group of LDP Dietmen calling themselves the 'Association of Comrades to discuss the Nation's Basic Issues', Sanseido was forced to change the text and, in a move more worthy of a farce if it had not been so serious, to replace the offending section by an essay on the musical *My Fair Lady*! They had of course first pressured the Ministry.[89]

In one case the Ministry did tone down some of the nationalistic language in the 'Latest History of Japan', compiled by another group calling themselves the 'National Congress to safeguard Japan', whose aim was to protect the country from 'masochistic, condemnatory' bias, but the compilers refused to mention that Emperor Hirohito had stated that he was not a god at the time of the Occupation. That was as recently as 1994 and the book was widely distributed at Shinto shrines, echoing the role of this purely Japanese religion or cult in the militarist period.

All this goes on in spite of the fact that Article 21 of the Constitution states that, 'No censorship shall be maintained', and if Japanese children continue to get a distorted view of their own country and others it is hardly surprising. Once again, the *tatemae* or how things appear on the surface and can be shown to foreigners has changed but the substance is another matter and since Japan has a 'role of law', in which judges are not independent of the government, rather than a 'rule of law' where judges should be free of political interference and do not owe their careers to a Ministry of Justice, it is extremely difficult to succeed in the claim that, for example, the textbook censorship system is unconstitutional. Even if a claim does succeed, there is always the possibility in a system like Japan's that other pressures can be brought to bear that will hinder its implementation. It has already been shown that in the 1950s the Minister of Education just went ahead and tightened up the censorship system in the face of the refusal of the Diet to pass the bill authorizing him to do so. Democracy *à la japonaise*?

In spite of these daunting obstacles and the tenacity of the opposing political forces, there are those who challenge the system: the most famous being Professor Saburo Ienaga, a 1937 graduate of the prestigious Tokyo University, whose struggle with the courts lasted over thirty years, from 1965 at least up to 1997, by which time he was aged 84.

Realizing that what he had been taught at school was very much the official line and that 'we were unable to learn what was going on in other countries', he had been 'really shocked' to discover about the Nanking massacre and the experiments carried out on live human beings by the army's notorious Unit 731. The high school history textbook he submitted to the Ministry in 1963 was rejected, which 'as a scholar, hurt me to be unable to write the truth ... many history scholars petitioned the Education Ministry to change the screening criteria. But it was not effective and I decided the only way to publicize the issue was to keep going to the courts'. He assembled a support group of 30,000 people and even published a monthly 'Textbook Suit News'. Indirectly, the Chinese and Korean protests over Japanese rewriting of history[90] helped his cause but in 1993 the Supreme Court ruled that screening of textbooks did not amount to censorship and did not violate freedom of expression.[91] In 1968 Ienaga's own 'The Pacific War 1931-1945' was published, though not of course as a textbook, and was translated into English the following year.[92]

In the most recent case in 1997 the authorities used the tactic of sitting as a 'petty bench', with only five out of the fifteen judges, declaring that they were 'unable' to rule on the main charge that textbook censorship was unconstitutional.[93] However, the presiding Supreme Court judge, Masao Ono, ruled against the government for censoring references to Unit 731, the chemical and bacteriological research unit at Pingfan in Manchuria, safely away from Japan with its members sworn to secrecy, that carried out horrific experiments on a far larger scale than those of the notorious Dr Mengele. The judge's words were: 'It is requested that the government refrain from intervening in educational content as much as possible.'[94] The government had always denied in the teeth of the evidence that there was any 'credible academic evidence' about Unit 731. To an American journalist Professor Ienaga had remarked that, 'To expose – that's the point. To expose the past, to expose censorship in our supposedly democratic system.'

So far from there being 'no credible academic evidence' about Unit 731, the evidence was available in comprehensive detail, even if it did not seep out until more than thirty years after the end of the war. The first book in English appeared in 1989 and was accompanied by a British television programme, in which the Unit's former printer, Naoji Uezono, who saw the most secret documents in his work, spoke at length. Photos in the book include the list of Unit 731's personnel, confiscated by the American GHQ after the surrender, portraits of some of the principal researchers, plans and buildings at Pingfan, or what was left after attempts to destroy the evidence by blowing them up.

On their visit to Japan, the two authors and their television team had attempted to interview doctors who had been members of the Unit and who had obtained prestigious and well paid jobs in medical schools and hospitals after the war. None agreed to be interviewed. As a matter of policy, the Japanese authorities have never pursued any of their own people for war crimes.[95] Five years later an American history professor, who by then had had access to both KGB and American archives, published a further account, with a map showing the extent of Unit 731's activities to include half a dozen sites in China and places as distant as Bangkok, Rangoon and Singapore.

Using the characteristic Japanese mechanism of group loyalty, no matter what the purpose involved, the Unit's commander, General Ishii, who was something of a local bigwig, had sworn his personnel to secrecy, which most of them have followed since 1945, with the exception of a minority that have spoken out. In the aftermath of the Second World War, which was almost immediately followed by the Cold War – for example, Stalin's tightening of control over his East European satellites, his attempt in 1948 to force the Western allies out of Berlin by blockading the city, not to mention his plans for using Japanese Communists and indoctrinated prisoners of war in Japan itself – meant that Unit 731's research findings were of great interest to both the USA and the USSR. General Ishii, who had first gone into hiding, and his personnel were offered immunity in return for information by the Americans, with the threat of interrogation by the Russians if they did not cooperate.

Ishii likewise played a cat-and-mouse game of asking the Americans what they wanted to know, so as to keep back bargaining chips for himself. Just what the Americans got is impossible to say. They were dealing with extremely cunning people who knew that their lives could be at stake. Thus, the clannish secrecy of the Japanese was compounded by what the Dutch judge at the Tokyo War Crimes Trials, Bert Röling, later commented on as follows: 'It is a bitter experience for me to be informed now that centrally ordered Japanese war criminality of the most disgusting kind was kept secret from the Court by the US government.'[96]

Some former Unit members expressed remorse in their old age, while others said they would do the same things again if it was necessary to win the war. According to Naoji Uezono: 'They screamed and screamed. But we didn't regard the *maruta* – literally "logs" i.e. the victims of experiments – as human beings. They were just lumps of meat.'[97] In 1982 the head of the Health and Welfare Ministry's Veterans Relief Bureau revealed in the Diet that Ishii was receiving a pension on the appropriate scale.[98]

A Japanese professor of science history, Keiichi Tsuneishi, is 'widely regarded as the leading expert on Unit 731', with his 1981 publication of 'The biological warfare unit that disappeared', *Kieta saikinsen butai*, shortly before Seiichi Morimura's more popular 'The devil's gluttony' *Akuma no hoshoku*. His publisher received threatening letters.[99]

Professor Tsuneishi also revealed details of poison gas shell production after obtaining papers from a former Japanese army officer who had kept them since the war. In February 1995, after the Chinese government had informed the UN that the Japanese forces had left behind about two million shells, the Japanese government was obliged to send a mission to China to deal with the problem.[100] The

Professor also referred to the mention by the Emperor's brother, Prince Mikasa, in his autobiography that he had visited Unit 731 at Pingfan. Asked if he thought that the Prince had told the Emperor 'what was going on there', Professor Tsuneishi replied: 'It is Japanese common sense to assume he told him.' The reference is to Japan's famous 'information sharing' mechanisms, especially to a brother and a superior. Unit 731's victims at Pingfan number at least 3,000 Chinese, Mongolians, Koreans and Russians. This does not include those, also of other nationalities, who suffered elsewhere.[101]

One of the Emperor's cousins, Prince Takeda, had visited Pingfan several times under the assumed name of Colonel Miyata, while his uncle, Prince Higashikuni, had visited it once. In 1939 the Emperor's younger brother, Prince Mikasa, attended a lecture by General Ishii in Tokyo.[102] In 1945 the latter had issued his staff with poison capsules but there is no indication that they were used.[103]

In 1993 residents of Shinjuku Ward in Tokyo and some former Unit 731 members brought a case to stop human bones of Mongoloid type that had been unearthed at the site of an army medical college said to have been connected with Unit 731 from being cremated without further examination. The case was rejected but the plaintiffs had organized an exhibition of documents and other items connected with the Unit at its various sites, including Shinjuku, where I lived at the time.[104] The documents included an English translation of the results of experiments released under the US Freedom of Information Act and others from China and the USSR. The following year the *Japan Times* published a photo of a senior officer of the Unit and others at sub-units in Manchuria[105] and a former colonel produced the written order he had issued in 1945 to destroy the evidence and documents relating to the Unit's activities.[106]

Between July 1993 and December 1994 a Unit 731 exhibition was shown at sixty-one places in Japan and statements by former members, with an outline of its activities, were published in paperback form in 1996.[107] In the same year, a Japanese scholar wrote about the Unit in an expanded English translation of his original Japanese work on Japanese war crimes.[108] In the light of all the information that was circulating, the Ministry of Education's long censorship campaign to deny the Unit's existence might seem surprising, were it not for its well known political agenda and that of unregenerate nationalist elements in the ruling party and pressure groups of the type already referred to.

Similar remarks apply to the Nanking massacre of 1937, which in 1994 the then Justice Minister (*sic*) and former head of the Defence Agency, Shigeto Nagano, had described as 'a fabrication.[109] The notorious LDP politician Shintaro Ishihara stated in an interview that the massacre was 'a story made up by the Chinese. It has tarnished the image of Japan but it is a lie'. This is the same Ishihara who wrote that the bond between the Emperor and his subjects 'transcended the bond between a head of state and its citizens' and that it expressed 'the uniqueness of Japan and the Japanese':[110] a racialist and fascistic outlook that still remains all too common in the sorts of governing circles in which people like Mr Ishihara move. Reacting as a Diet member in 1993 to Prime Minister Hosokawa's expression of regret for 'acts of aggression and colonial rule that had caused such widespread suffering', he remarked that 'Those indiscreet remarks without solid historical viewpoint deserve death.'[111]

Ironically, one of the most detailed accounts of the massacre, running to over 800 pages, was the diary kept by John Rabe, a Siemens representative and Nazi party organizer in Nanking. Rabe set up a safety zone to shelter Chinese and tried, unsuccessfully, to persuade the German government to urge restraint on the Japanese government.[112] Rabe and other witnesses testified at the war crimes trials in 1945 and contemporary records are believed to exist in the archives of the German diplomatic service.

Some 200,000 people – some say more – were killed over several days of savagery, of which considerable photographic and newsreel evidence remains. The *Nichi Nichi* newspaper reported the competition between two officers to behead Chinese, on 13 December 1937, 'scoring' 105 and 106 respectively. Both were themselves executed at the end of the war but the daughter of one of them complained in a nationalist magazine that he could not rest in peace while shameful lies were being spread that had 'ruined his reputation'.[113] For nationalists, even the euphemisms in the high school textbooks authorized by the Ministry of Education that 'Japanese troops were reported to have killed many Chinese, including civilians, and Japan was the target of international criticism' were too much.

After reading an article in a well known Japanese English-language magazine directed at foreign readers in a section on 'Debunking the rape of Nanking', a former British ambassador to Japan and author of several respected works wrote to the magazine. Under the heading of 'The rape of Nanking: a cover-up', he challenged what was just another attempt to rewrite history but the Japanese writer remained unrepentant.[114]

After Nanking, the worst massacre of civilians was at Manila near the end of the war. Another 100,000 died including those from neutral countries, killed 'because they were white'[115] another account of women and children interned by the Japanese in Sumatra mentions that Swiss and even Germans and Austrians were included.[116] After the war, Switzerland was one of no fewer than seventeen countries that obtained better compensation from Japan for the treatment of its civilian internees than Britain did for its prisoners of war; thanks to the Foreign Office, who instructed their staff to hush the matter up.[117] Japan's internment of even Axis civilians and their murder in Manila, also confirmed to me by a German informant, gives an idea of the ruthlessness with which the Japanese leaders, and not the leaders alone, pursued the war. It needs to be remembered in the context of what those who have promoted the idea of Japan as war 'victim' afterwards have been saying.

Some Japanese professors and journalists have followed up the reports of war crimes, at the cost to themselves of unpopularity and even physical danger: something that people who live in more open societies may find difficult to imagine, though they could understand the dangers of being a dissident under Communism. In Singapore, General Yamashita had ordered that all anti-Japanese Chinese should be killed and about 25,000 civilians were murdered, but a journalist, Takafumi Hishikari, who had been in Singapore in 1942 had been informed that a total of 50,000 were to be liquidated. Documents showing this were found in 1996 by Professor Hirofumi Hayashi. The officer ordered by Yamashita to supervise these massacres was Masanobu Tsuji:[118] to resurface after the war as an LDP Diet member in the 'new' Japan.

Reminiscent of the murders in the inter-war years of prime ministers and others who made themselves unpopular with the ultra-nationalists, the risks run by Japanese who draw attention to Japan's wartime behaviour were well illustrated by the case of Hitoshi Motoshima, the mayor of Nagasaki. Speaking on the anniversary of the attack on Pearl Harbor, he observed that, 'I think the Emperor bears some responsibility for the war': a remark that he refused to withdraw when pressed by LDP members. Eleven days later, 24 extremist groups roared through Nagasaki with loudspeaker vans demanding Motoshima's death as 'divine retribution'. Two days later sixty-two groups from all over Japan did the same thing.

But the extremists did not have it all their own way and within three days a newly formed Nagasaki Citizens' Committee for Free Speech had collected 13,684 signatures in support of their mayor. Then in January 1990 Motoshima was shot and nearly killed: an assassination attempt lauded in the extremist press as 'divine punishment'. Despite earlier death threats, Motoshima had no police protection, as LDP assemblymen had complained about the expense.

Motoshima himself had been in the wartime army but was also a Christian and he summed up the incident in a pithy comment: 'In Europe, people's feelings are based upon centuries of philosophy and religion but the Japanese only worship nature. This is what they have internalized. In a world ruled by nature, the question of individual responsibility does not come up.' He was not optimistic that this would ever change:[119] a significant remark, which all those who believe, or who want to believe, or have been told, that there is a 'new' Japan would do well to take seriously.

The apologists' view of Japan's wartime Greater East Asia Co-

Prosperity Sphere, or empire, was that its peoples were being liberated from European or American colonial rule, while the reality was that the latter was being replaced by Japanese rule. The economies of the area were to be mobilized to support Japan's war aims,[120] while the local populations were enslaved and their culture destroyed as useless in the modern age. Instead, they were to learn that modern culture meant Japanese culture.[121] The *tatemae*, or facade, was for instance as the government told the League of Nations, that Japan had 'no territorial designs on Manchuria', after it had seized control there.[122] Meanwhile Koreans and Taiwanese could be forced to serve in the Japanese army and civilians from the occupied territories, and of course prisoners of war, could be used as slave labour, both in Japan itself and elsewhere.

In 1945, for instance, 800 Chinese slave labourers at a copper mine in Japan, working for Kajima Gumi, now Kajima Corporation and one of the biggest construction companies, killed four of their brutal overseers and escaped. On their recapture, about fifty were tortured to death, in what is known as the Hanaoka incident. Of 986 Chinese, only 568 survived the war.

Afterwards, the Americans found Kajima employees trying to hide the evidence of the crime and arrested eight of them. For years a dispute over compensation rumbled on, with the company employing legalistic means – in a society where people supposedly disfavour the law! – to deny responsibility. Only in 1963 was a small monument put up, leading Tsuneo Yachita, a Japanese who felt that the affair should not be brushed under the carpet, to comment that, 'They are good at putting up memorial stones but when it comes to historical research and financial compensation, we have had no help at all.' The same tactics of denial and delay as used in the textbook censorship affairs, and indeed in other fields where the authorities want to procrastinate, will already be familiar. However in 1995 – fifty years after the end of the war – the Speaker of the Lower House of the Diet, Miss Takako Doi, formerly head of the Left-leaning Japan Socialist Party, attended a ceremony near Hanaoka in memory of those who were killed.

Resulting from a government directive in February 1944 referring to the labour shortage in Japan's munitions industry, 40,000 Chinese had been taken to Japan as forced labour, of whom 7,000 had died. In overall charge of wartime forced labour was Nobusuke Kishi, first arrested as a Class A war criminal in 1945 and then prime minister in 1957-1960.[123]

Miss Doi had been the first leading Japanese political figure to lay a wreath at the memorial to the civilian victims of the Japanese occupation of Singapore in 1942-1945. That was in 1994. Not even the popular, though LDP, Prime Minister Toshiki Kaifu had done so,[124] who in the years 1989-91 many Japanese hoped would turn out to be a possible reformer, only to have their hopes dashed by the LDP party machine.

Public awareness among the wartime Allied nations has understandably concentrated on such well known atrocities as the Burma-Thailand 'Death Railway',[125] the Bataan Death March and the ill-treatment of large numbers of civilians, including women and children but less has appeared outside Asia on the appalling sufferings of the Asian peoples supposedly 'liberated' by the Japanese. One estimate, for instance, of deaths among the Asian slave labourers on the Death Railway' is 100,000,[126] while another gives a casualty rate of 50 per cent,[127] compared to 12,399 out of 61,806 among the better organized prisoners of war.[128] As one British prisoner put it, 'It was possible. . . . to guess that these pathetic labourers would die in enormous numbers and be the biggest victims of the railway.[129] Another estimate was that of 260,000 Javanese sent to the railway and elsewhere, only 70,000 returned home. Those working on the railway included Burmese, Chinese, Indians, Malays, Thais and Vietnamese.

Acting for the Red Cross, the British government transferred ten million Swiss francs at prevailing rates via Berne to the Yokohama Specie Bank for the relief of POWs and civilian internees in Japanese hands but, as might have been supposed, the money was misappropriated for the Japanese war effort. The government did not get it back till 1952. [130]

For Allied prisoners of the Japanese the average death rate was 27 per cent, compared to 4 per cent for those captured by the other Axis powers.[131] The film *The Bridge on the River Kwai*, which compares unfavourably with the grimmer realism of films like *Schindler's List*, for instance, was described by one former prisoner as 'fine but fanciful'.[132] Specifically, it failed to reflect the courage and skill of the real Colonel Toosey in preventing even more deaths on the largest single project that POWs were forced to work on.[133]

In previous wars involving 'Western' prisoners i.e., Russians in 1905 and Germans in the First World War, the Japanese government had ordered the army to respect international rules in the treatment of prisoners but although the government had 'in principle' accepted the Geneva Convention and had told its enemies it would do so, it never ratified the Convention and made no effort to order the army at any level to comply with it. Aircrew in particular could expect little mercy.[134]

Wider awareness of Unit 731, most of whose victims were Asian, had to wait until long after the war, as did the tragedy of the 'comfort women', *ianfu*, or sex slaves of the Japanese forces, almost all of whose victims were again Asian. They included some 200,000 Korean women or girls, forced or tricked into sexual slavery.[135]

As with Unit 731 and other atrocities, the Japanese authorities first pretended not to have been involved and then used delaying tactics to avoid moral or financial responsibility. Until in 1992 Professor Yoshiaki Yoshimi discovered documents proving the government's involvement and, to his credit, made them public in the Asahi newspaper of 12 January 1992.[136] Even then, the Ministry of Justice claimed to have been unable to find the records. When a BBC reporter asked the chief government spokesman why this was, when Professor Yoshimi had been able to do so, the spokesman replied – after a long pause – that this was 'a very unfair question'.[137]

When pressed for direct compensation and an apology by Korean and other 'comfort women', the Japanese government then hid behind the proposal to establish an independent fund, which would have allowed it to maintain the fiction that it was not involved; adding insult to injury. This resulted in an International Public Hearing in Tokyo, with the participation of Professor van Boven of the Netherlands, a rapporteur for the UN Human Rights Commission;[138] followed by the visit of a team from the International Commission of Jurists, registered with the UN, to Japan in April 1993 to take statements.

At the same time, Japanese scholars and others proposed establishing a research centre to deal with issues like the 'comfort women', the Hanaoka incident, Unit 731 etc and a memorial hall 'for the souls of victims of Japanese militarism, as an educational resource for the next generation'.[139] Another Japanese historian, Yuko Suzuki and a former teacher, Rumiko Nishino, published books and spoke about the 'comfort women'; showing yet again that not everybody accepted the government line, or misinformation.[140]

The UN – on whose prestigious Security Council the Japanese government was keen to get a seat – then sent a three-person mission to Japan in 1995, meeting the Chief Cabinet Secretary, the Foreign Minister and former Korean 'comfort women'.[141] In a 37-page report it urged the government to apologize and to pay individual compensation to the victims and, if possible, to punish the wrongdoers. It condemned the government's plan of an independent Asian Women's Fund as inadequate: all of which led the government, as the *Japan Times* reported to feel 'displeased', and the prime minister, Ryutaro Hashimoto, also head of the nationalistic War-Bereaved Families Association, to state that the government would 'take any legal countermeasures necessary to fend off the requests'. A Japanese lawyer representing several victims who had already begun proceedings said that if the government did not agree with the mission's findings of 'extraordinary inhumanity', it should challenge them in the International Court of Justice at the Hague,[142] which it declined to do, preferring the well tried tactics of delay. By that time of course Japan had long since recovered from the poverty of the immediate post-war years.

Though Korean 'comfort women' were in the majority, adding to the considerable tensions between the two countries, Indonesians and others have also taken action against the Japanese government. Historians estimated that 60,000 Indonesian women had been forced into sexual slavery, of whom a quarter were still alive, according to a report in the *Japan Times* in 1996'[143] A group of women from the Philippines attempted to sue the Japanese government through the Tokyo District Court and one of them, Mrs Maria Henson, stated that, 'What we want is genuine compensation so that the Japanese government will restore our dignity.' Attacking the evasiveness of the textbook censorship system, she commented that, 'Future generations will read this (her experiences, translated into Japanese) even though the Japanese government will not allow the truth in textbooks.'[144] Two Korean women who had spoken at high schools in Japan also said afterwards, 'I feel anger towards the Japanese government ... I believe I would not be able to talk about such experiences even fifty years later.'[145] In some cases, the Japanese forces had sought to destroy the evidence by killing their victims and it is not difficult to imagine how painful it must have been for surviving victims to speak out, even fifty years later.

One Dutchwoman in particular, Mrs Jeanne Ruff-O'Hearne, did so for the first time at the International Public Hearing in Tokyo in 1992, when she described her terrible experiences.[146] She also spoke on British Channel 4 television on 1 August 1995 and 21 August 1997 with some of her fellow victims in the broadcast entitled 'Fifty years of silence'. Mrs Elly van der Ploeg who had travelled to Japan to bring a suit against the Japanese government was interviewed by the *Japan Times* in 1994.[147]

Exactly how many Dutch 'comfort women' victims there were is not clear. The first account to appear in the Dutch newspaper *Volkskrant*, by Mrs Keetje Ruizeveld spoke of a hundred at a camp at Kota Paris; another spoke of at least 52.[148] While a third mentioned 35 between the ages of 16 and 26 from a camp at Semarang,[149] who after appalling suffering were returned to the camp because of their determined resistance. It was only in 1992 that records at The Hague were made public.

The sources referred to here and others mention numerous other atrocities committed by the Japanese forces, some of which former Japanese soldiers wrote about to the press.[150] These include the planned massacre of all prisoners if the atomic bombs had not persuaded the Imperial Council to surrender.[151] That the Japanese authorities knew what they were doing is shown by a telegram sent from Tokyo to all camp commandants on 20 August 1945 ordering that, 'Personnel who have ill-treated POWs and (civilian) internees ... should at once be transferred ... or ... conceal(ed). ... Documents should be destroyed.'[152] That such people did in fact disappear was commented on in some prisoners' accounts.[153]

Two things need to be said about the behaviour of the Japanese forces. The first is the strong emotional influence of the ultra-nationalistic and racialist creed propagated by the authorities through such means as the Thought Bureau of the Ministry of Education, teaching that 'Japan is the divine country', quite different from 'Western' countries and superior to the peoples of Asia. Even a 'History of Japan' for tourists translated into English in 1939 stated that, 'The Imperial blood may be said to run in the veins of all Japanese'; while on 11 February 1940, the so-called anniversary of the founding of the nation by the mythical Emperor Jimmu 2,600 years previously, the *Japan Times and Mail* spoke of the 'promise of even greater attainments, a promise . . . in the deep consciousness of racial destiny that moves the soul of the race': a promise, as wartime propaganda had it, to bring other nations and races 'under one roof'.[154]

This fascistic creed is comparable to that of the Nazis and their idea of themselves as the *Herrenvolk*, the master race; which means that others do not matter and can be treated accordingly. A former prison camp interpreter told students in 1950 that he and his fellow soldiers were 'cultists for the Emperor', who would do anything in his name, as if they were under the same sort of spell as the followers of the Aum Shinrikyo cult were who attacked the Tokyo Underground with sarin gas on 20 March 1995.[155]

The second thing is the extreme 'military spirit' inculcated into soldiers and the way they were systematically brutalized: the reason that many Japanese, although not opposed to the war itself, nevertheless dreaded being called up.[156]

The basis of the system was absolute obedience, so that an order to use prisoners for bayonet practice for example was issued as if it came from the Emperor himself.[157] The practical purpose of the emphasis on 'spirit', which in connection with the racialist ideology and the warlike traditions of the past had a mystical ring at an emotional level, was to make up for any material deficiencies.[158] Taken together, the fascistic creed and the brutal system enslaved the Japanese themselves and those unfortunate enough to be at their mercy.

One of the most tragic examples was that of the Japanese civilian population of Okinawa, Saipan and other Pacific Islands, who either killed their own children and themselves because of what official misinformation had told them about the advancing American forces, or who wanted to give themselves up but were stopped by the Japanese army. Entitled 'Suicide island', a documentary about such mass suicides in 1944 was shown on British channel 4 television in the 'Secret History' series on 21 August 1977, while accounts have also appeared in the Japanese press. To this day, many Okinawans feel that they were sacrificed by the militarist regime in Tokyo,[159] and indeed that post-war governments in Tokyo have used them as the main sites of the big American bases, well away from the main islands, creating continued resentments of Tokyo.

What happened in the past does not necessarily mean that history will repeat itself but 'Westerners' especially, rather than Asians, should recognize the high degree of continuity between the nationalistic creed of the past and that of the present day, as expressed in the manipulation of myth and history by the Ministry of Education, the public views of leading LDP politicians and events such as the intimidation and attempted assassination of the mayor of Nagasaki. Hideaki Kase, the son of a former ambassador to Washington, in other words an educated man with international experience, and currently a well known commentator, wrote as recently as 1989 on the occasion of Emperor Akihito's accession: 'Japan's national character (*sic*) was formed before history was recorded. . . . When Japan was born, the Emperor was already a high priest and head of state. The Imperial family cannot be separated from Japanese mythology. The myths are identical to the birth of Japan. The Emperor is sacred because of his blood ties with the gods that created our nation.'[160] It shows the deep roots of this ideology in Japan: something that cannot just be turned off like a tap, least of all when it is being actively promoted.

The former German president, Richard von Weizsaecker, warned an audience at the National Education Centre in Tokyo in 1995 that a country that denies its own war past risks the dangers of repeating its crimes, being seen as unpredictable and as a threat by its neighbours. Specifically warning against insincere apologies, he remarked that, 'If they are not truly meant, it's better to refrain from them.'[161] In 1995 the British lawyer representing ex-prisoners' and internees' organizations from the UK, USA, Australia and New Zealand suing the Japanese government in Tokyo observed that Germany had paid a hundred times more in individual compensation than Japan.[162]

Shortly after the German president's warning, the then coalition prime minister, Tomiichi Murayama, an old Socialist in an extraordinary coalition with the LDP, had expressed his regret for 'Japan's colonial rule and aggression.'[163] But he did not have the vote of the government behind him and certainly not that of his unregenerate coalition partners. Among others, the *Sydney Morning Herald* had to conclude with regret that his expression was just 'a personal statement by a minor political figure outside the mainstream of Japanese political life':[164] he was in office as a stopgap between June 1994 and January 1996, when the nationalistic Ryutaro Hashimoto returned with the LDP. Similarly, the British press was outraged when the regret over the treatment of POWs that Murayama had expressed in a letter to the British prime minister, John Major,[165] was retracted under nationalist pressures.[166]

The former German president had gone on to refer delicately to Japan's 'internal battles about its interpretation' of recent history, mentioning that all Asian countries occupied by Japan during the war had a common view. 'This is a fact, not just with a historical but with a highly contemporary significance.' Germany would have been isolated internationally and 'internally at odds with itself' if it had not come to terms with the dark past of the Nazi period.

By comparison, it seems almost superfluous to point to the re-emergence after the Occupation of individuals and organizations most closely connected with the war, such as Nobusuke Kishi, wartime cabinet member responsible for forced labour and then prime minister in the 'new' Japan; Ryoichi Sasakawa, like Kishi another class A war crimes suspect, and then a post-war millionaire, allegedly out of profiteering from the war in Manchuria as well as post-war gambling on motorboat racing, and influential figure in ultra-nationalist circles, Masanobu Tsuji, closely involved in well known crimes, such as the massacres of Chinese in Singapore and of the wounded, doctors and nurses at the Queen Alexandra Hospital there, associate of the well known gangster and ultra-nationalist Yoshio Kodama[167] from 1940 onwards, and then Diet member in the 'new' Japan:[168] not forgetting all the LDP ministers and politicians who have kept on making faux pas about Japanese aggression, leading to protests abroad and very often their own resignation or retraction at home, and the noisy ultra-nationalist groups, who are obviously well funded and allowed the freedom of the streets.

The continuity from past to present was conspicuous in a case like that of Sasakawa's, who in 1931 founded his own ultra-nationalist group, the Patriotic Masses Party, *Kokusui Taishuto*, and flew to Rome to visit Mussolini, whom he greatly admired. After three years imprisonment in Sugamo Prison during the Occupation, he made a new fortune with official encouragement in motorboat racing: a fund partly at the disposal of the Ministry of Transport, showing his close connections with the interests of the bureaucracy. He then set up the Sasakawa Peace Foundation – something that might be described today as 'rebranding', as well as the Great Britain Sasakawa Foundation, and donated money to the World Health Organization to fight smallpox, for which he won the UN Peace Prize.

With an eye on a Nobel Prize, he cultivated politicians and made donations from his ample wealth to other causes, while simultaneously being accused of involvement with the *yakuza*, the gang members of organized crime syndicates. The Yomiuri newspaper, a leading journal, described him as a 'monster of modern times'. Seeing him on television in Japan, before his death in July 1995, receiving the salutes of his uniformed private army and listening to him explaining his philosophy, showed how little things had changed. When he was decorated by the wartime Emperor for his philanthropic work after the war, another recipient of the same order returned his decoration in disgust.[169] Like the wartime Emperor,

Sasakawa continued to be controversial even in death, when an argument broke out in the municipal assembly of the town of Minoo over whether public funds should be used for a memorial service. Those objecting to such a use of public money were defeated.[170]

Sasakawa's flamboyant profile made him known internationally, at least for those aspects of his career that it suited him to be known, but some of the most important connections showing the continuity between the overtly ultra-nationalist period and the present remain unknown to most people outside Japan.

One is the shrine at the Koa Temple near Atami to General Matsui, executed as a war criminal, whose troops were responsible for the Nanking massacre. In fact, he was in hospital at the time; leaving Prince Yasuhiko Asaka, an uncle of the Empress, in command. Said to have been personally shocked, he nevertheless took no action, like other commanders, and at his trial made no attempt to put the blame on a relative of the Imperial household.

Photos at Matsui's shrine showed one of Japan's most famous politicians, Shigeru Yoshida, prime minister from May1946 to May 1947 and from October 1948 to December 1954, paying his respects. In 1936 the army had blocked Yoshida's promotion to the cabinet on the grounds that he was too liberal[171] and he had been arrested by the *Kempeitai* in 1945 for advocating an end to the war.[172] This had commended him to the Americans but what the German journalist Günter Ederer saw and heard at the Koa Temple, including Yoshida's calligraphy on Matsui's memorial, made him doubt whether Yoshida had changed his ideas much since his days in Manchuria, or rather the puppet state of Manchukuo.

Near Hazu, not far from the industrial city of Nagoya, Ederer visited the 'memorial of the seven samurai' at Sangane-san, on a peak facing the Shinto shrine at Ise, which has a special connection as the holiest of holies to do with the Emperor system and where the incumbent must report major events to his ancestors. On the way, Ederer passed several other war memorials but the 'seven samurai' are the seven major war criminals, including General Tojo, executed as a result of the war crimes trials.

An inscription on one of the large granite slabs, by a prominent nationalist lawyer, Shohei Samonji, states how he had managed to steal the ashes of Tojo and the other war criminals with the help of crematorium staff so that they could be enshrined at the memorial. For Ederer, one of the most scandalous things was a granite pillar with the calligraphy of the post-war prime minister, Nobusuke Kishi, paid for by himself. Visitors to the memorial included groups of war veterans, members of ultra-nationalist organizations and organized crime syndicates, with whom they to some extent overlap: both priding themselves on their nationalistic fervour. Other memorials evidently in process of expansion were of a warlike nature, far removed from the officially peaceful image of the 'new' Japan. Ederer's book contains photos both of the 'memorial of the seven samurai', including the calligraphy of Prime Minister Kishi for instance, and of General Matsui's shrine at the Koa Temple.[173]

In contrast to these two memorials, which few foreign visitors have tracked down, Yasukuni Shrine in the centre of Tokyo is extremely public, even if some do not realize what its grounds contain and what its continuing resonances from the past are, which continue to make it a focus of controversy. The first is the enshrinement of Tojo and the other executed war criminals along with the ordinary war dead, which makes Yasukuni rather different from the Tomb of the Unknown Soldier for instance, contrary to what some apologists have tried to make out.[174]

Then there is the presence of the first locomotive to run on the Burma-Thailand 'Death Railway', which Tojo had ordered must be finished in sixteen months instead of the estimated five years needed: now a gathering place for Japanese railway regiment veterans and those who see it as a great engineering achievement. This has been commented on by prisoners who survived the railway[175] and by a journalist in *The Spectator*.[176] One veteran said he found the 'same Japanese racist superiority as fifty years ago and the blithe ignorance of the younger generation' deeply upsetting. In 1997 the London *Sunday Times* reported that British survivors of the railway were being obliged to plan a new museum and memorial because Japanese investors were planning to turn the site into a theme park around this 'triumph of construction'.[177] A wartime Japanese interpreter on the railway who protested to the Yasukuni Shrine authorities about the crass act of placing the 'Death Railway' locomotive in the Shrine grounds was ignored.

Compare this with the complaint by the Japanese government to the US in 1995 that one of the stamps in the set commemorating the end of the Second World War was to show the mushroom cloud over Hiroshima, which would 'hurt the sensibilities of its people'. In a stinging newspaper rejoinder, a Chinese writer who had lived through the war commented, 'What impudence! What cynicism!', pointing out that 'the Japanese have concealed the historical truth from their children by censoring textbooks and rewriting history'.[178] The US, now a large debtor to Japan, withdrew the stamp, while the Japanese government put pressure on Australia and New Zealand, also major trading partners, not to use the accepted term VJ Day for the end of the war in 1945 but to replace it by VP(acific) Day instead.[179]

As regimes like that of the old USSR knew, history can also be manipulated by physically destroying the evidence, as the Japanese at Pingfan etc. tried to do. Sugamo Prison, a prominent Tokyo landmark, where the war criminals had been incarcerated, was razed to the ground in 1971. In its place appeared 'Sunshine City', now a well known exhibition hall, which foreign visitors or even young Japanese would be most unlikely to associate with what was there before. The only reference to the past is a small stone slab with a message expressing the hope that 'the tragedies of war will not be repeated' which, as many have pointed out seems to imply that the war was something like a natural disaster such as an earthquake rather than something resulting from any deliberate action. On the reverse are the words 'praying for eternal peace'. In 1993 the *Japan Times* reported that a monument to the execution of war criminals in Tokyo's Toshima Ward could stay, in spite of an appeal to the Tokyo High Court on the grounds that the memorial 'honoured class A war criminals and violated the war-renouncing Constitution': so much for the official view.[180]

Yasukuni Shrine has weapons within its 'sacred ground' and even a memorial to the *Kempeitai*, the Japanese Gestapo. Imagine such a thing in Europe! By the 1980s *Kempeitai* veterans were congratulating themselves that they were among the most active ex-service organizations, while even Unit 731 had its association, called the *Seikonkai*, or 'Refined Spirit Association': a misuse of words that is almost beyond belief.[181]

Being so closely involved with the old Imperial Army and Navy and State Shinto, the national cult of the Emperor up to 1945, how governments behave in relation to Yasukuni Shrine sends out a symbolic message that is watched at home and abroad. Post-war governments kept a low profile until 1983 when the prime minister, Yasuhiro Nakasone, himself a wartime naval officer, visited the shrine at its spring festival and signed the register with his official title, though he refused to say whether his visit was official or not. The following year the government set up a committee to study the Yasukuni issue but it was unable to agree among its members.

The government then decided to go ahead anyway and in 1985 the Nakasone cabinet made an official visit to the Shrine on 15 August, the anniversary of the war's end: '. . . in other words, the government expressed the desire to reinstate the pre-war symbolic unification of religion and state',[182] but it was shocked by the strength of international condemnation, showing how out of touch it was, or perhaps how little it cared.

The Japanese Constitution prohibits the state from engaging in religious activities and from supporting religious institutions but the controversy continues. In 1994 the coalition prime minister, Tomiichi Murayama, called on cabinet members only to visit Yasukuni in a private capacity, which they said they would. The next year eleven out of twenty-one ministers abstained.[183] The London *Economist* at the time criticized '. . . the mistakes of America's post-1945 Occupation of Japan', which had 'failed to sweep away the leaders and symbols of the wartime government and to install new ones in their place'.[184]

At the same time, the Education Minister, Yoshinobu Shimamura, questioned the need for Japan to apologize for its wartime policies, which he was forced to retract, but reiterated that the Japanese (sic) were the most able people in the world: 'the nation's miraculous development in the post-war era has proved it'.[185] His remarks reflected those of another Education Minister, Seigo Okano, in the Diet in 1953, who stated that, 'I do not want to pass judgment on the rightness or wrongness of the Greater East Asian War (sic), but the fact that Japan took on so many opponents and fought them for over four years ... proves our superiority.'[186] Prime Minister Nakasone, again, provoked outrage with his remarks on the American mixture of races, while a senior Japanese official, quoted in 1982 by the *Wall Street Journal*, asserted that, 'The Japanese are a people that can manufacture a product of uniformity and superior quality because the Japanese are a race of completely pure blood, not a mongrelized race as in the US.'[187]

Similar remarks, expressed in terms of the alleged 'homogeneity' of the Japanese rather than in such overtly racialist language, were used by speakers at the EU-Japan Centre in Tokyo to explain innate Japanese advantages in group 'harmony' and quality control that fed into industrial performance.

What is significant about the frequency with which leading politicians and others who represent the official point of view make these remarks is their blithe assumption that they are self-evidently true. Though, as Professor Reischauer noted, Japan may appear to be an international country on the surface the bedrock of the 'master race' creed, disconcertingly reminiscent of the Nazi *Herrenvolk* idea, continues to give so much emotional satisfaction to so many. As a friend who worked as a manager in a Japanese company in Britain put it, one of the things that impressed him most about Japanese he came into contact with was how much they believed the official propaganda, but then it is flattering to believe that one 'is not as other men are', especially when this is actively encouraged by what George Orwell rightly called 'groupthink'. Rationalists might hate to admit it, but myth can give not only emotional satisfaction: it can also act as a powerful motivator with its own logic. That is what was meant earlier by 'value rationality'.

It was reported in 1995 that there had been some loosening of the Ministry of Education's censorship guidelines for history textbooks, though as before, the Ministry retains control and local education boards can only select books from among those passed by the Ministry's central control. On the other hand, the guidelines stressed respect for the national anthem and the national flag, observance of which at schools had created considerable disaffection. One publisher who proposed stating that '... the Japanese national flag has been taken by people of other Asian countries as a symbol of wartime aggression' and that it should be replaced, similar to what was done in Germany, was told to delete the passage. The estimated figure of twenty million Asian dead in the war was retained:[188] a figure that might be compared with that in Europe, which seems to attract more attention in the 'West' than what was Japan's responsibility. In 1998, for instance, the BBC repeated its television series on *The Nazis: a Warning from History*, while largely ignoring anything to do with Asia. It is not the way that people in Asia themselves see it of course.

According to a report published in 1997, textbooks are now allowed 'frank coverage' of subjects such as Unit 731, the Nanking massacre, up to a total of 160,000 victims, the 'comfort women' etc but many students will still not learn this part of modern Japanese history because it is not part of their university entrance exam curriculum. In fact, much of the harm has already been done, as the London *Spectator* noted in its review in 1992 of a television programme in which a Japanese government spokesman was interviewed, which showed 'the shocking level of ignorance among young Japanese about their nation's recent past, and the organized mendacity of the Japanese authorities in creating that vacuum'.[189] Japan's official war history, the *Senshi Sosho*, for example, a work in over a hundred volumes, does not mention prisoners of war at all.[190] What lessons can the young, especially those born years after the war, draw from the war if they are kept in virtual ignorance?

At a popular level there has been a spate of trashy revisionist novels, some of which show Japan winning the last war and colonizing America, and a surge in ultra-nationalist karaoke songs, some of which have surfaced in Hong Kong and other places in Japan's former wartime empire.[191] A major film company, Toei, has produced a film with the help of Tojo's granddaughter presenting him in a revisionist light. This led to protests by the Federation of Cinema and Theatrical Workers Unions that the film's 'depiction of Tojo as a person who protected the pride of the Japanese is a distortion of historical fact'.[192] In 1996 historians and pacificists opposed the revival of 'Marine Day', a wartime national holiday commemorating the navy. Indeed, seven of Japan's existing 'national' i.e. public, holidays have their roots in the nationalistic past,[193] with the revived National Foundation Day – the old *Kigensetsu* – being the most controversial.

There is no need to be surprised by these openly revisionist revivals and the political and ideological continuity that they represent. One of Japan's wartime foreign ministers, Mamoru Shigemitsu, for instance, was sentenced to seven years imprisonment in 1945 as a class A war criminal. By 1950 he was out of prison and by 1954 foreign minister again, and by 1956 negotiating with the Americans for the release of the war criminals still in Sugamo Prison.[194]

What is more surprising are the inhibitions that many people outside Asia seem to suffer from in speaking about the unreconstructed nationalists who either remained or got back into power in Japan after the Second World War. Others in Asian countries near

Japan and that experienced Japanese rule at first hand are more realistic in talking about things that others outside the region either do not know about or would prefer to forget. Lee Kuan Yew, the father of modern Singapore, for instance, had no hesitation in saying that whereas, 'There has been a catharsis in Germany. They've got rid of their sense of guilt, no longer trying to hide their past', in Japan it was, 'still very much a closet problem. There has been no catharsis'. Japanese peace-keeping forces were 'like giving liqueur chocolates to an alcoholic. Whatever they do, they go to the limits'.[195] Asian nations could never trust Japan as long as it could not acknowledge its mistakes.[196] Examples already mentioned of Japanese tendencies to 'go to the limits' in perverted forms of 'spiritual purity', that served as replacements for the wartime ethos, were the crimes of the Japanese 'Red Army' and Aum Shinrikyo, with its poison gas attacks.

These remarks were echoed in 1995 by a Filipino historian, Renato Constantino, with long Japanese experience who stated that, 'Japan refuses to confront the past . . . the old way of thinking lingers in the government', noting the large military budget and the aim of a UN Security Council seat, 'but you cannot cheat history. The truth will always come out', as in the 'comfort women' case.[197]

The Korean newspaper *Dong-A Ilbo*, commenting on the Nagano affair in 1994, one of many faux pas by a leading Japanese politician, asked, 'Why do such problems recur so often? We cannot but reason that it is because such perversion of historical facts reflects the subconscious attitude of the Japanese . . . the Nagano remarks have again revealed the deep-seated real thinking of the Japanese.'[198]

Comparing the attempted assassination of Prime Minister Hosokawa, one of the younger and more liberal LDP politicians in office for all of eight months in 1993–94 to whom some Japanese had looked for reform, by a nationalist opposed to any hint of a war apology, to the assassinations carried out by extremists in the 1930s, the Chinese Alliance for Memorial and Justice in the USA remarked that Japanese 'officials even try to distort and erase history'. The Alliance pointed out that Japan, which had walked out of the League of Nations when it had been condemned by the League for its seizure of Manchuria, now wanted a seat on its successor's Security Council.[199]

Speaking for Americans of Chinese ancestry, Dr Joseph Wong, noted the official visit of Prime Minister Hashimoto and cabinet members to the Yasukuni Shrine on 15 August 1996 and commented, 'Imagine if Chancellor Kohl of Germany publicly denied the Holocaust, then went to a Nazi shrine and paid tribute to Hitler and Goebbels.' In such circumstances, he described the Japanese government's aim of occupying a seat on the UN Security Council as grotesque and one that should be rejected.[200]

And what about Japanese people themselves? It is not difficult to discover that many are extremely frightened at any prospect of militarism, though since a frank admission of the past would be too much of a loss of face many prefer to sweep it under the carpet, or in some cases to shift the blame for their anxieties on to a convenient foreign scapegoat: the USA.

What they are often not facing up to is exactly what Lee Kuan Yew referred to; and who better than Jiro Hagi, the deputy director of the Japanese Defence Agency himself to put it into words, speaking as an insider: 'The Japanese people do not trust the Self-Defence Forces because they cannot trust themselves as Japanese. This is why they need the Constitution to block security efforts . . . we swing from one extreme (sic) to another. . . . When our energies are channelled in the right direction, this is fine, but when they are misused, terrible things happen. I also happen to think the Japanese . . . are racists.'[201] These remarks should be taken to heart by those pressing Japan to rearm even more than at present.

Following the remark about 'energies channelled in the right direction', it is not hard to see why Japan's post-war economic drive has led to Japanese society being compared to a society at war or why, to paraphrase Clausewitz, commerce and industry are the continuation of war by other means; though this is of course preferable to a shooting war.

This chapter began by asking, among other things, whether Japan has a democratic tradition. After the authoritarian regimes of the Tokugawa Shoguns lasting over two-and-a-half centuries and extending right up to the modern period in 1868, the oligarchy of the Meiji Period, and the militarists of the 1930s and 1940s, the answer should be obvious.

During hearings before the US Senate in 1951, General MacArthur expressed his view that the Japanese would be more receptive to democracy than the 'mature' Germans because the Japanese 'in spite of their antiquity measured by time, were in a very tuitionary condition . . . susceptible to following new models, new ideas. You can implant basic concepts there. They were still close enough to origin to be elastic and acceptable (sic) to new concepts'.[202] This view – paternalistic or naïve, depending on one's standpoint – implied that a sea change was being wrought by the Occupation, led of course by MacArthur. In defeat, there were many Japanese anxious to escape from the 'dark valley' of the militarist period but did MacArthur, who had wanted to leave Japan as early as 1948 in the hope of standing as a presidential candidate,[203] really believe it was realistic to expect changes of the magnitude he implied in his remarks to the Senate?

Given the way that the history of the recent past has been used, or rather misused, in Japan, the type of political system that it serves, and the images that so many Japanese have of themselves and others, what sort of business and economic system would be the outcome? It is the task of what follows to go into this further and ultimately to put forward possible scenarios of where it is all leading.

# ■ CHAPTER 4
# Power Holders – The Iron Triangle

(1) THE BUREAUCRATS: POLICY-MAKERS AND REGULATORS
*Will the Japanese ever be democratic? – European businessman.*

The Iron Triangle, known also to some as the Devil's Triangle, is a powerfully evocative image of the grip that the three controlling élites, namely the bureaucracy, big business and political bosses, have on Japan. These 'three biggest sources of power' and the collusive relations between them make up a system that differs from that prescribed by the Constitution i.e. 'a democratic state, ruled by a popularly elected representative government'. Conspicuous features are 'the dictatorship of the bureaucracy' and 'the ever-present influence of organized crime', which, coupled with domestic standards of living that do not reflect Japan's huge economic advances, make these achievements less attractive in the eyes of some Japanese.[1]

This does not mean that the three groupings always see eye to eye. In other words, they are not a monolith. Business may chafe under bureaucratic regulation, while appreciating that the bureaucracy protects them from intrusion into their cartels, especially by foreigners. Bureaucrats do not like politicians interfering in their decisions and helped to bring about the downfall of one of the most notorious LDP fixers, Shin Kanemaru, ostensibly no more than an ex-vice president of the party at the time but known popularly as 'the Don' for his skills in behind the scenes manipulation. On the other hand, politicians have been seeking to capitalize on the MOF's serious loss of popularity due to the financial crisis by getting their hands on the MOF's power: something that is easier said than done without inside knowledge and leverage.[2]

At a unifying level, there is general agreement about the direction in which Japan's politico-economic system should be aimed and how it should be run and it is within this famous 'consensus' that the three élites exist in a close symbiosis. The membership of the three élites and the vertical order running from those who have worked their way up to the top and control the levers of power down to those who aspire to get power in the future are clearly identifiable:[3] as are policies to promote the national economy, such as MITI's advocacy against Bank of Japan scepticism to protect and nurture the all-important motor industry, or the famous 'income-doubling' policy of the 1960s. For anyone interested in political theories of how different states are governed, Japan is a textbook example of rule by élites.[4]

For the bureaucrats the authority to issue or withhold licences is a major source of power. At the top of the table is the Ministry of Transport; '... with complete authority over land, marine and air transport ... and shipping charges', controlling entry to these industries. Despite all the talk about deregulation, it had authority over 2,017 types of licences in 1985, 1,966 in 1991 and still approximately the same number in 1994: not much change in nine years.

In fact, between 1985 and 1991 most ministries had actually increased the number of types of licences under their control. In that year MITI had 1,916 licences, MOF 1,210, the Ministry of Agriculture Fisheries and Food (MAFF) 1,315, the Ministry of Health and Welfare (MHW) 1,106, down to the Ministry of Education with 312. On top of these bare statistics, it must be remembered that a favourable response to an application for a licence depends on good relations with the bureaucrats, not just an objectively enforceable standard, since in many cases the way the regulations are drafted, by the bureaucrats themselves of course, allows them the maximum freedom of interpretation and delay, during which they may require considerable 'wining and dining'.[5]

Under the guise of protecting the public (from what?), preventing 'disorder in the market' or 'disorderly marketing' and guiding the economy in the public interest, the bureaucrats act to preserve cozy cartels in business, which the established companies and their managers certainly appreciate. In banking, for instance, officials who have no actual experience as bankers and who do not take responsibility for mistakes or failures are empowered to decide how many branches a bank may have and whether it should be allowed to open a new one.[6] In the road haulage and delivery business, bureaucrats decide how many vehicles a business has to have before it can obtain a licence and what rates it is allowed to charge: a barrier to entry in favour of the established firms. 'They made ten trucks the minimum because they didn't want to sanction lone wolves with one truck', complained the former president of one of Japan's best known express delivery companies. The regulations were supposed to have been liberalized in 1990 but operators could find little difference before and after that was not *tatemae*. Foreigners especially need to be very careful not to believe mere changes in words: they should only believe things when deeds follow and are maintained – not just as temporary sops that look good in public but which revert to type after a suitable interval.

In 1994 the Electricity Utility Industry Council proposed that the

1,000 permits needed to open an electric power station and the 2,700 reports to be provided to the government should be reduced to 1,700 and 40 respectively and that pre-start up checks should be reduced from about 3,800 to 1,000. The Council also proposed that home solar battery systems should be treated in the same way as televisions or other domestic appliances, with the manufacturers responsible for their safety; instead of being treated as electric power plants requiring licences similar to those just mentioned.[7]

Also in 1994 the regulations governing breweries were relaxed. Previously the minimum annual production quota under the Liquor Tax Law was 2,000 kilolitres but this was reduced to a mere 60 kilolitres, removing at least one entry barrier to small and foreign firms.[8]

The fine detail applied to the interpretation of regulations is often commented on. It took the Body Shop for example one-and-a-half years to get permission from the Ministry of Health and Welfare to market its banana shampoo in Japan, leading its local Japanese manager to remark that, 'Japan is one of the most restrictive countries that Body Shop operates in'.[9] Jacob's well-known biscuits, Custard Creams, underwent a very slight modification of ingredients in 1994 and were immediately banned. The modified ingredient was not on the official list.[10] I obtained several boxes from the British Embassy for the European managers at the EU-Japan Centre to enjoy during breaks and to learn about the all-pervasive regulatory system.

The control by the Ministry of Education over the content of textbooks and the curriculum, particularly 'ethics', has been referred to before and this control naturally extends to administrative matters. A municipal university, for instance, wanted to create a new section for business studies, requiring it to produce for the Ministry in Tokyo a full list of the staff to be appointed and what subjects they were qualified to teach. It also required the unfortunate dean of the faculty to make frequent visits to Tokyo with a colleague. Each time he would be told that what he had produced so far might be in order but that he would now have to produce something new that he had not previously been told about: a way of demonstrating the deference due to the Ministry, not to mention dragging things out.[11]

The possibilities for corruption in the system are obvious and the case of the road haulage licencing system led to yet another major scandal. This was the Sagawa Kyubin, or express delivery, case in 1992 in which the company had paid bribes to a large number of leading politicians to lobby for its interests. The background was the complex licencing system of the MOT whose Road Transport Law meant that operators were divided into territorial and route firms. To try and put it as simply as possible, Sagawa had established a nationwide group of companies with territorial licences but, under the Law, it was illegal to take partial loads at specified times on specified routes outside one's own territory because that would resemble route operation. When

Sagawa did this it was therefore breaking the law and, in addition, breaking the Labour Standards Law by making its drivers work excessively long hours. The theory was to balance supply and demand and to protect (whom?) against 'excessive competition'. A joke at the time was that Sagawa Kyubin's vehicles were busy delivering money to politicians. Even after the anti-competitive law had been changed, *Tokyo Business Today*, formerly *The Oriental Economist*, concluded that 'nothing has changed'.[12] Meanwhile, Yamato Kyubin had taken fifteen years to be licenced as a national carrier, while in the first two years after the change in the law, applications to start new road haulage businesses were down by 37 per cent, which hardly seemed like evidence of a real easing.

Millions of Japanese own cars and the system for their regulation is a good example of how the relationships between the three élites work. First, a person wanting to own a new car must provide evidence that there is an off-road parking space for it. Then there is a thorough official inspection after three years and every two years after that. Until the law was revised in July 1995, there was also a 'pre-inspection test' covering 102 items, although this was not part of the law but of 'administrative guidance', *gyosei shido*, from the ministry.

These two tests cost, needless to say, a considerable sum of money, with the 'pre-inspection test' being done at a normal garage that relied on selling and fitting parts for its income. In theory, the owner could then take the car him- or herself – or herself to the official inspection centre but it was said that the official inspectors were more lenient with cars driven in by someone working at the garage so that, according to *Tokyo Business Today*, there was the possibility of corruption.

Indeed, in 1982 when reform of the system was mooted, many of Japan's 80,000 garages, 60 per cent of which had fewer than five employees, lobbied the LDP's 'transport tribe', *zoku*, to prevent change to a system that suited them very nicely. There is evidence that the new law passed in 1995 has led to a reduction in motorists' costs, although an article written in 1997 says that it may take 'another five years before the results are clear'.

In addition to the official inspections, there are 12-month and 24-month inspections at the garage – it used to be six months – and the expense and trouble mean that many motorists trade in their cars before they get what would be considered old in many other countries. No one who has been to Japan can fail to notice the high proportion of new cars on the road, which by law are required to be washed daily, and this indirect method of forcing new models on to the market naturally suits the manufacturers. Meanwhile, many of the cars that have been traded in and are still in good condition because of the maintenance and inspection system can be shipped abroad. They go to markets as different as the Russian Far East via the port of Nakhodkha, New Zealand and increasingly Ireland, penetrating markets where second-hand cars are welcome and creating new demands for spares: again to the benefit of the manufacturers.

Because the Ministry of Transport has such tight regulation over vehicle ownership and running, its bureaucrats can 'parachute' into firms that they previously regulated, where they can use their personal connections with former colleagues and protégés in their comfortable retirement jobs. It is a cozy, some would say incestuous, system closed to outsiders where the enforcement of vaguely drafted laws gives the bureaucrats the maximum opportunity to reward compliance and to punish uncooperative behaviour.

Companies that make and repair cars give money to politicians to lobby for their interests, particularly to the LDP, the 'natural party of government' virtually without a break since 1945, and its 'transport tribe'. Obviously, the party that has the greatest and most influential network of supporters in government and industry has the greatest amount of patronage to deliver.

The whole system works on the basis of personal relations, lubricated by the large amounts of entertainment allowed under Japan's more-than-generous tax laws and gifts or favours of one sort or another that in different societies would be called bribes. It is the contrast between a system based on personal relationships and one based on impersonal contracts and unambiguous laws or, as Max Weber put it, a legal-rational order. It is not hidden from long-serving foreign businessmen in Japan but may be hidden by *tatemae* from other outsiders.

By those working the system and some apologists it may be explained in terms of warm human feelings, as against the alleged coldness or as the Japanese would say 'dryness' of Anglo-Saxon or Continental law, but it is all too obvious what the material gains of the different parties under the Japanese system are. As a commentator in the *Financial Times* put it, 'everyone except the consumer gets something out of it',[13] suggesting like many others that business in Japan exists for the producer rather than the consumer; in spite of the propaganda about the 'customer as king'.

This being so, some might expect Japanese consumers to revolt but although the crisis of the 1990s has made them look more carefully at prices than many already were, there is little sign of this happening. Many Japanese may grumble about the expense and inconvenience of the inspection system involved in running a car and are not unaware that it is part of a closed system for recycling money and power in a never-ending circle but to imagine that they are on the point of adopting free market economics and a different political system to go with it is a complete fallacy. The firm grip of the Iron Triangle and to an extent the bureaucracy's self-serving line that they are protecting the population from 'excessive competition', in the form of 'hire and fire' policies, unknown and perhaps unsafe foreign products etc.

provides psychological security. Inertia and anxiety about stepping outside the familiar bounds, as in the old phrase about 'clinging to nurse for fear of something worse', and the resignation implied in the common phrase *shikata ga nai*, 'it can't be helped', express popular perceptions that 'the system' is impregnable.

Who in this group-organized society with its tight web of interpersonal relations and its ruthless use of power, in for instance the security of a person's job and ability to earn a living, wants to be classified by others as a deviant and to risk being 'the nail that sticks up that is hammered down', in the frequently quoted phrase? In a society where children are taught to be like everyone else 'otherwise they will laugh at you' and where there is a strong social but not transcendental ethic, what internal moral support is there for leaving the security of the group? Japanese children are taught that individualism is nothing more than selfishness and has no positive qualities and those in more open societies who take individualism for granted should beware of projecting their own ways of thinking on to others.

Japan's militarist and wartime period provided plentiful evidence of the sadism that burst out in the treatment by Japanese superiors of their own subordinates, not to mention their foreign victims, and the other side of the coin, masochism, in the form of self-abasement, shows of humility and allowing oneself to be humiliated, remains conspicuous. Indeed, a former bureaucrat and qualified doctor sees masochism, often characterized as self-sacrifice, as a defining mark of Japanese society in general and the bureaucracy in particular; where 'newcomers earn recognition as fully-fledged members of Japan Inc.' not by real ability but by 'showing off the limits of the masochism of which they are capable', by, for instance, staying up overnight to draft legislation and working unreasonably long hours.[14] Kind-hearted but naïve people who believe that regimes that treat their people decently necessarily inspire the greatest loyalty only need to look at the regimes of wartime Japan, Hitler, Stalin etc, for whom so many were prepared to go through the fire, to see that this is another liberal illusion.

In fact, this is not the right question in Japan. At least until the crisis of the 1990s, the existing system has brought economic success to Japan on a scale that very few Japanese could have imagined in 1945 and even many of those who dislike the bureaucracy or the LDP admit that the guidance of the economy has been infinitely superior to the alternatives on offer, such as the then Japan Socialist Party and its unreconstructed Marxist theorists. In Japan, success is the measure of what is right and as a Japanese philosopher wrote three hundred years ago 'those who have won are invariably right and those who have been defeated are wrong': a maxim originally applied to war and now to business.[15] In other words, might is right. The power and success of the Iron Triangle are its justification and wise Japanese and those who want to survive know that they should not offend it.

1945 is a long time ago but to get an idea of the immense distance that Japan has travelled in terms of economic progress since then, it is worth remembering what one of America's leading Japan experts thought at the time. He was afraid that no matter what policies were adopted, Japan faced 'slow economic starvation'.[16] Indeed, a strong work ethic and the idea that Japan, with its large population and shortage of natural resources, is a basically poor country in an economically insecure position, is one that the authorities are keen to promote through the educational system.[17] It is designed to motivate this restless competitor towards further achievement. This does not help foreign relations, in the recurrent trade disputes for example, and at its worst encourages paranoia about the outside world.

To join ministries like MITI or MOF that have such an influence on directing the Japanese economy attracts many top university graduates and, as everyone in Japan knows, the royal road to the top in these key economic ministries is to have graduated from the law department of Tokyo University, for short Todai. This might seem a paradox in a system that disparages law on 'cultural' – in reality more political – grounds and where the Ministry of Justice intentionally restricts entry to the Legal Training and Research Institute, through which all future judges, prosecutors and lawyers must pass, under the ministry's control.[18]

In fact, the course at Todai's law school covers not only public and administrative law in a manner closer to politics than would be understood by law in the Anglo-Saxon sense, but also economics. Unlike in the business world, where the final university grade hardly matters in comparison with a job applicant's 'attitude', only the law school's top graduates can enter the bureaucracy. Others can still enter first rank companies, because the strength of the *Todai gakubatsu*, the Todai clique, will give them contacts in the ministries that will be useful for oiling the wheels in business. The figures showing the numbers of Todai graduates in the bureaucracy and the high positions they eventually occupy speak for themselves.[19]

Parents, especially the mothers who push their children to pass the exam to get into a 'good' university,[20] are keenly aware of the ranking order of universities and Todai law graduates are the élite of the élite. Mothers, who have a greater influence on their children's education, normally because fathers are out all the time at work, know how much graduation from a particular university determines career chances and that belonging to a specific clique is something that persists throughout life. The alleged tendencies of Oxford, Cambridge or Ivy League graduates to stick together are pale by comparison with the continuing strength of the Japanese *gakubatsu*, or cliques of graduates of the same university. Both the Japanese general managers in my time at the EU-Japan Centre were proud of being Todai law school graduates and were steeped in the bureaucratic mentality, though neither had got to the top. Nor were they especially popular with the rest of the staff.

The extreme concern in Japan's social order with rank and hierarchy was already alluded to.[21] Ministries, companies, universities are ranked in a well known order and it goes without saying how important rank within the bureaucracy is. The *gakubatsu* cliques are strengthened by the vertical relations of *sempai*, the senior and in his early years the mentor of the junior, *kohai*.

Something of the flavour of these top-down, hierarchical relations can be gauged from the following anecdote. In 1976 the president of All Nippon Airways, and a former MOT bureaucrat, had to appear as a witness in front of the Diet in connection with the Lockheed scandal. Journalists reported that he was shaking with rage because the Diet member questioning him had been his own junior when he, too, had been an official in the MOT.[22]

Something similar can be observed in university departments, where younger assistant professors will attach themselves to a senior professor who graduated from the same university in a patron-client relationship as they try and climb up the promotion ladder. It is a characteristically Japanese group formation based on a leader and his followers, found both in academic and political factions in their respective ways, and one which represents a split in the 'harmony'. In the business world, the top management should guard against such factionalism.

Reference was previously made to the transition from the authoritarian regime of the Shoguns, described by one Japanese political scientist as a 'feudal police state', to the authoritarian regime of the Meiji oligarchy, described as a 'centralized bureaucratic state',[23] and to the top-down gift of the Prussian style Meiji Constitution. Between then and 1945 it was made very clear that officials, literally of the Emperor, *Tenno no kanri*, owed their appointments and loyalty to the Emperor and that, as under the earlier Tokugawa regime, they were above ordinary people. As originators and enforcers of laws they still inspire a mixture of fear, prestige and irritation and to compare them with civil servants in other political systems who are supposed to take orders from their elected political masters can only lead to misunderstandings.

Meiji oligarchs like Hirobumi Ito were impressed by Bismarck's Germany and by what they learned from constitutional scholars like Rudolph von Gneist and the training that candidates for the bureaucracy received at Todai – Tokyo Imperial University until 1945 – and the officially designated school for administrators was also Prussian in inspiration. Between 1890 and as recently as 1947 no fewer than 91 per cent of the laws passed by the Diet originated in the bureaucracy.[24] Another Japanese commentator expressed the view that the period from 1868 to 1945 had 'a highly feudal character'.[25]

The hierarchical university order, with Tokyo's law school at the top as the point of entry to the top ministries, remains unchanged as a national job recruitment and selection system.[26] A top MITI official responsible for the direction of economic policy in the Economic Planning Agency recently described the school system as one that 'eliminated all pleasure from school life and destroys student creativity and individuality'.[27] This remark helps to explain the protests a few years ago under the dramatic slogan 'Abolish Tokyo University!'

During the premiership of Yasuhiro Nakasone from 1982 to 1987 there was supposed to be a great debate on education to make it less mechanical and more satisfying to individuals, though the use of this term was itself ambiguous, but the system remains unchanged. None of the three élites of the Triangle would be in favour of a more humanistic approach and the results of the debate were more emphasis on what it means to be Japanese and more discipline in schools.

This discussion on what originally sounded a proposal for reform was similar to another perennially-aired topic: the decentralization of Tokyo and, for example, the establishment of half a dozen regional capitals to replace it. But the reason why Tokyo is so centralized and why the major corporations must have their head offices there is precisely in order to be close to the ministries; quite apart from what the ministries themselves may think about it. Already in the 1960s a company like today's Sumitomo Corporation, with the Sumitomo Group's long association with Osaka and western Japan, found it necessary to have a 'second head office' in Tokyo. Todai and Tokyo go marching on, whatever the *tatemae* may be.

Here it needs emphasizing how difficult it may be for people used to Anglo-Saxon systems of government to grasp how much power Japanese bureaucrats wield; though somewhat easier for those accustomed to the French system of the Ecole Nationale d'Administration and the relations between élite bureaucrats, the *énarques*, and the graduates of the Grandes Ecoles in the private sector. When the Japanese authorities are trying to convince foreign negotiating partners or opinion-formers that the Japanese economy is fundamentally open and free market, on the evidence of the competition between, for example, motor manufacturers, electronics companies, trading companies etc. in their respective sectors, they will naturally seek to downplay the intervention of the bureaucracy in the economy. This is most obviously the case when the interlocutor is a leading proponent of free markets like the US but, as the examples shown here of bureaucratic regulation demonstrate, the Japanese authorities are being disingenuous.

This is not because, as official speakers have sometimes claimed, the mere figures for the total number of officials is relatively limited or because direct control over nationalized industries does not exist on the same scale as it did in Britain, for example, between 1945 and the start of privatization policies 'to roll back the frontiers of the state' under the Thatcher government. In 1993 there were said to be 360,000 bureaucrats in Japan's twelve ministries and eight major agencies. All told, 3.7 per cent of the population had national or local official status, which was described as a 'fairly low rate' among comparable industrialized countries,[28] but numbers alone cannot give an idea of how much power bureaucrats have. Details already given of the powers of regulation over business and industry expressed, for instance, by the number of licences that ministries require, plus 'visions' for the economy and the 'administrative guidance' at the ministries' disposal are more revealing.

To outsiders, and this includes many Japanese themselves, the ministries' way of operating may appear labyrinthine, with a 'complex web of administrative regulations', that only insiders can understand and are qualified to determine how they should be implemented.[29] Officials must, therefore, be approached with care.

The creation of a bureaucratic mystique is an important part of impressing the population with the power of the bureaucracy but the reality of bureaucratic power rests on a few simple facts. First, there is its origin in the political order of the 'centralized bureaucratic state' and the failure of the Occupation to reform it. Second is the 'national economic strategy' along the lines of Friedrich List's recommendations that have already been discussed, and the role allocated to the economic ministries in particular in putting the strategy into effect: a strategy whose characteristic ways of thinking and acting, in, for example, regard to foreign investment in Japan, technological autonomy, imports etc, has persisted well past the period of 'catching up' with other industrial competitors. Apart from that, would any bureaucracy voluntarily surrender its power and job opportunities by acquiescing in wholesale deregulation?

Third, is the mechanism of extra-legal 'administrative guidance', *gyosei shido*, at the ministries' disposal, likewise backed up by an extra-legal and informal power to reward compliance and punish recalcitrance. This 'guidance' commonly has what in other societies would be called the force of law and is frequently unwritten. This means that it is not transparent, so that it is easy to deny to, for example, foreigners that it has been given, and since it is extra-legal it cannot be challenged in the courts.[30] It easily constitutes 'an offer you cannot refuse'.

Fourth, the ministries enjoy the self-reinforcing mechanism of 'parachuting', *amakudari*, into jobs in the private sector on retirement, possibly at quite an early age. There they continue to cement relations between their old ministry and private firms, leading some to suspect that informally given, unwritten administrative guidance may constitute 'unfair dealings' between the two; but perhaps such third parties should have been more compliant and respectful themselves. It must be remembered that this mechanism functions within the context of a society characterized by exclusive in-groups and an extremely hierarchical structure.[31]

Since Japan's 'economic miracle' or high annual economic growth rates became conspicuous in the 1960s and Japanese manufactured goods began to flood export markets, leading to constant trade surpluses, people outside Japan have been wondering what it is all for. Nor have the trade surpluses stopped because of the financial crisis of the 1990s: quite the contrary. The *Financial Times* in 1998 announced 'Japanese trade surplus up 45 per cent': an amazing figure by any standards and one which the paper correctly observed was 'politically contentious', to say the least. While imports into Japan had fallen 9.3 per cent over the year, the trade surplus against the US was up 41 per cent and against the EU a staggering 75 per cent[32] Were the Japanese authorities – some would say again – exporting their way out of a crisis, or exporting unemployment? Meanwhile, an economist at the American Enterprise Institute stated that the Japanese government had said that extensive deregulation of the domestic economy, which could produce new investment opportunities was 'not possible'.[33]

There should have been no mystery about what it was all for. MITI's 'Vision of Japan for the 1990s' gives the answer as achieving international bargaining power and technological autonomy through industrial leadership;[34] commerce and industry having currently replaced military force as the way to project power internationally. What is it, for example, that backs the campaign to get a seat at the UN's top table, the Security Council, if not economic and hence political power? There is no agitation for this among the Japanese population as a whole, which rather fears the risks of UN entanglements, but LDP politicians hope such a gain of prestige would reflect well on them.

'Technological autonomy' harks back to List's vision of protecting and nurturing domestic industries, as in the highly successful motor industry case for instance,[35] and the mercantilism of 'catching up'. In the long run, consumers cannot consume unless they produce, so the domestic industrial and technological base must be protected: a fundamentally different outlook from that in Anglo-Saxon economies where foreign products that are, for whatever reason, more cost effective are allowed in to the detriment of local manufacturers, on the principles of free trade and the theory of comparative advantage, the proclaimed goals being consumer choice and consumer interests. Neither Japan's history of 'catching up', nor post-war reconstruction after 1945, nor its present political and economic structure lead the Japanese authorities to believe in these Anglo-Saxon ideas or the philosophy of Adam Smith. Some see MITI's 'visions' and the policies that implement them as part of Japan's 'age-old drive to preserve its exclusivity': a politico-economic aim, whose reality can only be distorted by those who project their own free-market thinking on to it.

Since MITI's 'visions' do not have the force of law in the Anglo-Saxon sense, outsiders can easily be persuaded that they are 'visions' and nothing more. But that is disingenuous. Would MITI's Industrial Structure Council spend time and effort on producing 'visions' if they were simply daydreams?

The answer was given when an American proposal was put to MITI that Japanese executives – note, not foreigners! – working for foreign companies in Japan should be included in the deliberations of the Industrial Structure Council. It was decisively rejected, with a sharp reply from a senior MITI official that it would be like asking for Japanese members to be included in meetings of the US National Security Council; underlining the national strategic aim of Japanese economic thinking.[36]

Of course MITI's 'Vision for the 1990s' may include some features designed to appeal to foreign governments, such as 'reduced working hours', which is clearly concerned with ensuring a so-called 'level playing field' in international competition, though there may be a temporary effect from the recession and 'land use reform', another equally image-building topic but one that is likely to remain blocked by the vested interests whom real reform would harm. One commentator considers that paying lip service to such proposals is mainly designed to reassure the American government that Japan is 'changing' in the direction of free market economics, now that there is a danger of people deciding that Japan's 'unique' politico-economic system cannot be treated in a normal free market way and must be treated differently i.e. less indulgently.[37]

MITI knows that others will read its 'visions' and one reason for its concern about being treated differently was the prominent attention paid to an article published in 1992 by Akio Morita, the then chairman of Sony. This worried that because Japanese companies employ different managerial practices, on things like working hours and shareholders' dividends for instance, they had a cost structure that European and American companies could not better and would eventually get sick of this unequal competition. What was interesting was the reaction of one of MITI's best known international trade negotiators. While not disagreeing with Morita's description of Japanese capitalism and managerial practices, he strongly warned that it was not politic to draw international attention to them: 'We must not provide a dangerous basis for the argument that says that Japan conducts itself by a different set of rules and must be treated differently.' What could be more obvious about the contrasts between American capitalism and Japanese economic management as enumerated by Morita, himself a highly successful international businessman, with the experience of his company in both the US, the UK, Continental Europe and elsewhere to draw on?[38]

Beginning with the need to rebuild after the Second World War and the desirability of raising living standards above their low pre-war level, Japan's national effort since 1945 has, for a number of other reasons as well, gone into the economy. Consequently the economic ministries responsible for directing and facilitating this effort[39] gained power to the extent that some consider that 'the politicians reign, but the bureaucrats rule'.[40]

Under the post-war Constitution, the Diet is supposed to be the supreme law-making body and bureaucrats are not supposed to take part in the legislative process. There is supposed to be a separation of powers; but bureaucrats had a clause inserted in the Cabinet Act, allowing them to propose bills, and another in the Diet Act formally allowing them to join Diet committees when their own proposals are up for consideration.

The result is that the bureaucracy '. . . has re-emerged as the dominant force behind Japan's legislative process' and 'drafts the vast majority of laws'. A bureaucrat pointed out that most Diet members, even if they saw law-making as their main function, would be incapable of doing so and that in any case their main job was to 'procure benefits for their local districts, like a new bridge or a bullet train'.[41] A well known instance was that of a rural area out in the rice-fields through which the original New Tokaido Line was scheduled to pass in 1964. This was in the constituency of a prominent LDP boss, Bamboku Ono, who put pressure on the then Japan National Railways to build a station there, which today stands there as his memorial: Gifu-Hajima station.

Under other political systems, it is the elected representatives that tell their civil servants what new policies they want implemented, even if the latter have a hand in drawing up the legislative proposals and it is the representatives that are responsible for defending their policies before the House. They do not just let bureaucrats speak in the House for them; though this practice is recently supposed to have ceased. Another crucial difference is that, as already mentioned, much Japanese legislation is deliberately vague, to give the bureaucracy the maximum leverage in deciding how to implement it in a particular case, while under other political systems it should be unambiguous.

What was meant above by the 're-emergence' of the bureaucracy was the failure of the Occupation to do more than purge some top officials, leaving the rest intact, although there were those who understood what this would mean. Writing in 1947, an American political scientist expressed his amazement that the bureaucracy was not mentioned as one of the institutions to be targeted for reform in order to produce 'responsible government', while correctly identifying the bureaucracy as 'the single organized group' with the power to frustrate this aim.[42]

Responsibility for 'democratizing' the bureaucracy rested with a single lieutenant, who in peacetime had worked in the US Civil

Service Commission, and who was also correctly disturbed by the bureaucracy's potential for frustrating the main aims of the Occupation and its ability to distort or sabotage the instructions it was now receiving. He passed a memorandum up to the head of the Government Section, a brigadier general.

Figures differ, but it is possible that only 719 officials were purged and it is not known how many were able to return when the Occupation ended. MITI 's senior officials in the 1950s and during the period of high economic growth in the 1960s had all worked in MITI's forerunner, the Ministry of Commerce and Industry, before 1945 and it would be naïve to imagine that they had undergone a Damascene conversion to free market thinking during the brief interlude of five years constituted by the Occupation.[43] As previously mentioned, the unreformed bureaucracy could hardly believe their luck when the departing Americans handed back such sweeping powers to them.[44]

Since that time there have been a number of occasions on which 'administrative reform' has been on the agenda but, like other perennial topics such as the 'decentralization' of Tokyo, nothing of substance has happened. In 1971 even the *Japan Times*, which is by no means a Leftist newspaper, lamented that General MacArthur had failed to 'reform Japan's bureaucratic structure', leaving it as deeply entrenched as it had been under previous regimes.[45]

Even the very day after the end of the war in 1945, a group calling itself the 'Committee on Post-War Problems' had met in Tokyo under the chairmanship of Saburo Okita. He later recalled that '. . . in time Japan will get back on its feet again . . . by new technology and economic power': the same aim as was to be reflected in MITI's 'vision' for the 1990s quoted above. This is hardly surprising, since Okita went on to become a senior official in the Economic Planning Agency and then, as ex-foreign minister, the 'acceptable face' of Japanese trade policy charged with soothing fractious foreign governments, who seldom understood that for all his eminence he had in any case no power to change things as they would have liked. But he was a good listener and an effective part of the authorities' public relations.[46]

Some people seem to find the idea of power as a goal, rather than material gain, difficult to grasp, although the two have a habit of going together but, as George Orwell observed, power can be an end in itself. Henry Kissinger, who was in a position to know, remarked that power was 'the ultimate aphrodisiac'. At home, the three constituents of the Iron Triangle dominate the population. Internationally, they increasingly set the agenda in trade and other relations, symbolized by Japan's biggest debtor, the US, giving in to official representations about Japanese 'sensibilities' and withdrawing the atomic bomb stamp from the set minted to commemorate the end of the war in 1945. Power is a significant good, to use the economists' term, in a society like Japan's that is acutely conscious of status and prestige, or 'face'. Some Japanese grumble about their great trade surplus with the US going to support American consumption, instead of improving their own domestic standard of living, but the Iron Triangle knows what it is doing: in this case adding to its leverage over the US. How far can one risk offending one's biggest creditor, when the latter could for example sell US government bonds?

'The West was both our model and our target' until the late 1960s, according to Masaya Miyoshi, then executive director of the Keidanren, the Federation of Economic Organizations and the most powerful business, commercial and industrial organization uniting the associations of manufacturers, commercial and financial firms across the entire field of the Japanese economy.[47] Because Japan's post-1945 effort went single-mindedly into the economy, evidenced by the conspicuous advances into overseas markets and international investment on an unanticipated scale, MITI's 'industrial policy' became a focus for discussion.

This policy was the practical expression of MITI's 'visions' and in its description as a 'new balance between intervention and freedom' was a significant pointer to the way in which Japan's politico-economic system operates.[48] More recently, this system has been described by a top MOF official as 'beyond capitalism' i.e. neither the Soviet style command economy nor Anglo-Saxon capitalism, with which the Japanese system is mostly compared, and definitely superior to the latter.[49] On the other hand, the case of the widely read article by Akio Morita mentioned above and the alarm it caused for one of MITI's most prominent trade negotiators demonstrates how officials will downplay the difference of the Japanese system, stressing instead its alleged similarities to Anglo-Saxon systems when it is politically advantageous to do so.

The decision of the Meiji oligarchy to 'catch up' with the 'West' by 'rich country, strong army' policies after 1868 has already been discussed and the method of doing so allocated a major role to the bureaucracy. The policy made Japan into what has been called a 'developmental state', with a way of thinking that still largely persists and the bureaucratic power structures that express it.[50]

A pre-war example of this policy was its application to the motor industry, where the domestic companies, Toyota and Nissan, were protected at the expense of Ford and General Motors, who had production quotas and restrictions on the use of foreign management imposed on them. Both gave up manufacturing in Japan in 1939.[51]

Starting again from a low position of weakness after the Second World War, the national economic strategy confirmed MITI's mission but although some officials are pleased to accept the praise as the founders of the economic miracle, this is not how Japan's engineers and shop floor workers in industry see it. But following on from the pre-war Regulation for Approving Excellent Automotive Parts and Materials, new ministerial guidance was given for the improvement of product quality in 1947, followed by the official establishment of the Japan Industrial Standard (JIS) in 1951. These steps showed the consistency of policy towards what was at the time a domestic 'infant industry'. MITI is, of course, not the only actor and shares the field with other important ministries like MOF in particular and private companies, represented by the power of the Keidanren and political lobbyists, in a game of continually shifting influences but to the outside world it is general policy to present a united front and certainly not to wash dirty linen in public.

Nonetheless, there is frequent tension between ministries with different interests to promote; not least because the wider the net of a ministry's control is, the more chances of 'parachuting' into comfortable retirement jobs its officials will have. The telecommunications industry, for example, is mainly regulated by MITI but part of it is under the control of the Ministry of Posts and Telecommunications and a gain for one is a loss for the other. The constant struggles to defend or gain territory are reminiscent of the game of *go* that was earlier alluded to.

In that sense the image of 'Japan Inc.' is an oversimplification, although in comparison with Anglo-Saxon systems it is obviously much more coordinated in terms of its overall strategic economic objective and the means designed to attain it, such as government-industry collaboration and cohesive industrial or trade associations. Part of the difficulty in pinning down the Japanese system may come from binary thinking, imagining that there are only two possible forms of politico-economic organization: a black and white contrast between the free market and the command economy, the latter typically associated with a dominant political ideology. But the Japanese system is not ideological as far as industrial policy is concerned, but pragmatic and practical and it is the job of the officials to help the process along;[52] naturally, they sometimes make mistakes.

Reacting in 1981 to an unusual criticism from the Fair Trade Commission, which is usually seen as a toothless watchdog in enforcing what is supposed to be American style anti-trust legislation, over its appliance of 'administrative guidance' to the oil industry cartel, MITI responded with its memorandum on 'The concept of administrative guidance'. This began by stating that, 'From the standpoint of the national economy' – an expression straight out of Friedrich List, not Adam Smith – 'it is important to implement the following measures in a prompt manner'; going on to enumerate them. The Japanese commentator quoting the example remarked that the memorandum 'appears to represent the attitude of each ministry of the national government'.[53]

No wonder that others see 'administrative guidance' – a nice euphemism – as 'comparatively unrestrained in any way ... by the judicial system'; which itself is not independent of the Ministry of Justice, which controls the careers of those working in it. This system of 'guidance' gives the bureaucratic élite immense power, enabling it to 'draft virtually all laws, ordinances, regulations that govern society'.[54]

The retired ambassador, Ichiro Kawasaki, similarly emphasized the 'strong position of the bureaucracy in formulating national policies' and that 'almost all of the important bills' originate in the ministries, leaving the Diet with what he called a 'perfunctory role' and politicians as 'brokers between the bureaucracy and special interests'.[55]

Because 'administrative guidance' is extra-legal it can hardly have an official definition but it has existed for over a century, even if the expression itself is more recent.[56] MITI's memorandum described its aim as 'implementing an effective measure in a flexible (*sic*) manner on the basis of agreement and cooperation of other parties, without excessive interference' – by whom is not clear. The memorandum then stated that 'administrative guidance has played an important role in the development of the Japanese economy and it will continue to be effective in the future' i.e. MITI would use it. A senior MITI official described it as permitting officials 'unlimited power to intervene administratively outside the system of law'.[57]

Especially when it is unwritten, the widespread use of 'guidance' from the ministries can easily be hidden from outsiders and these quotations by Japanese officials and commentators, not foreigners, show how disingenuous it is to pretend that the Japanese economy is run on purely free market lines, as some official spokesmen and foreign apologists try to make out. It is a characteristic method of conducting operations behind the screen, where face-to-face contact may be preferred to the written word because it permits those who are being guided to size up the tone and expression of the officials. The problems that all this poses for foreign business can be imagined.

The field covered by 'administrative guidance' was earlier said to be extremely wide and can be quite trivial. The Ministry of Posts and Telecommunications, for instance, issued guidance to broadcasters to save energy by closing down at midnight. All stations then closed between midnight and two a.m., leading to the comment that compliance was because of 'paternalistic human relations'. While this may have had something to do with it, including the wish not to be seen as 'the nail that sticks out which gets hammered down', those on the receiving end of guidance know that inside the velvet glove there is a mailed fist. In an allusion to Winston Churchill's characterization of the old Soviet Union, an editorial in the now unfortunately defunct *Tokyo Business Today* described the situation in Japan as 'a rule, surrounded by an ordinance, wrapped in a regulation'. Referring to the 'Iron Triangle, the collusion between bureaucrats, politicians and businessmen', it asked why people in Japan follow all these rules when they are not backed by law. Not surprisingly, the answer was the knowledge that refusal would be likely to lead to 'bureaucratic retaliation later . . . and perhaps in some unrelated business'. *Tokyo Business Today*, in fact, had made itself unpopular with the MOF by publishing a series of highly critical articles, including the suggestion that the MOF should be broken up. In the event, it was *Tokyo Business Today* that was closed down, ostensibly for losing money, though it was part of a well-off economic publishing group.[58]

How the 'rules' are implemented depends on the officials and since they have extra-legal *carte blanche* it follows that they may use quite extra-legal means to enforce them if they are opposed. They can easily make life difficult for a company by delaying or ultimately refusing authorization for a new venture or a new branch, cutting it out of information or contracts and if necessary blackmail.

The activities of the *sokaiya* were outlined earlier, one of whose specialities is to turn up companies' discreditable secrets. The ministries can threaten companies with an embarrassing loss of face and unfavourable publicity, which is often enough to secure their compliance, though in general officials would prefer to maintain the pretence that adhering to their 'guidance' is voluntary, a typical piece of *tatemae*.[59]

Here it should not be thought that only shady companies may have something to hide or that the word 'blackmail' with its obviously criminal connotations is being lightly used. It was pointed out earlier that the Big Four of the stockbroking industry, for instance, who might be thought to represent high standards, had been caught out in all manner of disreputable practices. In 1998 Japan Airlines, the country's leading first-rank company in the industry, was caught making payments to *sokaiya*, some of whom are now using the latest technology. They have launched websites on the Internet to spread information about companies that the latter would prefer to keep to themselves.[60]

A high MITI official estimated that 'more than half of all cases of corporate wrongdoing known to the police and MITI bureaucrats are covered up', and it takes little imagination to see how much of a hold this can give officials, or that what is revealed in the press is only part of the picture. Apart from the *sokaiya*, who are criminal corporate blackmailers, sensitive information, according to the MITI official quoted above, can come from a number of sources, such as MITI's own 'direct investigations, competitors, clients, the police, enemies in the business community and disgruntled employees'. Companies, I was told, have personnel whose job it is to deal with the *sokaiya* and the problems of disreputable secrets.

The ministries can also use 'divide and rule' tactics to enforce compliance by talking to the competitors in the relevant trade association so as to get a 'consensus' against a firm that looks as if it may step out of line; when it risks becoming 'the nail that sticks out that gets hammered down'. This, too, is not exactly free-market economics: more of a cartel, in spite of the, largely unenforced, provisions of the Anti-Monopoly Law. Officials can be quite ruthless in using these methods. In a rare case, the Supreme Court had ruled that 'administrative guidance' to pharmacies not to open branches was unconstitutional; but the Ministry of Health and Welfare simply told the pharmaceutical companies not to supply them. The example is given by a top MITI official.[61]

A famous earlier case was that of Sumitomo Metals, which in 1965 broke the 'industry consensus', or cartel agreement, by greatly increasing production after it had invested in new plant. Naturally this caused howls of protest from its competitors in the steel industry. MITI simply cut Sumitomo's allowance of imported coking coal. At that time, ministerial control over steel production was easily enforced because Japan's imports of 98 per cent of its iron ore and 90 per cent of its coal required licences under the existing exchange control regulations, while the Bank of Japan i.e. MOF, controlled the foreign borrowings of the steel companies.[62] Looking at it another way, one can easily understand the power that such regulations give to officials and why deregulation would threaten it. More recently 'guidance' was applied to a company that wanted to break the industry cartel by importing petrol from Singapore to sell at a lower price.[63]

In an interview in December 1995, Kenichi Ohmae, expressed the view that the degree of deregulation of the oil industry scheduled for March 1996 would not change much because, although anyone would in principle be free to open a filling station, MITI regulations on minimum capacity would necessitate an investment of a billion US dollars, while an 'outsider' would have to get supplies from the oil industry cartel; assuming that they would supply him. In his view, these would constitute insuperable barriers.[64]

The reference was to the scrapping of the 'Provisional Measures Law on the Importation of Specific Petroleum Refined Products' and to the revision of the 'Petrol Sales and Distribution Business Law'. With its excessive number of inefficient, small refineries, 25 per cent of which should be closed according to analysts, over-extended and over-staffed networks of filling stations, of which as many as half may not be profitable, and its huge amounts of debt, the oil industry cartel is not one of MITI's greatest successes.

Self-service has only recently been permitted and, as with the banks, rationalization has been put off. To date, the merger of Mitsubishi Oil and Nippon Oil has attracted attention because it will form the biggest oil company but both companies had already announced closures of petrol stations; in Mitsubishi's case one quarter of the total. The financial crisis and accompanying credit crunch have shown up this heavily regulated and feather-bedded business, which is certainly not unique in the distribution sector.[65]

So far, MITI's prestige in terms of the post-war development of the Japanese economy, particularly the manufacturing industry that has been the source of its prosperity, rather than distribution or services, for example, seems secure. The same cannot now be said of MOF, partly because of its reluctance to give up the 'convoy system' of keeping even the leakiest vessels in the various financial cartels afloat, and because of the corruption that has been revealed both within the ministry and the Bank of Japan. At the time of the *jusen*, or housing loan scandals, for instance, the revelation that former MOF officials were involved in the top management of these companies and were able to walk away with large pay-offs caused widespread anger.[66]

At the strategic level, the most frequently quoted example of 'administrative guidance' failing to be heeded by an industry was in the 1960s. At that time MITI believed that the large number of vehicle manufacturers would have to merge into smaller concentrations if they were to be strong enough to withstand foreign competition. Nissan and Prince did so but the others declined to follow their example. Now, with the increasing globalization of competition, the total number of large-volume manufacturers in the world is expected to decrease, which may in the end vindicate MITI's original policy. On the other hand, in an economy heavily dependent on oil imports, MITI failed in its aim of creating a first-class petrochemical industry spread among a number of companies such as Mitsubishi, Mitsui, Maruzen etc. in the major industrial groups or cartels.

The power at their disposal thanks to the system of 'administrative guidance' is by no means all that officials enjoy. Those in the top ministries especially i.e. MOF and MITI, are recognized as the élite of the élite produced by the grinding examination system and that and their power and influence give them a prestige in the wider society seldom found in other industrialized societies. On top of this is the system, unlike in many jobs in the private sector, that guarantees employment until retirement, although because of the seniority system applied in the bureaucracy, as already mentioned, or because of tempting offers elsewhere, many officials retire in their mid-fifties or earlier. This, as we have seen, is the famous system of *amakudari*, or 'descending from heaven' i.e. 'parachuting' into another job on retirement from the ministry that is in some way connected with it.[67]

*Amakudari* has been described as 'part of the glue holding together the notorious Iron Triangle of politicians, bureaucrats and businessmen'. A 1994 survey, for instance, found that 68.5 per cent of all executives of government affiliated special and public corporations were former senior officials of the ministries that are responsible for regulating them. A 1992-3 survey found that all the executives at 24 government corporations were former officials. At the time, there were altogether 79 government corporations, such as the Water Resources Development Public Corporation, the Japan Motorcycle Racing Organization, the Japan Foundation, the Power Reactor and Nuclear Fuel Development Corporation, Public Corporations for Expressways, large projects such as airports, bridges etc. etc.[68]

In the notorious *jusen* case, just mentioned, it was found that since the 1980s MOF officials had been getting 'lucrative posts with housing mortgage firms upon retirement from government service, twelve of them as a company chairman or president'. Former MOF officials 'headed five of the seven bankrupt housing loan companies at the time the firms accumulated most of their bad loans', during the 'bubble' economy. MOF then stopped sending retirees to these companies but one of the most recent had been the deputy commissioner of the National Tax Administration Agency: an interesting sidelight on the problem normally known as a possible conflict of interest. The National Personnel Authority, which oversees the personnel management of the ministries, has rules to prevent this but there are quite liberal exceptions.[69]

A Teikoku Databank survey in 1995 reported that one out of every 17 board members at major banks and stockbroking firms were retired bureaucrats, or 197 out of 3,332. Occupying these 'golden parachute' seats for retirees were 95 from MOF, 64 from the Bank of Japan, and 24 from other organizations: up by three at a point when banks were supposed to be restructuring to dispose of bad loans.[70]

A more critical report stated that, 'Survey reveals many retired bureaucrats are getting cushy jobs in the private sector.' This referred to the hiring for retirement jobs of former officials of the Board of Audit, where it was denied that this would result in any favours for the bodies employing them, although the latter could 'obtain access to government contacts and information'. However, an anonymous source stated that, 'We can't ignore requests from groups which want breaks in exchange for taking care of the old boys', and a professor of economics at Hitotsubashi, one of the most prominent private universities in the field, remarked that it was 'strange' having 'Board old boys working at groups receiving Board audits'.[71]

When the vice minister, the operational head of the ministry, resigns his peers must do the same, so that the new man has hierarchical seniority. The outgoing vice minister must then help his peers to find *amakudari* positions, very likely with the help of his seniors who have already moved on: it is the responsibility of the ministry, which obviously has an interest in furthering its network, to do this, not the responsibility of the individual. MITI vice ministers, for example, can become presidents and senior officers of Japan's leading companies, with benefits to both sides thanks to the closed loop of the relations between the ministry and the private sector firms it regulates.[72]

The procedure does not of course always go smoothly and firms do not always get the kind of person they want, or they may be reluctant to take anyone at all. In the case of the Centre for International Research and Development on Chemical-Free Farming, a public corporation regulated by the Ministry of Agriculture and Fisheries, the Corporation wanted three technicians as directors but the ministry had selected three *amakudari* from the office. After a heated argument in which almost all the talking was done by the MAFF official, who threatened to cancel the Corporation's permit, the Corporation was forced to accept the three officials from the office. It was a good instance of the 'offer you can't refuse' principle in operation. Fortunately, the Corporation representatives had had the good sense to tape-record the forty-minute argument.[73]

Writing in 1994 a commentator on political and economic issues reported that all government ministries had been asked to examine their public corporations and to state whether they planned to abolish any: 'not surprisingly, there was not a single plan for abolition'. The Administrative Reform Study Council had started its work over twelve years previously under the chairmanship of a prominent businessman but, 'Special public corporations and systems which were unnecessary twenty years ago are still around because bureaucrats want to protect their turf and politicians obtain votes and money by helping to maintain these organizations.'

At that time, top ex-bureaucrats headed one out of three banks and, although interest rates were supposed to have been liberalized, there was no competition whatever in this area.[74] Ministerial pressure was put on a private credit association, Jonan Shinyo Kinko, to exercise 'voluntary restraint' by cancelling its introduction of a new device to attract customers viz: a lottery on new time deposits enabling customers depositing over ¥100,000 to have a chance of earning cash prizes. Customers rushed to deposit ¥5 billion per day in new accounts, whereas Jonan had thought it would take six months to get ¥100 billion.

The ministry, which had known in advance of the scheme, had apparently not imagined that Jonan would go ahead without getting the green light and was 'stunned'. The president of the National Association of Shinkin Banks, not of course to be confused with the big city banks, criticized Jonan for 'deviating' from the cartel's unwritten rule to 'follow a uniform code of behaviour' and tried to force Jonan to cancel its new and evidently successful way of attracting deposits. For once, the Fair Trade Commission warned the Association not to interfere and other small banks and credit associations adopted strategies similar to Jonan's.[75] But as the later history of the big bank crisis has shown again, this action by a small entrepreneur has not changed the entrenched system and the role of MOF and its ex-officials in it.

When the third Administrative Reform Study Council met to re-examine thirty-four special public corporations it was boycotted by all the ministries, although the Council is an 'advisory body to the prime minister'. The ministries then worked on the LDP's Party Policy Research Council to adopt resolutions in the Diet supporting their rejection of the Council's hearing. Leading this move was the then MITI minister, and later prime minister Ryutaro Hashimoto, known for his nationalistic views and strong stance in trade negotiations. His comment to the Council's chairman was, 'Do you intend to destroy the LDP?' – underlining yet again the mutual advantages of the existing system of public corporations to the three sides of the Iron Triangle and the threat that deregulation would pose.

Like so much else in officialdom, *amakudari* is a complex business and may lead to more then one post-retirement job. Thus one of my contemporaries before coming to the EU-Japan Centre had been with the Japan Chain Store Association and with the Textile Industry Rationalization Council. Quite where he went after the Centre is not clear but once again he collected some good retirement money.

Strictly speaking, the move on retirement from the ministry to an agency or public corporation is known as a 'side slip', *yokosuberi*, and is not subject to any legal restrictions, for example, about potential conflicts of interest, and is not an item in government statistics.[76] However, in 1994 it was said that there were as many as two hundred 'former or active bureaucrats' in the regional administrations of Japan's forty-seven prefectures in the positions of governor, deputy governor or director of general affairs, allowing the Home Affairs Ministry a high degree of control rather like that of 'the Home Ministry of the past'. This was criticized as being the opposite of 'decentralization'.

MOF is the ministry that has had the greatest success in putting its 'OBs', old boys, into private corporations and it is also from MOF that the greatest number of candidates to enter the Diet come. These are typically high flyers who have to make their own way and join up with a faction, *habatsu*, in the LDP. While this is likely to be useful to the ministry it is not the ministry's job to fix up a retiree's political career, as it would be with other *amakudari*.

Ex-bureaucrats may make it to the cabinet and several have become important prime ministers. The latter include Japan's first prime minister after the Second World War, Shigeru Yoshida, from the Foreign Ministry: Nobusuke Kishi, 1957-60, from the former Ministry of Munitions and highly influential 'éminence grise' in post-war politics.[77] Hayato Ikeda, the architect of the 'income doubling' policy in the 1960s, from MOF: and Eisaku Sato, who presided over the Expo international exhibition in 1970, from the Ministry of Transport.

Ex-ambassador Kawasaki commented that officials from ministries such as MOF, MITI and Construction are successful because of the networks that they have already built up in politics and business. The background is the role of broker in 'pork barrel' or 'money politics'.[78] In 1990 there were seventy-two LDP ex-bureaucrat representatives in the Lower House of the Diet and thirty in the Upper House. Thus both in national and regional politics the ministries have their finger in the pie.[79]

It has often been pointed out that other industrial states have at different times adopted administrative measures to increase the competitiveness of their private industries, or to protect them, but the differences between such policies and those promoted by MITI for example lie in 'the degree of organization'.[80] In MITI's case, there has been both a cohesive overall programme with the strategic aim of promoting Friedrich List's 'national economy', together with the deployment of the intermediate tactical levels of organization, such as industry associations and cartels, to make the strategy effective. In the Japanese case, the one does not exist without the other.[81]

Those from Anglo-Saxon economies need to realize that an industry association is not a powerless talking shop and that cartels, though closed against outsiders, have had a significant role to play in a politico-economic structure of the Japanese type. Whether they have always been good for Japanese consumers is another matter. The results of this manufacturing industry-based strategy can be seen in the markets of the world.

Japanese officials have the power to make laws, in a way that gives themselves the maximum amount of power in their enforcement. They can issue, frequently unwritten, extra-legal 'administrative guidance' and, if necessary, put extreme pressure on those to whom it as addressed to make them comply. They can defend and extend their power by putting their high flying retirees in positions of influence in the private sector, public corporations and politics. Their power secures them prestige and levels of perks, such as entertainment allowances, 'wining and dining' either by outsiders hoping for information etc or by other officials, *kankan settai*, golf trips etc and black chauffeur-driven limousines on a scale and at a lower organizational level than would be normal in other systems. In or out of the office, their known power is an index of respect.

The bureaucracy, with its entrenched relationships within the closed networks of the Iron Triangle, is more then the first among equals of these three centres of power and is certainly not part of a system based on the free-market philosophy of Adam Smith.

## (2) BIG BUSINESS: WORK AS NATIONAL SERVICE
*Men who are engaged in industry and commerce are regarded very highly in Japanese society; these are the people who bear the banner of the national interest* – Japanese trading company executive.[1]

To understand why big business is one part of the Iron Triangle two essential facts must be borne in mind. The first is that business, as in the above quotation represents 'the national interest'; in other words, the immense effort made after 1945 aimed initially at survival and then at raising living standards, followed by the push to keep on expanding economic growth, which remains a national priority. The second fact is the power of Japanese management, in comparison with its competitors elsewhere in the industrialized world. An American researcher who worked in companies in Japan put it well: 'There is no doubt that it is the Japanese managers above all, who maintain most of their traditional prerogatives and hold the reins of power.' This applies both at the company level and in the wider political context.[2]

In a country like Britain, for instance, it is doubtful whether most people see businessmen and industrialists as bearing the banner of the national interest and as being engaged in a patriotic struggle that they should support. Many, on the contrary, would see them as people 'just out for themselves' and for years the leading attitude of the Labour Party has been anti-business; even if people do expect the jobs and prosperity that depend on economic success.

Psychologically, the mood in Britain after 1945 was to go back to a quiet life and established ways: the opposite of the officially sponsored campaign for economic growth and competitiveness at the same time in Japan, conducted sometimes with a frenetic urgency. Although the role of the Japanese bureaucracy in setting the scene for this campaign, by fostering and protecting industry for example, is undeniable, bureaucratic power alone could not have produced the economic miracle. That could only be done in factories and workshops, which explains the power of the voice of the big companies that dominate the business world and why it has to be listened to with respect.

Looking at the change in the balance of power between management and employees before and after the Second World War and the industrial relations legislation that followed it, management's power in Britain is obviously weaker than before, while in Continental countries there has been the spread of legal requirements for works councils and worker directors etc. Nor do employers' organizations like the Confederation of British Industries have the political links that their Japanese counterparts do.

To anyone familiar with the strict work discipline of Japanese factories in regard to attendance, time-keeping, work speed, the requirement to finish a job or to rectify mistakes in the employee's time without extra pay etc, the scant attention paid to work discipline in so much that has been written can only be described as a glaring omission. Even in the white collar sector, where such timing of work speeds etc would pose problems and where it is often alleged that efficiency is much lower than on the shop floor, management has the power to force employees to do unpaid overtime, popularly known as 'sabisu zangyo'; 'sabisu' i.e. service, being something that one does for nothing.[3]

An employee who took his employer up to the Supreme Court over his right to a long holiday in 1992 lost his case; the Court deciding that it was a matter for the employer's discretion. He was reprimanded and had his winter bonus, normally the largest, cut by the company. A spokesman for Nikkeiren, the Japan Federation of Employers' Organizations, a body specifically concerned with employee relations, praised the Supreme Court's decision.[4] As is relatively well known, many Japanese employees, especially managers who are ambitious to climb up the career ladder, do not take all the holidays that they are in theory entitled to, for fear of not being favourably evaluated by their superiors. Many companies have an 'attendance allowance' as a component of their pay systems paid when the employee is at work and not when he is absent.[5]

Particularly in large companies, it is the company and not the new entrant to it who chooses what job he should do, unless of course he has some strong technical qualification, and new entrants are not advised to express a preference but to let the company decide. Once in such a large mainstream company, there is little chance for the 'permanent' employee to get out if he is dissatisfied or frustrated in his career etc, as such companies have an implicit agreement not to poach staff from one another. This prevents labour mobility between the large firms and what would be the higher personnel costs that a market based on individual skills would bring. Being tied to the firm in such an 'internal labour market' is the price paid by 'permanent' employees for the famous long-term employment. Normally, the only way out would be to a lower grade and less prestigious firm, after incurring the opprobrium of having done something wrong, being unreliable, untrustworthy and so on.

This system only applies to the permanent staff in the large firms and not to the temporary or part time employees in them, who can be discharged at any time. Nor does it apply to the small firms. But the system gives management such a high degree of control over their employees, backed up by the emotional appeal of 'loyalty', which is a resonant value in Japan, that stories of how 'long term employment is finished' because of the recession should be treated with caution.

I once accompanied the manager of a large electronics factory on a visit to one of his supplier companies. The entire personnel was drawn up in rows, men on one side, women on the other. As we entered, they were literally called up to attention in military fashion, *kiotsuke!*, and listened in silence to the manager's explanation that competition was getting harder and that their cooperation was requested in helping his company.

The point is that the power of Japanese management, especially in industry, which has been and is the star of the Japanese economy, supported by its patriotic prestige and the evidence of its successes, is infinitely greater than in its 'Western' competitors. How this power extends beyond the workplace to take control of the employee's life was well expressed by an instructional videotape with the title 'The company comes first' and the choice of the phrase here 'work as national service', equivalent to the 'draft' in the USA, is a conscious one.

Like in the army, companies can and do post staff both within Japan and abroad and to try and object is not the way to help one's career. How common this is, is shown by the expression *tanshin funin*, meaning that the husband is posted away by himself from the family, perhaps at the other end of the country, but again it is the company, not the family, that comes first. Looking at it the other way from the viewpoint of Japanese management, already in a book published in 1974 the president of a bank in his annual message to his employees was warning about the dangers of relaxing their efforts and 'becoming a sorry spectacle of decline like Britain' which had sunk into consumerism.[6]

Neither the power of Japanese management nor its close involvement at the highest level of politics is new, though how it has come back from its lowest point during the first years of the Occupation and then re-established itself as a force in government circles is noteworthy. The *zaikai*, meaning something like the business world or circles, the financial world etc. is currently represented by four organizations, of which the Keidanren, the Federation of Economic Organizations, stands out as the voice of big business. According to one Japanese economic journalist, many in Japan believe that the *zaikai* are 'the nation's largest and most powerful pressure group'.[7] Looking at their present involvement in politics, not to mention the past, it is not difficult to see why.

Keidanren was notionally founded in 1946 but its predecessor, the Industrial Club, was established in 1917 with a membership of 185 open exclusively to companies in the first rank with a large capital. Businessmen used this financial power to seek election to the Diet, or parliament, and by 1930 about a third of Diet members were from the business world; and of this third 12 per cent were employed either by the Mitsui *zaibatsu* or the Mitsubishi *zaibatsu*, who competed against each other for political influence.[8] These two mammoth or oligopolistic industrial, financial and commercial groups 'were now hand-in-glove with the two chief rival political parties in the Diet'.

A popular joke was that when the Seiyukai party was in power it was a 'Mitsui government', while when its opponent, the Minseito, was in power it was a 'Mitsubishi government'. Similar to the present-day marriage connections between LDP politicians and leading figures in the construction industry, where who gets the contract is a major issue,[9] the minister of finance in the 1929 Minseito government, Junnosuke Inoue, was the son-in-law of the head of the Iwasaki family then in control of the Mitsubishi *zaibatsu* while the foreign minister, Kijuro Shidehara, was related to the same family.[10]

The situation may be compared with those countries where even the idea of a 'business government' would not be thought right. In fact the *zaibatsu* made themselves unpopular over allegations of profiteering during the depression of the 1930s, which was one factor in the spread of fascistic ideology and the rise of the military, but the closeness of big business and politics was a precedent for the situation after the end of the Occupation and yet another example of continuity from the 1930s and 1940s.

Another factor helping business to concentrate its power in a way that is also readily apparent today was the organization of cartels. For instance, the Paper Manufacturers Cartel was organized in 1880 – just twelve years after the start of the new Meiji regime in 1868 – and the Spinners' Association two years later; but this should not be thought of as a piece of history no longer relevant at the present time. After the boom during the First World War, when cartels lost some of their power to enforce 'orderly marketing', the government made cartels compulsory for major export industries in 1925 and passed the Vital Industries Control Law in 1931, controlling pricing and production. By 1937 industry was organized into 109 cartels and 1,173 industrial associations.

Compare this with the significance of cartels today, in everything but name, and industrial associations and the role that they play in what has been called Japan's present 'strategic economy'.[11] One is almost tempted to exclaim 'so what's new?' Anti-trust legislation was an American import after 1945 but, coming from a profoundly different political and economic background, it has generally remained a piece of *tatemae*: something that comes in handy for proclaiming that Japan's business and political system is based on free enterprise principles like any other, while seldom inconveniencing the usual way of doing things.

By 1928 the Industrial Club had grown to a thousand member companies. It was successful in lobbying for subsidies to heavy industry and changes in tariff rates and did its best to hinder labour legislation and universal suffrage, which was not introduced until the Occupation period. The Club was dominated by the *zaibatsu* and naturally represented the interests of big business, not the large number of small firms or for that matter agriculture. Its leaders came from the largest *zaibatsu* companies: a parallel today with the prominence of the *keiretsu* companies in the Keidanren. It sent trade missions abroad, again much like today, and to ILO (International Labour Office) conferences.

Following problems in the financial sector – how history repeats itself! – another organization of the main banks and financial institutions calling itself the Economic Association was set up in 1922 but it did not exclude the industrial firms and largely came to reflect the interests of big business as a whole. Indeed, one of the country's most influential businessmen from the Mitsui Holding Company, became chairman of both the Industrial Club and the Economic Association and when he was assassinated in 1932 the two organizations were merged. From then on the Economic Association was the voice of big business, although the Industrial Club still continues today at its premises in Tokyo as a club for businessmen in the usual sense of the word. The Economic Association then established the Employers' Association to deal specifically with labour problems.

These were, therefore, the origins of today's Keidanren, a characteristically Japanese portmanteau word standing for Keizai Dantai Rengokai, i.e., Federation of Economic Organizations, founded, or perhaps re-founded, in 1946, and of today's Nikkeiren, or Nihon Keieisha Dantai Renmei, i.e., the Japan Federation of Employers' Organizations, also dating from 1946. Being concerned with labour problems, as before, Nikkeiren's founding principles urged management to be 'fair but strong' in dealing with labour relations.

In addition to the Keidanren and Nikkeiren, the *zaikai* or business world has two other national organizations through which it can promote its agenda; the Japan Chamber of Commerce and Industry, representing the huge number of small and medium-sized enterprises (SMEs) – but under the control of the large industrial groups; and the Association of Corporate Executives, Keizai Doyukai, composed of individual, not corporate members, and not at the present time particularly influential. Within the structure of the national organizations there are regional and sectoral bodies. There are also powerful pressure groups, such as the Japan Medical Association, unusual in being a professional association at all, which has been extremely successful in pushing the interests of Japan's widespread network of private clinics and hospitals and its connections with the pharmaceutical industry.[12]

The pre-1945 groups of powerful companies, the *zaibatsu*, and their re-emergence in modified form as the *keiretsu* after the end of the Occupation were referred to in the previous chapter but to understand their power and that of the Keidanren it is necessary to go into further detail. The essential differences before and after the Occupation and why the two terms *zaibatsu* and *keiretsu* should not be confused can be summed up as follows: first, the removal of the centralized family control over the groups, leading to greater management control instead, even if in, for example, the Sumitomo Group several family members are active in the various companies[13]; second, the removal of the group holding companies and the distribution of the central capital among the group member companies, although the holding companies may be on the way back if it is judged that this would strengthen the companies financially and if the tax laws are revised accordingly; third, the Occupation purge of senior executives from the wartime period on the grounds that they had worked in tandem with the militarists, though just how many were reinstated when the Occupation ended in 1951 is an interesting question.

The expression 'dual economy' is current in Japan and refers to a two-tier structure.[14] The names of companies that are well known internationally normally belong to the large firms, frequently *keiretsu* member companies, in the top tier; rarely to the SMEs in the bottom tier, that the large firms nevertheless rely on as sub-contractors and suppliers. It goes without saying that the *keiretsu* are at the top of the hierarchy. Three of them, Mitsui, Mitsubishi and Sumitomo might be called 'classic' *keiretsu*, being based on long-standing *zaibatsu* antecedents well before the Second World War. They are also classic in the sense of being 'horizontal' keiretsu i.e. clusters of a considerable number of major corporations around their own bank. The other 'horizontal' *keiretsu* are Fuyo, formerly Yasuda, Sanwa and the Dai-Ichi Kangyo Bank Groups.

The presidents of these groups meet monthly to discuss matters of mutual concern, including, for instance, political funding. Together with their interlocking share-holdings and directorships, the groups form charmed circles inaccessible to outsiders – one of the complaints of the American SII (Structural Impediments Initiative) talks[15] while their strength in terms of the numbers of their directly affiliated companies, their sales and profitability underline their dominant position at the top of the hierarchy. In 1992 the presidents' monthly meetings of the classic *keiretsu* alone, Mitsui, Mitsubishi and Sumitomo, consisted of the heads of 29, 24 and 21 major corporations: an index of cohesive strength.

In addition to the six 'horizontal' *keiretsu*, there are ten 'vertical' *keiretsu* in other words, groups of affiliates and suppliers dependent on a major manufacturer, or of companies dependent on a bank or other major corporation. They also include such well-known names as Hitachi, Industrial Bank of Japan, Matsushita, Nippon Steel, Nissan, Seibu, Tokai, Tokyu, Toshiba-IHI, and Toyota.[16]

In the electrical and electronics industry there are what have been called distribution *keiretsu* of tied shops, often run by retired employees of the manufacturers, which only sell the products of one of the big makers. The most famous is Matsushita with no fewer than 25,000 exclusive outlets, followed by Toshiba with 12,500, Hitachi with 10,000 and Sanyo with 6,000. These extensive oligopolistic networks, which provide after service and deal discreetly with complaints, help the companies to maintain prices and make it difficult for newcomers to break into the market. The companies do, of course, sell through other outlets, such as department stores, but as with the other keiretsu it is a good strategy for maintaining their oligopolistic position, whatever the *tatemae* about free competition may be.

When it is realized that *keiretsu* executives dominate the four organizations through which the business world acts as a pressure group, by holding most of the top positions in the Keidanren, Nikkeiren, the Japan Chamber of Commerce and Industry (JCCI) and Keizai Doyukai, the power of big business can easily be understood. Part of the strategy includes using this power to provide *amakudari* posts for bureaucrats on their retirement from the ministries, as has already been discussed in the preceding section, on the 'you scratch my back, and I'll scratch yours' principle. Towards the politicians, the important part of the strategy is the provision of political funds by the Keidanren and the sectoral organizations principally, but not exclusively, to the preferred 'natural party of government', the LDP.[17]

In 1992 Keidanren's membership was made up of 120 associations and 940 corporate members. Both of its two governing councils were dominated by executives from *keiretsu* companies: the average age of the twelve vice-chairmen being 75, reflecting Japanese ideas about hierarchy and the time it takes to get to the top in these companies – something to remember when being told stories about how young people these days are different etc. Keidanren had no fewer than 44 committees, reporting to its board of directors and passing on recommendations to the government. The president, popularly known as 'the prime minister of business', is appointed by his predecessor and is typically 'a powerful personality of great economic and political clout'.[18] In a survey of the companies listed on the first section of the Stock Exchanges in 1991 the first person their presidents said they would listen to was Gaishi Hiraiwa, president of Keidanren, followed by Eiji Suzuki, former chairman of Nikkeiren, and Akio Morita, then chairman of Sony.[19]

The Keidanren can take the initiative in new projects that may later be sponsored officially. In June 1968 for instance the Keidanren established its Space Activities Promotion Council, which was followed by the government's Space Activities Commission shortly afterwards. Dr Koji Kobayashi of NEC and the Keidanren had the task to project 'a long-term vision for space development in Japan and to lobby the government for the budgetary allocations necessary for its achievement'.[20]

Apart from its research on topics of importance to big business in particular and the Japanese economy in general, Keidanren acts almost like an official body in sending high-level delegations to foreign countries to negotiate agreements, which would then be followed up by the government. Naturally, it has a close relationship with MITI, cemented for instance by *amakudari* jobs, and MITI's Industrial Structure Council is chaired by the Keidanren chairman. This ensures that MITI's 'visions' are not just academic daydreams but are strongly influenced by what the top management of big business wants.[21] It goes without saying that the Keidanren has a keen interest in industrial policy and in 1980, for example, it requested a bigger budget for science and technology to help private firms.[22]

With the sole exception of the Socialist government of Tetsu Katayama from May 1947 to March 1948, the LDP or a coalition, such as that of Tomiichi Murayama between June 1994 and January 1996, that it could manipulate, the LDP has been in power ever since the end of the Second World War. The LDP is inevitably the Keidanren's preferred 'natural party of government' and has largely provided the sort of stable political environment and support for business that the Keidanren wanted. Under this regime, the power of the unions, as well as of the Socialist and Communist parties, has been restrained.

The Keidanren's fear of Socialism might seem exaggerated but even in the tightly policed state that wartime Japan was there were signs of disaffection, while in the immediate post-war period there was great labour unrest and the attempt in 1947 to hold a General Strike. There was the covert support of the Soviet Union for its clients in Japan and the attempt to use indoctrinated prisoners of war to stir up revolt on their return from the USSR. There was the 'production control' movement in several well known companies when employees took over the management of, for example, the Keisei Railway, running from Tokyo to what is now Narita Airport.[23] In 1945 Prince Konoe, prime minister from 1937 to 1941, presented his 'memorial' to the Emperor in which he set out in sober detail why Japan at that point seemed 'ripe for revolutionary transformation' and why the war should be ended before there was 'a Communist revolution'.[24] After the years of repression of the 1930s and 1940s it would perhaps be natural to expect such an explosion, especially in a country like Japan with its tendencies to value extreme forms of commitment rather than the golden mean, as the sarin gas affair, the 'Red Army', the suicide of Yukio Mishima etc. unfortunately demonstrate.

This has not meant that the Keidanren has always seen eye to eye with the LDP or hesitated to upbraid it, as when in 1954 it reprimanded the Diet for its behaviour over the shipbuilding scandal. But for the Keidanren the bottom line has always been that in order to preserve the status quo the LDP must control at least two thirds of the seats in the Lower House of the Diet. Fearing in 1955 that it would be impossible to check the Socialists, who had won 156 seats in the Upper House, the Keidanren itself pushed through the merger of the then Liberal and Democratic parties into the present day LDP; creating what is now known as the '1955 system'. The president of the

Keidanren at the time, Kogoro Uemura, who had been a top planner of Japan's war effort, played a leading role in the merger; providing another instance of continuity from the old days.[25]

The Keidanren had been 'more determined than ever to push the merger of the two conservative parties' when it saw that the election of February 1955 had not produced the majority it had hoped for and the following year when organized business judged that the merger was still not working out properly it decided that further action was necessary. At a conclave behind closed doors at the Tokyo Kaikan, a well known downtown meeting hall, seventy leaders from the business world decided that the prime minister, Ichiro Hatoyama, would have to go. Keidanren's president, Taizo Ishizaka, bluntly declared that 'the affairs of state cannot be entrusted to an invalid' and demanded the prime minister's resignation at a meeting with the LDP secretary-general, the executive board chairman and the secretary of the party's policy committee; although the real reasons for Keidanren's attitude were said to include Hatoyama's negotiations with the Soviet Union, restoring diplomatic relations after the war, and disapproval of the actions of Hatoyama's right-hand man, Ichiro Kono.

This was the period of the Keidanren's greatest influence over the LDP when it could, as a Japanese commentator noted, 'bring down a government when it concludes that the prime minister has outlived his usefulness and become a definite liability'. As well as Hatoyama, even Yoshida, the first post-war prime minister and a strong-willed and skilful politician, and Kishi, the survivor from the pre-war days in Manchuria, the wartime years and his arrest by the Occupation authorities as a Class A war criminal, 'all had no recourse but to yield to the irresistible pressure of organized business'. What the Keidanren could give, it could also take away. Kishi's mistake was to make himself unpopular over the handling of the US-Japan Security Treaty issue, which resulted in large-scale riots in 1960 and the cancellation of President Eisenhower's visit to Japan.

During the period of high economic growth in the 1960s another prime minister, Hayato Ikeda, of 'income doubling' fame, remarked that 'the government is the captain and the *zaikai*, the business circles, the compass of the ship' i.e., business sets the course of the ship of state, which in a state devoted to economic growth is quite logical. With the success of his policy, Ikeda was able to bring the ship into port, while those mentioned above who for one reason or another failed to do so as organized business had hoped found themselves relieved of their command.

Writing in 1968, the Japanese commentator saw the role of business in the 'triumvirate', or Iron Triangle, as much more important than before the Second World War. It funds politicians, who require huge sums of money first to get elected and then to advance their political careers: it is 'well represented in the cabinet, advisory councils, the Diet and the LDP'; and through control over parts of the media it can influence the population as a whole.[26] This type of closeness of the Keidanren and the politicians shows how utterly inappropriate it would be to imagine that employers' organizations elsewhere, like the Confederation of British Industry for example, could be taken as an analogy.

The Keidanren is powerful and respected but its glory days of merging parties and making and breaking prime ministers are for the moment at least in the past. Between May 1946 and April 2000 Japan has had no fewer than twenty-six prime ministers but a number who followed Sosuke Uno in rather rapid succession after 1989 were the victims of scandals, factional rivalries and behind the scenes manipulation by other LDP power brokers, rather than of the Keidanren. Different Keidanren presidents have also seen things differently. Eishiro Saito from Nippon Steel, president from 1986 to 1990,for instance was publicly attacked for failing to show leadership and for not being assertive enough in his dealings with politicians.

Of course, politicians would like to get as much money from Keidanren as possible, and may threaten to raise corporate taxes as a way of twisting its arm, which on the other hand explains why not all Keidanren members are keen on getting too close to the LDP. With regard to the bureaucracy, companies may not wish, as they say in Japan, 'to wake a sleeping child' and risk the permits, licences etc. that they need to do business, or the possibility of having their accounts examined more closely. Business for its part does not want to have government interfering in its affairs, while getting what it wants from government by means of its trade associations and advisory councils, as in the space industry example. Many business and political leaders have a common educational background and also marriage and family ties.[27]

In the early post-war years prime minister Yoshida was informed that, 'You see to it that the proper policies are shaped and we will see to it that you do not need to worry about money'[28] and despite the periodic disagreements the Keidanren and its member companies have remained the main paymaster of the LDP. Not every Keidanren president, however, has seen things in the same way and in 1974 Toshiwa Doko stated that he was a 'strong believer in a free economy' and that what he objected to was 'the recent trend towards money power'. Perhaps what he meant was that business was tired of handing over large sums for what looked like unnecessary election campaigns and that the politicians should do more in return. At all events, the LDP campaign fund fell from ¥18,879 million in 1974 to ¥10,081 million in 1976. Prior to that, in 1974, the LDP secretary-general had allocated candidates for *keiretsu* and other large companies to support and pressure was put on employees and their families to vote for them.[29]

In 1989 the LDP secretary-general, requiring an extra ¥15 billion for the Lower House elections of February 1990 which he was not confident of winning, directly threatened the motor industry, asking them 'which policy they thought was wiser': an increase of several billion ¥ in taxes that would hurt their business or a contribution of ¥5 billion to the LDP, which would help to keep the latter in power with the various advantages to them etc. It was the classic 'offer you cannot refuse'. To get round the formal limitations on the size of political contributions, the twelve city banks and three long-term credit banks provided ¥15 billion on lenient terms.[30] The secretary-general was then Ichiro Ozawa, later to become famous as the author of *Blueprint for a new Japan* and someone to watch in Japan's convoluted political world.[31]

The 1990 list of the nine major sectoral contributors to political funds acting on behalf of the Keidanren and of the twenty-three major corporate donors showed the Petroleum Association of Japan at the top, with US $628,000 to the LDP and US $62,000 to the then Social Democratic Party of Japan, since merged into the New Frontier Party. The next two were the Japan Iron and Steel Federation and the Japan Automobile Manufacturers' Association, highly influential in negotiations with the EU over quotas for example.

The Mitsubishi Bank headed the corporate list, which was a roll call of the largest firms in industry, banking, construction and so on. The Bank followed the standard pattern, with funds of US $605,006 to the LDP and US $48,000 to the DSP.[32]

These are not, of course, anything like the total of funds that the LDP received only declared funds from the business world. Other ways of raising funds belong to the discussion on politics and by definition are not necessarily easy to identify.

In 1995 managers in the electric power industry were invited to contribute 'on a voluntary basis' to a fund to raise ¥1 billion for the LDP as part of a total of ¥10 billion to be collected by the Keidanren. The latter had been asked for the money by the LDP so as to repay a loan of ¥10 billion that the party had received from the banks in order to fight the 1993 election. The electric power industry had previously adopted a policy of rejecting requests from political parties but, as a member of the Keidanren, was obliged to contribute all the same.[33]

During the *jusen*, or housing association, scandal in 1996 the LDP and its allies asked the Keidanren to help find ways to reduce the amount of public money that would have to be spent to liquidate these bankrupt companies by getting the banks to pay more. But the Keidanren president, Shoichiro Toyoda of Toyota Motors, rejected calls for the top executives of the banks who had founded the *jusen*, or housing and loan companies as they would be called in the US, to resign. 'Most bank representatives saw this as a government attempt to interfere in their business',[34] which would have been personally inconvenient for more than a few of them.

As already noted, the Keidanren and the LDP do not always see eye to eye although as far as 'money politics' and the awarding of contracts, investment funds etc are concerned they have a symbiotic relationship. Each fights its own corner and to get what it wants needs each other, even if in their heart of hearts businessmen resent having to pay contributions that resemble an extra tax. To the outside world, the institutions that support Japan's national economy may be presented as a seamless monolith, particularly in comparison with what people in pluralistic societies are used to, but inside there is the pursuit of sectional interests within the overall framework.

To publicize its concerns in English, the Keidanren works with the Keizai Koho Centre, translated as the Japan Institute for Social and Economic Affairs and described as a private institute, which publishes two magazines, *Economic Eye* and *Speaking of Japan*. Keizai Koho Centre's current chairman is Shoichiro Toyoda, president of Keidanren, and its editorial board has included Keidanren officials, MITI and Foreign Ministry officials, professors and journalists. As well as contributions by those outside Japan, it has included pieces in accord with official information campaigns to justify Japanese trade practices,[35] such as, 'No need to apologize. Explaining Japanese industrial policies'.

While the Keidanren is the most powerful big business pressure group both in regard to domestic politics and foreign business, Nikkeiren, the Japan Federation of Employers' Organizations, with its specific responsibility for labour relations policy has played a major role in this field on several key occasions since its rebirth in 1946. According to ILO (International Labour Office) figures the unionization rate of Japanese employees in 1995 was 24 per cent, having declined by 16.7 per cent over the previous ten years. While Japan has the image of docile workers, divided up into unions based on one enterprise or even one factory, there were severe disputes at well known companies like Toshiba in the immediate post-war period earlier referred to, and later at, for example, the Mitsui Miike coalmines and most dramatically at Nissan Motors in 1953.

The Nissan dispute was dramatic in its breakdown of work discipline, and in the intimidation by union militants of junior managers at work and of 'unreliable' workmates and their families at home, but its real significance lay in management's success in using the tactic of organizing a 'second union' to defeat the original union that had been taken over by the militants.[36] This decisively shifted the balance of power in management's favour, in which Nikkeiren had played a major part, as it also had in defeating the attempt to organize an industry-wide union, Densan, not restricted to one company, in the electric power industry.[37]

Except for the Seamen's Union and the Teachers' Union, unions in Japan are not organized so as to combine all carworkers, all bank employees, all railwaymen etc. on an industry-wide basis but are organized on an 'enterprise' basis. What is often not understood is that not all companies, or factories, only have one union each: hence the expression 'second union', which is otherwise unintelligible.

In the Nissan case, the management organized the 'second union' in opposition to the original militant union and were told by Nikkeiren that they were fully supported. Nikkeiren's president, Hajime Maeda, published warnings to other companies that the sort of troubles Nissan was experiencing would spread to them if they did not stand firm and in July 1953 he told the Nissan management that they had Keidanren's backing in resisting the union.

Nikkeiren was not known to some as 'fighting Nikkeiren' for nothing and these were not just empty words. Nikkeiren arranged for the Industrial Bank of Japan and Fuji Bank to make loans to Nissan, for other firms to give work to Nissan's sub-contractors during the strike and for its competitors not to take advantage of Nissan's difficulties by increasing their market shares: a good example of the 'we're all in the same boat' philosophy. Nikkeiren 'provided legal assistance when Nissan closed its factories, fired the union leaders and had them arrested'.[38]

In the view of a Japanese authority, 'Management has had the upper hand in most of Japan's industrial relations since the 1960s'. In some cases it has been a good tactic to leave the old union splinter group alongside the new 'second union' organized and supported by management, as a harmless way of letting off steam, but some foreign companies have been plagued by them. Ironically, one case was at the Delegation of the European Communities in Tokyo over the sacking of a temporary employee: perhaps serving to remind foreign companies that they should not take Japanese unions for granted.[39]

After the oil shock of 1973, a time of sudden price rises, large wage increases and economic panic with goods disappearing from the shops, the still nationalized Japan National Railways experienced several strikes and even sabotage. When JNR was privatized in 1987, the authorities seized the opportunity to get rid of the militants when the overmanned business had to be slimmed down. Late into the 1990s they could still be seen on television demonstrating for compensation.[40]

In 1995, Nikkeiren called for a wage freeze at the time of the 'spring labour annual offensive', *shunto*, the regular annual wage bargaining round, claiming that there had been no improvement in productivity. Takeshi Nagano, the president said that manufacturing companies must be prevented from leaving Japan for countries with lower labour costs, which would have resulted in the 'hollowing out', or *kudoka*, of industry and inevitable rises in unemployment.[41]

His successor the following year, Jiro Nemoto of the NYK shipping line, reiterated the call, stating that employment, economic growth, the balance of trade, and commodity prices should be kept in balance and that 'there were sound economic as well as social arguments for putting employment first'. He admitted that the official unemployment statistics understated the real figure and that they would rise unless wages were restrained,[42] though the leaders of Honda and Nippon Steel did not agree with his assessment.[43] But the wage freeze message was consistent.

Between the Keidanren and Nikkeiren on the one side and between the Japan Chamber of Commerce and Industry (JCCI) on the other there is a gulf in the amount of influence the latter wields, due to the latter's membership consisting of small and medium-sized enterprises (SMEs) and it being a federation of 488 local chambers of commerce. Its origins go back to the Tokyo Chamber of Commerce established in 1878 but its president was purged under the Occupation and it was not reinstated until 1950.

Although representing the bottom half of the 'dual economy', its direction is in the hands of the large companies that the SMEs work for. At the time of writing its president is Rokuro Ishikawa of one of the biggest construction companies, Kajima Corporation, connected with the Sumitomo *keiretsu*. Before that, its most notable president was Shigeo Nagano, president of the world's largest steelmaker, Nippon Steel; and quite a contrast with the JCCI's membership of SMEs.[44]

Nagano's status as head of Nippon Steel persuaded the government to set up a scheme for providing SMEs with small loans, provided they obtained the approval of the local chamber of commerce, but SMEs are in an unenviable position. They bear the brunt of any business downturn and are mostly heavily dependent on the companies they supply, often through shareholdings and the transfer of technology. There are many stories of SMEs not being free to choose who they work for and of being threatened with extinction by their customers if they try and expand their business elsewhere: so much for the free enterprise system.[45]

Every year MITI's Small and Medium Enterprise Agency publishes its White Paper on SMEs, showing the considerable differences in wage levels between SMEs and first class companies and the high bankruptcy rates among SMEs: a figure virtually indistinguishable from the total bankruptcy figures for all firms, at least until the recent crisis.[46] In his article on the 'Feudal world of Japanese manufacturing', one unusually outspoken SME proprietor describes the top-down relations between the big manufacturers and their suppliers and how 'cost down' pressures bear down heavily on the SMEs, in spite of the levels of fast delivery, quality and reliability that they have to provide.[47] Even a Confederation of British Industry mission to Japan in 1961 which was trying to get to grips with the realities of Japan's industrial performance recognized the role of the SMEs in underpinning the entire industrial system and reported that 'in matters of delivery and payment, sub-contractors are clearly driven on a very tight rein': if anything, an understatement.[48]

What is still not sufficiently appreciated is the essential role of the SMEs in the key industries like cars and electronics and the organization by the big companies of their sub-contractors and suppliers into hierarchical chains that are under their firm control.[49] A car, for instance, consists of some 50,000 parts, of which companies like Toyota and Nissan buy in about 60 per cent, so familiarity with the big names of Japanese industry alone gives a distorted impression.

So it should be no surprise that MITI's figures show that 70 per cent of employees in manufacturing work in the SMEs. Germany also has a strong SME sector but a Japanese-German comparison of the average size of manufacturing firms in 1994 showed that the Japanese average was 'very small indeed'. While the German average was 186 employees, in Japan it was only 93.[50] It is a pity that more European and American writings have not paid attention to the significance of entrepreneurs[51] and SMEs in assessing Japanese competitiveness and why, although they are so numerous, they are so under the thumb of the big companies.

The last of the four business organizations, Keizai Doyukai, the Association of Corporate Executives, is different from the three others in that it has individual, not corporate, members and in being the most recent. It was established in 1946 and is more of a forum for the discussion of topics like the responsibilities of business, its future directions etc. rather than being a pressure group *per se*. Its leaders have come from the large firms but since the death of a former strong president in 1978 it has lost influence. In 1991 its then president was forced to apologize for making remarks that were critical of the LDP's inability or unwillingness to pursue political reform.[52]

In the case of the bureaucracy, it was said that the royal road to recruitment was to get into Tokyo University and to show the 'right attitude' at the selection interview. Education in Japan was also described as a 'national recruitment system', widely understood as such by parents at large and much more rigid in its determination of future careers and jobs than in many other industrial societies. As many have pointed out, it has proved well adapted to providing the companies with a literate, numerate and well drilled workforce in the years since 1945, based on the effort and memory needed to get through the rote learning of the 'exam hell', *shiken jigoku*.

For several years I tested the English language proficiency of recent entrants to a major *keiretsu* company, whose universities were listed by their names. The company's policy was to recruit from half a dozen universities at the top of the university hierarchy, so anyone who wanted to enter the managerial stream in this company, and many like it, had to get into one of these universities first. Those who failed the entrance exam the first time round, could either spend a year cramming to take it again or would have to enter a company lower down in the pecking order. Parents and students are well aware that the university entrance exam is the big cut-off point and many schoolchildren are driven so hard because their future depends on it. A European manager at the EU-Japan Centre commented that it was 'a very cruel system'.[53]

Those who graduate from third-rate universities, of which there are quite a few, will only be accepted by low-grade companies, while those who finish their education after high school are destined for non-managerial jobs. Companies maintain close links with the universities they recruit from and a graduate who subsequently performs poorly reflects discredit not just on himself but on his university, and professor. It can be a potent form of social control.

Those at the bottom of the pile in terms of exams passed must survive as best they can in the world of the SMEs, that pay less, have less prestige and cannot afford the 'long-term employment' and fringe benefits of the big companies. SME employees are in a labour market little different from anywhere else, while the 'permanent staff' in the big companies, hired directly after finishing their education, are in the company's own 'internal' labour market. The degree of job security they enjoy, although affected to some extent by the recession, is what they are paying a high price for in terms of the degree of company control over their lives both in and outside the workplace, which many people in other societies, including managers, would not like. It needs emphasizing that even the largest companies employ temporary and part-time staff, many of them women, who are paid less than the 'permanent staff', can be discharged at any time and are not eligible to join the company's union etc. Moreover, it needs to be remembered that for regular staff union membership is automatic: it is not a personal decision.

Exact figures are hard to come by, but the best estimates of employees having the relative security of a job until the normal company retiring age of sixty is no more than 20 per cent. These people are undoubtedly important but it is a pity that so many official speakers and others talk and write as if they are the majority and that their job security is the main reason for Japanese companies' economic performance. It is misleading to say the least.

But the whole point of the national recruitment system is its effect as a motivator, driving the young to perform by way of cramming schools and exams to get on the ladder leading to the managerial stream in a first-class company. For the most capable and ambitious, there is the prospect of rising high up the competitive ladder to the top, which in a *keiretsu* company can mean becoming the company's representative on Keidanren and perhaps eventually the Keidanren president.

It has often been said that this is a highly meritocratic system but the remark requires qualification. In the professions there is a stronger tradition in Japan of son following father than in Europe or America and under the heading 'All in the family: nepotism in Japanese corporate management', Japan's leading English-language business magazine pointed out in 1992 to the degree of family control in major corporations. A total of 121 well-known companies were listed, some with more than one family member on the board. The list included such internationally known companies as Kajima, Tokyu and Takenaka in construction: Pioneer, Omron and Makita in electronics and appliances: Canon, Minolta and Seiko (Hattori) in precision industries: Toyota, Suzuki and Aisin in the motor industry: Kikkoman, Kagome and Ezaki Glico in the food industry: Takeda, Shionogi and Eisai in pharmaceuticals: Shiseido and Lion in cosmetics and toiletries: Brother, Fanuc and Tadano in machinery: Takashimaya, Daimaru and Isetan in department stores: Ito-Yokado in chain stores; and Tokyo Gas and Chubu Gas.[54]

The complete list showed how widespread the practice is among companies of the first rank, said to number about 250 out of 1,264 listed on the first section of the Stock Exchange, while among SMEs the owner who hands on the business to his son is a familiar figure everywhere. In a survey of the presidents of the listed first-class companies, the same magazine had found the previous year that 45.9 per cent found the appointment of company presidents on a hereditary basis 'acceptable as long as the person appointed is appropriate'. Those opposed to the practice of 'public firms continuing in what is seen as the equivalent of private ownership' amounted to 42 per cent, while those most strongly opposed who stated that 'the practice should be discontinued' made up 10.9 per cent.[55]

According to a Japanese researcher who compared social mobility and education in Japan, the US and the UK, there is also doubt as to whether the situation in Japan is as different as has been said. To attend cramming schools and the top private universities in Japan costs money and once the pattern has been established it tends to repeat itself. For many people that is how they get the chance to become members of the business élite, represented at the top by the Keidanren.[56] Of the company presidents in the survey just mentioned, 19.6 per cent came from Tokyo University, while nearly half came from the four top universities of Tokyo, Keio (private), Kyoto, and Waseda (private). Their average age was 61.7 years, compared to 62.0 five years previously, showing the time it takes in established Japanese corporations to get to the top.

The top-down control of the big manufacturers over the hierarchy of the SMEs that supply them and the dominant position of the *keiretsu* companies at the peak of the pyramid of the Japanese economy, running all the way down to the smallest workshops, account for the powerful clout of the Keidanren in the political arena. The competitive force that maintains this power is the national recruitment system of educational achievement and the determination by companies of whether job applicants have the 'right attitude'. Yet to look at this way of pushing the young who aim to get into the top companies from an early age by forcing them to study long hours and take extra lessons at cramming schools does not by itself explain the advances of Japanese companies on world markets.

No selection process is perfect, and companies that are selecting their 'permanent staff' will be as careful as possible to avoid embarrassing mistakes afterwards, but merely giving people job security is no guarantee that they will be productive. Bureaucratic organizations, of which the former nationalized industries in Britain were a notorious example, are often known for their poor performance, and Japan's overmanned white collar sector is not without its examples either. What is missing from the equation are the qualities that make a successful entrepreneur, such as drive and the ability to spot new market openings,[57] together with strong work discipline and the constant watching of how employees are performing.

Partly because it is not the done thing in Japan for people to put themselves forward, even when others are well aware who holds the power; partly because of the constant harping on consensus and harmony and the importance of maintaining the fiction of group effort when it is really strong management that sets the tone, especially when the entrepreneurial founder of the company is involved; and partly perhaps because it would be foolish to reveal the roots of competitiveness to others, the role of strong business leaders and tight work discipline has been constantly understated. When company discipline is firmly enforced, it does not have to be pointed out all the time, which is perhaps an additional reason why it has not received more attention in books about management in Japan. In a sense, it is what the educational system has taught pupils to expect before they even enter a company.

Despite the antiquity of some of the *keiretsu* companies like Mitsui and Sumitomo, it is often forgotten that many of Japan's best known manufacturing companies were not established until quite recently. YKK, today the world's biggest maker of zip fasteners, for instance, was founded by Tadao Yoshida, the son of a poor family, in 1934: his inspiration was the life of Andrew Carnegie.[58] Also familiar with Andrew Carnegie's story was Yoshisuke Aikawa, the founder of Nissan in 1933.[59] Toyota Motors was founded by Kiichiro Toyoda in 1935.[60] Soichiro Honda set up his first company in 1927. Konosuke Matsushita, also from a poor family and without a university education but widely recognized as one of Japan's greatest entrepreneurs started his first business in 1917 and ended up by heading Matsushita Electric, one of the 'vertical' *keiretsu*. There were many others whose names are less well known abroad.

After the Second World War there was another crop of entrepreneurial companies, of which the best known internationally is probably Sony, which started out with virtually nothing except its own drive to innovate and its engineering skills. In other fields there were the sports goods maker ASICS, begun by Kihachiro Onitsuka in 1949 after many struggles,[61] the security systems company now known as SECOM established by Makoto Iida in 1962,[62] and the Kyoto Ceramics Company, Kyocera, set up by Kazuo Inamori, also from a poor background, in 1959 and today the world 's largest producer of ceramic packages for the integrated circuits industry.[63]

These business leaders, whether before or after the Second World War, can be said to be the Henry Fords of Japan and it is a pity that, with some exceptions, Japanese companies have often been represented as 'faceless'. In a recent comment on Kazuo Inamori's career, the *Financial Times* remarked that it had been 'marked by a single-minded devotion to the businesses he has founded and confidence that they will succeed', and an unusual willingness to speak out in a business world and wider society where conformity is the rule; but then he has been extremely successful. Of course, by no means all companies are still led by their entrepreneurial founders but the best are led by successors who can motivate and control their organizations to make them productive. Others have become bureaucratic and one reads in the press about their efforts to refocus and restructure themselves.

It has been said that in the Japanese business world it is industry that comes first and finance second. Consequently, it is above all manufacturing that, to quote the trading company executive at the beginning of this section, 'bears the banner of the national interest' as the prime creator of the nation's wealth. This is not to disparage the other firms, in trading or services for example, or to imply that the Keidanren is solely a manufacturer's lobby but it does mean that something more than a narrow financial focus is necessary in order to avoid a distorted view of the Japanese economy at the present time and where it is going. The Keidanren and the whole idea of work as national service to support the national economy on which everyone's survival depends will remain important components of the Iron Triangle.

## (3) THE POLITICIANS: SMOKE-FILLED BACKROOMS
*Japan has first-rate industries; and tenth-rate politicians* – popular Japanese saying.

Because Japan appears to be a 'modern' state in the technical sense, many who do not know it at first hand assume that is also modern in the political sense. But outsiders from Western Europe or North America, for instance, should not project their own ideas of representative democracy on to Japan's political apparatus. Merely assuming that words used to label things, like 'elections, parties, prime minister etc.' mean the same things as elsewhere is to seriously distort the realities of how politics in Japan actually work. This is something that cannot be repeated too often.

The British prime minister, for example, has considerable power to select and to reshuffle his cabinet as he pleases. He can order British forces into action. The Japanese prime minister's power is greatly limited by having to choose for his cabinet a balance of members of the different factions within his party. His job is more to do with administration than policy. The threat to his position comes from the *kuromaku*, the 'wire pullers', ostensibly in the same party but in competing factions: not from the opposition.

Thus, the second cabinet in 1990 of one of the Liberal Democratic Party's (LDP) more publicly acceptable 'front men', Toshiki Kaifu, prime minister for a brief spell from August 1989 to November 1991, was balanced between the factions according to their power. Seven ministers were from the Takeshita faction: five from the Abe faction: five from the Miyazawa faction: four from the Watanabe faction; and three from the Komoto faction.[1] The job of trying to hold together five separate groups all scheming for power can be imagined. Finally, when the arch-manipulator himself, 'Don' Shin Kanemaru, who had first supported Kaifu, judged that he had outlived his usefulness, he was 'ruthlessly' thrown out of office. He was replaced by Kiichi Miyazawa as premier (1991–93), one of the old guard who was considered a safe pair of hands.[2]

What the Japanese prime minister says in the international arena is severely limited by his dependence on the special interest groups, especially as far as money is concerned, and the bureaucrats. In the case of the LDP this primarily means industry and the financial lobby, followed by the farm lobby, the small shopkeepers and so on.[3] He will generally try and say something nice for foreign consumption but, assuming he even wanted to, he would be unable to, for example, implement the market-opening measures that other countries are always demanding.[4]

The former ambassador Ichiro Kawasaki was quoted as saying that politicians were simply 'brokers, or middlemen, between the government and special interests', such as between the garages that regularly inspect private cars and the Ministry of Transport, the general construction companies, *zenekon*, and the Ministry of Construction, the banks and insurance companies and the Ministry of Finance, the farmers and their Ministry etc. In other words, politicians are more concerned with fixing up deals, to bring contracts and money to their local area or to benefit their own personal careers, than with policy as normally understood.[5]

The bureaucrats rule whereas the politicians reign, as they say in Japan, and the special interest groups need the help of the politicians in lobbying for contracts, subsidies and protection from competition. Ultimately the Diet passes the legislation, although this, too, can be got round by means of the ministries issuing 'administrative guidance', as already described. Indeed, the technique of using 'administrative guidance' as a means of camouflaging what the government is doing and of preserving 'harmony' in the Diet is a recognized strategy but not one that belongs to normal parliamentary democracy. It is rule by extra-parliamentary means.[6]

To enter politics, to get elected and to advance in a faction to the point of attracting one's own followers requires five qualities in a leader: 'one to four are money, and the fifth is political ability'. This was the view of a Japanese writer fifty years ago and as a present-day commentator notes, 'Money is still the crucial ingredient in political success.' The collection of LDP funds through business organizations like the Keidanren has already been described and the special interest groups naturally reciprocate the politicians' favours in the expected way. This is the basis of 'pork barrel' or 'money politics' in Japan[7]

Because this is built into the system, the expression 'structural corruption' is often heard in Japan; or sometimes more poetically 'black mist'. This predominantly affects the LDP since, as the party that has been in virtually uninterrupted power in one form or another since the end of the Second World War in 1945 – a fact which itself requires explanation and comment – they naturally have the greatest power of patronage at their disposal. They are in an inherently corrupt business, connected with the *boryokudan* or 'Japanese Mafia', who can raise money and act as 'enforcers'. This is because of 'Japan's opaque business and political systems which conduct important transactions out of the public eye . . . a surefire recipe for graft and corruption on a massive scale'.[8]

Another well-known Japanese political commentator defined this as '. . . a vast arena where social coordination takes place without ever going through the channel of organization. . . . Everything from naked violence, terror and intimidation, to the subtler pressures exerted by *oyabun* (bosses – frequently in a criminal sense since the Tokugawa Period onwards). . . . These are the methods of solving the problem by means of *direct* human relations'.[9] A contemporary example is the attack by gangsters on Juzo Itami, who in his film *Mimbo no onna*, 'A taxing woman', had shown them up as the unromantic thugs they are.

What is perhaps surprising is that, thanks to films like *The Godfather*, the connections between organized crime and 'tenth-rate politicians' in other parts of the world are widely known; while the Japanese authorities have been quite successful in presenting Japan as a 'crime free' country with a modern political system. One reason for this is that with the few recent exceptions of films directed by 'Beat' Takeshi Kitano, only the most artistic or best Japanese films have been shown outside Japan. There are plenty of gangster movies, with the *oyabun* or godfathers of the crime syndicates and their henchmen, but either the distributors do not think there is a market for them in Europe or the US or they are cooperating in a policy of self-censorship by not showing material abroad which might reflect unfavourably on Japan's official image. In the US the 1960s Robert Mitchum and Ken Takakura film *The Yakuza* was an exception.

In Japan itself the media constantly report the endemic corruption of political life but it must be asked what the purpose of doing so is. The *Japan Times* for instance reported under the headline 'Public ennui greets scandals' that the nation 'appears inured to fresh news of corruption' and doubted whether it would 'draw much public attention or spur real reform'.[10] The item concerned a real estate dealer, Mitsuhiro Kotani, described at the time of his previous arrest in August 1990 for manipulating share prices as a 'member of the private political fundraising group' of prime minister Nakasone (1983-7). He was then charged with extortion, by threatening to sell his shares in the well known manufacturer Janome Sewing Machine Co. to gangsters unless the company gave him a loan. The *Japan Times* observed that there was 'a persistent web of ties between politicians, stock and property speculators and banks'.

When bribery and corruption become too blatant, the LDP's tactic has been to call for 'political reform', though they are themselves among the biggest culprits. This has happened when some of the big fish are arrested or forced to stand down; as with prime minister Tanaka (1972-4), prime minister Takeshita (1987-9), and the biggest behind-the-scenes manipulator of them all, 'Don' Shin Kanemaru, theoretically just the former LDP vice president until 1992 but in fact the *kuromaku*, or kingmaker. On television there are dramatic pictures of the accused being put under arrest, followed by a suitable period of 'sound and fury' in the media; ultimately 'signifying nothing' more than the usual *tatemae*, until the same thing happens again. An experienced foreign commentator quipped that his files showed the LDP's 'reform' slogans for 1976, 1979, 1982, 1987, 1989 and 1992: 'at least no one can claim that the LDP is inconsistent'.[11]

Why does the system seem so impregnable? Among the reasons given are the lack of a credible opposition and, as someone else who knew Japan well wrote, the 'lack of political philosophy, coupled with continual pragmatic compromising . . . at least in the West, opposition parties offer realistic alternatives'. That was written in 1979 but remains true today.[12]

Other reasons are the apathy or lack of interest in politics *per se* on the part of those who disapprove of the system but see reform as hopeless because of the dense network of mutually supporting vested interests in its way. An attitude of resignation is common. Others, of course, profit in a small way from the system or are caught up in the group relations that characterize so much of Japanese society. More seriously, when one considers how and why voters vote, there is the problem of what is a 'Western' political system superimposed on Japanese social and political behaviour and ideology. Hence it remains an elaborate charade of *tatemae*, a 'pseudo-democracy' or a sham, with similar words for voting, elections etc but denoting something very different in practice.[13]

Japan's first Constitution dates from the Emperor's proclamation of 1889, during the 'opening' of the country, and its second from the Occupation year of 1947. Until as recently as 1994 Japanese experts defined the two characteristics of the election system as 'multi-member districts' i.e. as many as up to five representatives all for the same one constituency, and 'unequal apportionment' i.e. electoral districts not having equal numbers of voters in relation to their populations. The two characteristics are not accidental and they continue to be among the influences on Japanese politics today; though they are by no means the only influences, as some who think naïvely about 'political reform' appear to think.

The Meiji oligarchs of the new regime after 1868 did not want anything more than a restricted parliamentary system and chose the Prussian-type Constitution of 1889 as best suited to their purposes. Having up to five representatives for the same district – up to the revised electoral law of 1994, first used in 1996 – meant that the keenest competition was between the candidates of the same, or 'government', party, the LDP; rather than the notional opposition, with the possible exception of the election of 1947 in the chaotic conditions of the early post-war period. 'Unequal apportionment' continues to mean that movements of population, typically from the country to the cities, are not reflected in the lists of electors; or to put it another way, it takes fewer votes to win in the country than in the cities.

This is good for the LDP, for whom rural communities organized on traditional lines are a strong source of support; and for the Social Democratic Party of Japan, formerly the Japan Socialist Party, for whom public employees 'in the biggest industry in the rural areas are important'. It was only a few years ago that the then Socialist president, Takako Doi, announced on television that the Party would not allow 'a single grain of foreign rice to enter Japan': a remark aimed at rural voters rather than urban consumers. By comparison, the 'Clean Government Party', Komeito, supported by the allegedly Buddhist Soka Gakkai sect, the Japan Communist Party and, until its merger, the Democratic Socialist Party were seen as predominantly urban.[14]

As far back as 1909 the Lower House of the Diet had proposed a proportional representation system but the Upper House had rejected it. From the standpoint of the Meiji oligarchs and the bureaucracy, the advantage of having several candidates competing amongst themselves for the, for example, three to five seats in the same district was that this competition helped to prevent the formation of large, unified parties. It ensured that the already existing factions in the same party would continue to fight among themselves. The strategy of the bureaucrats was that 'without any big, organized party, the bureaucracy can have more power than the politicians': a classic strategy of divide and rule. Not surprisingly, there are some present-day politicians who would like to reverse this but that is much easier said than done.

The most notable is Ichiro Ozawa, related by marriage to two LDP kingmakers, and before that a protégé of prime minister Tanaka. 'In contrast to the typical Japanese politician, Ozawa possesses the logic, vision and determination valued by other nations': as clearly shown in his own *Blueprint for a New Japan*. Said to be 'up to his eyeballs in money politics', he is close to the construction industry and has cultivated relations with MOF bureaucrats. He is also said to have made his mark in certain American government circles and is obviously highly ambitious but he is widely criticized for his 'arrogance', which can be a damning indictment in Japan where at least the pretence of humility is the accepted form, and is not 'a typical Japanese politician'.[15]

Proportional representation was again proposed after the Second World War, this time by the leader of the Socialist Party. He was told by the home affairs minister, Zenjiro Horikiri, himself a former bureaucrat, that this would be 'premature'. Apparently, the time that had elapsed between 1909 and 1945 was not long enough. So the bureaucrats' policy of keeping the 'power of political parties weak' continued as before. One Japanese commentator considers that bureaucrats generally scorn politicians and direct their main efforts towards their symbiotic relations with finance and industry, where they can find *amakudari* retirement jobs for themselves.[16]

In theory, all electoral districts should have the same number of voters, based on the census taken every five years, but the Constitution regards a discrepancy of 1.51 to one as allowable. LDP people tend to take this imbalance as justified, which is not quite the same thing. In the 1963 election, for instance, the imbalance, due to moves in the population, had widened out to 3.55 to one. When this was challenged in the Tokyo High Court, the decision was that this inequality was 'unfair but Constitutional' and that the result of the election should stand: yet another example of the Alice in Wonderland principle that 'a word means what I want it to mean', such as Constitutional for instance. The judgement itself should surprise no one, since judges are not independent and owe their careers to the government i.e. the LDP, the 'natural party' of government in one form or another.

The 1960 census should have been completed in time for the 1963 election but was delayed (sic), although it did reduce the gerrymandering of electoral districts to 'only' 2.19 to one by simply adding nineteen representatives. Under Japanese election law, it is the representatives themselves who are responsible for reallocating seats. Since the majority are from rural areas, where the population is draining away, what possible incentive can they have for setting up reallocation committees which would threaten their own seats? Thus, gerrymandering helps to keep the LDP in power as an apparently permanent government.

To say *'plus ça change, plus c'est la même chose'* would be an understatement. The 1990 census showed that the inequality in electoral districts had widened out again to 2.77 to one, when the reapportionment was made two years later. According to the *Japan Times*, it was three to one in some case.[17] Under the headline 'An extraordinary situation', an Australian professor in Japan was moved to comment on the paper's headline of 'Voting inequality ruled illegal but results valid'; pointing out that if the inequality was illegal, then the election should have been held again.[18]

As before, this was not, of course, done and it is hardly surprising to find books with titles like 'Japan's pseudo-democracy' [19] or to see Japanese-style democracy as being more like that of a one-party state: a 'Kabuki drama' or, according to one Japanese professor, 'karaoke democracy' in which the singers come and go but the tunes are always the same.[20]

In spite of the anxieties about the advance of Communism in the period of post-war disruption, the feebleness of the opposition has helped the LDP to the extent that it has become a self-fulfilling prophecy. Because the Left has been seen to have no credible policies for the economy[21] or convincing leaders and has engaged in futile dogmatic arguments over 'monopoly capitalism' etc, it has been continually out of power. Because it has been out of power, it has no experience and has gained little competence or credibility in the eyes of the voters, many of whom do not actually like the LDP, but most of whom are concerned with their own economic fortunes.

Until relatively recently, the LDP's reputation for economic management has been secure and to judge its corruption etc. by the criteria of a superficially 'Western' political system resting on the foundations of Japanese society and a different set of expectations would be misleading. This is not an argument for saying that the one is as good as the other, as some Japanese and foreign relativists make out, but corruption in any system is still corruption and one would have to be blind not to see the difference.

For years the old Japan Socialist Party, with its Moscow connections and its hankerings until late in the day for North Korea, was also marked by its impractical stand towards the 'Self Defence Forces': somewhat comparable to 'Old Labour' in Britain in fact. Until 1984 it opposed anything to do with the Forces at all but then came up with the formula that they were 'unconstitutional but legal': another Alice in Wonderland form of words, similar to the one that the LDP were employing about gerrymandered elections. Apparently, the meaning was that although the Forces contravened the famous Article 9 of the 'peace' Constitution of 1947, renouncing 'war as a sovereign right of the nation' so that 'land, sea and air forces, as well as other war potential will never be maintained', since the Diet had approved the Forces they were nevertheless legal.[22]

This was the viewpoint represented by the old Socialist prime minister, Tomiichi Murayama, in his extraordinary coalition with the LDP in the eighteen months between June 1994 and the return to power of the LDP under its nationalistic prime minister Ryutaro Hashimoto in January 1996. Both coalition parties had been desperate to get their hands on power and Murayama had abandoned his opposition to the Forces, whose existence he had strongly opposed up to that point. Already a year in advance, one of Japan's best known political commentators was prophesying that 'Murayama's days are numbered'.[23]

On being asked to go to the Foreign Ministry, a Tokyo taxi driver asked where it was: something difficult to imagine if it had been MITI or MOF. A common Japanese saying is that 'there are no votes in foreign policy', meaning that a Dietman has to look after the 'pork barrel' interests of his local electors. Outsiders have seen the policy as a successful example of 'merchant's diplomacy' i.e., sell as much as possible to anybody. Under South Africa's apartheid regime, for instance, Japanese passport holders had 'honorary white' status.

For many people, the one serious exception has been the US-Japan Security Treaty, whose renewal in 1960 caused a widespread popular explosion and led to the downfall, though not the exit from politics, of prime minister Nobusuke Kishi. US-Japan relations as such are not the main focus here but from the Occupation onwards the LDP has pragmatically followed American security policy,[24] while taking ruthless advantage of America's huge open markets. The paradox of Japan, the great creditor, being defended by America, now the great debtor, has not been lost on knowledgeable Americans with years of business experience in Japan.[25]

The popular explosion of 1960 over the 'Ampo', or Security Treaty, was based on a fear of being sucked into Cold War conflicts beyond Japan's borders, exploited by radical student and other Leftist groups. From the violent militarism of the 1930s and 1940s, many Japanese had a naïvely utopian vision of Japan as an Asian Switzerland; as if Japan could now withdraw into its shell and isolate itself psychologically from the outside world: a parallel with the two hundred and fifty years or so of the 'closed country' before 1868. Most were blissfully ignorant that Swiss neutrality involved compulsory military service and the maintenance of considerable war potential, as theoretically outlawed by the Constitution.

The reality was that the US-Japan Security Treaty was ratified in 1960, after the big organized crime syndicates with 100,000 men at their disposal had helped the government to contain the rioting. To coordinate these efforts, a meeting was held between Yoshio Kodama, representing the crime syndicates, and Tomisaburo Hashimoto, LDP secretary-general at the time of the attempt on the life of ambassador Reischauer.[26]

Kodama had a pre-war criminal record, had been engaged in plundering platinum and diamonds in China through his own Kodama Organization and had been arrested as a suspected war criminal at the time of the Occupation. He had largely funded the Liberal Party of prime minister Ichiro Hatoyama (1954-6). In the shadowy and to a large extent overlapping world of gangsters and ultranationalist Rightists he was president of the notorious 'Greater Japan Patriotic Federation'.

At an early stage in the Lockheed scandal, Kodama had been hired by Lockheed in secret in 1958 to help sell military aircraft and contacted Yasuhiro Nakasone, who had to resign as LDP secretary-general when this became known in 1976: it did not of course prevent Nakasone from becoming prime minister in 1982-7. Kodama's trial over the Lockheed scandal was cut short by his death. He rejected the truthfulness of Lockheed documents, claiming that they were the work of 'vengeful US imperialists'.

Tomisaburo Hashimoto – not to be confused with prime minister Ryutaro Hashimoto in 1996-8 – belonged to the faction of prime minister Kakuei Tanaka (1972-4). Prime minister Tanaka was the biggest fish to be caught in the Lockheed scandal and was arrested in July 1976 – on the orders of the head of a rival faction, Takeo Miki (1974-6). Tomisaburo Hashimoto, then transport minister, who had naturally participated in the decision to buy Lockheed aircraft, and his parliamentary vice minister were then arrested in September 1976.[27]

Needless to say, the Lockheed case was but one example of this way of doing business in order to ensure a sale. Indeed it was followed by the McDonnell Douglas case of 1979 but it was the most notable case known to the public until the Recruit scandal of 1989. The Lockheed scandal provided a good opportunity for prime minister Tanaka's numerous political enemies to get rid of him[28], while in the Recruit scandal it was prime minister Takeshita (1987-9) who had to resign, though this did not stop him from becoming another powerful wire-puller behind the scenes.

McDonnell Douglas had paid as much in 1979 to the head of the Defence Agency as Lockheed had to Tanaka before it but the affair did not make the same impact. As so often in Japan, there is generally more to it than meets the eye; particularly in a state where what counts is the role of law as used by the state, or those in power, not the rule of law.

In power, prime minister Tanaka's big idea had been 'the remodelling of the Japanese archipelago': a scheme in which his own building and construction companies would naturally have had a key role. Described as a 'rags to riches' politician, who had started his working life on building sites, the Tokyo Regional Taxation Bureau stated that the sum he left on his death of ¥11.9 billion was 'a record amount for a Japanese prime minister'. His daughter, who was at the time the LDP's head of the Science and Technology Agency – an unusual post for a woman in Japanese politics – 'denied that the complex structure of the family companies was designed to evade paying taxes', recalling similar cases elsewhere. Few Japanese politicians seem to die poor.[29]

One thing that stands out from these happenings in 'the opaque business and political systems' in which such transactions are carried on in the smoke-filled backrooms is the tight web of relations between politicians, businessmen, fixers, bureaucrats and even shadier figures from the world of organized crime. This makes these networks impervious to outsiders, whatever may be declared to the contrary for foreign consumption.

The construction industry, which is a major source of funds for politicians, is a good example. Like the bureaucratic system for inspecting private cars mentioned earlier, it is a system in which 'everyone gives and everyone takes', along the three sides of the Iron Triangle. Like the chain of dependent origination in Buddhist philosophy, it has no beginning and no end but for the sake of convenience it is simplest to refer first to the politicians, especially to those belonging to the LDP's 'construction tribe', or *zoku*. They help to award contracts to the companies they favour, by maintaining the inner circles of the bid-rigging groups, which are only open to selected companies: thus preserving the status quo and preventing what in the view of the Iron Triangle is 'excessive competition' or 'disorder in the market'.

In return, the firms that get the contracts provide the politicians with money and help at election time, as already mentioned in the case of companies being invited to support candidates etc. The bureaucrats give 'cooperative' companies useful information and overpriced contracts that help them to make more money, while the companies reciprocate with *amakudari* retirement jobs and other favours, such as the well known 'wining and dining', golf trips and so on. The bureaucrats assist the politicians by protecting or putting pressure on the construction companies as required, through the means of the licence system, while the politicians protect the bureaucrats' vested interests and secure budgets for the so-called 'bridges to nowhere' that have already been discussed. It is a system of mutually supporting cronyism, though each group will naturally try to get the best of the deal.[30]

The Japanese term for bid-rigging, *dango*, is well known in Japanese business and, given all the vested interests that profit from it, is not likely to disappear in a hurry. It annoys foreign companies and has become an item in US-Japan trade negotiations. Sometimes foreign companies may get token contracts.

Like the Japanese distribution system, which employs huge numbers of small shopkeepers that are a significant constituency for the LDP, the *dango* system also has the aspect as a means of social policy to keep down unemployment; not to mention of keeping money flowing to the LDP. The argument is that real, open competition would force the companies to compete on price, which would put many of the smaller ones out of business. A speaker from the Federation of Construction Contractors expressed the view that it might be possible 'to restrict illegal political donations for a while but there's not the slightest chance of permanently eradicating shady donations and *dango*; these practices are part of the very structure of the industry' and, it might be added, the collusive relations between the politicians, the bureaucrats and the companies.[31]

Looking at business-political marriages and the sons of Dietmen and ministers following in their fathers' footsteps further emphasizes how things are literally 'kept in the family'. Shin Kanemaru, who died in 1996, was the senior figure of the LDP's 'construction tribe' and a former construction minister; as well as being the most celebrated fixer in the smoke-filled backrooms. His son was married to the eldest daughter of former prime minister Takeshita, himself a skilled *kuromaku*, or behind the scenes manipulator. Takeshita's youngest daughter was married to the son of Takenaka Komuten, one of the Big Five of the Japanese construction companies; while Takeshita's half brother was married to the daughter of the founder of Fukuda Construction Co., another major contractor. The daughter of ex-prime minister Nakasone was married to the heir apparent of Kajima Construction Co., Japan's largest. Ichiro Ozawa, the ambitious politician whose book and political manoeuvrings have caused a stir, is married to another daughter of Fukuda Construction Co. In the cases of the two political marriages into this family, the 'go-between' who arranged them was none other than former prime minister Tanaka, himself brought down by the Lockheed scandal. What is significant is the high level at which these marriages were arranged and there are more cases where Dietmen run their own businesses.[32]

Especially in the case of sons whose fathers are either nationally or locally famous, entering the Diet can be likened to taking over a going concern. It is a head start when it is remembered how much it costs to get elected. In 1990 no fewer than 41 per cent of Lower House representatives had followed their fathers into the Diet and were known as second generation, or *nisei*. Thirteen representatives were third generation, while two were even fourth generation. There are many other family connections between generations: the name, reputation, contacts and inherited wealth all being important.

Bureaucrats often despise second generation Dietmen, whom they see as having the mentality of local chamber of commerce people toward the spoils of the political system. There is also some snobbery among élite bureaucrats, who graduated from the top national universities like Tokyo and Kyoto, towards second generation politicians who had to go to other universities instead; although second generation politicians have included such figures as the ex-prime ministers Miyazawa, Hosokawa and Hata, and the 'shadow Shogun' Ichiro Ozawa.[33]

The *tatemae*, or theory of electoral funding, is that there are legally determined limits but it is another open secret that many times more is spent, although 'the disclosure reports to the Home Affairs Ministry are usually carefully falsified'.[34] It is another instance similar to that of the false accounting in the financial sphere where everyone knows the figures are meaningless and yet the rituals are still performed. Why then is the cost of a political career so high?

There is an old joke that the LDP is neither liberal, nor democratic nor even a party. It is a collection of factions, *habatsu*, which modifies some of the propaganda about everything in Japan being consensus and harmony. In its day, the Japan Socialist Party also had factions but being almost permanently out of power its factions could not be compared in terms of practical significance with the LDP, the 'natural party of government'.

LDP factions scarcely reflect any ideological differences and their key decisions are 'made by the factional leaders in secret':[35] not, for example, by the prime minister on his own. The faction leaders are people with money and power and the ability to attract more money and followers who hope that by attaching themselves to him their own political careers will prosper. Factions are 'probably the basic fact of life in Japanese politics'.[36]

The intensity of LDP factional struggles comes from the fact that whoever is elected president of the LDP becomes prime minister. The election itself is a formality, as the result has already been 'sewn up' by the deals in the smoke-filled backrooms by the faction bosses and fixers, as with ex-prime minister Kaifu for example, who was both put into and out of office by these methods. In the business world, such pre-decision manoeuvrings are known as *nemawashi*, literally binding up the roots, so that the 'harmony' of the formal decision-making process is not disturbed. The hard bargaining that may precede the achievement of this harmony should be kept hidden.

Consistent with behaviour in other Japanese groups, absolute loyalty is expected from the followers, while the leader or boss can distribute patronage down to the junior members, who need his help to make any headway in politics. Bureaucrats know that they should 'move their antennae like those of an insect in the direction from which power emanates',[37] identifying which factions are up, which are down and which are moving one way or the other. By openly answering questions to ministers in the Diet for them and making themselves useful, they can gain influence which will stand them in good stead if they are themselves aiming at a political career on retirement from the ministry.

When the merger of the former Liberal and Democratic Parties was carried out under Keidanren pressure in 1955, creating the '1955 system', the two parties already had three factions each. The merged LDP then had six factions, four of which were led by bosses who were prime ministers at one time or another. Over the years, some factions split or were dissolved but in 1991 there were still six LDP factions vying for power against each other in the multi-seat electoral districts of that time.[38] One was led by the disgraced ex-premier Takeshita, who continued as one of the most experienced behind-the-scenes operators, and another by Kiichi Miyazawa, prime minister in 1991-3 and then finance minister during the financial crisis of the 1990s.

In the fifty-five years between the end of the Second World War in 1945 and 2000, Japan had no fewer than twenty-five prime ministers, with one caretaker, as the following list shows. The longest in office, Eisaku Sato, from 1964-72, owed his position to his skill in playing off one factional rival against another:[39] also to the death of his predecessor and of two more rivals. He had a *yakuza* bodyguard at his disposal, while other politicians hired gangsters to make sure that their election meetings passed off without incident:[40] a precaution similar to companies' use of *sokaiya* at the annual shareholders' meeting to deflect awkward questions.

What is obvious from the list is the dominance of the LDP and its return to power after its tactical coalition with the Socialists under Murayama in 1994, in spite of its difficulties in having for the present lost its majority in the Upper House. Even in Katayama's Socialist government in 1947 there were some from the Right, including the later prime minister Takeo Miki. This did not make for an atmosphere of trust among the factions.[41]

## JAPAN'S PRIME MINISTERS 1946-2000

| | | | |
|---|---|---|---|
| May 1946 | Shigeru Yoshida | July 1980 | Zenko Suzuki |
| May 1947 | Tetsu Katayama (Socialist) | Nov. 1982 | Yasuhiro Nakasone |
| Mar. 1948 | Hitoshi Ashida | Nov. 1987 | Noboru Takeshita |
| Oct. 1948 | Shigeru Yoshida | June 1989 | Sosuke Uno |
| Dec. 1954 | Ichiro Hatoyama | Aug. 1989 | Toshiki Kaifu |
| Dec. 1956 | Tanzan Ishibashi | Nov. 1991 | Kiichi Miyazawa |
| Feb. 1957 | Nobusuke Kishi | Aug. 1993 | Morihiro Hosokawa (ex-LDP) |
| July 1960 | Hayato Ikeda | Apr. 1994 | Tsutomu Hata (ex-LDP) |
| Nov. 1964 | Eisaku Sato | June 1994 | Tomiichi Murayama (Soc.-LDP coalition) |
| July 1972 | Kakuei Tanaka | | |
| Dec. 1974 | Takeo Miki | Jan. 1996 | Ryutaro Hashimoto |
| Dec. 1976 | Takeo Fukuda | Aug. 1998 | Keizo Obuchi (fatal illness) |
| Dec. 1978 | Masayoshi Ohira (deceased) | Apr. 2000 | Yoshiro Mori |
| June 1980 | Masayoshi Ito (caretaker) | | |

Rivalry among the LDP factions is in pursuit of power, not ideology, which in a sense has been Japan's strength from 1945 onwards. Governments have got on with the job of promoting economic growth by pragmatic means, making politicians more like business promoters, including of course of their own interests, but leaving many Japanese dissatisfied.

This can be compared with other systems where there is, as Akio Morita of Sony found to his polite bafflement, the pride of American businessmen in an 'adversarial relationship between government and business'. He stated frankly that 'the bureaucracy, which actually runs the government' was something that Japanese business had a relationship with that was 'basically supportive'.[42] From another point of view, the American ambassador John Allison stated in 1954 that there was 'no basic conviction for or against the free world or Communism' and that Japan's leaders would pursue any course 'to advance Japanese interests': the Japanese government was neither ally nor partner and only interested in getting the maximum out of the relationship with the US at the lowest possible cost. It seems hardly necessary to point again to the pragmatic, economic orientation of Japanese politics since 1945.[43]

On the face of it, Japanese elections should be cheap but, as with so many other things in Japan, the more you dig into them the more you find beneath the surface. Before an election, wooden boards go up with numbered spaces neatly squared off into equal-sized lots for the photos of the candidates, with their names and parties but no campaign messages. Small loudspeaker vehicles tour the streets announcing their candidate's name and politely requesting the voters' support, but again with no statements of policy. Paid political advertising on television, radio and hoardings is forbidden as is, at least in theory, door-to-door canvassing, and the emphasis is on personalities, not policies

At election meetings candidates present themselves to the voters wearing their best suits and extra length white gloves, which might lead a cynic to suppose that this is because their hands are so dirty. In 1980 a former construction minister remarked that to be elected you had to spend ¥100 million in the six months before the election was called and another ¥100 million during the official campaign period. Insiders reckoned that to retain a Lower House seat most candidates would spend at least ¥100 million but that newcomers would need twice that; which is where the faction boss would come in. In the Upper House it was calculated that what had been the figure of ¥500 million, or US $1.7 million, needed to get elected in 1974 had risen to ¥700 million in 1980. In 1977 a Japan Socialist Party (JSP) member announced that she was standing down because she could not find ¥100 million for even a minimal campaign: the JSP was largely supported by the unions.[44] It has been calculated that on a per capita basis the cost of elections in Japan is ten times higher than in the US.[45]

Politicians have to build up a successful supporters' association, *koenkai*, in their districts and keep the supporters happy so that they will continue to vote the right way. The tradition of doing and receiving favours in Japan based on the social principle of *on* or obligation is well known but is also rather like having credit in the bank that one can draw on later. All these things cost money.

Dietmen have their salary, an allowance for the salaries of two secretaries, plus funds for travel but most Dietmen want more than two secretaries and the official expense allowances are the tip of the iceberg. A Social Democratic Party of Japan (SPDJ) member who joined the Murayama coalition in 1994 was astounded to discover that it was the custom for him to pay an extra ¥350,000 a month to Diet employees such as chauffeurs, bodyguards and receptionists: though this was not counted as part of their salaries.[46] Shigeyo Hayasaka, an adviser for over twenty years to prime minister Tanaka, Japan's 'god of votes', stated that new LDP Dietmen would need to raise ¥100 million a year to pay their way, while more senior faction members would need twice that amount. Part of Hayasaka's job was to raise funds for the faction and to distribute bundles of cash to its members: some of whom received it 'with tears in their eyes' at election time. In the 1986 Lower House election, for example, the LDP gave each of its 311 official candidates up to ¥30 million each, while in 1990 it spent an estimated ¥200 billion, or US $1.3 billion: a staggering sum.

Under the multi-seat electoral district system, competition between the rival LDP factions occurred in all 130 districts; which included vote-buying. In Chiba Prefecture near Tokyo an LDP Dietman, Toru Uno, was charged with buying some 110,000 votes at ¥2,000 each, but he was not the only one to fall under suspicion.[47] The emergence of

Kakuei Tanaka as prime minister in 1972 was largely due to his wholesale bribery of 'neutral' factions in his fight against his rival, Takeo Fukuda. It was said that he had 'the best friends money can buy'; but also many enemies.

A faction chief, Michio Watanabe, and former minister spoke about LDP Dietmen's expenses to the Foreign Correspondents Club in Tokyo in 1988. Most Dietmen had ten to fifteen secretaries (!), costing a total of ¥10 million a month in salaries. These were not just people sticking stamps on envelopes but in many cases confidants deeply involved in all sorts of activities of the Dietman, representing him at funerals, weddings, shrine and school ceremonies and visits to hospitals etc. to make donations. Quite a few Dietmen have been secretaries in their time, like prime minister Kaifu who was secretary to prime minister Miki before him, while several second generation Dietmen have been secretaries to their own fathers before succeeding them: a good way of learning the ropes.

When things go wrong with receiving shares etc, it is often the secretary who gets the blame, as was seen most dramatically in the Recruit scandal.[48] Each visit to a school, hospital, wedding ceremony etc. required the Dietman or his secretary to make a donation, which he ignored 'at his peril' if he wanted to be re-elected. Watanabe's comment, which some might find a bit cynical, was that the voters got 'the political system they deserved'.

In 1989 the Asahi newspaper ran a series of articles pointing out how expensive a political career was. LDP Dietmen were said to attend an average of thirty ceremonies, receptions, funerals etc. a month, with one Tokyo representative claiming to put in an appearance at as many as three hundred a month! Of course under other political systems, private corporations, trade unions and individuals contribute to parties but what distinguishes the situation in Japan is the sheer amount of money involved. Thus a gala for prime minister Takeshita and his LDP faction paid for by the construction industry in 1987 raised US $14 million. The same evening, a fund-raising event for President Reagan raised US $500,000 – and that was considered a good result. There are many other means by which politicians can raise money and their value in recommending companies to helpful bureaucrats increases as they climb up the greasy pole. In such cases a note of recommendation on their business card is said to be worth ¥300,000.

'Party tickets' either to fund-raising parties or to 'policy seminars', whether attended by the purchasers of such tickets or not, bring in a good income. Speculation on the Stock Exchange – see previous remarks about reimbursing influential clients for losses – is another way of making money and if anything goes wrong there is normally the secretary 'who did this without my knowledge' to take the blame. This happened with Ryutaro Hashimoto when he was finance minister in 1991 in the affair of the bogus Fuji Bank certificate of deposit;

before he became prime minister in 1996 of course. Kickbacks and favours of one sort or another are common from dubious businesses connected with gambling. These include the ubiquitous pachinko, or pinball parlours – Japan's most lucrative leisure industry – which are connected with and 'protected' by organized crime and which, since they also avoid paying too much tax, do not want people asking awkward questions.[49] Even the 'clean' prime minister Kaifu, on whom some people had pinned their hopes of reform, received ¥5 million from the pachinko industry. He also had the use of a flat at a nominal rent in the prestigious Sanbancho Mansion, just round the corner from the EU-Japan Centre. The former Socialist chairwoman, Takako Doi, likewise received money from the pachinko industry; and so did the unfortunately named 'Clean Government Party', Komeito.[50]

Another business owing its lucrative profits to gambling was the Sasakawa motorboat racing business, which was a 'slush' fund for the Ministry of Transport and which after Sasakawa's death the ministry was keen to extend more direct control over. For MITI the equivalent was the Japan Bicycle Association, involved in racing, which under MITI's aegis supplied some of the Japanese money for the EU-Japan Centre, no doubt 'voluntarily' as they say. It has already been mentioned in the context of the machine-tool industry.[51]

Given the importance of getting on the career escalator by going to the right university, under the national recruitment system,[52] it is hardly surprising that parents worried about their sons passing the entrance exam may enlist the help of their local Dietman in getting him in 'through the back door', *uraguchi nyumon*, as it is called, by bribery. This is said not to apply to the top government universities like Tokyo and Kyoto but to others, including sometimes medical schools (*sic*).

All-pervading 'structural corruption' and the huge amounts of money that change hands because of it are the characteristics of Japanese politics. The Lockheed scandal and the Recruit scandal have been mentioned several times in passing but these were simply the most notable examples of what is a continuous process. It has included practically 'everyone who was anyone' in the LDP who, as the entrenched power holders, were and are the people who have things that other people want in their gift.

As the Lockheed and Recruit examples show, prime ministers have regularly been included. This started with the first post-war prime minister, Shigeru Yoshida, who obtained money from the coal industry in return for help with its reconstruction. Hitoshi Ashida and Takeo Fukuda were indicted over the Showa Denko chemical fertilizer company scandal in 1948. Nobusuke Kishi was strongly suspected of profiteering from deals in South East Asia over loans, aid concessions etc. and Hayato Ikeda and Eisaku Sato were among those involved in the shipbuilding scandal of 1954.[53]

As I found in the 1960s, people existing on an ordinary 'salaryman's' money found these flagrant breaches extremely irritating but seemed resigned to them, without the moral fervour that might have been expected elsewhere. Others, perhaps by a process of doublethinking, seemed to believe that government, as in the old Confucian idea, was essentially virtuous, though if they listened to the media at all they would have known that it was not just a case of a few rotten apples in the barrel. What might be considered paradoxical is the extreme contrast between the popular self-image of Japanese people as personally honest and the endemic corruption of their public life.

The Lockheed scandal[54] only arose in the highly-publicized way it did because of an American inquiry into bribes paid by US firms abroad and Lockheed's admission that it had (had) to bribe Japanese politicians to the tune of ¥2.5 billion in 1973-4, without which its bid would have failed against that of its competitor, McDonnell Douglas. Lockheed was represented by the Big Nine general trading company Marubeni and McDonnell Douglas by Mitsui. All Nippon Airways (ANA) had originally decided in McDonnell Douglas's favour but Marubeni was a contributor to prime minister Tanaka's faction and ANA had already received favours in return for its political contributions. These included licences to fly on profitable domestic routes. When, therefore, Lockheed and Marubeni together offered the prime minister ¥500 million, he then told the Ministry of Transport, who had to licence the purchase, to issue administrative guidance to ANA to buy Lockheed Tristars instead. It was a good example of the complex relations and manipulations of Japanese domestic politics on which the success or failure of a foreign company's sales efforts may depend. Since the pretence is that the market is open and that bribery does not exist, many foreign companies may be in the dark about the difficulties they face.

Prime minister Tanaka had always been an LDP outsider and, apart from his factional enemies, many did not like his brash style of collecting votes and money. In 1983 the Tokyo District Court sentenced him to four years imprisonment and a fine of what he had received from Lockheed of ¥500 million but he further alienated people by not showing the *tatemae* of ritual repentance. This was considered poor form. Also convicted were Tanaka's secretary, the former chairman and two directors of Marubeni corporation and ten others. An ironic footnote to the trial was the complaint of a Mitsui vice president that Tanaka had not 'kept his word' after he thought he had Tanaka's agreement to buy from his client, McDonnell Douglas. Perhaps he had, as the old joke puts it, made the mistake of 'taking yes for an answer'.

Even before the Lockheed affair surfaced, Tanaka had been forced to resign as prime minister in 1974 because of his land deals that allowed him to profit from his knowledge of forthcoming development projects. He had been saved in 1976 by the heads of three of the factions, who had told the then prime minister, Takeo Miki, that he would be removed from office if he allowed the public prosecutor to pursue further investigations. It was a good example of the weakness of a prime minister in the face of determined factional opposition.

In the Lockheed affair, Tanaka was released on bail and, if he had not been seriously ill, he would have had the last laugh. The LDP hardly lost any votes and he himself was re-elected; theoretically as an independent without any party affiliation. His majority was the largest of any Lower House member. He remained 'the decisive kingmaker for the cabinets of prime ministers Ohira, Suzuki and Nakasone': showing once again that the role of the *kuromaku*, the puppet master behind the scenes, is often more important than that of the prime minister, who is the figurehead. Tanaka's electoral district of Niigata in Northern Japan was well known for the amount of new bridges, roads, tunnels, railways and other public works that it owed to his time in politics. He was, in a word, an 'excellent' Dietman.

Following the Lockheed scandal, the next big one was the Recruit 'incident' or 'problem', to use the standard euphemisms.[55] The Recruit Company was set up by Hiromasa Ezoe, then a student at Tokyo University, in 1960. Starting with advertisements in university newspapers, he then found a gap in the market for information on job opportunities: something of keen interest to university students within the national recruitment system.

Branching out into real estate four years later, he also purchased two Cray supercomputers and provided on-line housing and other information with the help of NTT (Nippon Telegraph and Telephone Co.). While producing his 'Recruit Book' of employment opportunities for students and a comparable book about universities and colleges for high school pupils, his company projected the image of an up-to-the-minute data processing and information technology firm. By 1987 his company had 6,200 employees, with a turnover of ¥270 billion, and he himself had become Japan's 29th largest taxpayer with an income of ¥1.3 billion. In 1986 he had been appointed by prime minister Nakasone as a member of the expanded government Tax Council, although his membership had been approved by Noboru Takeshita, the leader of a rival faction.

Ezoe, like prime minister Tanaka, came from a humble background and craved status. He was not on a par with the LDP's old guard, even though he had got into all three business organizations: the Keidanren, where he had the title of Councillor: Nikkeiren, where he was a managing director; and Keizai Doyukai, where he was a trustee. As might be expected, he made political contributions and cultivated the ministries most useful to his business: Education, Labour and the Ministry of Posts and Telecommunications.

To increase his influence, Ezoe used the recognized tactic of offering

¥1.25 million of unlisted Recruit shares at a nominal price to a selected list of politicians, bureaucrats and businessmen in 1984. This enabled them to make large tax-free windfall profits when the shares later came on to the market, because unlisted shares are priced in comparison with other companies' shares without considering their actual market potential. Since Ezoe's company was doing well, the recipients were on a winner: he would hardly have offered them otherwise.

He then used the same strategy in 1986, offering ¥1.5 million in unlisted shares to men of influence on a selected list, including twelve LDP Dietmen and five from the opposition parties.

'Don' Shin Kanemaru funnelled money to the Socialists, the Democratic Socialists and the 'Clean' Government Party, Komeito, enabling him to head off open confrontations in the Diet. As Takeshita said, Kanemaru was 'a good arbitrator when things went wrong. He settled things'. On New Year's Day, a traditional occasion for showing loyalty and for asking for favours, journalists were surprised to find the secretary-general of the Socialist party at Kanemaru's house with Mrs. Kanemaru pouring saké for him.

In April 1989 Hikosaburo Okonogi, who as the then chairman of the LDP's Diet Affairs Committee had given the Socialists ¥2 million, ostensibly for tickets for a Socialist fund raising party, voiced an unusual public complaint. The press quoted him as saying that he was 'furious that they didn't know how to behave': apparently, the Socialists had not sent even a thank-you note. In other words, there was nothing unusual in giving money to a party theoretically in opposition but they should have observed the social niceties.

In 1995 the LDP justice minister in the coalition government under Tomiichi Murayama had to resign when news of the secret loan he had received from a 'new religion' of ¥200 million, at that time US $1.99 million, leaked out. He had promised to oppose his own government's proposals to tighten up the regulations over religious organizations, following the sarin gas attacks by the Aum Shinrikyo sect, while the main opposition group had undertaken not to ask 'embarrassing questions' about the loan.[56] Ezoe's inclusion of opposition Dietmen in his list of those receiving unlisted shares is consequently not as unusual as it might seem.

When the news of the unlisted shares got out, initially over a building contract in 1988, those involved were said to include former prime minister Nakasone, the LDP secretary-general and would-be prime minister Shintaro Abe, and the former prime minister Kiichi Miyazawa. Ezoe himself went into hospital and refused to answer questions: a standard ploy in such cases. Miyazawa tried to put the blame on an aide but had to resign. Hisashi Shinto, chairman of NTT had to resign. It was said that he needed money to get political help for his newly privatized company, in which the government still held

65 per cent of the shares, to fend off competition. On his arrest, he remarked that, 'I tripped on a small stone'. His rivals within NTT had apparently been leaking information. It was also said that ex-premier Nakasone had pressured him into buying two Cray supercomputers, for resale to Ezoe at a reduced price, but Nakasone was not indicted.[57]

The new justice minister (*sic*), Hasegawa, and the Economic Planning Agency minister resigned, followed by the vice ministers for Education and Labour. Prime minister Takeshita admitted to receiving ¥151 million, then US $1.6 million, of unlisted Recruit shares and to 'forgetting to report' another ¥50 million, or US $381,000. To be a faction leader means having the power to attract large sums of money, which then attracts followers. Nakasone had received at least ¥140 million and Abe and Miyazawa over ¥100 million each but the prosecution's problem was to prove that these were corrupt inducements for favours received. Dietmen cannot be held for questioning while the Diet is in session and top politicians cannot be asked to give evidence voluntarily, since everything is done through their secretaries. Takeshita's secretary and confidant of thirty years committed suicide. Nakasone did testify before the Diet but denied knowing anything. Takeshita resigned as prime minister and was replaced by a largely unknown 'front man' whom he could control, Sosuke Uno.

Other lesser personalities were indicted. Rothacher lists thirteen leading LDP politicians who received pre-flotation Recruit shares, two Democratic Socialist Party Dietmen, one Japan Socialist Party Dietman and one 'Clean' Government Party Dietman, with the amounts mentioned. One well known LDP politician, Yohei Kono, compared being involved in the Recruit scandal to getting a speeding ticket: everyone except cyclists does it and the few who get caught are unlucky. Altogether forty-three politicians, bureaucrats, businessmen and journalists resigned. There were altogether twelve prosecutions but the difficulties of proving that bribes had led to favours may be imagined.

Because of the political limits placed on the prosecutor's power the affair, like others before and since, gradually blew over and things returned to normal. Ezoe himself had political ambitions and was preparing the ground by making donations to Nakasone, whose faction he planned to join, and also to Takeshita and Abe for not objecting. His companies were investing in Iwate Prefecture, where he planned to stand, but these ambitions were frustrated. He was the only defendant not to get a suspended prison sentence; but then he was an outsider, not a politician, and media attacks had suggested that he was of *burakumin*, or outcaste, origin.

What was unfortunate for the LDP was that the affair occurred at a time when there was widespread resentment at the introduction in April 1989 of the consumption, or value-added, tax of three per cent, to plug a gap in the budget. This hit people in their pockets and provided a glaring contrast with what others could make just by being given unlisted Recruit Co. shares. Takashi Kato, former vice minister of Labour, had bought 3,000 unlisted shares in September 1986 and had made a profit of ¥6.9 million when he sold them in November. Katsuyo Ikeda, deputy secretary-general of the 'Clean' Government Party, Komeito, was given a loan by Ezoe's own subsidiary, First Finance Co., and made a profit of ¥10 million between September 1986 and the following month. Prosecutors discovered that Takeo Fujinami, former LDP chief cabinet secretary under Nakasone, had bought a house in December 1986 for ¥132 million without the visible means to do so.

One recent history of post-war Japan refers to the Recruit scandal debacle as 'the end of the Ancien Regime' but in what sense can this be true?[58] After the 'front man' Sosuke Uno, who came to grief in of all things a sex scandal, and Toshiki Kaifu, Kiichi Miyazawa of the LDP's old guard became prime minister in 1991 and was joined by others in his cabinet who had received Recruit money but were now apparently 'purified'. Evaluating politics in Japan by projecting the concepts of parliamentary democracy used elsewhere is as bad a mistake as projecting the principles of free market economics on to the national economic policy. In fact, the two are inseparable. Money politics, factionalism, corruption, the deals done by the various interconnected in-groups in the smoke-filled backrooms are not aberrations from the normal pattern of Japanese politics: they are the normal pattern.

To believe otherwise is to fall into the trap of believing that disclosures in the press or political realignments mean the same as they would under other political arrangements; or of believing that 'public opinion' in the 'Western' sense of the word exists in the same way. Takeshita's secretary, who committed suicide over the Recruit affair, left behind a note to his old high school newspaper, in which he said that, 'Behind the scenes of this peaceful democracy (*sic*) are the same bloody power struggles to the death that were waged time after time by medieval warlords.'

The constant scandals that occur are a matter of historical record and how many are there that do not see the light of day?[59] The case of the Sagawa Kyubin Express Delivery Company that needed to get licences to operate its business has already been referred to.[60] In it Shin Kanemaru admitted receiving illegally ¥500 million, then some US $4 million, and was fined the maximum penalty under the law of US $1,600. He claimed the money was not for him personally but for his faction. He was arrested on charges of income tax evasion in March 1993 but pleaded not guilty and died of a stroke in March 1996, aged 81. Former prime minister Nakasone described his political tactics as 'very classical'.

The Japanese 'journalist of the year' wrote in 1977 that,

'Entertainment, gift-giving and bribery play a greater part in business and politics in Japan than in any other country in the world. This is a way of life which people who want to deal with or to understand the Japanese should keep well in mind.'[61]

The now unfortunately defunct *Tokyo Business Today*,[62] formerly the *Oriental Economist*, described the machinations linking the three pillars of the Iron Triangle as a '. . . structural problem, a system of mutual assistance for vested interests', from which outsiders, Japanese and even more foreigners, are excluded. Specifically mentioned were the difficulties in entering certain markets, '. . . the suppression of free competition . . . and corruption of society as a whole'. Hiroshi Fukunaga, the editor, declared that '. . . the nation will never be truly modernized and can never begin to call itself international' while this system of interlinked closed circles persisted and described prime minister Miyazawa's aim of making Japan a 'lifestyle superpower' as an illusion.

The authorities' rewriting of history has already been mentioned and after textbooks for 1989 had been published a supplementary civics textbook to bring junior high schools up to date on the Recruit scandal, the resignation of prime minister Takeshita etc, had already been distributed to some 2,000 schools it was then withdrawn. It was accused of 'lacking neutrality' because it stated the names of politicians involved in the scandal: it was replaced instead by something on the consumption tax.[63]

Political journalism is also co-opted into the process of news management by the authorities. Many journalists spend years assigned to the same politician, industry or ministry etc. This gives the politician or bureaucrat the opportunity to give them inside information not for publication and other favours; in return for which he expects a favourable press.

The reason why this differs from what happens elsewhere is the existence of the '*kisha*, or journalists clubs': yet another form of exclusive in-group, which a politician like Shin Kanemaru was an expert at making work for him. His press corps became his confidants and understood the threat that Nakasone represented to him, and by extension to their own careers. A member of Nakasone's press club would not have been welcome at a meeting with Kanemaru, where he would have seemed more like a spy. Failure to follow the rules of the club would mean expulsion and a consequent drying up of information with severe results for anyone under the system of restricted job mobility, the price for long term employment, for any individual quixotic enough to break ranks with his in-group.[64]

Hiroaki Tase, a senior reporter with the Japanese equivalent of the *Financial Times*, criticized the 'unhealthy proximity between the media and politicians', pointing out that the press seldom engaged in serious political criticism and was therefore immature. Given the nature of Japanese politics as a system of brokering deals in the domestic arena, this is not surprising.[65] He had come to his new view of what the press should be during four years in Washington, where he found the press more open, analytical and critical. He supported the abolition of the cozy cartels of the *kisha* clubs and their form of self-censorship.[66] They are believed to number in the region of six hundred.[67]

*Kisha* clubs have strict rules on membership, on what may be published and when and have not been open to foreigners.[68] They generally serve to promote orthodox views of politics for domestic consumption and a more or less idealized image of Japan for foreigners, though it has to be said that there was an improvement in the treatment of news in the quality press between the 1960s and the 1990s. Hiroshi Fukunaga, editor of *Tokyo Business Today*, warned that English-language magazines aimed at foreign audiences 'are expected to portray the country's *positive* aspects, or at least not to dig too deeply into unseemly matters'.[69] They may therefore include considerable doses of misinformation, for example, that the majority of employees have so-called 'lifetime employment', or that Japan is a 'crime-free' country, with a rule of law similar to that in other modern states.

The functioning of the *kisha* clubs was clearly evident in the manipulation of news by the authorities in one of the most serious events of recent years, referred to earlier: the Aum Shinrikyo sarin gas attacks at Matsumoto and particularly in the area of Kasumigaseki in central Tokyo, the hub of bureaucratic Japan, in March 1995. The television news simply announced that 'now we will go over to our reporter at the Tokyo Metropolitan Police press club', who seemed merely to repeat what the police were giving out, without comment or analysis. There was no criticism of the police failure to take any notice of neighbours' complaints about what was going on at Kamikuishiki, near Mount Fuji, at Aum's chemical factory over several months, or of Aum's dubious land deals. Nor were there questions about why the police had tried to force an innocent man, Yoshiyuki Kono, to confess, including by browbeating his son, when he and especially his wife had been victims of the attack. He had not been arrested or charged and later complained about the media's campaign of harassment based on tips given to them by the police. Three television stations did in fact apologize.[70] The police did not.

Before their arrest, several leading members of the Aum Shinrikyo cult, such as the 'lawyer', or PR expert, Fumihiro Joyu, were treated as media celebrities, appearing many times on television and once, to its shame at the Foreign Correspondents Club.[71] Instead of being treated as possible suspects in crimes that had caused death and injury and as representing an organization that was already known to practice kidnapping, extortion and brainwashing, to name but a few, they were treated as if they were serious partners in a philosophical discussion. At least one French journalist told an Aum representative to his face that he was lying.

Mitsuyuki Okawa, a managing director of Tokyo Broadcasting System television, told a Diet inquiry that his station had not shown videotapes to Aum leaders of an interview with a lawyer, Tsutsumi Sakamoto, to whom distraught parents had come about the disappearance into Aum of their children. Sakamoto had been on the point of pursuing Aum, when he, his wife and small baby had been murdered. Tokyo Broadcasting was then forced to admit that they had lied to the Diet and that they had shown the tapes to the Aum leaders; without informing the police.[72] It was later revealed that the murders of the Sakamoto family had been ordered by the so-called 'guru', Shoko Asahara himself.

To this catalogue of deplorable media behaviour was then added an event that anyone who saw it on television is unlikely to forget: the murder in full public view outside Aum's Tokyo office, with police manning the crowd control barriers, of Hideo Murai, Aum's 'science minister' and highly qualified chemist. Strangely, the murderer made no attempt to escape. It was rumoured that Aum was involved in drugs and that the *yakuza* wanted Murai out of the way before he could talk; but it is highly unlikely that the full story will ever be revealed. As a former Kyodo News Service reporter and professor of Tokyo Women's Christian University observed: 'It's not surprising the media don't criticize the police, because most media organizations are members of press clubs. If they did so, the police would retaliate by not leaking information to them.'[73]

Partly because of such basic problems as having, for example, financial news, delayed until Japanese journalists have been given it first, some foreign journalists have reluctantly been partially accepted by *kisha* clubs, though to what extent is not clear.[74] There is also the problem that if they are really accepted into the club, they will be forced to obey its restrictive rules: not surprisingly many foreign reporters are strongly opposed to doing so. They risk having to submit to what another Japanese journalist described as a 'system that fosters collusion through prior scripting of who will report on what and how it will be reported': it is not a system consistent with press freedom.[75]

Censorship of matters concerning the Emperor is the responsibility of the Imperial Household Agency, a government department, and can extend to the Japanese-language versions of foreign publications. The original edition of *Newsweek* on 27 May 1993 appeared with a photograph of Masako Owada on the cover with the title of 'the reluctant princess' on her marriage to the Crown Prince: her father was a senior Foreign Ministry official. In the Japanese-language edition, the title had been changed to the non-controversial 'birth of a princess'. Photos of Rightists were dropped; as was an account of their connections with gangsters and LDP politicians and how some wanted to 'restore the Emperor to full divinity'. The whole article was cut by more than a half.[76]

Surprisingly, the one thing added to the article was that Masako Owada's grandfather had taken over a company called Chisso Corporation, responsible for one of the worst post-war pollution scandals, Minamata. This had involved the physical intimidation by gangsters of the victims and literally years of trying to get compensation.[77]

The Japanese edition of *Newsweek* is published not by an American company but by a company largely owned by Suntory, the large Japanese whisky, beer and drinks company, which did not wish to antagonize 'the Imperial Household Agency, right-wing fanatics, the *yakuza* or LDP politicians'. Meanwhile the *Japan Times* had presented the differing views of professors and others on the rites of accession performed by Emperor Akihito under the heading 'Role of Emperor in society is still unclear'.[78]

How arduous it can be for the ordinary person to obtain public information was shown by a Supreme Court ruling of 1995 on a case brought five years earlier by a plaintiff who wanted to photocopy the political fund balance sheets of altogether eight groups. The Home Affairs Ministry had refused this permission, which the Osaka District Court had upheld in December 1991. One year later the Osaka High Court had ruled in favour of the plaintiff's appeal but the Ministry had told the election committee to take the case right up to the Supreme Court. The Supreme Court had then decided that although the Political Funds Control Law guaranteed the right to see documents and to copy them by hand, there was no right to photocopy them! The plaintiff described the decision as 'ridiculous' and as symbolizing the immense distance ordinary people would have to travel before they would be able to 'watch over' politics.[79] It was a nice example of the 'role of law' in working at the behest of political interests and of legalistic nit-picking; proving again that the 'cultural' dislike of using the law that we have so often been told about does not get in the way of the most hair-splitting legalism when there is a political motive.

In November 1994 the electoral system for the Lower House of the Diet was revised and was used for the first time in the October 1996 elections. In place of the old multi-seat constituencies with several representatives, often from the same party, there are now three hundred single-seat constituencies, elected on the first past the post principle. A further two hundred seats in eleven separate regions are elected by proportional representation. Each voter has two votes, one for each type of seat, and marks the name of his or her preferred candidate on a printed paper: under the old system, the preferred candidate's name had to be written by the voter on the paper. An unusual feature of the system is that candidates may stand for both types of constituency.

The new system was the result of a compromise under the remarkable coalition of the LDP and the other parties supporting the government headed by the old Socialist Tomiichi Murayama.[80] The LDP and the Ozawa group favoured the single-seat constituencies, with the anti-LDP parties favouring proportional representation, based on what they judged to be their best interests. According to one theory, single-seat constituencies should produce a new kind of politics in Japan, along the lines of the two-party system in Britain (?) and the US, although this is not at all certain, as examples like Canada and India show.[81] One may also doubt whether deeply ingrained political behaviour can be so simply changed; assuming of course that such is the intention.

For the LDP the attraction was that electing one rather than several representatives for the same district would cost less and that it would to some extent serve to remove the stigma from its image after the Lockheed scandal, the Recruit scandal, the Sagawa Kyubin scandal and all the rest.[82] The LDP had regularly dangled the carrot of political reform in front of the voters (see Note 11 above), and when prime minister Ohira suddenly died in office in June 1980 the idea was presented again by a party heavyweight, Masayoshi Ito, who had not been involved in the Recruit scandal, when he was approached again in 1987 after the fall of prime minister Takeshita, who had had to resign because of Recruit.

Ito would have been a reassuring figure but he was aged seventy-five and had diabetes. Knowing that he would be used to fill a gap, he attempted to impose his own conditions. These included a full two years term as premier for himself, the elimination of multi-seat constituencies and – horror of horrors – the resignation from the Diet of thirteen LDP politicians directly connected with Recruit and the abolition of the factions.

To imagine Japanese politics in general and the LDP in particular without factions seems like a contradiction in terms and it is no surprise that the LDP bosses rejected Ito's terms and chose instead Sosuke Uno as a new front man.[83] After him and Toshiki Kaifu, whose treatment by Shin Kanemaru has already been mentioned, Kiichi Miyazawa, who had been involved in Recruit and who was one of the people Ito had thought should resign, became prime minister and it looked as if Japan's political life was returning to normal.

What was the result of the election carried out under the new rules in October 1996? Despite the sheer scale of the Recruit scandal, the LDP's Lower House vote went up from 211 to 239. Though it failed to get an absolute majority in the 500 seat House, it was, in the words of a Japanese political scientist 'the hidden winner: the losers (being) the camp of those who supported electoral reform'.[84] The LDP Ryutaro Hashimoto's cabinet of November 1996 consisted entirely of LDP members, while an Asahi newspaper poll of July 1966 had found that

65 per cent of voters put personalities before parties: with an increase among young voters opting for personalities – 76 per cent. These results must have been quite gratifying for the LDP, especially as a hardline prime minister, not the reform-minded Kaifu, was now back in power. Hashimoto, a strong fundraiser and president of the Japan War-Bereaved Families Association, consistently opposed even the notion of Japanese aggression in the Second World War and was a second-generation Dietman, strongly entrenched in the LDP's 'welfare tribe': a classic LDP representative in fact.[85]

During the 1996 election all parties had issued vague statements supporting deregulation and administrative reform but yet again 'without any systematic proposals': something foreign governments should take note of. The commentator just quoted above doubted whether 'most voters are burning with desire for administrative reform and all the rest of it' and foresaw the likelihood of a new period of LDP rule.

Hashimoto himself had failed in April 1985 to report ¥160 million collected at a fund-raising party for which Recruit had bought ¥400,000 worth of tickets. As prime minister in 1997, he was forced to apologize for the 'confusion' that his appointment to the cabinet of Koko Sato had caused: Sato having been given a suspended two-year prison sentence for taking bribes at the time of the Lockheed scandal. It was said that Hashimoto had been obliged to accept Koko Sato under pressure from former prime minister Nakasone, the *'de facto* leader of another LDP faction', showing that 'the factions wield as much power as ever they did'. Sato had to step down.[86]

In an interview in December 1997 the LDP secretary-general, Koichi Kato, likewise conceded that 'the role of the factions in securing cabinet posts for their members has actually grown'. He also doubted whether a two-party system would develop, describing Japan as not being 'a country where people debate' on the basis of clear opinions concerning, for example, policy matters. He was optimistic that the new system would work to the advantage of the LDP in the long run and agreed that the LDP 'is the only party to have benefited from the new system'.[87]

Others have also commented that '. . . policy issues have not been a major concern in most post-war Japanese general elections',[88] and that, 'In today's political world, the rule of the LDP is unchallenged.'[89] A Japanese reporter for the *Financial Times* found that, '. . . Japan's ruling LDP is gaining a reputation for being indestructible.'[90]

Indeed, before getting carried away by the rhetoric of 'change' that a revision of the electoral law might seem to imply, it is wise to ask what difference is to be expected when the rest of the political environment is still there unchanged. One example is the so-called 'second' or supplementary budget, which remains in the gift of the government and until recently did not even have to be accounted for to the Diet.

This is not just another budget to adjust to changed economic conditions during the financial year, as can be found in other countries, but something quite different. Known since 1953 as the Fiscal Investment and Loan Programme (FILP), or *zaito*, it uses money from the post office savings system, postal life insurance schemes and compulsory savings in state pension funds. Post office savings, introduced in the last century, have traditionally had a special attraction because the rate of interest has been set higher than that of the banks by the Ministry of Finance; to the frustration of the banks.[91] Until 1988 it was an open secret that the same person could open several accounts in different names, since savings up to a certain level were tax-free, making this a popular form of tax evasion. Other advantages were that by 1994 post office branches had 24,000 automatic cash machines for deposits and withdrawals, more than the largest commercial banks, and unlike banks did not charge for making transfers anywhere in Japan. Post office savings in Japan have promoted the savings habit more than postal savings in most countries.

The 'second' budget is over half and perhaps as much as two-thirds the official budget and FILP money is spent on projects such as airports and toll roads, which are supposed to be profitable because FILP funds are supposed to be returned with interest. But when 'bridges to nowhere' are being built for political reasons and to stimulate the economy, or the building companies, which are big contributors to the LDP, the need for profitability gets left behind.

Recently, a bridge costing ¥18 billion was opened: serving just 353 people on an obscure island. The Honshu-Shikoku Bridge Authority is losing ¥45 billion a year because the interest it has to pay is double the tolls it collects: it now owes the FILP ¥2.1 trillion. The Japan National Railways Settlement Corporation set up when the National Railways were privatized in 1987 had greater debts ten years later than when it started: ¥23.5 trillion, or five per cent of GDP. The new combined bridge and tunnel across Tokyo Bay was financed with ¥1.4 trillion of FILP debt. All these debts bear down on the unfortunate taxpayer, already groaning under the weight of the housing association, *jusen*, the ¥60 trillion (so far) for the banks' debts and the consumption tax etc.[92]

The *Financial Times* recently described Japanese public finance as a web that is 'complex, opaque and huge', in which the 'off balance sheet items' and 'hidden losses' add up, as was seen earlier with the problems of the banks and their *tobashi* methods of hiding losses, to unquantifiable amounts.[93] The FILP deals with huge amounts, like the ¥400,000 billion of postal savings and pension funds:[94] four times the assets of the world's largest commercial bank, the Bank of America, or to put it another way, more than the GDP of Germany.[95] No wonder another Japanese journalist reported that the 'second' budget was known to MOF officials as the 'abode of the demons'. The parallel between the 'complex, opaque and huge' system of public finance with the political system, with all its openings for corruption and obfuscation on the 'I'll scratch your back and you scratch mine' principle, hardly needs emphasizing.

As long ago as 1994 Japanese journalists criticized this system whereby the post office, in effect the world's largest bank, collects the money and passes it on to the Ministry of Finance, who then lends it out on the basis of behind-the-scenes political priorities for 'bridges to nowhere', the public corporations, staffed by people from within the closed circle, like the Japan Housing Corporation etc, and other sorts of projects. A scheme whereby one ministry, the MPT, lends to another, MOF, despite their occasional turf wars, was described as 'bizarre', while the money ends up to the benefit of different public and private sector uses. A prophetic comment in 1994 was that, 'No one group is in control of the entire process, and that may be the biggest problem of all.'[96]

Politically, some 18,000 post offices are franchises, working on a commission for savings collected and stamps sold. The postmen who deliver the letters know who has moved, enabling staff to visit local households periodically. The post offices represent a powerful vested interest and, as the *Financial Times* noted under the headline 'Postmasters who beat the banks and deliver votes',[97] postmasters are influential people. Many are rich local people who bought the title when the service was first established and it has been estimated that Japan's 24,000 postmasters control 80,000 votes each: the postmasters' association and the postal unions support the LDP financially.[98]

Especially in rural areas, postmasters have proved effective lobbyists for getting public money for local projects, and consequently good vote gatherers for the LDP. Many key politicians have served as ministers of posts and telecommunications and ex-MPT officials are keen to get *amakudari* retirement jobs, or in some cases to enter the Diet. This naturally cements the three sides of the Iron Triangle. In the leadership election in September 1995, the postmasters ensured that people voted for Ryutaro Hashimoto and not for Junichiro Koizumi. Mr Koizumi had proposed privatizing the post office![99]

Looking at the networks of mutually supporting linkages that serve to keep the whole web of vested interests in control and the amount that is negotiated out of sight in the smoke-filled backrooms, it should be obvious how hard it would be to change the political side of the Iron Triangle without changing all the rest of the bureaucratic and business sides.

Even such a person as Kenichi Ohmae, former head of McKinsey Japan and often described as the country's leading business guru, seems not to have appreciated the point. Standing as a Tokyo gubernatorial candidate in April 1995, he admitted being disconcerted by how 'ugly . . . Machiavellian and dirty' the political pressures were.

He had made his name with the idea of the 'borderless world' and discovered instead just how inward-looking Japan's Establishment was. He was personally attacked in the media: something that anyone who does not repeat the official line that Japan is the best of all possible worlds can expect. Ruefully commenting on his failure to secure more than a fraction of the members he had aimed at for his political reform group, he observed that, 'The Ministry of Education has done a wonderful job of persuading 120 million Japanese that their fate is handed down to them by the government. I am having an uphill battle persuading people this is not so.'[100]

In the event, the election for Tokyo governor was won by Yukio Aoshima, a comedian who in the 1960s had impersonated a bad-tempered old woman in a popular television series, *ichiwaru baasan*. In Osaka, another popular comedian, 'Knock' Yokoyama, was elected as governor: not exactly an endorsement of conventional politicians. 'Knock' Yokoyama was re-elected in 1999 but Yukio Aoshima in Tokyo, after battling the LDP machine as well as the city's other problems, stood down after his four years.

To some, his successor was also a comedian but of a different sort. Having made the slogan 'The Japan that can say no' famous, he campaigned in Tokyo under the slogan 'A Tokyo that can say no'. This was the well known nationalist figure, Shintaro Ishihara. Among the things he was saying 'no' to was the continued presence of the Yokota air base in the Tokyo suburbs, while casting doubt on the value to Japan of the US-Japan Security Treaty: something outside the remit of a Tokyo governor. In the conditions of the recession, some saw him as a more sinister expression of nationalism.[101]

The chapter started by quoting the popular Japanese saying that 'Japan has first-rate industries; and tenth-rate politicians'. When listening to all the nice-sounding platitudes about 'cooperation, mutual understanding, peace, harmony' etc. for international consumption, people should remember that Japanese politics are firmly domestically focused and that 'there are no votes in foreign policy'. A foreign journalist with considerable experience in Japan wrote that LDP politicians who have worked the system virtually without interruption since the end of the Second World War in 1945 were people who could not 'make a persuasive speech or present a clear policy, because they never had to'. On the other hand, they were 'masters of back-handed fund-raising, closed-door intrigue, and impenetrable double-talk'.[102]

Anyone from abroad who is not aware of this difference between the *tatemae* presented in front of the screen and the *honne* hidden behind it is lost; which unfortunately includes quite a few foreign businessmen, officials and politicians. They should remember the old Japanese saying that 'fair words please fools'.

■ CHAPTER 5

# Will It Ever Change?

*We Japanese feel we have been pretty successful. Why should we change ? Others who are doing worse than us should change, not us*
– Kazuo Nukazawa, managing director, Keidanren, 1993.[1]

Here – I am tempted to say for once – we get a straight answer to the question of Japan changing but who asks such a question and why do people keep on asking it with such persistent expectation? Do people in other Asian countries ask it? Seldom – and let us remember that they are closer to Japan; and not just geographically.

So the question predominantly expresses the wishful thinking of those in the Western world who cannot see beyond the confines of their own free market and liberal democratic thinking, especially in Anglo-Saxon societies. Naturally, they want Japan to 'change', since this would fit in with their own ideas of how an advanced society should work and would save them the trouble of having to get to grips with Japan's political and business systems as they really are.

The Japanese authorities are naturally aware of this wishful thinking and of what people would like to hear about 'change', frequently understood in the uncomplicated sense of becoming 'more like us', and have been quite successful in playing up to it. One loses count of how many times articles with titles like 'Japan at the crossroads' appear, hinting that real change is just around the corner in attitudes towards 'internationalization' in business or politics, if only the foreigners will be patient just a little longer. The oft-repeated line that 'Japan is changing' – as if other societies did not – is banal and there has been little indication of change on the scale of what occurred in Britain or America during the 1960s, for instance.

Some then argue that 'young people are different now', and want to enjoy their lives instead of giving all their time and energy to the company. But what is the reality? At a time of rising unemployment, management again has very much the whip hand and those leaving school or university, becoming what the Japanese call proper 'social beings', *shakaijin*, in contrast to students, know that if they want to succeed in the company, or even get a job at all, they must conform to the company system. They cannot afford to be 'the nail that sticks out that gets hammered down'. Once inside the company system, with its degree of control over their time, including what in other countries would be the time outside official working hours, and the years it takes to reach senior management level, they become indistinguishable from their predecessors. Though they may enjoy the four years of university as the one chance between the 'exam hell' of the school system and working all hours in the company, there is little evidence that most have serious doubts about merging themselves in the task of the company and 'bearing the banner of the national interest'.

Naturally, there are always a few exceptions or dropouts but what difference to the system as a whole do they make? Staying twenty-five years or more in a company and attaining the minimum promotion level commensurate with length of service, while keeping one's ideas to oneself, changes nothing. Those who believe that young employees are going to change the key policies of either the companies or the bureaucracy are deluding themselves. They forget the slow process continuing over years of work, during which they are being watched and assessed by their seniors, whereby these organizations ensure the continuity of their policies and practices. By the time when young employees have fought their way to the top, which is where the key decisions are made, they are no longer young.

One also needs to be aware of the web of relationships and 'face' that bind the graduate job-seekers who make up the managerial élites in the big companies and in the bureaucracy to their universities: a web that puts them under much greater pressure than elsewhere. The employment handbook of a leading private university puts the matter well, explaining that:

> One cannot change his job in midstream simply because it does not suit him. . . . Not only is the graduate an employee of a firm but he is also considered a life-long representative of his university. A bad reputation can result . . . in disastrous effects for all the students that follow. He is, therefore, always under an obligation to his university to be obedient and loyal.[2]

In some Western business and political circles the desire to be reassured that the frequently discussed 'differences' are really just superficial 'misunderstandings', to use one of the favourite words employed by the Japanese authorities, is so strong that it blots out what Japan's economic leaders have quite unequivocally said. Naohiro Amaya, who retired from MITI as vice-minister, stated that:

> Post-war Japan defined itself as a cultural state holding the principles of liberalism, democracy and peace, but these were only superficial

principles, *tatemae*; the fundamental objective, *honne*, was the pouring of all our strength into economic growth.³

In a nice piece of understatement, particularly in the context of the previous discussions of Japan's politico-economic systems, Amaya made the pithy remark that, 'We violated all the traditional economic concepts. . . . The realization of the myth that if you entrust things to the market mechanism, the invisible God's hand will bring about a rational result is quite limited.'⁴

What this meant in practice was described by another MITI official, who explained that, 'Free competition has a stifling effect (*sic*). We must not allow it to be used in distributing the benefits of high growth, wages and profits':⁵ hence the common observation that in Japan 'only the companies are rich, the people are poor', and the comments of Akio Morita of Sony that the companies do not pass on enough of their earnings to employees and shareholders. Yet the former American Vice-President Dan Quayle, in a speech in New York, attacked the idea that the Japanese economy was not 'subject to the same market forces as American or European companies'.⁶

In another speech, this time to the OECD, another former MITI vice-minister, Yoshihisa Ojimi, explained that:

> After the war, Japan's first exports consisted of such things as toys or other miscellaneous merchandise and low quality textile products. Should Japan have entrusted its future, *according to the theory of comparative advantage*, to these industries characterized by an intensive use of labour? That would perhaps be rational advice for a country with a small population of five or ten million. But Japan has a large population. *If the Japanese economy had adopted the simple doctrine of free trade* and had chosen to specialize in this kind of industry, it would almost permanently have been unable to break away from the Asian pattern of stagnation and poverty. MITI decided to establish in Japan industries which require intensive employment of capital and technology, industries that *in consideration of competitive cost should be the most inappropriate for Japan*, industries such as steel, oil refining, petrochemicals, automobiles, aircraft, industrial machinery of all sorts, and electronics, including electronic computers. From *a short run, static viewpoint*, encouragement of such industries would seem to conflict with economic rationalism. *But from a long run viewpoint*, these are precisely the industries where income elasticity of demand is high, technological progress is rapid, and labour productivity rises fast. It was clear that without these industries it would be difficult to employ a population of a hundred million and raise their standard of living to that of Europe and America.⁷

What could be clearer than that? The statement makes it plain that Japan's policy was based on the rejection both of free trade and the theory of comparative advantage; not only in a purely economic sense but also in terms of the all important web of bureaucratic, big business and political relations that make up the Iron Triangle that has already been outlined. Yet many in the 'West' who should know better persist in the face of the evidence in believing that the Japanese politico-economy runs on free market lines or dream up fancy abstract theories about the inevitability of 'convergence'.

Why do they think the Japanese authorities would deliberately undermine their own power and abandon their way of doing things which has served them so well, if not perhaps always the population as a whole? Isn't it high time we listened to the powerful heads of MITI who have explained in unambiguous terms what they did, such as rejecting free market philosophy and the 'stifling effect' of free competition, and why they did so?

There is, of course, nothing new in these policies, except that the industrial and commercial power that Japan has built up since the 1960s makes it more urgent to understand what is behind them,[8] After the 'opening' of Japan in 1868 the policy was to enable Japanese companies themselves to produce the goods and services that the foreign companies that were at that time ahead of them were producing and to have no further need of them.

Some may say, including of course Japanese propagandists, that Ojimi's speech was made in 1970 and that 'it is all different now'. That ignores the significant roles of the bureaucrats and political interest groups in managing the economy, seen as clearly today in the use of public money in the financial sector or the awarding of contracts for 'bridges to nowhere' etc. as it ever has been. Anyone who thinks that the Japanese economy functions purely according to abstract economic principles should talk to experienced foreign businessmen in Japan and others who have been there long enough to know that it is not just a question of economic determinism apparently without any political involvement. Of course the Japanese way has its costs, as the use of public money to pay off the debts of the banks or the former National Railways etc. show, but these can usually be pushed off on to the unfortunate Japanese man or woman in the street.

Showing again how little has changed, the declaration of the European Council in March 1985 '. . . expressed severe concern about aspects of trade and economic relations' with Japan and the 'disappointing outcome' of the consultations between the EU Commission president, Jacques Delors, and prime minister Nakasone. In that year Japan 'registered the largest trade surplus (over US $50 billion) ever achieved by any one country in history'. The 1986 Moorhouse report to the European Parliament noted the particular surplus in manufactured goods and that Japan's 'initial need . . . to finance imports . . . of raw materials ... had long since been superseded by a global export offensive ... to maximize ... international market penetration at the expense of foreign producers worldwide'[9].

In 1999 the *Financial Times* and other papers were again constantly bringing out dramatic figures on Japanese exports and imports: 'Japan trade surplus soars to £74 billion higher'. The surplus against the EU was up 26 per cent: imports were down 12 per cent. With the US the surplus reached ¥6,700 billion, the highest since 1987, described by the deputy United States Trade Representative (USTR) as, 'A serious global issue and an extremely serious issue in our relationship with Japan.'[10] Yet there were still those who failed to understand the nature of Japan's 'global export offensive' and the use in the recession of the 1990s of the strategy of exporting one's way out of a recession, seen, for instance, in steel exports to the US.

Meanwhile, the mercantilist 'one-way street' policy persists, as perfectly summed up by the official quoted earlier who warned that, 'Foreign companies cannot come into Japan for free'. As recently as 1998 a Japanese retail sector analyst commented that, 'On the surface things have changed. Japan can say to the US that deregulation has occurred. In reality, nothing has changed, and in fact the regulations have actually become more strict.' Regulations here refer to MITI's previous Large Scale Store Law (*Daitenho*): an important issue for foreign exporters since such chain stores are more likely to handle their goods than the myriad of family run small businesses. As already noted, the shift of regulatory authority from MITI to local governments makes the situation worse because the local political interests are themselves hand in glove with the local shopkeepers. As another Japanese analyst noted, 'These are things they (foreign companies) cannot defend themselves against'.[11] So the Japanese government gets the propaganda benefit of such 'deregulation', while not merely leaving the basic problem untouched but actually making it worse.

No wonder the former director for Japanese affairs of the office of the USTR asked in 1993, 'Do trade agreements work?'[12] Since the American administration erroneously believes that the Japanese market operates on free market principles , which as Messrs. Ojimi, Amaya and other officials – who it can be safely assumed are not 'Japan bashers' – have publicly denied, this seems highly unlikely: especially when there is not the same continuity or institutional memory on the American or European side. The rapporteur on trade and economic issues with Japan to the European Parliament under the heading 'Odds stacked against breaking into Japan' in the *Financial Times* likewise referred again to the regulatory and structural barriers to European goods, in spite of the years of negotiation.[13]

The fundamental mistake is to believe that the Japanese economy 'responds more or less in the same way and to the same stimuli as the US economy', or the more free market European economies i.e.

consumer-oriented objectives within the context of what are not virtual one-party states.[14] Western governments grasp this in regard to defence but fail to see the future strategic consequences of letting others dominate their machine-tool and high-technology industries: a dominance which affects national power rather than purely economic performance, not merely now but in the future as well because of the loss of technical competence.[15]

In a review of 'Law and trade issues of the Japanese economy: American and Japanese perspectives', an American contributor pointed to the danger of mistaking the rhetoric of 'liberalization' or 'deregulation' for substance in other words of mistaking *tatemae* for *honne*. 'Let there be no mistake: the Japanese bureaucracy has no background of liberalism towards foreigners, foreign business, or foreign products in any situation where foreigners have the edge. Discrimination has long been the rule.'[16] Japanese people working abroad use foreign products every day but if they are to be imported into Japan, then they must be regulated, and the domestic interests protected.

The language of trade agreements is itself a problem. In the US-Japan agreement of June 1995 on automobiles and car parts, the American president claimed that this time Japan had undertaken 'a significant step to fundamental change' – that word again! – 'this agreement is specific. It is measurable'. At the same time, the Japanese prime minister stated that, 'Japan had adhered to the principle that we oppose managed trade . . . we have successfully excluded all of the numerical targets', the actions of companies belonging to, for example, the Keidanren, being 'beyond government reach': a nice irony when trade had always been managed by Japan's ruling élites.[17]

Regardless of who was 'right' in the above case, the flat contradiction of their views is glaring. One reason is the use of what the Japanese call *tamamushi iro*: language which like the iridescent colours of the 'jewel' beetle changes from purple to green to brown, depending on the angle that one views them from. It is an evocative image of the ambiguous language used by politicians and, in this case, trade negotiators.[18] Thus, there is little substantive progress and the scene is set for further mutual recriminations and endless talking shops, which the Japanese authorities know very well how to finesse.

During the Cold War, Western governments were used to the idea that the basic political stance of the Kremlin did not change and that what was required was patient negotiation over the years, as in the Strategic Arms Limitation Talks for example. They also knew that even if Soviet officials left the scene those that replaced them were there to represent the same political and strategic aims, in which they had been brought up. Western governments knew that they were not dealing with a democratic system but one in which the continuous institutional memory and fixity of purpose on the other side had to be taken into account; yet they frequently fail to see that the same need for consistency of purpose and institutional memory can apply to economic nationalism as well as to a shooting war. They are prone to think that because there is a new prime minister or cabinet 'Japan has changed utterly', as the naïve editorial of the Wall Street Journal put it on 21 June 1993, without an understanding of the background to Japanese politics. These indeed are the 'Fallacies of Political Change' that an ex-USTR saw wishful thinkers in the West deluding themselves with.[19]

During the Cold War it was easy to understand the nature of the Communist system and the threat posed by its military machine but it requires a further intellectual effort to understand the nature of Japan's 'non-capitalistic market economy', as Eisuke Sakakibara called it in his *Beyond Capitalism. The Japanese Model of Market Economics*, and the threat posed by its industrial and commercial machine.[20] What has not made it easier is that so few economists and economic commentators have actually lived in Asia and cannot therefore be aware of the context within which Japan's advance has taken place and what its strategy is. 'Japanese leaders . . . see the Japanese economy mainly as an instrument of power. . . . But with few exceptions, business publications have utterly failed to provide their correspondents with the solid cultural and linguistic training needed.'[21]

Before the Second World War the successful local assembly operations of Ford and General Motors in Japan were seen by the government as a hindrance to the development of the Japanese motor industry and as a drain on the balance of payments. Legislation was introduced with the express aim of making it impossible for them to continue and they were forced to give up.[22] After the War and having finally got out of its trade deficits to become the world's biggest creditor, one can be reasonably sure that the government would not tolerate becoming a debtor again. It would be too much of a loss of power, and 'face'.

While it is salutary that the Western press should finally report the shenanigans in the Japanese financial and political world for what they are, now that the 'bubble' has burst, there is the danger that the wider picture will be put out of balance by too much emphasis on the financial side. The acquisition by GE Capital in January 1999 of a number of leasing and other companies for £4.2 billion was described as 'the largest ever by a foreign buyer in Japan'.[23] GE Capital's president was obviously pleased that his company had 'been allowed (*sic*) to take one hundred per cent control . . . a big shift' and to ring-fence its acquisitions against the possibility of facing hidden losses that might be revealed later due to false accounting.[24]

That is all very well but what happens in five or ten years time when the pressure is off Japanese companies and they no longer need foreign money and foreign methods, or for instance when one of GE's ring-fenced life companies goes bankrupt because of the previous Japanese management and the Japanese public thinks that GE nevertheless has a duty to pick up the tab? One can easily imagine the campaign against the 'cold' and legalistic foreigners. Under a political system where the state uses the law as it pleases, once 'the bamboo that bends with the wind snaps back', the foreign firms could be under pressure. 'Virtually every acquisition in the financial sector has run into problems': not only about hidden losses but about who is to run the firm.[25] In Japan it is one thing to sign a contract and another to make an acquisition work as the foreign buyer wants, when its environment in every sense and the vast majority of its personnel are Japanese.

What this regulatory environment can mean even to Japanese firms was shown in the headline 'Japanese insurers may sue Ministry over lost funds', over their losses in the now nationalized Nippon Credit Bank (NCB). The insurers complaint was that 'we were forced to invest in NCB according to a formula drawn up by the authorities': a formula resulting in losses for them of ¥97 billion, or £516 million, allegedly due to the Ministry of Finance concealing the true state of affairs at NCB.[26]

More dramatic, and in the view of some unlikely, has been the decision of a major foreign firm, Renault, to get involved in the troubled affairs of Japan's number two motor manufacturer, Nissan. This is not the first time that Nissan has been in trouble,[27] due to poor management decision making and structural problems, such as too many outlets selling too few cars in contrast to its powerful rival Toyota. Daimler Chrysler looked at Nissan but liked neither the figures it saw nor the company's resistance to change.[28] For the large capital injection urgently needed by Nissan, said to have £15 billion's worth of debts, Renault got 35 per cent of the company and the right of veto but not outright control.[29]

Some see potentially serious weaknesses on both sides and the atmosphere at Nissan and within Japan is, as might be expected, not favourable. A former MITI official called the foreign acquisition 'a national disgrace' and a blot on the whole Japanese motor industry.[30] The French government's continuing stake of 44.2 per cent in Renault was also a cause of disquiet. Nissan's president, criticized for the way in which it put a large part of the company up for sale – *miuri*, 'to sell one's body' in Japanese thinking[31] – resigned. But Renault is at the beginning of a process which Ford took some twenty years working at with Mazda. Whatever happens, it is clear how little Japanese attitudes have changed in regard to foreign participation in business in Japan; though when it is the other way round it is called 'industrial cooperation' and the suggestion that Japanese firms in Europe or America were being discriminated against in some way would cause strong resentment.

Press emphasis on the opportunities apparently available in the financial sector – 'one third of the world's savings, most of it stashed in dozy local banks or the postal savings system, earning derisory rates on interest'[32] – despite the lack of proper accounting and other dubious practices, tend to understate Japan's strengths in manufacturing. A senior American manager with long experience in Japan commented on how this misperception struck him each time he travelled home. People forget that Japan's economy is 70 per cent of East Asia's: seven times as large as China's for example. In November 1998 it had US $240 billion in foreign currency reserves and a US $130 billion current account surplus; backed by a well trained and skilled industrial workforce under tight management control and technological strengths in product areas for which there is strong export demand, such as cars and electronics, in which it continues to rack up enormous trade surpluses.

Foreign misperceptions of Japanese economic weakness extending from the financial sector to the economy as a whole, despite cases such as Nissan's, are not unwelcome to the Japanese authorities as they help to make Japan appear less of a competitive threat and to encourage the complacent stories that Japan is 'finished'.[33] But do Japan's material, technological and intangible assets, including, for instance, work ethics, make it look as if this is the case? We have only ourselves to blame if we underestimate the competitor.

Morihiro Hosokawa, prime minister from August 1993 to April 1994 and chairman of the Subcommittee for Better Quality of Life, summed up the contrast between 'Japan, the economic giant and on the other side, the poverty of the lives of ordinary Japanese people'.[34] A senior member of Japan's National Institute of Public Health commented that, 'Japan is not really a developed country; industry has developed but the country as a whole has not. Our economic growth rate and GNP may well make the government proud, but the living conditions of the people should cause it shame.'[35] The work ethic in a country where most people still have low expectations and do not expect all the state welfare benefits as of right, plus long annual holidays and regulated working hours, with the statutory payment of overtime, is generally higher than in much of European industry, for instance; and the authorities are determined to keep it that way.

Economies do not run simply on the basis of totting up columns of figures and those who are used to living in open, liberal and market-oriented societies need to make a considerable effort of imagination to understand what it is like to work in a country with a long history of authoritarian rule and poverty; where there is no sense of individualism as is taken for granted elsewhere and where the economic philosophy is based on the principles of Sun Tzu and Friedrich List. Control in such a society is not just restricted to the field of 'the national economy' but covers the role of social management of 'the State in everyday life', emphasizing group interests and group identity: the 'we Japanese' attitude,[36] as in the remarks of Kazuo Nukazawa at the beginning of this chapter, which effectively embrace the majority of the population.

What businessmen and trade negotiators see as a 'one-way street' is not just an economic phenomenon but is paralleled by a 'closed shop' mentality, the aim of which as so often in the past has been to keep out not only foreign products but foreign ideas. It is the Meiji slogan of 'Japanese spirit, Western technology' all over again. Anyone who doubts this, should read *Cartels of the Mind*, which details how foreign influences in the press, the law and elsewhere are kept out.[37] The author refers to what he calls 'Japan's overblown particularism', in other words the authorities' insistence that Japan's 'uniqueness' among all the countries of the world is beyond other peoples' understanding, and of course the slightest criticism. Harking back to the long period when Japan was virtually a closed country under the Tokugawa, some Japanese refer to this mentality as a *shimaguni konjo*, or 'island country complex'.

Starting with Japan's 'top-down' decision in the late nineteenth century to industrialize on the same level as the other established Powers, the new Meiji regime needed an ideology to mobilize and control the population, giving them a special idea of who they were. This was the *Nihonjinron*, or ideology of Japaneseness, which makes at least three major assumptions. First, it is assumed that the Japanese constitute a 'culturally and socially homogeneous racial entity, whose essence is virtually unchanged from prehistoric times to the present'. Second, it is taken as self-evident that the Japanese 'differ radically from all other known peoples': largely by avoiding any meaningful comparisons with them. Thirdly, the Japanese are 'consciously nationalistic, displaying . . . hostility to any mode of analysis which might seem to derive from external, non-Japanese sources',[38] This is the ideological background to Japanese trade policy and to discrimination against foreign business in Japan.

Why are the Japanese authorities '. . . so unconcerned about the double standard of its trading policy? It has to do with the ultimate values of Japanese political life – or what can be called the lack of them . . . sheer power (is) the main test of what is "fair" . . . the established power'.[39] Looking at Japan's trade policy and official attitudes towards inward investment without a thorough understanding of how power works in Japan is a major fallacy.

Even such a good friend of Japan as Professor, later Ambassador, Reischauer pointed out its 'inward-looking' attitude and wondered whether this would continue to make it 'an international odd man out': a view consistent with the self-regarding narcissism of the *Nihonjinron*. Thus because the sense of individuality in this form of group organization is taboo, 'it finds its narcissistic' satisfaction 'through the socially sanctioned idiom of an evoked racial, disindivualized uniqueness', contrasted with the 'monolithic otherness' of all countries that are not Japanese.[40] This serves the élites' aims of insulating the population mentally from others and of promoting the group organization and group thinking, as some Japanese as well as George Orwell put it, that the country is famous for.[41]

Inculcating the feeling of 'apartness', mechanisms of control such as the school system propagate 'ideologies to try and convince the public that social conditions in the country are the result of anything – culture, history, language, national character, climate and so forth – other than politics'.[42] Hence the constant harping on 'culture' and narcissistic representations of 'difference' in books on Japan, especially those written for foreign consumption.

According to Kenichi Ohmae, even the word 'Japanese' has been given an 'abstract, metaphysical meaning', as in the myth of 'the Japanese brain' or of 'racial unity', which serve to distinguish Japan from the rest of the world and which are discussed in the books about 'Japanese uniqueness'. What this means at the level of international trade or politics is that, 'Japan's classification of the world's countries is the natural outcome of its own self-image. . . . The Japanese divide the world into two types: resource rich countries that promise to alleviate Japan's mineral poverty, and consumer countries that provide markets for manufactured products'.[43] Behind the rhetoric about 'internationalization', economic nationalism and thinking of the *Nihonjinron* type, 'The real religion of the Japanese is Nihonism. They believe in their nation first and all other faiths and ideologies are only sects of this one basic religion.'[44]

Despite what top MITI officials such as Yoshihisa Ojimi and Naohiro Amaya had already revealed to the OECD and elsewhere about Japan's trade and economic strategies, there came a moment in 1990 when the Japanese Foreign Ministry 'feared that accurate knowledge among foreigners about the structure of Japanese capitalism might lead to countermeasures against Japanese business activities, and it sought through propaganda and dirty tricks to prevent this from happening'.[45] Anyone who does not repeat the official line could be singled out for personal attacks[46] but it seemed as if the ministry was worrying about nothing. In 1993 Eisuke Sakakibara, at that time director general of the Ministry of Finance's international finance bureau and popularly known as 'Mr Yen', went on to publish his *Beyond Capitalism*, in which he proclaimed not merely the difference but the superiority of the Japanese way of doing things.[47] Four years later he went on to point out in the London *Economist* that 'pessimism about the Japanese economy is overdone'. We cannot say that we have not been warned.[48]

So where is Japan going? Will the changes that the wishful thinkers in Europe and more particularly the US continue to hope for materialize? Whether the Japanese authorities have an official policy aimed at world economic domination is immaterial in the sense that its 'global economic and political strategy' impel it in this direction in an unending quest for power, security and prestige. This arises out of the interests of the three ruling élites and the web of relations between the bureaucrats, the leaders of big business and the politicians. The effect is to make Japan a headquarters nation in the world economy', leaving the US, as an American expert put it, as a 'puzzled bystander':[49] puzzled because of the official pretence or inability to see that the two economies do not work on the same lines. This is despite warnings such as that of James Fallows in 1989 that there is a 'basic conflict between Japanese and American interests' arising from 'Japan's inability or unwillingness to restrain the one-sided and destructive expansion of its economic power'.[50] Given the distrust of Japan that exists in Asia, this has potential consequences beyond the purely economic.

In the EU and USA Japanese firms undertake lobbying and PR campaigns to create a favourable atmosphere for themselves that would not be possible for American and European firms in Japan's closed environment. In 1990 for instance the Foreign Ministry in Tokyo called three hundred of Japan's leaders to a meeting and told them to increase their local donations in the US: for which the 'the Japanese government announced that it would give large tax deductions' to those that did so.[51] In Europe and USA Japanese firms like to publicize how many jobs they are creating in their transplants. But if that were the whole story why is there such an imbalance between Japanese direct investment abroad and foreign direct investment in Japan and why is there such an absence of official involvement in welcoming foreign investors with the sorts of investment incentives that other countries provide?

For many years foreign countries were not allowed to get more than 49 per cent of a joint venture and even when they were allowed to get 51 per cent or more they were likely to remain outside the charmed circle of Japanese business and official relations.[52] In fact the rejection as a matter of policy of foreign inward investment dates back to 1874, when the Ministry of Finance defied the London financial establishment by preventing a British-owned timber company from raising capital, forcing its withdrawal from Japan.[53]

The necessity of seeing Japanese policy in its politico-economic context, not just a purely economic context, has been consistently discussed here, and it is in the latter case that many of the misinterpretations lie. From that it follows that a major change in Japan's economic thinking would be impossible without a commensurate change in the political system: something that did not happen even under the Occupation. At that time, the first post-war prime minister,

Shigeru Yoshida, noted in his diary that the Occupation 'with all its power and authority behind its operation, was hampered by its lack of knowledge of the people it had come to govern, and even more so perhaps, by its generally happy ignorance of the amount of requisite knowledge it lacked'.[54] Fifty years later an influential Japanese scholar considers that the '1940 system', with its industrial cartels, bureaucratic regulation, restrictions on competition, and 'industrial patriotic associations' i.e. unions, established in the 1940s to mobilize the country for war is the reason why Japan is 'still fighting the Second World War' in some respects.[55]

Also fifty years later, a retired Japanese ambassador

> ... wondered whether Japan has ever been a modern democratic nation even after 1945, in the true sense of the word.... Individualism is what has been lacking in our society. Individualism lies at the foundation of a modern democratic society.... Without individualism, the establishment of what I would like to define as 'the public domain' in our society will not be possible. Japan has so far failed to transform itself into a truly democratic nation because of the absence of this concept of the public domain.[50]

Dr Leo Esaki, one of the few Japanese Nobel Prizewinners, but who had worked in America, similarly considered that the Japanese 'never challenge the unknown. There is a lack of a spirit of exploration. Eventually you come down to the lack of individualism'.[57] Eisuke Sakakibara wrote in 1997 that, 'Western individualism has failed to take root ... the goal is not personal but corporate gain.'[58] 'Corporate' or 'national' is important because it underlies Japanese company life, which might be compared with something in between school and the army in other societies.

Meanwhile, the Japanese press in 1996 reported that the Japanese public had had 'three unelected governments in a row': the 'old order' was back.[59] That gives some idea of the problem for those outside Japan hoping for change in economic relations based on an equivalent political change.

On the international scene the Japanese authorities continued to pursue their goal of a seat on the United Nations Security Council (UNSC) by contributing large sums of money but without, as Lee Kuan Yew of Singapore put it, undergoing the real 'catharsis' over their behaviour in Asia before and during the Second World War. This attempt to buy power and prestige is reminiscent of the attempts by the political fixer Ryoichi Sasakawa, after his release from prison during the Occupation, to buy the Nobel Peace Prize by making large donations from the different funds he set up with the proceeds from his dubious business activities.

By 1993-94 the Japanese government had only ratified seven of the twenty-five UN Human Rights Conventions and no more than a similar proportion of the ILO (International Labour Office) conventions.[60] In the 1960s, for instance, an ILO delegation had visited Japan led by Erik Dreyer to see whether the freedom of employees to associate was being observed but there was little result. It has to be asked what a formal government ratification is worth.

The Japanese writer of an article entitled 'No right to join the club' did not believe that the government's request to the UNSC was based on popular demand and poured scorn on its attempt to obtain 'special exemptions and privileges, on the grounds that it is unique among the nations of the world'. He also doubted whether it had 'a global strategy for maintaining' the peace.[61] Ironically, the Japanese Foreign Ministry's Recruitment Centre for International Organizations had to admit that the UN's figures for Japanese personnel at its headquarters and twenty-five related organizations was 'the lowest among the world's major industrialized nations'.[62] The main reason was the difficulty in making one's way in a career back in Japan once one had been outside the Japanese employment system, which normally requires moving up through the ranks from the end of education onwards for this kind of job.

In 1994 Yohei Kono, the foreign minister, had been obliged to confirm the existence of a twenty-five-year-old government paper admitting that, 'Japan will assure a policy of not having weapons for the time being. But it should always maintain the economic and technical potential to produce them.'[63] Japan's employment of dual-use plutonium in its considerable nuclear power station system has caused protests and alarm, not least over accidents, while three per cent of the plutonium pile has remained 'unaccounted for'.[64] Japan also has a rocket programme.

A knowledgeable EU Commission official who experienced at first hand in the Tokyo Delegation the problems of 'sticking carefully to the worthy rules of the GATT (General Agreement on Trade and Tariffs) while one by one strategic industries are being annihilated or forced into subjugation' by an 'intelligent, persistent and determined trading partner, willing to outflank and outsmart all gentlemen's agreements put in the way of its global economic domination', foresaw the consequences for the future competitiveness and living standards of the EU and USA.[65] Likewise a former USTR saw that the Japanese authorities 'tend to view settlements as merely one phase in a prolonged negotiation. Thus, many do not realize the resources required to monitor and implement trade agreements in order to produce concrete results'.[66] In discussion, the former EU ambassador in Tokyo, confirmed that getting an agreement on paper was the least of the problem and that when it came to implementation '. . . it was as if one had to start all over again right from the beginning'.

In March 1995, the Japanese authorities published a deregulation programme consisting of 1,091 items but Alain Coine, president of Rhône-Poulenc in Tokyo described it as 'meaningless': pointing out that it was full of ambiguous phrases like 'will be considered' or '. . . to be reviewed. . . . We are afraid that things under consideration will remain under consideration for many years'. In other words, this was classic bureaucratspeak for saying what foreign business would like to hear but with no intention of doing anything about, for example, '*keiretsu* corporate relations', as mentioned by the president of the European Business Council.[67] The EU Commission in Brussels also expressed its dissatisfaction.

The following year, the EU Commission published a 99-page *Summary of market access problems in Japan* together with a 127-page *List of EU deregulation proposals for Japan* but after all the stories about 'Japanese snow is different', to keep out the French and Italian ski manufacturers, the alleged discovery by Japanese officials of the 'Mediterranean fruit fly' in Rotterdam harbour, to keep out the Dutch bulb and cut flower exporters,[68] the eventual acceptance of Dutch peppers and tomatoes but the Ministry of Agriculture's refusal to accept the same products from fields a few miles away in Belgium or 'even to give a clear indication of the procedure to be followed to obtain import authorization' all show the endless possibilities for using delaying tactics to protect the local competition.[69]

On 23 February 1999, the *Financial Times* reported that the American government had negotiated 35 trade pacts but that 'only a handful had been successful'. 'Stymied by WTO rules and global economic concerns, Washington has scant chance of reversing a 33 per cent rise in its deficit with Japan'; part of the reason being Japan's 'highly cartelized society' and that there are many issues not covered by the WTO, 'particularly competition policy'. That is a fatal flaw when trying to deal with the web of relations between companies in Japan and the wheels within wheels of their relations with bureaucrats, politicians and local interest groups. No wonder that the paper reported that '. . . Washington has threatened, demanded, exhorted and nagged, but the US merchandise trade deficit has continued to climb.'[70]

Sir Roy Denman, former EU commissioner, sees the 'variety of devices, from technical standards to cartels and arrangements between companies' that lie at the heart of Japan's 'one-way street' trading practices as a 'problem for the world trading community'. In 1982 the EU Commission had proposed joint action to Washington but were told the US did not want to 'gang up' against Japan. The EU replied that this was not their intention but that they simply wanted to ensure that those getting the benefit of the world trading system had their markets open to imports.[71] Now some, but by no means all, Europeans are congratulating themselves on having found a more 'subtle' approach to trade negotiations, which Japanese officialdom should have less trouble in dealing with. They must be laughing up their sleeves at not having to deal with two trading blocs whose common interests outweigh their differences at the same time: that could have put them under real pressure. Meanwhile, the US government had changed its mind, and now proposed joint action to the EU. But the latter, content with its so-called 'subtle' approach, was unfortunately no longer interested.

Since 1945 Japan's rulers have played a very successful game of trading on 'Western' ignorance of the intertwined relations of its political economy, while mobilizing its own people for national economic effort, and benefiting from the world trading system and the 'divide and rule' strategy towards its competitors. It has been very cleverly done, even if others in Asia have fewer illusions than many 'Westerners' seem to about what Japan's leaders have been up to.

Exaggeratedly handwringing reports still emanate both from Japanese officialdom's 'cooperative' channels of information and from 'Western' media accounts that reflect the mechanical 'bean counter' calculations that should have been dismissed years ago by more attention to first-hand reports by experienced foreign analysts within Japan itself. Instead of relaxing in the belief that Japanese competition is not quite what it was from the 1960s to the bursting of the 'bubble', it would be better to understand the politico-economic system as it is instead of dreaming that it is the same as that with which neo-classical economists are familiar, or that it is in process of 'converging'.

In the July 2000 Lower House elections, the government of the new LDP prime minister, Yoshiro Mori, lost 38 seats, bringing its total to 233 out of 480[72] but, as one British newspaper put it, the LDP would still be likely to 'retain a commanding role in the coalition'. In spite of the apparently unfavourable arithmetic, its 'Italian style business-political corruption' would be able to deliver the desired results. Yuko Obuchi, daughter of the recently deceased Keizo Obuchi, quickly recalled from her language studies abroad, would be likely to inherit his seat, providing a further example of the dynastic side of Japanese Diet politics already referred to.[73] In other words: no change.

During the election campaign, it emerged that Mr Mori had acted as a go-between, an important role in Japanese society, for the marriage of the son of a former *yakuza* boss four years previously. His explanation was that he had replied to 'a request from an important associate'.[74] To Shinto priests and supporters he stated that Japan was a 'divine country centred on the Emperor' a remark 'reminiscent of the (State) Shintoist ideology that justified Japan's aggression in the Second World War'. After protests from opposition groups and the Chinese Foreign Ministry, which said that Japan should 'learn the lessons of history', Mr Mori stated that he had not meant 'to give the wrong impression'.[75]

He was reported to be very much in the tradition of the head of a faction, *habatsu*, involved in the pork-barrel lobbying for a high speed train line for his constituency, linked to two known financial scandals, and more at home in 'the familiar smoke-filled rooms' than in international affairs. His emergence as prime minister confirmed that 'there are no votes in foreign policy' and the unchanging nature of the LDP, effectively the 'natural party of government', whatever the electoral arithmetic might suggest.[76]

The idea of 'The End of History', arising out of a Western intellectual background, with its comforting notions that free markets and liberal democracy have decisively won the argument and that history is consequently at an end, was yet again confounded. Rather the power élites' skilful realization of a 'nationalist economic programme, structured in its tools and mercantilist in its ends' shows that it will be a very long time before Francis Fukuyama's dream is realized; if indeed it ever is.[77]

In spite of the many promises to reform the, undoubtedly problematic, financial system, there is a similar lack of substantive change. 'Restructuring' is an officially approved buzz word but the head of the Financial Reconstruction Commission (FRC) announced that, 'There may have been an impression that we are backsliding recently but that is not the fact', though without saying in more precise terms what was intended.[78] His predecessor, Michio Ochi, had the month before reassured bank and credit union officers that they would receive sympathetic treatment 'if audits by the Bank of Japan and the government's bank watchdog were too strict'. This indiscretion, said to reflect the LDP's point of view, cost him his position; showing the dangers of speaking with *honne* instead of *tatemae*. An American analyst in Tokyo expressed a fear widespread among foreign institutions that 'the LDP is seriously putting aside any serious reform agenda'.[79]

During the bidding to take over the nationalized Nippon Credit Bank (NCB), the Ministry of Finance (MOF) passed over a higher bid from the American institution Cerberus in favour of a lower bid from the Tokyo-based Softbank, a non-bank company. Foreign observers wondered whether MOF's FRC had been swayed by 'nationalist concerns'.[80]

Kimitaka Kuze, described as a 'top financial regulator', was obliged to resign in August 2000 after only 27 days in office, after allegations that he had received ' US $5.3 million in perks and fees from a major bank, a construction company and a religious organization'. He was aged no less than seventy-one at the time. The case was said to have been another blow to Yoshiro Mori's 'already shaky government'. It was yet another instance, if more were needed, of 'business as usual'.[81]

As recently as February 2000 what was billed as 'Japan's first hostile domestic bid' (*sic*) was defeated. The target, Shoei, an electronics and real estate company was defended by the Fuyo *keiretsu*, who attacked the Japanese bidder for being 'unnecessarily aggressive' and for 'undermining traditional Japanese loyalty'. The bidder retorted that, 'Japan Inc. is not a market; it's a members club', confirming what many foreign businessmen in Japan have long thought.[82] The first foreign company to win a hostile bid – in 1999! – was Cable and Wireless, a British company that beat NTT for the IDC telecommunications group.

It bears repeating here that the purpose is not to pronounce on whether Japanese companies should adopt the practice of hostile bids or not, which is for them to decide, but to look at the evidence of whether they are 'converging' with Anglo-Saxon practice or not. The evidence for the latter is slight.

Following the hostile official reaction to Renault's holding in Nissan, it is hardly surprising that Carlos Ghosn, the 'cost killer' sent to revive the troubled company's fortunes, has also been the object of criticism from the union, the Keidanren, shareholders, employees and dependants. His plan of October 1999 was to close five factories, with job losses of 21,000 at a time of higher than usual unemployment. It led to union protests at the company's headquarters in Tokyo. 'In the Japanese way of thinking, Ghosn's plan is unforgivable. . . . There has never been anything like this before. Companies have gone bankrupt rather than do this', was one union comment. Ghosn promised to find alternative work for those laid off and financial incentives for them to relocate but there was scepticism that this was realistic.[83]

Hiroshi Okuda, president of Keidanren and also president of Nissan's much stronger rival, Toyota, criticized Ghosn's plan, apparently in favour of a 'third way' between traditional Japanese capitalism and laissez-faire capitalism. Toyota's human relations director commented that there were moves to 'reform traditional Japanese business practices but not necessarily towards Western-style capitalism', i.e. not in the direction of the Anglo-Saxon model. It was his belief that, 'As long as we make improvements on a daily basis, we don't need major surgery.'[84] The remark reflected one of the fundamental principles of the Quality Control movement: constant incremental improvements on a gradual basis to the existing model, rather than the dislocation of a sudden step change. It shows commitment to the existing model that has been continually refined and has a rationale of its own.

Meanwhile, local residents in Murayama, one of the sites destined for plant closure in March 2001, saw Renault's move more as a 'hostile takeover'.[85] Ghosn was publicly criticized at a shareholders meeting for his alleged unfamiliarity with Japanese ways (personal communication).

The problems that Japanese accounting practices, such as *tobashi*, window-dressing etc, pose for foreign commentators who are not naturally familiar with them have already been discussed. At the national level there are likewise severe problems in knowing which sets of statistics, if any, to believe. No fewer than one thousand people are employed at two different government bodies, MITI's Economic Planning Agency (EPA) and the Management Co-Ordination Agency respectively, whose two sets of statistics do not tally in regard to such a matter of crucial importance as to whether the Japanese economy is in recession or not. Here they have been criticized for presenting 'conflicting signals' and for being 'dangerously inaccurate'.[86]

Shortly beforehand it had been reported, again in the *Financial Times*, that MOF was preparing for the '... first full balance sheet of (national) assets and liabilities for complete transparency in describing the fiscal position': hitherto said to be '... one of the most opaque in the industrialized world'.[87]

Major difficulties included capturing 'the full extent of hidden (*sic*) government liabilities in the complex financial situation', the exclusion or otherwise of regional government accounts, and an accurate assessment of pension liabilities, bearing in mind the rate at which Japan's population is ageing. The political sensitivity of openly publishing such information is obvious and the reason why it will be interesting, to say the least, to see what actually happens. For the present, the Japanese economy can continue to enjoy the advantages of being effectively camouflaged.

While there was constant attention paid both in Japan and abroad to the hard time Japan was said to be having, the country's foreign currency reserves rose to US $300 billion in April 2000: up from US $240 billion in 1998.[88] Currently, the all-important Yen-dollar exchange rate is ¥108 to the dollar, or ¥161 to the pound, so that the Yen is still strong compared to what it was in 1970 for example i.e., no less than ¥360 to the dollar. Indeed the Japanese government has been trying hard at the G7 and other meetings to persuade other governments to cooperate in the depreciation of the Yen, in order to help Japanese exports!

In a similar manner to the post-1945 period, when a life and death crisis impelled the Japanese population to economic reconstruction and advance, the present slowdown compared to the boom years after the 1960s, though nothing like the immediate post-war years, will lead to a further increase in Japanese competitiveness. This will continue to be based on the pursuit of economic nationalism and the pragmatic use of institutions and strategies that have served Japan's rulers so well. Technology and products will naturally change but the underlying strengths of the system, whose utility has been proven to the satisfaction of those in charge, in international competition will be preserved. In business language, Japan will be back, were it not for the fact that it has never really been away, as its cars on the world's roads and the plethora of its products in the shops and markets of the world demonstrate more eloquently than any dry theories.[89] Any commentator or competitor who believes in the comforting notion that 'Japan is finished' should think again.

Without stretching the point, a number of comparisons have been drawn between Italy and Japan and at a key moment in Italian history, the Risorgimento, Giuseppe di Lampedusa's famous Sicilian novel, *The Leopard*, has the line to the effect that, 'We must change in order to remain the same': the impression given by Japan in its power structure, national economy, bureaucracy and ideology.[90]

But the last word should go to a distinguished elder statesman, not from Europe or America, but from Asia, with experience of Japanese methods. Lee Kuan Yew, Senior Minister of Singapore, commented that, 'Singapore, unlike Japan, did not have the same irreversible attachment to the blueprint by which it was built.'[91]

## Yen to the Dollar 1949 to 2000

The appreciation of the Yen, *endaka*, from ¥360 to the dollar upwards

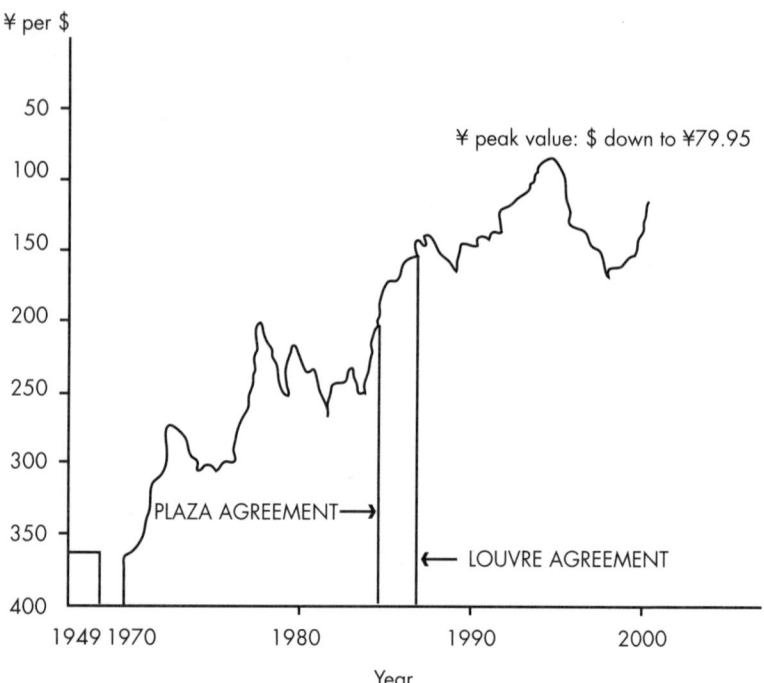

Plaza Agreement September 1985
Louvre Agreement February 1987

Sources: Hsu, R.C., *Reading, B.*, Financial Times

# Japanese Terms

The two most important are:

| | |
|---|---|
| tatemae | facade, pretence, official fictions, the surface, (the 'right thing to say') |
| honne | real intentions or meanings, substance, the facts |
| amakudari | 'descent from heaven' i.e. bureaucrats parachuting from their Ministry into private companies they have just been regulating |
| bonasu | 'bonus', but not in normal English sense. Payments up to 3-5 times the normal monthly salary at fixed times, seen as regular income |
| boryokudan | 'violent groups' i.e. organized crime syndicates |
| burakumin | 'village people' i.e. outcaste groups |
| dango | 'bid rigging', especially in building industry |
| endaka | 'upward revaluation of' ¥, especially after 1985 |
| go | popular equivalent of chess, based on invasion of territory |
| gyosei shido | 'administrative guidance' from officials, 'an offer you cannot refuse' |
| habatsu | political faction, in cabinets and parties |
| hai | yes = 'I hear you', frequently mistranslated as 'I agree with you' |
| juku | cramming school, especially for younger pupils |
| karoshi | death by overwork |
| keiretsu | oligopolistic major company groupings since the 1950s, covering commerce and industry. Typically bank-centred. Interlocking directors etc. |
| kento shimasu | 'We'll study it', officialese for 'forget it' |
| kisha kurabu | journalists' clubs i.e. exclusive self-censoring in-groups |
| kojinshugi | individualism, synonymous with selfishness |
| kuromaku | behind the scenes manipulators |

| | |
|---|---|
| madogiwazoku | 'Tribe sitting by the window', i.e. company managers put by the window without work. Method of enforcing retirement |
| MOFtan | person responsible at banks for relations with Ministry of Finance |
| muzukashii | 'it's difficult', i.e. out of the question |
| sokaiya | type of gangster specializing in blackmailing and/or 'protecting' companies |
| tamamushii iro | ambiguous language of trade negotiators, politicians etc, from jewel beetle whose colour changes depending on the angle it is viewed from |
| tobashi | 'passing over' accounts, i.e. hiding losses |
| yakuza | gangster, member of organized crime syndicate |
| yobiko | cramming school, especially for university entrance exams and retakes |
| zaibatsu | till 1945 the main oligopolistic company groupings, covering commerce and industry, typically with bank-centred holding company. Dissolved under the Occupation, including the previous family control, but reconstituted as keiretsu |
| zaiteku | 'financial technology' i.e. investment speculation by manufacturers, especially during the 'bubble economy' |
| zaito | the Finance Investment and Loan Programme i.e. the 'Second Budget' of projects, expenses etc. typically reflecting special LDP interests |

# References

**INTRODUCTION: JAPAN'S ECONOMIC NATIONALISM**

1. i. Choate, P. *Agents of influence.* Knopf, New York. 1990. p. 31.
   ii. Hrebenar, R. J. *The Japanese party system.* Westview, Boulder (Colo. ) 1992. p. 57.
   iii. Johnson, C. *Japan: who governs?* Norton, New York. 1995. pp. 77-8, 214-9.
   iv. Kubota, A. 'Big business and politics in Japan, 1993-95'. In Jain, P. and Inoguchi, T. eds. *Japanese politics today.* Macmillan Australia. 1997. pp. 124-43.
2. Schaller, M. *Altered states: the US and Japan since the Occupation.* Oxford University Press, New York. 1997. p. 7.
3. Nakagawa, Y. and Ota, N. *The Japanese-style economic system.* Foreign Press Centre, Tokyo. 1981.
4. Fingleton, E. *Blindside.* Simon and Schuster, London. 1995. pp. 3-6, 11-14, 25-9.
5. Schaller, M. *op. cit.* p. 221.
6. Japan survey. *Financial Times,* London. 14 July 1998.
7. Rothacher, A. *The Japanese Power Elite.* Macmillan, London. 1993.
8. Many translations e. g. Sun Tzu. *The art of war.* Hodder and Stoughton, London. 1995. Sun Tzu. *The art of war for executives.* Commentary Krause, D. G. Brealey, London. 1996.
9. Cf. Trevor, M. H. 'Japan: what international managers should know'. In *Pacific Rim Management 1996.* American Management Association, New York. 1996.
10. Schaller, M. *op. cit.*
11. Eatwell, J. *Whatever happened to Britain?* BBC, London. 1982. pp. 72-5.
12. 'Local governments impose own rules on large stores'. *Japan Times,* Tokyo. 26 October 1995.
13. *Financial Times,* London. 25 June 1998.
14. *Financial Times,* London. 6 August 1998.
15. Sazanami, Y. , Urata, S. and Kawai, K. *Measuring the cost of protection in Japan.* Institute for International Economics, Washington. 1995.

16 'For Kantor, the Motorola case says it all'. *Financial Times*. London. 17 February 1994.
17 Van Marion, M. F. *Liberal trade and Japan: the incompatibility issue*. Physica, Heidelberg. 1993. p. 49.
18 'Brittan disappointed'. *Sunday Times*, London. 16 March 1995. *Financial Times*, London. 15 March 1995.
19 *Japan Times*, Tokyo. 4 April 1995.
20 Miyamoto, M. 'Government of the bureaucrats, by the bureaucrats, and for the bureaucrats', In *Tokyo Business Today*. Tokyo. February 1996.
21 Fukushima, G. S. 'Underestimating Japan'. In *Tokyo Business Today*, Tokyo. June 1993.
22 *Financial Times*, London. 27 July 1998.
23 i. Reading, B. *Japan: the coming collapse*. Orion, London. 1992.
 ii. Woronoff, J. *Japan: the coming economic crisis*. Yohan, Tokyo. 1992.
24 *The Great Hanshin Earthquake*. Japan Times, Tokyo, special report. 1995.
25 *Terror in the heart of Japan*. Japan Times, Tokyo, special report. 1995.

## 1 A CRISIS OF CONFIDENCE

1 Financial Times survey. Japanese industry: slowdown has laid bare the myth of industrial might. *Financial Times*. London. 16 December 1997.
2 Alletzhouser, A. *The house of Nomura. The inside story of the world's most powerful company*. Bloomsbury, London. 1990. pp. 155-61.
3 Hall, I. P. *Cartels of the mind*. Norton, New York. 1998. pp. 45-79.
4 Rothacher, A. *The Japanese power elite*. Macmillan, London. 1993. pp. 103-8.
5 i. 'The lesson of history'. *Financial Times* London. 5 July 1995. The Japanese calendar follows the Emperor's reign e. g. Showa Period 1926-89, for the reign of Emperor Hirohito, since his demise the Showa Emperor. The reign of Emperor Akihito has the name Heisei. Consequently Heisei 1 = 1989.
 ii. 'Japan reaps what it sowed. Crisis in the financial system has its roots in flimsy regulation and poor policy making'. Leading article. *Financial Times*, London. 1 December 1997.
6 Interview with Lee Kuan Yew, Senior Minister, Singapore. *Sunday Times*, London. 6 October 1996.
7 'What would Confucius say now?' *Economist*, London. 25 July 1998.
8 Reading, B. 'Japan's system is the culprit. The need is for reform, not reflation'. *Financial Times*, London. 8-9 August 1998.
9 (Alice in) 'Wonderland accounting'. Leading article. *Financial Times*, London. 26 November 1997.
10 i. Entries under 'sokaiya, underworld business, business ethics' in Hsu, R. C. *The MIT Encyclopaedia of the Japanese economy*. MIT, Cambridge, Mass. 1994.
 ii. Entries under 'sokaiya' in Kaplan, D. E. and Dubro, A. *Yakuza: the explosive account of Japan's criminal underworld*. Addison-Wesley, New York. 1986. Macdonald, Futura, London. 1987.
 iii. 'Paying for peace among Japanese shareholders'. *Financial Times*, London. 30 June 1982.
 iv. Dawkins, W. 'Corporate Japan passes the AGM (annual general meeting) test'. *Financial Times*, London. 28 June 1996.

# REFERENCES

11 Alletzhouser, A. *op. cit.* p. 286.
12 Katayama, O. 'The importance of being honest'. *Look Japan*, Tokyo. October 1996.
13 i. 'Banks' bad loan disclosure: not quite transparent'. *Tokyo Business Today*, Tokyo. August 1993.
   ii. 'Fudged figures'. 'The hidden truth behind the mask'. *Financial Times*, London. 18 June 1999.
14 i. Sakurada, K. 'Who can you trust?' *Tokyo Business Today*, Tokyo. October 1994.
   ii. Robinson, M. 'Making a killing'. *Tokyo Journal* Tokyo. December 1994.
15 Sakurada, K. *ibid.*
16 Tanaka, F. 'The impact of introducing international accounting standards'. *Tokyo Business Today* Tokyo. May 1993.
17 Sataka, M. 'Corporate code of silence: auditors keep it all in the family'. *Tokyo Business Today*. November 1993.
18 *Economist*, London. 11 April 1998.
19 'Annual rituals known as shareholders' meetings'. Editorial. *Tokyo Business Today*. August 1991.
20 *Financial Times*, London. 4 June 1998.
21 Fay, S. *The collapse of Barings*. Random House, London. 1996. p. 1.
22 i. 'Wall Street *shokku*' (shock). *Economist*, London. 30 September 1995.
   ii. *Financial Times*, London. September 27,29. 4 October 1995.
   iii. *Japan Times*, Tokyo. 5 October. 4,24,26 November 1995.
   iv. *Sunday Times*, London. 1 October 1995.
23 'Daiwa executive indicted in US. New charges show how manager helped hide losses'. *Japan Times*, Tokyo. 29 December 1995.
24 i. 'Door closes on Daiwa's US network'. *Financial Times*, London. 6 February 1996.
   ii. For chronology of events, see *Japan Times*, Tokyo. 4 November 1995.
   iii. 'Ministry reluctant to testify on Daiwa'. *Japan Times*, Tokyo. 16 February 1996.
   iv. 'Daiwa pleads guilty in US: agrees to pay US $ 340 million fine'. *Japan Times*, Tokyo. 1 March 1996.
25 'Banks' problem loans may reach ~ ¥140 trillion'. *Japan Times*, Tokyo. 30 November 1995.
26 Hartcher, P. *The Ministry*. Harvard Business School, Cambridge, Mass. 1998.
27 Miyamoto, M. *Straitjacket society. An insider's irreverent view of bureaucratic Japan*. Kodansha, Tokyo. 1994. p. 50.
28 'Banks' unrecoverable or endangered loans estimated at ¥79 trillion'. *Nikkei Weekly*, Tokyo. 8 December 1997.
29 Tett, G. and Wighton, D. 'Japan admits scale of bad loans'. *Financial Times*, London. 13 January 1998.
30 Tett, G. 'Gangsters threaten US investors buying Japanese debt'. *Financial Times*, London. 16 April 1998.
31 Sumitomo Corporation. *From the history of Sumitomo*. Sumitomo Corporation, Osaka. 1980. p. 3.
32 Inohara, H. *Human resource development in Japanese companies*. Asian Productivity Organization, Tokyo. 1990. pp. 31-2, 41.

33  i. Arai, S. *Shoshaman*. University of California, Berkeley. 1991.

ii. Prindle, T. K. ed. and trans. *Kinjo, the corporate bouncer and other stories from Japanese business*. M. E. Sharpe, New York. 1989. Weatherhill, N. Y. 1992.

34  Dodwell Marketing Consultants. *Industrial groupings in Japan*. Dodwell, Tokyo. Annual.

35  i. *Financial Times*, London. 28 June 1996. 18,20,27 February 1997. 3 February, 27 March, 11, 12 May, 13 August 1998.

ii. *Sunday Times*, London. 16,23,30 June 1996.

36  Dawkins, W. 'The rising Yen: it was not always thus'. *Financial Times*, London. 24 June 1994.

37  Fukushima, G. S. 'Understanding Japan'. *Tokyo Business Today*, Tokyo. June 1993.

38  Wood, C. *The bubble economy: the Japanese economic collapse*. Tuttle, Tokyo. 1992. p. 19.

39  Kunihiro, M. 'The Japan as Number One syndrome'. *Japan Echo*, Tokyo. Vol. Xi. No. 3. 1984.

40  Eurostat. *The European Union and Asia*. Eurostat, Luxembourg. 1995.

41  'Japan on the brink'. *Economist*, London. 11 April 1998.

42  Kaplan, D. E. and Dubro, A. *op. cit.* pp. 278-302.

43  Cutts, R. L. 'Power from the ground up: Japan's land bubble'. *Harvard Business Review*. May-June 1990.

44  Wood, C. *op. cit.* p. 35.

45  Lewis, M. 'Kamikaze capitalism'. *Spectator*, London. 2 June 1990.

46  Cutts, R. L. *ibid*.

47  Alletzhouser, A. *op. cit.* pp. 183-209.

48  Tett, G. 'Man in the news: Akira Mikuni'. *Financial Times*, London. 29-30 November 1997.

49  Wood, C. *op. cit.* 'Securities companies'. 'Broking scandals'. pp. 93-139.

50  'The Nomura scandal. Familiar sins'. *Economist*, London. 15 March 1997.

51  Dawkins, W. 'Nomura's HQ raided in probe of suspected gang links'. *Financial Times*, London. 26 March 1997.

52  i. 'Tea-time raid'. *Economist*, London. 29 March 1997.

ii. Alexander, G. 'Nomura takes a beating in gangland'. *Sunday Times*, London. 27 April 1997.

53  'Investor protection fund lacks safeguards'. *Financial Times*, London. 25-6 July 1998.

54  i. 'Mr. Clean'. *Economist*, London. 26 April 1997.

ii. 'A useful scandal'. *Economist*, London. 24 January 1998.

55  Hollerman, L. *Japan's economic strategy in Brazil: challenge for the United States*. Heath, Lexington. 1988.

56  Woronoff, J. *Japan's commercial empire*. Macmillan, London. 1984. Sharpe, N. Y. 1985.

57  Halliday, J. and McCormack, G. *Japanese imperialism today. 'Co-Prosperity in Greater East Asia'*. Penguin, Harmondsworth. 1973.

58  Hu, Y-S. *National attitudes and the financing of industry*. Policy Studies Institute, London. 1975.

# REFERENCES

59 Johnson, C. *Japan: who governs? The rise of the developmental state.* Norton, New York. 1995.

60 Reading, B. *Japan: the coming collapse.* Orion, London. 1993. p. 227.

61 Trevor, M. H. *Japan's reluctant multinationals.* Pinter, London. 1983. pp. 151-2.

62 *The Times*, London. 22 November 1996.

63 *Wall Street Journal*, New York. 21 November 1994.

64 *Financial Times*, London. 10 December 1997.

65 Schultz, R. Review of 'Japanese takeovers: the global contest for corporate control' by Kester, W. C. (Harvard Business School, 1991). *Tokyo Business Today*, Tokyo. April 1991.

66 Shimizu, N. *Tokyo Business Today*, Tokyo. January 1995.

67 Morita, A. *Made in Japan.* Fontana, London. 1987. p. 262.

68 Emmott, B. *The sun also sets. Why Japan will not be Number One.* Simon and Schuster, London. 1989. p. 125.

69 MITI. *Small business in Japan. White Paper on small and medium-sized enterprises (SMEs) in Japan.* SME Agency, MITI, Tokyo. Annual.

70 Nakamoto, M. 'From noodles and rockets to shareholder value'. *Financial Times.* , London. 21 March 1998.

71 Nakamoto, M. 'Japan's LDP reverts to bad old ways'. *Financial Times*, London. 27 March 1998.

72 Lorenz, A. 'Euro pile up'. *Sunday Times*, London. 9 March 1997.

73 'Japanese car exports. Tokyo says Brussels has agreed to a higher quota'. *Financial Times*, London. 26 March 1998.

74 i. Nakamoto, M. 'Japanese (domestic) vehicle sales fall'. *Financial Times*, London. 7 March 1998.

ii. Simonian, H. and Griffiths, J. 'Japanese car-makers target Europe'. *Financial Times*, London. 4 March 1998.

75 Abrahams, P. 'Japan's current account surplus soars to £ 7. 64 billion'. *Financial Times*, London. 14 April 1998.

76. i. Moorhouse, J. and Teasdale, A. *Righting the balance: a new agenda for Euro-Japanese trade.* Conservative Political Centre, London. 1987.

ii. European Business Community (EBC), Tokyo. *White Paper on commerce and industry.* EBC, Tokyo. 1998.

77 Courtis, K. S. *The purge of Japan's economy. The most difficult phase ahead.* Deutsche Bank Capital Markets (Asia), Tokyo. 17 August 1992.

78 Sander, H. 'Out of Asia. Japanese banks and companies head home'. *Far East Economic Review*, Hong Kong. 16 April 1998.

79 *Financial Times*, London. 3,4-5 April 1998.

80 *Financial Times*, London. 7 August 1998.

81 Fukushima, G. S. 'A new era in US-Japan relations?' *Tokyo Business Today*, Tokyo. January-February 1993.

82 *Japan Times*, Tokyo. 22 December 1995.

83 *Japan Times*, Tokyo. 19 January 1996.

84 Kaplan, D. E. 'Bullets for bankers. How do you get gangsters to pay back what they owe?' *Tokyo Journal*, Tokyo. February 1995.

85 i. Imashiro, M. *Outcome of the privatization of the Japanese National Railways (JNR).* Daito Bunka University, Tokyo. 1991.

ii. 'National Railways astronomical deficit'. *Journal of Japanese Trade and Industry*, Tokyo. No. 5. 1983.

iii. Minister targets JNR debt'. *Japan Times*, Tokyo. 16 January 1996.

iv. Hutton, B. 'Japan's private railways signal danger ahead'. *Financial Times*, London. 15 April 1998.

86 *Financial Times*, London. 21 August 1998.
87 'Japanese bank rescue may use public funds'. *Financial Times* London. 21 August 1998.
88 *Financial Times*, London. 10 August 1998.
89 'LTCB fudge'. Leading article. *Financial Times*, London. 19 August 1998.
90 'Japanese prime minister to withhold results of national bank audit'. *Financial Times*, London. 18 August 1998.
91 'Japan to scale back high profile probes into financial corruption'. *Financial Times*, London. 25 May 1998.
92 *Financial Times*, London. 13 January 1998.
93 Van Wolferen, K. *The enigma of Japanese power*. Tuttle, Tokyo. 1993. pp. 2-3, 548-88 *passim*.

## 2 MYTHS AND REALITIES

1 'Cars that got the Japanese going'. *Sunday Times*, London. 31 October 1993.
2 Halberstam, D. *The Reckoning. How Japan beat the United States in the auto industry war and rewrote the rules of international business competition*. Bantam Books, New York. 1987. p. 645.
3 QC Circles: a bluecollar revolution'. *Focus Japan*. JETRO, Tokyo. Vol. 7. No. 7. July 1980.
4 Woronoff, J. *Japan's commercial empire*. Sharpe, Armonk N. Y. 1984. Macmillan, London. 1985.
5 Orr, R. M. 'US-Japan relations: patterns set in the past'. *Tokyo Business Today*, Tokyo. November 1993.
6 Schaller, M. *Altered states the United States and Japan since the Occupation*. Oxford University Press, New York. 1997. p. 9.
7 Schaller. *op. cit.* pp. 18, 38.
8 Hollerman, L. 'International economic controls in Occupied Japan'. *Journal of Asian Studies*, USA. Vol. XXXVIII, No. 4. August 1979.
9 Van Wolferen, K. *The enigma of Japanese power*. Tuttle, Tokyo. 1993. pp. 15, 462.
10 Eatwell, J. *Whatever happened to Britain?* BBC, London. 1982. pp. 72-4.
11 i. Fukushima, G. S. 'Tales from a trade veteran' *Journal of the American Chamber of Commerce in Japan*, Tokyo. January 1991.

ii. 'Revisionism and US-Japan relations'. *Japan Close-Up*, Tokyo. September 1991.

iii. Fukushima, G. S. Regular column in *Tokyo Business Today*, Tokyo. 1992-5.

12 i. Wolf, M. J. *The Japanese conspiracy. The plot to dominate industry worldwide – and how to deal with it*. 'MITI, the bike races and the great machine tool debate'. Empire Books, USA. 1983. New English Library, London. 1984. pp. 48-65.

ii. 'The Business', *Financial Times magazine*. London. 8 April 2000.

# REFERENCES

13  Fingleton, E. *Blindside*. Simon and Schuster, London. 1995. pp. 342-51.
14  i. Woronoff, J. *Japan as anything but Number One*. Yohan, Tokyo. 1990. pp. 215-9.

  ii. Hall, i. P. *Cartels of the mind. Japan's intellectual closed shop*. W. W. Norton, New York. 1998. p. 13.
15  Miyamoto, M. *Straitjacket society. An insider's irreverent view of bureaucratic Japan*. Kodansha International, Tokyo. 1994. pp. 174-6.
16  MITI. *White Paper on small and medium enterprises in Japan*. MITI Small and Medium Enterprise Agency, MITI, Tokyo. Annual.
17  Abegglen, J. C. *The Japanese factory: aspects of its social organization*. Free Press, Glencoe Ill. 1958.
18  Abegglen, J. C. and Stalk, G. *Kaisha: the Japanese corporation. How marketing, money and manpower strategy, not management style, make the Japanese world pace-setters*. Harper and Row, New York. 1985.
19  Cole, R. E. *Japanese blue collar: the changing tradition*. University of California, Berkeley. 1971.
20  Ohmae, K. *Beyond national borders: reflections on Japan and the world*. Kodansha International, Tokyo. 1987. pp. 2-3.
21  Wolf, M. J. *op. cit*. p. 124.
22  DeVos, G. and Wagatsuma, H. *Japan's invisible race. Caste in culture and personality*. University of California, Berkeley. 1967.
23  Hicks, G. *Japan's hidden apartheid: the Korean minority and the Japanese*. Ashgate, Aldershot, Hants. 1997.
24  Entry under 'employment discrimination' in Hsu, R. C. *The Encyclopaedia of the Japanese economy*. MIT, Cambridge, Mass. 1994.
26. i. Sun Tzu. *The Art of War for executives*. Commentary Krause, D. G. Brealey, London. 1996.

  ii. McNielly, M. *Sun Tzu and the Art of Business. Six strategic principles for managers*. Oxford University Press, New York. 1996.

  iii. Sun Tzu. *The Art of War*. Foreword by Clavell, J. Hodder and Stoughton, London. 1995.
27  Dale, P. N. *The myth of Japanese uniqueness*. St Martin's Press, New York. Routledge, London. 1990.
28. i. European Business Community (EBC), Tokyo. *White Paper on commerce and industry*. EBC, Tokyo. 1998.

  ii. European Commission, Brussels. *Summary of market access problems in Japan*. Brussels, 1996.

  iii. European Commission, Brussels. *List of EU deregulation proposals for Japan*. Brussels, 1996.

  iv. Moorhouse, J. and Teasdale, A. *Righting the balance: a new agenda for Euro-Japanese trade*. Conservative Political Centre, London. 1987.

  v. Fallows, J. 'Containing Japan'. *Atlantic Monthly*, Boston Mass. Vol. 263. No. 5. May 1989.

  vi. Fingleton, E. *op. cit*. pp. 261-2, 266-7.

  vii. Prestowitz, C. V. *Trading places*. Tuttle, Tokyo. 1991. pp. 448-485.
29  Herzog, P. *Japan's pseudo-democracy*. Japan Library, Folkestone, Kent. 1993. p. 205.

30  Trevor, M. H. *Japan's reluctant multinationals*. Pinter, London. 1983. p. 136. n. 19.
31  Woronoff, J. *op. cit.* p. 288.
32  Hofstede, G. *Cultures and organisations: software of the mind*. Harper, Collins, London. 1994. pp. 177-204, 226-30.
33  'WTO (World Trade Organisation) to rule on Japanese liquor taxes dispute'. *Financial Times*, London. 28 September 1995.
34  'Japanese love taste for whales'. *Daily Telegraph*, London. 9 November 1996.
35  Fingleton, E. *op. cit.* p. 345.
36  Kawasaki, I. *Japan unmasked*. Tuttle, Tokyo. 1969.
37  Kamata, S. *Japan in the passing lane. An insider's account of life in a Japanese auto factory*. Allen and Unwin, London. 1983.
38  Miyamoto, M. *op. cit.*
39  Hofstede, G. *op. cit.* pp. 66-7, 260.
40  Nakane, C. *Japanese society*. Penguin, Harmondsworth, Middx. 1973. pp. 1-23.
41  Samuels, R. J. *'Rich nation, strong army': national security and the technological transformation of Japan*. Cornell University. 1994. 320-41.
42  Hall, I. P. *op. cit.* pp. 11-4.
43  Woronoff, J. *op. cit.* p. 280.
44  McCormack, G. *The emptiness of Japanese affluence*. M. E. Sharpe, Armonk N. Y. 1996. pp. 78-86.

## 3 A 'NEW' JAPAN?

1  Dale, P. N. *The myth of Japanese uniqueness*. St Martins Press, New York. Routledge, London. 1990.
2  Garon, S. *Molding Japanese minds: the state in everyday life* Princeton University. 1997. p. 237.
3  Reischauer, E. O. *The Japanese today: change and continuity*. Tuttle, Tokyo. 1988. p. 394.
4  Hall, I. P. *Cartels of the mind*. Norton, New York. pp. 12,180.
5  Reischauer, E. O. and Fairbank, J. K. *East Asia: the great tradition*. Houghton Mifflin, Boston. Tuttle, Tokyo. 1958. p. 648.
6  Hearn, L. *Japan: an attempt at interpretation*. Tuttle, Tokyo. Reprinted 1955. p. 117.
7  Herzog, P. *Japan's pseudo-democracy*. Japan Library, Folkestone, Kent. 1993. pp. 196-207.
8  Fairbank, J. K. , Reischauer, E. 0. and Craig, A. M. *East Asia: the modern transformation*. Houghton Mifflin, Boston. Tuttle, Tokyo. 1958. p. 815.
9  Storry, R. *A history of modern Japan*. Penguin, Harmondsworth, Middx. 1961. pp. 23-4.
10  Eisenstodt, G. 'Myths and mummies'. *Financial Times*, London. 29-30 August 1998.
11  Reischauer and Fairbank *op. cit.* p. 464.
12  Reischauer and Fairbank *op. cit.* pp. 450-518.
13  *Japan Times*, Tokyo. 7 June 1995.
14  Quoted in *Japan Times*, Tokyo. 17 June 1995.

## REFERENCES

15 Harries, M. and S. *Soldiers of the sun: the rise and fall of the Imperial Japanese Army*. Random House, New York. 1991. p. 25.
16 i. *Japan Times*, Tokyo. 21 January 1992.
   ii. Hicks, G. *Japan's war memories: amnesia or concealment?* Ashgate, Aldershot, Hants. 1997. pp. 30-1.
17 Bailey, P. J. *Postwar Japan: 1945 to the present*. Blackwell, Oxford. 1996. p. 120-2.
18 Van Wolferen, K. *The enigma of Japanese power*. Tuttle, Tokyo. 1993. pp. 378-80.
19 Nakane, C. *Japanese society*. Penguin, Harmondsworth, Middx. 1973. pp. 22, 107.
20 Mitchell, R. H. *Censorship in Imperial Japan*. Princeton University. 1983. p. 8.
21 Nakane, C. *op. cit.* pp. 24-65.
22 Reischauer and Fairbank. *op. cit.* p. 619.
23 See note 12 of chapter 2 above.
24 Hearn. *op. cit.* pp. 254-5.
25 Van Wolferen. *op. cit.* p. 273.
26 Storry. *op. cit.* p. 101.
27 Harries, M. and S. *op. cit.* p. 19.
28 i. Fairbank, Reischauer and Craig. *op. cit.*
   ii. Livingston, J., Moore, J. and Oldfather, F. *The Japan Reader: 1, Imperial Japan 1800-1945*. Penguin, Harmondsworth, Middx. 1976.
29 Hearn. *op. cit.* pp. 483-4.
30 Livingston, Moore and Oldfather. *op. cit.* p. 175.
31 Hearn. *op. cit.* pp. 415-6.
32 Fairbank, Reischauer and Craig. *op. cit.* p. 576.
33 i. Storry. *op. cit.* pp. 116, 120, 229-33.
   ii. Herzog. *op. cit.* pp. 19-20.
34 Fairbank, Reischauer and Craig. *op. cit.* p. 276.
35 Tipton, E. K. *The Japanese police state: the Tokko in interwar Japan*. Athlone, London. 1990. pp. 44, 74, 83-4.
36 Lamont-Brown, R. *Kempeitai: Japan's dreaded military police*. Sutton, Stroud, Glos. 1998.
37 i. Hackett, R. F. 'The Meiji leaders and modernization: the case of Aritomo Yamagata'. Jansen, M. B. ed. *Changing Japanese attitudes towards modernization*. Princeton University. 1969. pp. 253-61.
   ii. Harries, M. and S. *op. cit.* pp. 23-5,36.
   iii. Norman, E. H. 'Conscription and the opposition to it'. Livingston, Moore and Oldfather. *op. cit.* pp. 171-6.
38 Harries, M. and S. *op. cit.* p. 49.
39 Livingston, Moore and Oldfather. *op. cit.* pp. 211-30.
40 Harries, M. and S. *op. cit.* p. 129.
41 Storry. *op. cit.* p. 127.
42 *Japan Times*, Tokyo. 26 July 1994.
43 Harries, M. and S. *op. cit.* pp. 66-7.
44 Fairbank, Reischauer and Craig. op. cit. pp. 482-3.

45 Storry. *op. cit.* pp. 205-6.
46 *Ibid.* p. 168.
47 *Japan Times*, Tokyo. 26 August 1995.
48 Personal communication.
49 i. *Japan Times*, Tokyo. 14 October 1995.
   ii. *Mainichi Daily News*, Tokyo. 14 October 1995.
50 *Japan Times*, Tokyo. 14 August 1994.
51 Storry. *op. cit.* pp. 159-164.
52 *Japan Times*, Tokyo. 29 October 1991.
53 Harries, M. and S. *op. cit.* p. 177.
54 Irokawa, D. *In search of modernity*. Free Press, New York. 1995.
55 Fairbank, Reischauer and Craig. *op. cit.* p. 601.
56 Harries, M. and S. *op. cit.* pp. 271-5.
57 Duus, P. , Myers, R. H. and Peattie, M. R. *The Japanese wartime empire 1931-45*. Princeton University. 1966. p. xii.
58 Horan, W. H. *Visions of infamy*. St Martin's Press, New York 1991.
59 *Japan Times*, Tokyo. 21 November 1994.
60 Ventura, R. *Underground in Japan*. Cape, London. 1992. Afterword by Buruma, I. pp. 185-93.
61 Fairbank, Reischauer and Craig. *op. cit.* p. 811.
62 Bix, H. P. 'Japan's delayed surrender: a reinterpretation'. Hogan, M. J. ed. *Hiroshima in history and memory*. Cambridge University. 1996. pp. 108-15.
63 Dower, J. W. *Japan in war and peace*. New Press, New York. 1993. pp. 344-5.
64 Gibney, F. ed. *Senso: the Japanese remember the Pacific War*. Letters to the editor of the Asahi newspaper. Sharpe, Armonk, NY. 1995. pp. 287-8.
65 Storry. *op. cit.* p. 185.
66 'Tojo ordered A-bomb in 1943'. *Japan Times*, Tokyo. 21 July 1995.
67 *Japan Times*, Tokyo. 23 and 27 July 1995.
68 'Japan pursued its own atomic bomb. Fifty scientists worked frantically'. *Japan Times*, Tokyo. 20 July 1995.
69 Dower. *op. cit.* pp. 55-100.
70 *Japan Times*, Tokyo. 28 July 1995.
71 'Toxic gas plant still uneasy topic'. *Japan Times*, Tokyo. 17 January 1995.
72 Dower. *op. cit.* p. 147. n. 5.
73 'Japan still haunted by Hiroshima fifty years on'. *Daily Telegraph*, London. 28 July 1995.
74 Berger, M. 'Japan defiant till the end'. *Sunday Times*, London. 6 August 1995.
75 Warner, L. and Sandilands, J. *Women beyond the wire*. Arrow, London. 1997.
76 Edwards, J. *Banzai, you bastards*. Souvenir Press, London. 1990. pp. 140-1. Japanese translation: *Kutabare jap yaro*. Komishi Shobo, Tokyo. 1992.
77 *Nippon Times*, Tokyo. 15 August 1945. Reprinted in *Japan Times*, Tokyo. 15 August 1995.
78 Dower, J. W. 'The bombed: Hiroshima and Nagasaki in popular memory'. Hogan, M. J. ed. *op. cit.* pp. 123-4.
79 Hicks. *op. cit.* 1997.

# REFERENCES

80  *Daily Telegraph*, London. 28 July 1995.
81  *Japan Times*, Tokyo. 21 August 1994.
82  Dower, J. W. In Hogan ed. op cit. pp. 128,137-41.
83  Dower, J. W. *Japan in war and peace. op. cit.* p. 121.
84  *Asahi Evening News*, Tokyo. 17 February 1996.
85  i. Obituary. *The Times*, London. 20 July 1995.
    ii. Kaplan, D. E. and Dubro, A. *The yakuza: the explosive account of Japan's criminal underworld*. Addison-Wesley, New York. 1986. Macdonald, Futura, London. 1987. pp. 96, 98-100, 108, 133, 152-3, 252, 320-4, 328, 340.
86  Hicks. *op. cit.* p. 98.
87  Livingston, Moore and Olfather. *op. cit.* p. 149.
88  *New York Times*. 17 June 1994.
89  Herzog. *op. cit.* p. 20.
90  *Japan Times*, Tokyo. 31 July 1995.
91  *Japan Times*, Tokyo. 17 March 1993.
92  Ienaga, S. *The Pacific war 1931-1945*. Pantheon, New York. 1978.
93  *The Times*, London. 30 August 1997.
94  Smith, P. 'The closed shop'. *The Nation*, USA. 24 November 1997.
95  Williams, P. and Wallace, D. *Unit 731*. Hodder & Stoughton, London. 1989. p. 57.
96  Harris, S. H. *Factories of death: Japanese biological warfare 1932-1945 and the American cover-up*. Routledge, London. 1994.
97  Harries, M. and S. *op. cit.* p. 361.
98  Williams and Wallace. *op. cit.* pp. 302, 287-92.
99  Tsuneishi, K. Interview. *Tokyo Journal*, Tokyo. May 1994.
100 *Japan Times*, Tokyo. 25 May 1995.
101 *Japan Times*, Tokyo. 11 August 1992.
102 Daws, G. *Prisoners of the Japanese: POWs of World War II in the Pacific*. Morrow, New York. 1994. p. 336.
103 Harris, S. H. *op. cit.* pp. 141-3, 176.
104 *Japan Times*, Tokyo. 24 July and 6 December 1994.
105 *Japan Times*, Tokyo. 15 February 1994.
106 *Japan Times*, Tokyo. 5 July 1994.
107 Gold, H. ed. *Unit 731 testimony*. Yen Books, Tokyo. 1996.
108 Hogan, M. J. ed. *op. cit.* p142.
109 Tanaka, Y. *Hidden horrors: Japanese war crimes in World War Ii*. Westview Press, Boulder, Cob. 1996. pp. 135-65, 238.
110 Buruma, I. *The wages of guilt: memories of war in Germany and Japan*. Vintage, Random House, London. 1995. pp. 122, 256-7.
111 Goodwin, M. J. *Shobun: a forgotten war crime in the Pacific*. Stackpole Books, Mechanicsburg, Pa. 1995. p. 140.
112 i. Hijiya-Kirschnereit, i. 'Nanking in Japanese literature'. *DIJ newsletter No. 2. October 1997*. German Institute for Japanese Studies, Tokyo. 1997.
    ii. Wickert, E. ed. *The good German of Nanking. The diaries of John Rabe*. Knopf, New York. 1998. Little, Brown, London. 1999.

113  i. Buruma. *op. cit.* pp. 112-35.

ii. Chang, I. *The rape of Nanking: the forgotten Holocaust of World War II.* Basic Books, New York. 1997.

iii. Gibney, F. ed. *op. cit.* pp. 60-1.

iv. Tanaka, Y. *op. cit.* p. 80.

v. Documentary film: '*In the name of the Emperor*'. Chang, C. and Tong, N. Film News Foundation, New York. 1995.

114  Cortazzi, Sir H. 'The rape of Nanking: a cover-up'. *Japan Echo Vol. XVII*i. *Autumn 1991.* Tokyo. 1991. pp. 1-4.

115  Daws. *op. cit.* p. 323.

116  Warner and Sandilands. *op. cit.* p. 179.

117  UN treaty office documents. 'Secret pact denied POWs better deal'. *Sunday Times*, London. 31 May 1998.

118  *Japan Times*, Tokyo. 11 March 1996.

119  i. Buruma. *op. cit.* pp. 249-50, 254-5.

ii. *Daily Mail*, London. 8 December 1989.

120  Kobayashi, H. 'The post-war legacy of Japan's wartime empire'. In Duus et al. *op. cit.* p. 324.

121  Goodman, G. K. ed. *Japanese cultural policies in Southeast Asia during World War II.* Macmillan, London. 1991.

122  Duus et al. *op. cit.* p. xix.

123  Buruma op cit. pp. 276-81.

124  *Japan Times*, Tokyo. 29 June, 1 and 6 July 1995. *Financial Times*, London. 10 August 1995.

125  Kershaw, G. *Tracks of death.* The Book Guild, London. 1992.

126  Duus et al. *op. cit.* p. xxxviii.

127  Daws *op. cit.* p. 220.

128  Davies, P. N. *The man behind the bridge: Colonel Toosey and the River Kwa*i. Athlone Press, London. 1991. p. 195.

129  Lomax, E. *The railwayman.* Vintage, Random House, London. 1996. p. 106.

130  i. Huie, S. F. *The forgotten ones: women and children under Nippon.* Angus & Robertson. Pymble, NSW. 1991. p. 3.

ii. 'Japan stole cash sent to aid starving POWs'. *Sunday Times*, London. 3 September 1995.

131  Tanaka *op. cit.* pp. 2-3.

132  Alexander, S. *Sweet Kwai, run softly.* Merriotts Press, Bristol. 1995. p. 251.

133  Davies *op. cit.*

134  Harries, M. and S. *op. cit.* p. 479.

135  i. Hicks, G. *The comfort women.* Yen Books, Tokyo.

ii. Howard, K. ed. *True stories of the Korean comfort women.* Cassell,London. 1995.

136  *Japan Times*, Tokyo. 25 July 1995.

137  Buruma *op. cit.* p. 195.

138  Executive Committee, International Public Hearing. *War victimization and Japan. International public hearing report.* Toho Shuppan, Tokyo. 1993.

139  *Japan Times*, Tokyo. 20 April 1993.

## REFERENCES

140 *Asahi Evening News*, Tokyo. 22 January 1995
141 *Japan Times*, Tokyo. 23 July 1995.
142 *Japan Times*, Tokyo. 7 February 1996.
143 *Japan Times*, Tokyo. 14 February 1996.
144 *Japan Times*, Tokyo. 4 February 1996.
145 *Japan Times*. Tokyo. 25 November 1995.
146 Executive Committee, International Public Hearing. *op. cit.* pp. 60-8.
147 *Japan Times*, Tokyo. 19 July 1994.
148 Hicks. *The comfort women. op. cit.* pp. 34, 111, 128-9.
149 Tanaka *op. cit.* pp. 92-3.
150 Gibney *op. cit.* pp. 65-84 *passim.*
151 i. Alexander *op. cit.* pp. 2, 207-8.
 ii. Daws *op. cit.* pp. 279, 324-7.
 iii. Dean, P. S. W. 'A guest of Japan - uninvited and invited'. *Proceedings 120. The Japan Society*, London. Autumn 1992.
 iv. Edwards *op. cit.* pp. 172-5.
 v. Warner and Sandilands *op. cit.* pp. 250-1.
152 i. Daws *op. cit.* p. 337.
 ii. McCormack, G. and Nelson, H. *The Burma-Thailand railway.* Allen & Unwin, Australia. 1993. p. 77.
153 Edwards *op. cit.* p. 252.
154 Dower. *War without mercy. op. cit.* pp. 221-4.
155 *Japan Times*, Tokyo. 12 November 1995.
156 Harries, M. and S. *op. cit.* pp. 101-2.
157 i. Gibney *op. cit.* pp. 27-31, 54-5.
 ii. Harries, M. and S. *op. cit.* 478-84.
158 Harries, M. and S. *op. cit.* p. 322.
159. i. Hicks. *Japan's war memories: amnesia or concealment? op. cit.* pp. 61-2.
 ii. *Japan Times*, Tokyo 25 June and 31 October 1995.
160 Quoted in Buruma. *op. cit.* p. 257.
161 *Japan Times*, Tokyo. 8 August 1995.
162 *Japan Times*, Tokyo. 1 February 1995.
163 *Japan Times*, Tokyo. 16 August 1995.
164 Quoted in *Japan Times*, Tokyo. 22 August 1995.
165 *Japan times*, Tokyo. 13 August 1995.
166 *Sunday Times*, London. 13 August 1995.
167 Johnson, C. *Japan: who governs?* Norton, New York. 1995. p. 195.
168 Daws *op. cit.* P. 374.
169 i. Obituary. *The Times*, London. 20 July 1995.
 ii. Obituary. *The Guardian* London. 8 August 1995.
170 *Japan Times*, Tokyo. 12 September 1995.
171 Reischauer, Fairbank and Craig. *op. cit.* p. 595.
172 Storry *op. cit.* p. 254.

173 Ederer, G. *Das leise Lächeln des Siegers*. Econ Verlag, Düsseldorf. 1991. pp. 305-17.
174 Daws *op. cit.* p. 375.
175 i. Alexander *op. cit.* pp. 273-4.
   ii. McCormack and Nelson *op. cit.* pp. 9,157.
176 Byrne, D. 'This is your torturer'. *The Spectator*, London. 29 July 1995.
177 *Sunday Times*, London. 5 January 1997.
178 Huimin, Z. 'China still haunted by images of war'. *Japan Times*, Tokyo. 21 May 1995.
179 Doyle, L. 'Pacific victory for political correctness hurts veterans'. The *Guardian*, London. 8 August 1995.
180 *Japan Times*, Tokyo. 29 September 1993.
181 Buruma *op. cit.* pp. 221-S.
182 Hardacre, H. *Shinto and the state 1868-1988*. Princeton University. 1989. pp. 150-1.
183 *Japan Times*, Tokyo. 13 July 1994. 12 August 1995.
184 'The symbols of Japan's past'. *The Economist*, London. 3 June 1995. p. 25.
185 *Japan Times*, Tokyo. 10 August 1995.
186 Duus et al. *op. cit.* p. xl.
187 Dower. *War without mercy. op. cit.* p. 315.
188 'New textbooks carry enhanced war information'. *Japan Times*, Tokyo. 29 June 1995.
189 *The Spectator*, London. 2 May 1992. p. 41.
190 Daws *op. cit.* p. 25.
191 i. 'Japan rewrites the war'. *Sunday Times*, London. 12 March 1995.
   ii. 'Karaoke singers glorify Japan's brutal conquest of Asia'. *Daily Telegraph*, London. 27 July 1996.
192 'War criminal or patriot: Tojo's heirs rock Japan with World War II revisionism'. *Wall Street Journal*, New York. 30 April 1998.
193 'Japanese holiday angers pacifists'. *Daily Telegraph*, London. 20 July 1996.
194 i. Bailey, P. J. *op. cit.* p. 33.
   ii. Daws *op. cit.* pp. 374-5.
195 Harvey, R. *The undefeated: the rise, fall and rise of Greater Japan*. Macmillan, London. 1994. pp. 516-7.
196 Harries, M. and S. *op. cit.* p. 491.
197 Quoted in *Japan Times*, Tokyo. 24 August 1995.
198 Duus et al. *op. cit.* p. xlvii.
199 Chinese Alliance for Memorial and Justice, USA. 'A country that does not recognise its wrongs cannot do right'. *New York Times*. 17 June 1994.
200 'Japanese war criminals honored as heroes'. *New York Times*. 15 December 1996.
201 Buruma *op. cit.* p. 33.
202 Dower. *War without mercy. op. cit.* p. 303.
203 Schaller *op. cit.* p. 14.

REFERENCES

## 4 POWER HOLDERS – THE IRON TRIANGLE

(1) THE BUREAUCRATS: POLICY-MAKERS AND REGULATORS

1. Uchida, M. 'The Iron Triangle. Bureaucrats, businessmen and politicians at the core of corruption'. *Tokyo Business Today*, Tokyo. November 1993.
2. Baker, G. 'Politicians clash with bureaucrats'. *Financial Times*, London. 9 February 1996.
3. Rothacher, A. *The Japanese power elite*. Macmillan, London. 1993.
4. Mosca, G. *The ruling class*. Greenwood, London. 1980.
5. i. Hara, E. and Uchida, M. 'Bureaucratic power: MOT dispenses rights as it sees fit'. *Tokyo Business Today*, Tokyo. January/February 1993.

    ii. Reading, B. 'Japan's system is the culprit. The need is for reform, not reflation'. *Financial Times*, London. 8-9 August 1998.
6. Tsutsui, Y. *Effectiveness of branch regulation in Japanese banking*. Hitotsubashi University, Tokyo. March 1989.
7. 'MITI panel: cut red tape for electric utilities'. *Yomiuri Shimbun*, Tokyo. 2 December 1994.
8. Okamoto, N. 'Three cheers for the microbeers'. *Look Japan*, Tokyo. March 1997.
9. Fisher, A. 'Yes, we have no bananas'. *Financial Times*, London. 19 July 1994.
10. Deer, B. 'Tokyo's men from the ministry really take the biscuit'. *Sunday Times*, London. 7 August 1994.
11. Personal communication.
12. i. Takahashi, E. et al. 'MOT: Ministry of Tyranny'. *Tokyo Business Today*, Tokyo. March 1994.

    ii. Inoue, R. 'In for repairs'. *Look Japan* Tokyo. May 1997.
13. Reading, B. *Ibid*.
14. i. Miyamoto, M. 'Envy, discrimination and masochism: the foundation of Japanese society'. *Tokyo Journal*, Tokyo. May 1993.

    ii. Miyamoto, M. *Straitjacket society: an insider's irreverent view of bureaucratic Japan*. Kodansha International, Tokyo. 1994. pp. 139-41.
15. Braddon, R. *The other Hundred Years War: Japan's bid for supremacy 1941-2041*. Collins, London. 1983. p. 191.
16. Lyons, N. *The Sony vision*. Crown, New York. 1976. p. 76.
17. Ohmae, K. *Beyond national borders. Reflections on Japan and the world*. Kodansha International, Tokyo. 1987. pp. 2-3.
18. Van Wolferen, K. *The enigma of Japanese power*. Tuttle, Tokyo. 1993. p. 281.
19. i. Johnson, C. *MITI and the Japanese economic miracle: the growth of industrial policy 1925-1975*. Tuttle, Tokyo. 1982. pp. 57-62.

    ii. Koh, B. C. *Japan's administrative elite*. University of California, 1989. pp. 86-7, 97.

    iii. Rothacher *op. cit*. pp. 128-30.
20. De Vos, G. A. *Socialization for achievement*. University of California. 1973.
21. Nakane, C. *Japanese society*. Penguin, Harmondsworth. 1973. pp. 24-89.
22. Johnson, C. MITI *op. cit*. p. 59.
23. Koh *op. cit*. p. 14.
24. Pyle, K. B. *The making of modern Japan*. Heath, Lexington, MA. 1996. pp. 122-5.

25　Tsuji, K. ed. *Public administration in Japan*. University of Tokyo. 1984. p. 5.
26　Van Wolferen *op. cit.* pp. 380-2, 466.
27　Sakaiya, T. *What is Japan? Contradictions and transformations*. Kodansha International, Tokyo. 1993. p. 37.
28　Rothacher *op. cit.* pp. 117-8.
29　Koh *op. cit.* pp. 117-8.
30　Shiono, H. 'Administrative guidance'. Tsuji, K. ed. *op. cit.* p. 213.
31　Nakane, C. *Ibid*.
32　i. Abrahams, P. 'Japanese trade surplus up 45 per cent', *Financial Times*, London. 22 October 1998.

　　ii. 'Current account surplus up 52 per cent'. *Financial Times* London. 2 November 1998.
33　Makin, J. 'The West may have to tolerate more imports'. *Sunday Times*, London. 29 November 1998.
34　Sakakibara, E. *Beyond capitalism: the Japanese model of market economics*. Introd. Prestowitz, C. V. University Press of America, Lanham, MD. 1993. pp. viii-ix.
35　Cusumano, M. *The Japanese automobile industry*. Harvard University. 1985.
36　Prestowitz, C. V. *Trading places. How America is surrendering the future to Japan and how to win it back*. Tuttle, Tokyo. pp. 245-6, 257-9.
37　Neff, R. 'Prospects for progress'. *Journal of Japanese Trade and Industry*, Tokyo. No. 5. September-October 1990.
38　Johnson, C. *Japan: who governs? The rise of the developmental state*. Norton, New York. 1995. pp. 59-62.
39　Huber, T. M. *Strategic economy in Japan*. Westview, Boulder, CO. 1994.
40　Johnson, C. 'The people who invented the mechanical nightingale'. *Showa: the Japan of Hirohito*. Proceedings, American Academy of Arts and Sciences. Vol. 119. No. 3. Summer 1990.
41　i. Miyamoto, M. *Straitjacket. op. cit.* pp. 11, 32, 120-1.

　　ii. Herzog, P. J. *Japan's pseudo-democracy*. Japan Library, Folkestone, Kent. 1993. pp. 262-3.

　　iii. Hutton, B. 'Bridges to nowhere'. *Financial Times*, London. 25-26 April 1998.
42　Maki, J. 'The role of the bureaucracy in Japan'. Livingston J. , Moore, J. and Oldfather, F. *The Japan Reader: 2, Postwar Japan 1945 to the present*. Penguin, Harmondsworth, Middx. 1976. pp. 28-32.
43　Koh *op. cit.* pp. 37-SO.
44　i. Hollerman. Chapter 2, note 8.

　　ii. Horsley, W. and Buckley, W. *Nippon, new superpower: Japan since 1945*. BBC, London. 1990. p. 49.

　　iii. Van Wolferen *op. cit.* p. 459.
45　Quoted in Johnson, C. *Japan: who governs? op. cit.* p. 120.
46　i. Horsley, W. and Buckley, W. *op. cit.* pp. 38-9, 46.

　　ii. Van Wolferen, K. *op. cit.* p. 462.
47　Braddon, R. *op. cit.* p. 64.
48　Nakagawa, Y. and Ota, N. *The Japanese-style economic system. A new balance between intervention and freedom*. Foreign Press Centre, Tokyo. 1981.

# REFERENCES

49 Sakakibara, E. *Ibid.*
50 Johnson, C. *Japan: who governs? The rise of the developmental state. Ibid.*
51 Dodwell. *The structure of the Japanese motor components industry.* Dodwell Marketing Consultants, Tokyo. 1979. pp. 4-10.
52 Magaziner, I. C. and Hout, T. M. *Japanese industrial policy.* Policy Studies Institute, London. 1980.
53 Shiono. op cit. pp. 211-2.
54 Johnson, C. *Japan: who governs ? op. cit.* p. 13.
55 Kawasaki, I. *Japan unmasked.* Tuttle, Tokyo. 1969. p. 197-9.
56 Shiono. *op. cit.* p. 204.
57 Sakaiya. *op. cit.* pp. 37-9.
58 i. Editorial. *Tokyo Business Today*, Tokyo. November 1993.
   ii. 'Inside MOF: the men from the ministry'. *Tokyo Business Today*, Tokyo. Parts 1-5. January-May 1995.
59 i. Van Wolferen *op. cit.* p. 450.
   ii. Chapter 1, note 10.
60 i. 'JAL admits to racketeer link'. *Financial Times*, London. 18 August 1998.
   ii. 'Racketeers: guilty verdicts in DKB trial'. *Financial Times,* London. 20 October 1998.
61 Sakaiya, T. *Ibid.*
62 Magaziner, i. C. and Hout, T. M. *op. cit.* pp. 49-50.
63 Entries under 'administrative guidance, industrial policy' in Hsu, R. C. *The MIT Encyclopaedia of the Japanese economy.* MIT, Cambridge, Mass. 1994.
64 *Capital magazine*, Germany. December 1995.
65 i. 'Decontrols posing shake-up in service stations' services'. *Japan Times*, Tokyo. 15 August 1995.
   ii. Ito, T. 'All hands to the pumps'. *Look Japan*, Tokyo. April 1997.
   iii. Harney, A. 'Japanese petrol industry needs tiger in its tank'. *Financial Times* London. 26 November 1998.
   iv. Abrahams, P. 'A sector in need of slick action'. *Financial Times*, London. 29 October 1998.
66 'Finance Ministry old boys at heart of *jusen* problem'. *Japan Times*, Tokyo. 19 January 1996.
67 Koh *op. cit.* p. 257.
68 i. Chinone, K. 'Parachuting into paradise'. *Tokyo Business Today*, Tokyo. June 1994.
   ii. '*Amakudari* positions widespread'. *Japan Times*, Tokyo. 4 November 1994.
69 See note 66 above.
70 'Bureaucrats still landing on boards. One in 17 bank, brokerage seats a "golden parachute" for retirees'. *Japan Times*, Tokyo. 14 October 1995.
71 'Old boys not yet quite out to pasture'. *Mainichi Daily News*, Tokyo. 13 October 1995.
72 Johnson, C. MITI *op. cit.* pp. 65-73.
73 'Over "golden parachute" issue: recorded tape reveals vividly how bureaucrat pressed group'. *Asahi Evening News*, Tokyo. 12 June 1990.

74 Yayama, T. 'The bureaucrats stand pat'. *Japan Times*, Tokyo. 6 December 1994.
75 'MOF: cocky, sensitive and edgy'. Editorial, *Tokyo Business Today*, Tokyo. February 1995.
76 Koh *op. cit.* 235-47.
77. i. Rothacher *op. cit.* pp. 145-8.
    ii. Van Wolferen *op. cit.* p. 459.
78 Kawasaki, i. *Ibid.*
79 Rothacher *op. cit.* p. 72.
80 Woronoff, J. *Japanese targeting. Successes, failures, lessons.* Macmillan, London. 1992. pp. 4-5.
81 Huber *op. cit.* p. 43.

(2) BIG BUSINESS: WORK AS NATIONAL SERVICE

1 Funaki, Y. 'Japanese management and management training'. *BACIE Journal*. London. January 1981.
2 Cole, R. E. *Work, mobility and participation: a comparative study of American and Japanese industry*. University of California. 1979. p. 252.
3 'Bank employees found working more for less'. *Mainichi Daily News*. Tokyo. 30 January 1992.
4 Wagstyl, S. 'Employees' lot dealt blow by Japanese court'. *Financial Times*, London. 24 June 1992.
5 Ballon, R. *The Japanese employee*. Sophia University, Tokyo. 1969. pp. 126-34.
6 Rohlen, T. P. *For harmony and strength: Japanese white-collar organization in anthropological perspective*. University of California. 1974. p. 51.
7 Tanaka, Y. 'The world of the zaikai'. Hyoe, M. and Hirschmeier, J. eds. *Politics and economics in contemporary Japan*. Kodansha, Tokyo. pp. 64, 65-78.
8 Hirschmeier, J. and Yui, T. *The development of Japanese business 1600-1980*. Allen and Unwin, London. 1981. pp. 179, 184-8, 325-332.
9 Choate, P. *Agents of influence*. Knopf, New York. 1990. p. 31.
10 Storry, R. *A history of modern Japan*. Penguin, Harmondsworth,Middx. 1960. pp. 172, 177.
11 Huber, T. M. *Strategic economy in Japan*. Westview, Boulder, Colo. 1994. pp. 12-3, 38-44.
12 Steslicke, W. A. *Doctors in politics: the political life of the Japan Medical Association*. Praeger, New York. 1973.
13 Rothacher, A. *The Japanese power elite*. Macmillan, London. 1993. p. 189.
14 i. Hirschmeier, J. and Yui, T. *op. cit.* pp. 321-5.
   ii. Huber, T. M. *op. cit.* p. 15.
15 Hsu, R. C. *The MIT encyclopaedia of the Japanese economy*. MIT, Cambridge, Mass. 1994. pp. 341-2.
16 Dodwell Marketing Consultants. *Industrial groupings in Japan*. Dodwell, Tokyo. Annual.
17 I, Hsu, R. C. *op. cit.* pp. 198-202.
   ii. Keenan, J. *Unlocking Japan's distribution system in the '90s*. Canada Communication Group, Ottawa. 1994. pp. 36-42.

# REFERENCES

iii. Reading, B. *Japan: the coming collapse*. Orion, London. 1992. pp. 226-8.

iv. Rothacher, A. *op. cit.* pp. 31,183-216.

18 Hirschmeier, J. and Yui, T. *op. cit.* p. 326.

19 'Japanese CEOs: how they view their jobs and life'. *Tokyo Business Today*, Tokyo. December 1991.

20 Kobayashi, K. *The rise of NEC*. Blackwell, Oxford. 1989. pp. 94-5, 153.

21 Huber, T. M. *op. cit.* p. 15.

22 Fransman, M. *The market and beyond*. Cambridge University. 1990.

23 Kawanishi, H. ed. *Japan im Umbruch. Gewerkschafter berichten über Arbeitskämpfe der Nachkriegsära*. WSI des Deutschen Gewerkschaftsbundes, Düsseldorf. 1989.

24 Dower, J. W. *Japan in war and peace*. New Press, New York. 1993. pp. 103, 104-54.

25 Horsley, W. and Buckley, R. *Nippon, new superpower: Japan since 1945*. BBC, London. 1990. p. 46.

26 Yanaga, C. *Big business in Japanese politics*. Yale University. 1968. pp. 20-1, 68-70, 148-51.

27 Taira, K. *Economic development and the labour market in Japan*. Columbia University. 1970. p. 226.

28 Hirschmeier, J. and Yui, T. *op. cit.* p. 327.

29 Japan Times, Tokyo. 27 August 1974. Quoted in Woronoff, J. *Japan, the coming social crisis*. Lotus, Tokyo. 1982. pp. 224-5.

30 i. Reading, B. *op. cit.* p. 243.

ii. Rothacher, A. *op. cit.* pp. 30-i.

31 Ozawa, i. *Blueprint for a new Japan*. Kodansha International, Tokyo. 1994.

32 'The Liberal Democratic Party: despite scandals they still reign'. *Tokyo Business Today*, Tokyo. October 1991.

33 'Electric industry staff asked to donate ¥1 billion to LDP'. *Japan Times*, Tokyo. 24 November 1995.

34 'Keidanren's help sought for *jusen*'. *Japan Times*, Tokyo. 5 March 1996.

35 Ikeda, Y. 'No need to apologise. Explaining Japanese industrial policies'. *Speaking of Japan*, Tokyo. Vol. 4. No. 38. February 1984

36 Halberstam, D. *The Reckoning. How Japan beat the United States in the auto industry war and rewrote the rules of international business competition*. Bantam Books, New York. 1987. pp. 147-57, 165-9.

37 Kawanishi, H. *Enterprise unionism in Japan*. Kegan Paul, London. 1992. pp. 77, 119.

38 Cusumano, M. A. *The Japanese automobile industry*. Harvard University, Cambridge, Mass. 1985. P. 155.

39 Van Wolferen, K. *The enigma of Japanese power*. Tuttle, Tokyo. 1993. pp. 89-90.

40 Kawanishi, H. *op. cit.* p. 150.

41 'Freeze on wages urged. Nikkeiren adopts tight policy for spring talks'. *Japan Times*, Tokyo. 13 January 1995.

42 *Financial Times*, London. 6 February 1996.

43 *Financial Times*, London. 27/28 February 1996.

44 i. Rothacher, A. *op. cit.* pp. 227-8.

ii. Tanaka, Y. loc. cit. pp. 72-4.

45 Sakai, K. 'The feudal world of Japanese manufacturing'. *Harvard Business Review*. November-December 1990.
46 MITI. *White Paper on small and medium enterprises in Japan*. MITI Small and Medium Enterprise Agency, MITI, Tokyo. Annual.
47 Sakai, K. and Sekiyama, H. *Bunsha: improving your business through company division*. Taiyo Industry Co. , Tokyo. 1985.
48 Horsley, W. and Buckley, R. *op. cit.* p. 65.
49 Dodwell Marketing Consultants. *The structure of the Japanese motor components industry*. Dodwell, Tokyo. 1990.
50 Waldenberger, F. 'Firms and markets: why is Japan different?' German Institute of Japanese Studies, Tokyo. *Miscellanea. Working Paper No. 8. May 1994*. pp. 16-7.
51 *Entrepreneurship: the Japanese experience*. PHP Institute, Kyoto. 10 issues, 1982-3.
52 Rothacher, A. *op. cit.* pp. 74-5, 228.
53 De Vos, G. *Socialization for achievement*. University of California. 1973.
54 *Tokyo Business Today*, Tokyo. November 1992.
55 Ishida, H. *Social mobility in contemporary Japan: educational credentials, class and the labour market in a cross-national perspective*. Stanford University. 1993.
56 i. Sakai, K. *Lives in the making: the story of a manufacturing family*. Intergrace, Tokyo. 1991.

   ii. Sakai, K. and Russell, D. *To expand, we divide*. Intergrace, Tokyo. 1993.
57 Kamioka, K. *Japanese business pioneers*. Times Books, Singapore 1986.
58 Iwabori, Y. *The management of YKK: Yoshida's business philosophy*. Senko Kikaku, Tokyo. 1978.
59 Kojima, N. 'Yoshisuke Aikawa: the man who built Nissan'. *Journal of Japanese Trade and Industry*, Tokyo. No. 6. 1987.
60 i. Dymock, E. 'Toyota fruit of the loom'. *Sunday Times* London. 18 January 1987.

   ii. Toyoda, E. *Toyota: fifty years in motion*. Kodansha, Tokyo. 1987.
61 Tanaka, H. *Personality in industry: the human side of a Japanese enterprise*. Pinter, London. 1988.
62 Shimazaki, H. T. *Vision in Japanese entrepreneurship: the evolution of a security enterprise*. Routledge, London. 1992.
63 i. 'Tale of the *sugi* seeds. Kazuo Inamori tells Michiyo Nakamoto why Japan must be more entrepreneurial'. *Financial Times*, London. 1 December 1995.

   ii. Nakamoto, M. 'Kazuo Inamori: single-minded devotion'. *Financial Times*, London. 30 November 1998.

(3) THE POLITICIANS: SMOKE-FILLED BACKROOMS

1 Hrebenar, R. J. *The Japanese party system*. Westview, Boulder, (Colo). 1992. p. 267.
2 Kanemaru obituary. 'Fallen godfather of Japan's LDP', *Financial Times*, London. 29 March 1996.
3 Keenan, J. *Unlocking Japan's distribution system in the '90s*. Canada Communication Group, Ottawa. 1994. pp. 43-7.

# REFERENCES

4 Stelzer, I. 'Why Japan won't keep trade promises'. *Sunday Times*, London. 15 April 1990.
5 Kawasaki, I. *Japan Unmasked*. Tuttle, Tokyo. 1969. p. 198.
6 Krauss, E. S. , Rohlen, T. P. and Steinhoff, P. G. eds. *Conflict in Japan*. University of Hawaii. 1984. p. 284.
7 i. Hrebenar *op. cit.* p. 514.
   ii. Wada, J. *The Japanese election system*. Routledge, London. 1996. p. 2.
8 'Not such strange bedfellows: the LDP and the underworld'. *Tokyo Business Today* Tokyo. December 1992.
9 Maruyama, M. *Thought and behaviour in modern Japanese politics*. Oxford University. Expanded edition 1969. p. 264.
10 *Japan Times*, Tokyo. 6 March 1991.
11 Orr, R. M. 'Three scenarios for the LDP'. *Tokyo Business Today*, Tokyo. January 1993.
12 Hirschmeier, J. Introduction. *Politics and economics in contemporary Japan*. Kodansha International, Tokyo. 1979. p. ix.
13 Krauss, E. S. 'Conflict in the Diet: toward conflict management in parliamentary politics'. Krauss et al, *op. cit.* pp. 243-293.
14 Wada *op. cit.* pp. 9, 11, 48, 53, 82.
15 i. Ozawa, I. *Blueprint for a new Japan*. Kodansha International, Tokyo. 1994.
   ii. Matsuyama, Y. 'Eleven questions about the Murayama administration'. *Journal of Japanese trade and industry*, Tokyo. No. 6. 1994.
16 Inoguchi, T. 'Japanese bureaucracy: coping with new challenges'. Jain, P. and Inoguchi, T. eds. *Japanese politics today: beyond karaoke democracy*. Macmillan Australia. 1997. p. 106.
17 *Japan Times*, Tokyo. 15 August, 1992.
18 *Japan Times*, Tokyo. 3 February 1993.
19 Herzog, P. J. *Japan's pseudo-democracy*. Japan Library, Folkestone, (Kent). 1993.
20 Jain and Inoguchi *op. cit.* pp. 1-2.
21 *Ibid* p. 18.
22 Hrebenar *op. cit.* p 95.
23 Morita, M. 'Change in the wind: Murayama's days are numbered'. *Tokyo Business Today*, Tokyo. May 1995.
24 Bailey, P. J. *Postwar Japan: 1945 to the present*. Blackwell, Oxford. 1996.
25. i. Fukushima, G. S. 'Three visions of Japan'. *Tokyo Business Today*, Tokyo. October 1994.
   ii. Orr, R. M. 'Why should the American military remain in Japan?' *Tokyo Business Today*, Tokyo. June 1993.
26 i. Kaplan, D. E. and Dubro, A. *Yakuza: the explosive account of Japan's criminal underworld*. Addison-Wesley, New York. 1986. Macdonald, London. 1987. pp. 102-110.
   ii. Terzani, T. 'Wir sind die Erben der Samurai'. *Der Spiegel*, Hamburg. Nr. 26-27. 1990. p. 110.
27 Rothacher *op. cit.* pp. 14, 33, 98, 104-8, 119.
28 Van Wolferen, K. *The enigma of Japanese power*. Tuttle, Tokyo. 1993. pp. 179-82.
29 *Japan Times*, Tokyo. 27 September 1994.

30 Mamiya, J. 'The Iron Triangle and corruption in the construction industry'. *Tokyo Business Today*, Tokyo. November 1993.
31 Mamiya, J. 'Government and contractors prove: it takes two to *dango*'. *Tokyo Business Today* Tokyo. July 1995.
32. i. Choate, P. *Agents of influence*. Knopf, New York. 1990. p. 31.
   ii. Rothacher *op. cit.* pp. 50-1, 75-6.
33 Uchida, M. 'Iron Triangle', bureaucrats, businessmen and politicians at the core of corruption'. *Tokyo Business Today*, Tokyo. November 1993.
34 Hrebenar *op. cit.* p. 59.
35 *Ibid* p. 268.
36 Baerwald, H. H. 'Parties, factions and the Diet'. Hyoe, M. and Hirschmeier, J. eds. *Politics and economics in contemporary Japan*, Kodansha International, Tokyo. 1983. pp. 21-63.
37 Odawara, A. 'The union of the LDP and the bureaucracy'. *Japan Echo*, Tokyo. Vol. XI, No. 4. Winter 1984.
38 Fujiyasu, M. 'The Liberal Democratic Party: despite scandals they still reign'. *Tokyo Business Today*, Tokyo. October 1991.
39 Hrebenar *op. cit.* p. 259.
40 Van Wolferen. *op. cit.* p. 134.
41 Bailey *op. cit.* p. 115.
42 Morita, A. *Made in Japan*. Dutton, New York. 1986. p. 178.
43 Schaller, M. *Altered states: the US and Japan since the Occupation*. Oxford University Press, New York. 1997. p. 71.
44 Hrebenar *op. cit.* pp. 60-5, 260.
45 Choate *op. cit.* pp. 28-33.
46 'Unwritten rules tax ministers. Greasing bureaucrats' palms a legacy of the LDP era'. *Japan Times*, Tokyo. 1 September 1994.
47 i. Hrebenar *op. cit.* p. 61.
   ii. Holstein, W. J. *The Japanese power game: what it means for America*. Scribner's, Macmillan, New York. 1990. p. 144.
48 Rothacher *op. cit.* pp. 52-60.
49 Reading, B. *Japan: the coming collapse*. Orion, London. 1992. p. 134.
50 i. Hrebenar *op. cit.* pp. 75, 263
   ii. Holstein *op. cit.* pp. 135, 139.
51 Wolf, M. J. *The Japanese conspiracy. The plot to dominate industry world-wide and how to deal with it*. Empire Books, USA. 1983. New English Library, London. 1984. pp. 48-65.
52 Azumi, K. *Higher education and business recruitment in Japan*. Columbia University. 1969.
53 Van Wolferen *op. cit.* p. 179.
54 i. Jain and Inoguchi *op. cit.* pp. 114 115.
   ii. Reading *op. cit.* pp. 253-4.
   iii. Rothacher *op. cit.* pp. 102-8.
   iv. Van Wolferen *op. cit.* pp. 167-87.
55. i. Herzog *op. cit.* pp. 175-95, 205.
   ii. Holstein *op. cit.* pp. 109-121.

## REFERENCES

    iii. Hrebenar *op. cit.* p. 75.
    iv. Reading *op. cit.* pp. 158, 263-71, 282-4.
    v. Rothacher *op. cit.* pp. 102-22.

56 'Japan's government shaken as justice minister resigns'. *Financial Times*. London. 10 October 1995.
57 Holstein *op. cit.* pp. 111-2.
58 Bailey *op. cit.* p. 170.
59 Herzog *op. cit.* pp. 152-95, 268-70.
60 'Fallen political kingmaker'. *Japan Times*, Tokyo. 29 March 1996.
61 Shiba, K. *Oh Japan! Yesterday, today and probably tomorrow.* Norbury, Tenterden, Kent. 1979.
62 'The Kanemaru scandal and its roots in the Japanese system'. *Tokyo Business Today*, Tokyo. November 1992.
63 Herzog *op. cit.* p. 207.
64 Holstein *op. cit.* p. 113.
65 Sato, K. 'Media's role, ties to Establishment in spotlight'. *Japan Times*, Tokyo. 19 January 1994.
66 Terazono, E. 'A hack out of the old block'. *Financial Times*, London. 18 August 1994.
67 'A working list of the *kisha* clubs'. *No. 1. Shimbun. Journal of the Foreign Correspondents Club*, Tokyo. Vol. 18. No. 6. June 1968.
68 Hall, I. P. 'Segregated scribes. The foreign correspondents'. *Cartels of the mind. Japan's intellectual closed shop.* , Norton, New York. 1998. pp. 45-79.
69 Fukunaga, H. 'Time to break the MOF taboo'. *Tokyo Business Today*, Tokyo. January 1995.
70 'TV stations apologise to Matsumoto man'. *Japan Times*, Tokyo. 7 June 1995.
71 Fukunaga, H. 'Aum sweet Aum: the cult that shook Japan'. *Tokyo Business Today*, Tokyo. June 1995.
72 i. 'TBS denies showing tape to cultists'. *Japan Times* Tokyo. 20 March 1996.
    ii. Bracket, D. W. *Holy terror. Armageddon in Tokyo.* Weatherhill, New York. 1996. p 11.
73 Moriguchi, K. 'Cultists held on misdemeanour charges'. *Japan Times*, Tokyo. 15 April 1995.
74 'Agency fights to get access to press club'. *Japan Times,,* Tokyo. 25 May 1993.
75 Takahashi, Y. 'And that's the way it is. Or is it ?' *Look Japan*. Vol. 41. No. 469. Look Japan, Tokyo. April 1995.
76 Ushio, S. 'Japan's sacred cows prove too much for Newsweek's editors'. *Tokyo Business Today*, Tokyo. August 1993.
77 i. Upham, F. K. 'Environmental tragedy and response'. *Law and social change in post-war Japan*. Harvard University. 1987. pp. 28-77.
    ii. Huddle, N. , Reich, R. and Stiskin, N. *Island of dreams. Environmental, crisis in Japan*. Autumn Press, New York, Tokyo. 1975.
78 Kitazume, T. 'Role of Emperor in society is still unclear'. *Japan Times*, Tokyo. 3 November 1990.
79 'Suit over public-information access fails. Ban upheld on photocopying political-fund documents'. *Japan Times*, Tokyo. 25 February 1995.

80  Stockwin, J. A. A. 'Reforming Japanese politics: highway of change or road to nowhere?' Jain and Inoguchi *op. cit.* p. 90, n. 7.
81  Wada *op. cit.* p. 17.
82  Rothacher *op. cit.* pp,120-2.
83  i. Herzog *op. cit.* pp. 190-1.
    ii. Reading *op. cit.* pp. 250, 256, 270.
84  Sato, S. 'LDP redivivus: the failure of electoral reform'. *Japan Echo*, Tokyo. Spring 1997.
85  Fukunaga, H. 'Ryutaro Hashimoto: tough guy at the helm once again'. *Tokyo Business Today*, Tokyo. November 1995.
86  'Another apology from Hashimoto'. *The Economist*, London. 27 September 1997.
87  'The agenda of a Liberal Democratic Party leader'. Koichi Kato interviewed by Gerald L. Curtis. *Japan Echo*, Tokyo. December 1997.
88  Jain, P. C. and Todhunter, M. 'The 1996 general election: status quo or step forward?' Jain and Inoguchi *op. cit.* pp. 224-38.
89  'Japan under the new LDP'. Kiichi Miyazawa interviewed by Fumiya Shinohara. *Japan Echo*, Tokyo. June 1998.
90  Nakamoto, M. 'LDP shrugs off its electoral setbacks to extend its stranglehold on power'. *Financial Times*, London. 18 December 1998.
91  Maya, M. 'Rise in the postal savings worries commercial bankers'. *Japan Times*, Tokyo. 19 November 1992.
92  i. 'Japan's other debt crisis'. *The Economist*, London. 12 December 1998.
    ii. Kosaka, M. 'The paradox of Japanese politics'. *Japan Echo* Tokyo. Vol. XV. No. 4. 1998.
93  Tett, G. 'After the banks. Japan's public finances are in a mess'. *Financial Times*, London. 1 February 1999.
94. i. Calder, K. E. *Strategic capitalism. Private business and public purpose in Japanese industrial finance*. Princeton. 1993. pp. 59-62, 279-83.
    ii. Harvey, R. *The undefeated. The rise, fall and rise of Greater Japan*. Macmillan, London. 1994. pp. 398-9.
    iii. Hsu, R. C. *The MIT Encyclopaedia of the Japanese economy*. MIT, Cambridge, Mass. 1994. pp. 139-40, 230-1, 277-8.
    iv. Pyle, K. B. 'Economic nationalism'. *The making of modern Japan*. Ch. 14. Heath, Lexington, Mass. 1996. pp. 247-8.
95  Terazono, E. 'Japan wrestles with budget demon'. *Financial Times*, 28 August 1995.
96  Kakinuma, S. and Nakamura, M. 'Japan's national mega bank also sells stamps'. *Tokyo Business Today*, Tokyo. September 1994.
97  Baker, G. 'Postmasters who beat the banks and deliver votes. Growing complaints of unfair competition in deposits'. *Financial Times*, London. 31 October 1995.
98  Prestowitz, C. V. *Trading places. How America is surrendering its future to Japan and how to win it back*. Tuttle, Tokyo. 1989. p. 239.
99  'Return to sender'. *The Economist*, London. 18 October 1997.
100 Dawkins, W. 'Borderless guru hits brick wall. Politicians are not so keen on reform !' *Financial Times, London*. 5 April 1995.

101 'Japan: the man who keeps saying no'. *The Economist*, London. 10 April 1999.
102 Sayle, M. Quoted in Rothacher *op. cit.* p. 274.

## 5 WILL IT EVER CHANGE?

1 Quoted in Fingleton, E. *Blindside*. Simon and Schuster, London. 1995. p. 49.
2 Quoted in Thomas, R. *Japan: the blighted blossom*. Tauris, London. 1989. p. 151.
3 Quoted in Pyle, K. B. 'The Japan question: power and purpose in a new era'. American Enterprise Institute Press. Washington. 1992. p. 36.
4 Quoted in Prestowitz, C. V. *Trading places*. Tuttle, Tokyo. 1989. p. 248.
5 Quoted in Sakakibara, E. *Beyond capitalism. The Japanese model of market economics*. University Press of America. 1993. p. 9.
6 *op. cit.* Quoted in Introduction by Prestowitz, C. V. p. xii.
7 Quoted in Eatwell, J. *Whatever happened to Britain?* BBC, London. 1982. pp. 89-90.
8 cf. Johnson, C. *MITI and the Japanese Miracle*. Tuttle, Tokyo. 1982.
9 Moorhouse, J. MEP. Report on trade and economic relations between the EC and Japan. *European Parliament Working Documents A 2-86/86. PE 101. 033 fin.* 10 July 1986. pp. 5-6.
10 'Japan trade surplus soars to £74 billion high'. *Financial Times*, London. 26 January 1999.
11 *Financial Times*, London. 14 July 1998.
12 *Tokyo Business Today*, Tokyo. November 1993.
13 Moorhouse, J. MEP. Letter to *Financial Times*, London. 15 December 1997.
14 Horsley, W. and Buckley, R. *Nippon, new superpower*. BBC, London. 1990. pp. 163-8.
15 Prestowitz, C. V. *Trading places*. Tuttle, Tokyo. 1989. pp. 116-7
16 Fukushima, G. S. Review of 'Law and trade issues of the Japanese economy'. *Journal of Asian Studies,* Washington. Vol. 47. No. 4. November 1988.
17 Huber, T. M. *Strategic economy in Japan*. Westview, Boulder, Co. 1994. pp. 93-157.
18 Fukushima, G. S. 'It's *tamamushi iro* again!' *Tokyo Business Today*, Tokyo. September 1995.
19 Fukushima, G. S. 'Fallacies of political change'. *Tokyo Business Today*, Tokyo. September 1993.
20 Sakakibara *op. cit.*
21 Fingleton *op. cit.* pp. 6, 343.
22 Dodwell Marketing Consultants. *The structure of the Japanese motor components industry*. Dodwell, Tokyo. 1979. pp. 5-6.
23 Tett, G. 'GE Capital seeks further Japan buys'. *Financial Times*, London. 23 February 1999,
24 *Financial Times*, London. 25 January 1999.
25 *Financial Times*, London. 'Making tracks for Japan'. 4 February 1999.

26 *Financial Times*, London. 20/21 February 1999.
27 i. Cusumano, M. *The Japanese automobile industry*. Harvard University. 1985.
   ii. Halberstam, D. *The reckoning*. Bloomsbury, London. 1986.
28 *The Economist*, London. 20 March 1999.
29 *Sunday Times*, London. 21 March 1999.
30 Harney, A. 'Nissan chiefs at crossroads with long, weary journey ahead'. *Financial Times*, London. 23 March 1999.
31 Gibney, F. 'Nissan calls for a tow'. *Time Magazine*. 15 March 1999.
32 *The Economist*, London. 9 January 1999.
33 Fukushima, G. S. 'Perception gap hurts US and Japan'. *Los Angeles Times*. 13 November 1998.
34. Hosokawa, M. 'An examination of the existing gap between foreigners' perceptions of Japanese wealth and the actual situation'. *Japan Close-Up*, Tokyo. September 1991.
35 Quoted in Huddle, N. and Reich, R. *Island of Dreams*. Autumn Press, Tokyo. 1975. p. 78.
36 Garon, S. *Moulding Japanese minds. The State in everyday life*. Princeton. 1997.
37 Hall, i. P. *Cartels of the mind. Japan's intellectual closed shop*. Norton, New York. 1998.
38 Dale, P. N. *The myth of Japanese uniqueness*. Routledge, London. 1986. p. i.
39 Fallows, J. 'Containing Japan'. *The Atlantic Monthly*, Boston. Vol. 263. No. 5. May 1989.
40 Dale *op. cit.* p. 141.
41. i. Miyamoto, M. *Straitjacket society*. Kodansha International, Tokyo. 1994.
   ii. Miyamoto, M. 'Bureaucracy's magic mirror'. *Japan Times*, Tokyo. 7 February 1994.
   iii. Miyamoto, M. 'Envy, discrimination and masochism are the foundation of Japanese society'. *Tokyo Journal*, Tokyo. May 1993.
42 Johnson, C. 'The people who invented the mechanical nightingale'. *Showa: the Japan of Hirohito*. Daedalus. Proceedings of the American Academy of Arts and Sciences. Summer 1990. p. 86.
43 Ohmae, K. *Beyond national borders*. Kodansha International, Tokyo. 1987. pp. 3-4, 67-8.
44 Hirschmeier, T. and Yui, T. *The development of Japanese business 1600-1975*. Allen and Unwin, London. 1975. p. 296.
45 Ennis, P. *Tokyo Business Today*, Tokyo. January 1990. Quoted in Prestowitz, C. V. 'New directions of US-Japan relations in a new era'. *Japan Close-Up*, No. 6. Kansai Economic Federation. March 1993.
46 Fingleton *op. cit.* pp. 180-86.
47 Sakakibara *op. cit.*
48 Sakakibara, E. 'The once and future boom'. *The Economist*, London. 22 March 1997.
49 Hollerman, L. 'The headquarters nation'. *The National Interest*, Washington. Fall 1991.
50 Fallows, J. *op. cit.*
51 Choate, P. *Agents of influence*. Knopf, New York. 1990. p. 143.

# REFERENCES

52 Lawrence, R. Z. 'Japan's low levels of inward investment'. *Foreign Direct Invest*ment. Ed. Froot, K. A. National Bureau of Economic Research. University of Chicago. 1994.

53 Fingleton *op. cit.* p. 137-41.

54 Quoted in Prestowitz *op. cit.* p. 240.

55. i. Noguchi, Y. 'The persistence of the 1940 setup'. *Japan Echo Special Issue*, Tokyo. 1977.

ii. Tsukada, N. and Fukunaga, H. 'In Japan the war is over but the 1940 system lives on'. *Tokyo Business Today* Tokyo. September 1995.

56 Seki, E. *Speech to the Japan Society,* London. March 1996.

57 Quoted in Thomas *op. cit.* p. 93.

58 Sakakibara, E. 'Change and continuity in modern Japan'. *Japan Echo Special Issue* Tokyo. 1997.

59. i. 'Three unelected governments in a row . *Financial Times*, London. 8 January 1996.

ii. 'LDP's return to power leaves voters bewildered'. As above.

iii. 'The old order returns in Japan'. *Straits Times quoted in Japan Times*, Tokyo. 18 January 1996.

60 McCormack, G. *The emptiness of Japanese affluence*. Sharpe, Armonk. 1996. p. 197.

61 *Tokyo Business Today*, Tokyo. December 1994.

62 'Hard reality beats out idealism. International organizations drawing few Japanese'. *Japan Times*, Tokyo. 30 June 1995.

63 'Japan minister gives assurance on nuclear arms. Document revealed nuclear option was studied'. *Financial Times*, London. 4 August 1994.

64. i. 'Leakproof?' *The Economist*, London. 20 January 1996.

ii. Harvey, R. *The undefeated: the rise, fall and rise of Greater Japan*. Macmillan, London. 1994. pp. 578-82.

65 Rothacher, A. *Europe's Japan problem: Japanese corporate strategies and the Western response*. European University Institute, Fiesole. 4 June 1992.

66 Fukushima, G. S. 'Washington door-knock'. *Tokyo Business Today*, Tokyo. May 1995.

67 'European executive hits decontrols'. *Japan Times*, Tokyo. 4 April 1995.

68 Van Marion, M. F. *Liberal trade and Japan: the incompatibility issue*. Physica, Heidelberg, 1993. pp. 49-50.

69 Fielding, Sir L. *Lecture of 14 November 1995 to the Japan Society,* London.

70 'US short of answers as Japan trade gap swells'. *Financial Times*, London. 23 February 1999.

71 Denman, Sir R. 'US-Japan trade dispute may lead to WTO bust up'. Letter to *Financial Times*, London. 2 June 1995.

72 Time. 14 August 2000.

73 *Daily Telegraph*. 23 June 2000.

74 'Japan's voters wafted along by divine wind'. *Sunday Times*. 25 June 2000.

75 'Divine Japan gaffe recalls war policies'. *Daily Telegraph*. 17 May 2000.

76 'Japan's leader'. *Financial Times*. 5 April 2000.

77 Fukuyama, F. *The End of History and the Last Man*. Hamish Hamilton, London. 1992.

78 'Japan "not backsliding" on financial reforms'. *Financial Times*. 7 March 2000.
79 'Japanese minister forced to quit after bank gaffe'. *Financial Times*. 26-27 February 2000.
80 'Softbank group in negotiations to buy NCB'. *Financial Times*. 25 February 2000.
81 *Time*. 14 August 2000.
82 i. 'Japan's first domestic hostile bid is defeated'. *Financial Times*. 15 February 2000.

 ii. 'Shoei's woes give Japan's management a rude awakening'. *Financial Times*. 3 February 2000.

 iii. 'Challenging Japan's cozy corporate culture'. *Time*. 7 February 2000.
83 'Union protest challenges Renault'. 'Job cuts shock Nissan town'. *Financial Times*. 25 January 2000.
84 'Beauty and beast of the new Japan'. *The Guardian*. 15 February 2000.
85 *Financial Times*. 25 January 2000.
86 i. 'Recession or recovery: the figures don't add up'. *Financial Times*. 13 March 2000.

ii. 'Japan plans to overhaul statistics'. *Financial Times*. 17 March 2000.
87 'Japan plans consolidated national accounts'. *Financial Times*. 8 February 2000.
88 'The sun also rises'. *Sunday Times*. 16 April 2000.
89 Fingleton, E. *In praise of Hard Industries. Why manufacturing, not the information economy is the key to future prosperity*. Houghton Mifflin, Boston. 1999.
90. Garon, S. *op. cit.* p. 237.
91 i. 'Preparing to compete in the wider world'. *Financial Times*. 28 March 2000.

 ii. Lee Kuan Yew. *The Singapore Story. Memoirs of Lee Kuan Yew*. Singapore Press Holdings. Times Editions. 1998. pp. 53-83.

# Bibliography

Abegglen, J. C. *The Japanese factory: aspects of its social organization*. Free Press, Glencoe, Ill. 1958.

Abegglen, J. C. and Stalk, J. *Kaisha: the Japanese corporation. How marketing, money and manpower strategy, not management style, make the Japanese world pacesetters*. Harper & Row, New York. 1985.

Alletzhouser, A. *The house of Nomura*. Bloomsbury, London. 1990

Alexander, S. *Sweet Kwai, run softly*. Merriots Press, Bristol. 1995.

Arai, S. *Shoshaman: a tale of corporate Japan*. University of California. 1991.

Bailey, P. J. *Postwar Japan: 1945 to the present*. Blackwell, Oxford. 1996.

Ballon, R. *The Japanese employee*. Sophia University, Tokyo. 1969.

Brackett, D. W. *Holy terror: Armageddon in Tokyo*. Weatherhill, New York. 1996.

Braddon, R. *The other 100 Years War: Japan's bid for supremacy 1941-2041*. Collins, London. 1983.

Buruma, I. *The wages of guilt: memories of war in Germany and Japan*. Vintage, Random House, London. 1995.

Calder, K. F. *Strategic capitalism. Private business and public purpose in Japanese industrial finance*. Princeton University. 1993.

Chang, I. *The rape of Nanking: the forgotten Holocaust*. Basic Books, New York. 1997.

Choate, P. *Agents of influence. How Japan's lobbyists in the United States manipulate America's political and economic system*. Knopf, New York. 1990.

Cole, R. E. *Japanese blue collar: the changing tradition*. University of California. 1971.

Cole, R. E. *Work, mobility and participation: a comparative study of American and Japanese industry*. University of California. 1979.

Cortazzi, Sir H. 'The rape of Nanking: a cover-up'. *Japan Echo Vol. XVIII. Autumn 1991* Tokyo.

Courtis, K. S. *The purge of Japan's economy. The most difficult phase ahead*. Deutsche Bank Capital Markets (Asia). Tokyo. 17 August 1992.

Cusumano, M. A. *The Japanese automobile industry*. Harvard University. 1998.

Cutts, R. L. 'Power from the ground up: Japan's land bubble'. *Harvard Business Review*. May-June 1990.

Dale, P. N. *The myth of Japanese uniqueness.* Routledge, London. 1990.

Davies, P. N. *The man behind the bridge: Colonel Toosey and the River Kwai.* Athlone, London. 1991.

Daws, G. *Prisoners of the Japanese: POWs of World War II in the Pacific.* Morrow, New York. 1994.

Dean, P. S. W. 'A guest of Japan, uninvited and invited'. *Proceedings 120. Japan Society, London.* Autumn 1992.

De Vos, G. and Wagatsuma, H. *Japan's invisible race. Caste and culture in personality.* University of California. 1967.

De Vos, G. *Socialization for achievement.* University of California. 1973.

Dodwell Marketing Consultants. *Industrial groupings in Japan.* Dodwell. Tokyo. Annual.

Dodwell Marketing Consultants. *The structure of the Japanese motor components industry.* Dodwell, Tokyo. 1979.

Dower, J. W. *Japan in war and peace.* New Press, New York. 1993.

Dower, J. W. *War without mercy. Race and power in the Pacific War.* Pantheon, New York. 1986.

Duus, P. , Myers, R. H. and Peattie, M. P. *The Japanese wartime empire 1931-45.* Princeton University. 1966.

Edwards, J. *Banzai, you bastards.* Souvenir Press, London. 1990. Japanese translation *Kutabare jap yaro.* Komishi Shobo, Tokyo. 1992.

Ederer, G. *Das leise Lächeln des Siegers.* Econ Verlag, Düsseldorf. 1991.

Eatwell, J. *Whatever happened to Britain?* BBC, London. 1982.

Emmott, B. *The sun also sets. Why Japan will not be Number one.* Simon & Schuster, London. 1989.

*Entrepreneurship: the Japanese experience.* PHP Institute, Kyoto. 10 issues 1982-3.

European Business Community (EBC). *White Paper on commerce and industry.* EBC, Tokyo. 1998.

European Commission, Brussels. *List of EU deregulation proposals for Japan.* 1996.

European Commission, Brussels. *Summary of market access problems in Japan.* 1996.

Eurostat. *The EU and Asia.* Eurostat, Luxembourg. 1995.

Executive committee, International Public Hearing. *War victimization and Japan.* International public hearing report. Toho Shuppan, Tokyo. 1993.

Fairbank, J. K. , Reischauer, E. O. and Craig, A. M. *East Asia: the modern transformation.* Tuttle, Tokyo. 1958.

Fallows, J. 'Containing Japan'. *Atlantic Monthly,* Boston. Vol. 263. No. 5. May 1989.

Fay, S. *The collapse of Barings.* Random House, London. 1996.

Fingleton, E. *Blindside. Why Japan is still on track to overtake the US by the year 2000.* Simon & Schuster, New York. 1995.

Fingleton, E. *In praise of Hard Industries. Why manufacturing, not the information economy is the key to future prosperity.* Houghton Mifflin, Boston. 1999.

Fransman, M. The market and beyond. Cambridge University. 1990.

Fukushima, G. S. Review of 'Law and trade issues of the Japanese economy'. *Journal of Asian Studies.* Washington. Vol. 47. No. 4. November 1988.

# BIBLIOGRAPHY

Fukushima, G. S. 'Tales from a trade veteran'. *Journal of the American Chamber of Commerce in Tokyo*. 1991.

Fukuyama, F. *The End of History and the Last Man*. Hamish Hamilton, London. 1992.

Garon, S. *Moulding Japanese minds: the state in everyday life*. Princeton University. 1997.

Gibney, F. 'Nissan calls for a tow'. *Time* Magazine. 15 March 1999.

Gibney, F. ed. *Senso: the Japanese remember the Pacific War*. Letters to the editor of the Asahi Newspaper. Sharpe, Armonk, New York. 1995.

Gold, H. ed. *Unit 731 testimony*. Yen Books, Tokyo. 1996.

Goodman, G. K. ed. *Japanese cultural policy in SE Asia during World War II*. Macmillan, London. 1991.

Goodwin, M. J. *Shobun: a forgotten war crime in the Pacific*. Stackpole Books, Mechanicsburg, PA. 1995.

Halberstam, D. *The reckoning. How Japan beat the US in the automobile industry war and rewrote the rules of international business competition*. Bantam, New York. 1987.

Hall, I. P. *Cartels of the mind. Japan's intellectual closed shop*. Norton, New York. 1998.

Halliday, J. and McCormack, G. *Japanese imperialism today. 'Co-prosperity in Greater East Asia'*. Penguin, Harmondsworth, Middx. 1973.

Hardacre, H. *Shinto and the State 1968-1988*. Princeton University. 1989.

Harries, M. & S. *Soldiers of the sun: the rise and fall of the Imperial Japanese Army*. Random House, New York. 1991.

Harris, S. H. *Factories of death: Japanese biological warfare 1932-45 and the American cover-up*. Routledge, London. 1994.

Hartcher, P. *The ministry*. Harvard Business School. 1998.

Harvey, R. *The undefeated: the rise, fall and rise of Greater Japan*. Macmillan, London. 1994.

Hearn, L. *Japan: an attempt at interpretation*. Tuttle, Tokyo. Reprint 1995.

Herzog, P. *Japan's pseudo-democracy*. Japan Library, Folkestone, Kent. 1993.

Hicks, G. *The comfort women*. Yen Books, Tokyo. 1995.

Hicks, G. *Japan's hidden apartheid: the Korean minority and the Japanese*. Ashgate, Aldershot, Hants. 1997.

Hicks, G. *Japan's war memories: amnesia or concealment* ? Ashgate, Aldershot, Hants. 1997.

Hijiya-Kirschnereit, I. 'Nanking in Japanese literature'. *DIJ newsletter No. 2, October 1997*. German Institute for Japanese Studies, Tokyo.

Hirschmeier, J. , and Yui, T. *The development of Japanese business 1600-1980*. Allen & Unwin, London. 1981.

Hofstede, G. *Cultures and organisation: software of the mind*. Harper, Collins. London. 1994.

Hogan, M. J. ed. *Hiroshima in history and memory*. Cambridge University. 1996.

Hollerman, L. 'International economic controls in occupied Japan'. *Journal of Asian Studies, USA. Vol. xxxviii, No. 4. August. 1979*.

Hollerman, L. *Japan's economic strategy in Brazil: challenge for the United States*. Macmillan, London. 1985.

Holstein, W. J. *The Japanese power game: what it means for America*. Scribners, Macmillan, New York. 1990.

Horan, W. H. *Visions of infamy*. St Martins Press, New York. 1991.

Horsley, W. and Buckley, W. *Nippon, new superpower: Japan since 1945*. BBC, London. 1990.

Howard, K. ed. *True stories of the Korean comfort women*. Cassell, London. 1995.

Hrebenar, R. J. *The Japanese party system*. Westview, Boulder, Co. 1992.

Hsu, R. C. *The MIT encyclopaedia of the Japanese economy*. Massachusets Institute of Technology. 1994.

Hu, Y-S. *National attitudes and the financing of industry*. Policy Studies Institute. London. 1975.

Huber, T. M. *Strategic economy in Japan*. Westview, Boulder, Co. 1994.

Huddle, N. , Reich, R. and Stiskin, N. *Island of dreams. Environmental crisis in Japan*. Autumn Press, New York, Tokyo. 1975.

Huie, S. F. *The forgotten ones: women and children under Nippon*. Angus & Robertson, Pymble, New South Wales. 1991.

Ienaga, S. *The Pacific War 1931-45*. Pantheon, New York. 1978.

Inohara, H. *Human resource development in Japanese companies*. Asian Productivity Organisation, Tokyo. 1990.

Irokawa, D. *In search of modernity*. Free Press, New York. 1995.

Ishida, H. *Social mobility in contemporary Japan educational credentials, class and the labour market in a cross-national perspective*. Stanford University. 1993.

Iwabori, Y. *The management of YKK: Yoshida's business philosophy*. Senko Kikaku, Tokyo. 1978.

Jain, P. and Inoguchi, T. eds. *Japanese politics today*. Macmillan, Australia. 1997.

Jansen, M. B. ed. *Changing Japanese attitudes towards modernization*. Princeton University. 1969.

Japan Times. *The Great Hanshin earthquake*. Special report. Japan Times, Tokyo. 1995.

Japan Times. *Terror in the heart of Tokyo*. Special report. Japan Times, Tokyo. 1995.

Johnson, C. *Japan - who governs? The rise of the developmental state*. Norton, New York. 1995.

Johnson, C. *MITI and the Japanese economic miracle: the growth of industrial policy 1925-1975*. Tuttle, Tokyo. 1982.

Johnson, C. 'The people who invented the mechanical nightingale'. *Showa, the Japan of Hirohito*, Proceedings, American Academy of Arts and Sciences. Vol. 119, No. 3. Summer 1990.

Kamata, S. *Japan in the passing lane. An insider's account of life in a Japanese automobile factory*. Allen & Unwin, London. 1983.

Kaplan, D. E. and Dubro, A. *Yakuza. The explosive account of Japan's criminal underworld*. , Futura, London. 1987.

Kawanishi, H. *Enterprise unionism in Japan*. Kegan Paul, London. 1992.

Kawanishi, H. ed. *Japan im Umbruch. Gewerkschafter berichten über Arbeitskämpfe der Nachkriegsära*. WSI des Deutschen Gewerkschaftbundes. Düsseldorf. 1989.

Kawasaki, I. *Japan unmasked*. Tuttle, Tokyo. 1969.

Keenan, J. *Unlocking Japan's distribution system in the '90s*. Canadian Communication Group, Ottawa. 1994.

Kershaw, G. *Tracks of death*. Book Guild, London. 1992.

Kobayashi, K. *The rise of NEC*. Blackwell, Oxford. 1989.

Koh, B. C. *Japan's administrative elite*. University of California. 1989.

Krauss, E. S. , Rohlen, T. P. and Steinhoff, P. G. eds. *Conflict in Japan*. , University of Hawaii. 1984.

Lamont-Brown, R. *Kempeitai: Japan's dreaded military police*. Sutton, Stroud, Glos. 1998.

Lawrence, R. Z. 'Japan's low levels of inward investment'. Froot, K. A. ed. *Foreign Direct Investment*. National Bureau of Economic Research. University of Chicago. 1994.

Livingston, J. , Moore, J. and Oldfather, F. *The Japan reader: Vol. 1. Imperial Japan 1800-1945*. Penguin, Harmondsworth, Middx. 1976.

Livingston, J. , Moore, J. and Oldfather, F. *Vol. 2. Postwar Japan to the present*. Penguin, Harmondsworth, Middx. 1976.

Lomax, E. *The railwayman*. Vintage, Random House. London. 1996.

Lyons, N. *The Sony vision*. , Crown, New York. 1976.

Magaziner, I. C. and Hout, T. M. *Japanese industrial policy*. Policy Studies Institute, London. 1980.

Maruyama, M. *Thought and behaviour in modern Japanese politics*. Oxford University. 1969.

McCormack, G. *The emptiness of Japanese affluence*. Sharpe, Armonk, New York. 1996.

McCormack, G. and Nelson, H. *The Burma-Thailand railway*. Allen & Unwin, Australia. 1993.

Mitchell, R. H. *Censorship in Imperial Japan*. Princeton University. 1983.

MITI. *Small business in Japan*. White Paper on small and medium-sized enterprises (SMEs) in Japan. SME Agency, MITI. Tokyo. Annual.

Miyamoto, M. *Straitjacket society. An insider's irreverent view of bureaucratic Japan*. Kodansha International, Tokyo. 1994.

Moorhouse, J. MEP. Report on trade and economic relations between the EC and Japan. *European Parliament Working Documents A 2-86/86. PE 101. 033 final*. 10 July 1986.

Moorhouse, J. MEP, and Teasdale, A. *Righting the balance: a new agenda for Euro-Japanese trade*. Conservative Political Centre, London. 1987.

Morita, A. *Made in Japan*. Fontana, London. 1987.

Mosca, G. *The ruling class*. Greenwood, London. 1980.

Murakami, H. and Hirschmeier, J. eds. *Politics and economics in contemporary Japan*. Kodansha International, Tokyo. 1979.

Nakagawa, Y. and Ota, N. *The Japanese style economic system. A new balance between intervention and freedom*. Foreign Press Centre, Tokyo. 1981.

Nakane, C. *Japanese society*. Penguin, Harmondsworth, Middx. 1973.

Ohmae, K. *Beyond national borders: reflections on Japan and the world*. Kodansha International, Tokyo. 1987.

Ozawa, I. *Blueprint for a new Japan*. Kodansha International, Tokyo. 1994.

Prestowitz, C. V. *Trading places. How America is surrendering its future to Japan and how to win it back*. Tuttle, Tokyo. 1991.

Prindl, T. K. ed. and trans. *Kinjo, the corporate bouncer and other stories from Japanese business*. Sharpe, Armonk, New York. 1989.

Pyle, K. B. *The making of modern Japan*. Heath, Lexington, Mass. 1996.

Reading, B. *Japan, the coming collapse*. Orion, London. 1992.

Reischauer, E. O. and Fairbank, J. K. *East Asia: the great tradition*. Tuttle, Tokyo. 1958.

Reischauer, E. O. *The Japanese today: change and continuity*. Tuttle, Tokyo. 1988.

Rohlen, T. P. *For harmony and strength: Japanese white-collar organization in anthropological perspective*. University of Columbia. 1974.

Rothacher, A. *Europe's Japan problem: Japanese corporate strategies and the Western response*. European University Institute, Fiesole, Florence. 4 June 1992.

Rothacher, A. *The Japanese power elite*. Macmillan, London. 1993.

Sakai, K. and Sekiyama, H. *Bunsha: improving your business through company division*. Taiyo Industrial Company, Tokyo. 1985.

Sakai, K. and Russell, D. *To expand, we divide*. Intergrace, Tokyo. 1993.

Sakai, K. *Lives in the making: the story of a manufacturing family*. Intergrace, Tokyo. 1991.

Sakai, K. 'The feudal world of Japanese manufacturing'. *Harvard Business Review*. November-December 1990.

Sakaiya, T. *What is Japan ? Contradictions and transformations*. Kodansha International, Tokyo. 1993.

Sakakibara, E. *Beyond capitalism: the Japanese model of market economics*. Introd. Prestowitz, C. V. University Press of America, Lanham, MD. 1993.

Samuels, R. J. *'Rich nation: strong army': national security and the technological transformation of Japan*. Cornell University. 1994.

Sazanami, Y. , Urata, S. and Kawai, K. *Measuring the cost of protection in Japan*. Institute for International Economics, Washington. 1995.

Schaller, M. *Altered states: the United States and Japan since the Occupation*. Oxford University Press, New York. 1997.

Shiba, K. *Oh Japan! Yesterday, today and probably tomorrow*. Norbury, Tenterden, Kent. 1979.

Shimazaki, H. T. *Vision in Japanese entrepreneurship: the evolution of a security enterprise*. Routledge, London. 1992.

Steslicke, W. A. *Doctors in politics: the political life of the Japan Medical Association*. Praeger, New York. 1973.

Storry, R. *A history of modern Japan*. Penguin, Harmondsworth, Middx. 1961.

Sumitomo Corporation. *From the history of Sumitomo*. Sumitomo Corporation, Osaka. 1980.

Sun Tzu. *The art of war*. Hodder & Stoughton, London. 1995.

Sun Tzu. *The art of war for executives*. Commentary Krause, D. G. Brealey, London. 1996.

Sun Tzu. McNeilly, M. *Sun Tzu and the art of business. Six strategic principles for managers*. Oxford University Press, New York. 1996.

Taira, K. *Economic development and the labour market in Japan*. Columbia University, New York. 1970.

Tanaka, H. *Personality in industry: the human side of a Japanese enterprise*. Pinter, London. 1988.

# BIBLIOGRAPHY

Tanaka, Y. *Hidden horrors: Japanese war crimes in World War II*. Westview, Boulder, Co. 1996.

Thomas, R. *Japan: the blighted blossom*. Tauris, London. 1989.

Tipton, E. K. *The Japanese police state: the Tokko in interwar Japan*. Athlone, London. 1990.

Toyota, E. *Toyota: fifty years in motion*. Kodansha International, Tokyo. 1987.

Terzani, T. 'Wir sind die Erben der Samurai'. *Der Spiegel*, Hamburg. Nr. 26-27. 1990.

Trevor, M. H. 'Japan: what international managers should know'. *Pacific Rim Management 1996*. American Management Association, New York. 1996.

Trevor, M. H. *Japan's reluctant multinationals*. Pinter, London. 1983.

Tsuji, K. ed. *Public administration in Japan*. University of Tokyo. 1984.

Tsutsui, Y. *Effectiveness of branch regulation in Japanese banking*. Hitotsubashi University, Tokyo. 1989.

Upham, F. K. *Law and social change in postwar Japan*. Harvard University. 1987.

Van Marion, M. F. *Liberal trade and Japan: the incompatibility issue*. Physica, Heidelberg. 1993.

Van Wolferen, K. *The enigma of Japanese power*. Tuttle, Tokyo. 1993.

Ventura, R. *Underground in Japan*. Cape, London. 1997.

Wada, J. *The Japanese election system*. Routledge, London. 1996.

Waldenberger, F. 'Firms and markets: why is Japan so different?' German Institute of Japanese Studies, Tokyo. *Miscellanea. Working paper No. 8. May 1994*.

Wickert, E. ed. *The good German of Nanking. The diaries of John Rabe*. Little, Brown, London. 1999.

Williams, P. and Wallace, D. *Unit 731*. Hodder & Stoughton, London. 1989.

Warner, L. and Sandilands, J. *Women beyond the wire*. Arrow, London. 1997.

Wolf, M. J. *The Japanese conspiracy. The plot to dominate industry worldwide - and how to deal with it*. New English Library, London. 1984.

Wood, C. *The bubble economy: the Japanese economic collapse*. Tuttle, Tokyo. 1992.

Woronoff, J. *Japan as anything but Number One*. Yohan, Tokyo. 1990.

Woronoff, J. *Japan, the coming economic crisis*. Yohan, Tokyo. 1992.

Woronoff, J. *Japan, the coming social crisis*. Lotus, Tokyo. 1982.

Woronoff, J. *Japan's commercial empire*. Macmillan, London. 1984.

Woronoff, J. *Japanese targeting. Successes, failures, lessons*. Macmillan, London. 1992.

Woronoff, J. *Japan's wasted workers*. Lotus, Tokyo. 1991.

Yanaga, C. *Big business in Japanese politics*. Yale University. 1968.

PERIODICALS

*The Economist*, London.
*The Financial Times*, London.
*The Guardian*, London.
*The Japan Times*, Tokyo.
*Japan Echo*, Tokyo.
*Look Japan*, Tokyo.

*The Spectator*, London.
*The Sunday Times*, London.
*Time* Magazine, London edition.
*The Times*, London.
*Tokyo Business Today*, formerly *The Oriental Economist*, Tokyo.
*Tokyo Journal*, Tokyo.

# Index

'administrative guidance' 5, 24, 58, 146, 152–6, 158, 160, 196, 232
Aisin 177
Allison, Ambassador 192
All Nippon Airways 144, 196
*amakudari* 6, 8, 146, 156–9, 167, 168, 184, 189, 208, 232
Amaya, Naohiro 63, 210–1, 212, 214, 220
*Art of War* xii, xiii, 24, 64, 90, 218
Asia xxiii, 1, 4, 5, 27, 28, 42, 45, 57, 63, 66–7, 72, 76, 91, 108, 124, 133, 134–5, 210, 216, 225
ASICS 179
Ataka takeover 30
Aum Shinrikyo xxv, 72–3, 127, 135, 168, 198, 202–3
Austria 121

'bean counters' xi, 37, 48, 218, 225
'Black Ships' 77, 93
BMW 32
Brazil 28
Brittan, Sir Leon xix, 39
Brother 177
business schools 48

Cable & Wireless 227
California xiv, 17, 18, 21
Canon 177
capitalism, Anglo–Saxon ix, xi, 32, 33, 40, 46, 48, 145, 147–8, 151, 152, 159, 160, 210, 227
capitalism, Japanese xi, xv, 33, 40–1, 148, 151, 211–5, 217, 221, 226–7

Carnegie, Andrew 178
China 27, 36, 80–2, 91, 94–5, 99, 103–5, 106, 108, 111, 119–20, 123, 131, 218, 225
Chubu Gas 177
Colbert xv
Cold War xv, 19, 46, 49, 64, 119, 187, 215–6
Communism xv, 58, 67, 71, 73–4, 93, 102, 104, 115, 168, 185, 192
comparative advantage xv, 147, 212
Confucius 5
'convergence' 37, 81, 213

Dai-Ichi Kangyo 166
Daimaru 177
Daiwa Bank 12–3, 15, 33
Daiwa Securities 2, 9, 23, 27
*dango* 189, 232
Democratic Socialist Party 184, 198–9
Denman, Sir Roy 1, 224
Dodge, Joseph 47

Eisai 177
Electricity Utility Industry Council 138–9
*endaka* xx, 19, 27, 59, 231, 232
EU xi, xiii, xvi, xxii–iii, 2, 20, 28, 36, 39–40, 42, 57, 58, 65, 69, 139, 213, 221, 224
EU Delegation, Tokyo xxiv, 173, 223
EU exports 21, 29, 35, 147, 196, 213–4
EU–Japan auto agreements 34–5, 43, 171

269

EU-Japan Centre, Tokyo xi, xiii–iv, 4, 8, 11, 24, 50, 55, 57, 61–2, 66, 133, 139, 143, 159, 195
European Business Community (EBC), Tokyo xix, xx, 224
Ezaki Glico 177

Fanuc 177
FILP 'second budget' 206–7
Ford 31–2, 77, 151, 179, 216, 217
France xv, 46, 57, 83, 100, 145, 217
Fuji Bank 173, 194
Fukuda 189
Fuyo 227

*gaijin* (foreigners) 3, 67
General Motors 151, 216
Germany 70–1, 96, 99, 100, 108, 121, 128, 133, 135–6, 144, 175, 183
Glaxo 30
*go* (game) 27–8, 34, 152, 232
'Greater East Asia Co-Prosperity Sphere' 28, 106–7, 122–3

Hanix 9
Hayek, Friedrich 41
Hearn, Lafcadio 78, 88, 93, 96
Hitachi 54, 166
Hollerman, Leon 47
Honda 32, 174, 178
*honne* xviii, 41, 45–6, 52–4, 209, 215, 226, 232
Houdaille 49–50, 195

incompatibility of business systems viii, 32
individualism 5, 52, 60, 71, 93, 122, 219, 222
Industrial Bank of Japan (IBJ) 22, 166, 173
Industrial Revolution 77, 89, 92
information as competitive weapon (see also *tatemae*) xii, 4, 43, 48, 51, 64, 70
Iron Triangle xii, xx, xxii–iii, 4, 17, 137, 141, 142, 145, 150, 163, 156, 160, 161, 169, 179, 188, 201, 208, 213, 220
Isetan 9, 177
Ishihara, Shintaro 120–1, 209
Isuzu 33
Italy 46, 225, 229

Ito-Yokado 177

Japan – accounting practices 5–7, 9, 10, 14, 30, 207,
Air Lines 7
Bank of 1, 2, 15, 39, 138, 155–6, 157, 226
'Big Bang' xvii, 8, 26–7
Big Business xi, 15, 36, 103, 161–79, 213, 221
'bubble' economy x, xxi, xxiv, 18–22, 33–5, 54, 58, 216, 225
bureaucrats xi, xvi, xix, xxv, 3, 5, 8–9, 11, 14, 23, 45, 47, 53, 58, 62, 69, 70, 137–60, 161, 175, 184, 189, 190, 191
cartels ix, 2, 3, 137–8, 152, 156, 158, 159, 164, 201, 219, 224
censorship 58, 60, 87, 89, 110, 113, 115–8, 120, 126, 131, 138, 201–3
company unions 31, 54, 162, 168, 172–3, 176, 227
consumers associations xxii
deregulation xvii, xix, 35, 138, 146–7, 214, 215, 224
Diet xx, 25, 39, 104, 121, 133, 149, 159, 163–4, 168, 170, 181, 184, 186, 193–4, 197, 199, 208, 225
electoral system 181, 183–5, 190, 192–4, 204–6
Emperor xx, 65, 78–82, 84, 94–8, 103, 105–6, 108–9, 111, 117, 120, 122, 127–8, 129–30, 144, 153, 168, 203–4, 225
employment conditions 4–6, 140, 148, 161–3, 176, 210–1, 218
entrepreneurs 91, 138, 158, 175, 178–9
Establishment 43, 44, 52, 80, 209
family-controlled companies xvii, 177
feudalism 5, 11, 89, 144, 174
foreign exchange reserves 218, 228
groupism xiv, 71–2, 220
industrial banking 29
'internationalization' xvii, 39, 65, 68, 210, 220
joint ventures 29, 30–2, 221
journalists (*kisha*) clubs xx–i, 3, 51, 176, 201–3, 222, 232

# INDEX

labour markets 66, 157, 162, 174–6, 210–1
law xvi–ii, xx, 10–1, 24, 67, 118, 132, 139–40, 141, 144, 152–4, 160, 161–2, 204, 217
licencing system xvi–ii, xix, 138–40, 158, 170, 196
management power xiv, 161–2, 173, 177–8
mercantilism xv, 147, 214, 226
mergers and acquisitions 8, 30, 31–2, 155, 226–7
military forces 72, 84–5, 97, 99, 135–6, 186
minority problems xiii, 61
'1955 System' 168–9, 191
non–tariff barriers xix, 35, 64
normative values 56–7, 60–1, 64–5, 67, 71, 73, 74, 75–6, 83–4, 85–6, 90, 93, 95–6, 122, 133, 142, 143–4, 191
nuclear capability 110, 223
official slogans 95–6, 219
official statistics 14, 228
organized crime 6, 7, 9, 20–1, 22, 25, 67, 137, 181–2, 187, 195, 204
outcastes xiii, 61, 88–9, 199, 232
part-time employees 54, 162, 176
'permanent' employees 16, 54, 162, 176
political corruption 25, 60, 104, 140, 141, 158–9, 170, 181, 185–6, 188–9, 193–4, 195, 197–200, 207–8
political factionalism xii, 40, 159, 180, 190, 197, 226, 232
political violence 103–4
politico-economic system ix, xi, 14, 32, 37, 43, 60, 67, 100, 141–2, 145–6, 148, 152, 157, 172, 188, 200, 201, 213, 220, 221
politics xi, xvii, xx–i, 3, 40, 95–8, 137, 153, 163–4, 180–209, 221
postal savings 207–8
public corporations 157–8, 208, 218, 228
restless competitor 37, 143, 161
small and medium firms (SMEs) 27, 33, 43, 54, 99, 162–3, 166, 173, 174–6, 177
social control 40–1, 75, 87, 89, 95, 98, 176, 218–9

stereotypes ix, xxii–iii, 5, 32, 37, 43, 45, 50, 56, 60, 65
stock exchange 1, 6, 8, 25, 36, 46, 51, 167, 177, 194
temporary employees 54, 162, 176
ultra-nationalism 76, 79, 82, 84, 101, 106, 109, 115, 127, 130, 134, 187, 204, 209
union federations 134
'uniqueness' xiv, 64, 68, 71, 78, 80, 98, 147–8, 219
university cliques 143–4, 177
war victim' 108, 110–1, 112–3, 121
Japan Bicycle Association 50, 195
 Chamber of Commerce 165, 167, 174
 Communist Party 104, 184
 Economic Foundation 63
 External Trade Organization (JETRO) xvi, 28, 43, 63
 Industrial Standard 43, 151–2
 -Italy Auto Agreement 43
 Medical Association 165
 National Railways (JNR) xxi, 3, 38, 149, 173, 207, 213
 Problem xi, 5, 43, 73
 Socialist Party 2, 98, 142, 168, 183, 184, 186, 190, 193, 195, 198–9
Japanese Red Army 85, 135, 168
*jusen* (see also scandals) xxi, xxiv, 6, 20–1, 38, 171, 207
Just in Time (JIT) systems 19
JVC 33

Kagome 177
Kajima 177, 189
Kanemaru, Shin ('Don') 24, 137, 180, 182, 189, 198, 200, 201, 205
Keidanren 151, 152, 163, 165, 167, 168–70, 172, 174, 191, 197, 210, 215, 227
*keiretsu* 2, 9, 15, 29, 100, 165, 167, 170, 174, 175, 176, 178–9, 227, 232
Keizai Doyukai 165, 167, 175, 197
Keizai Koho Centre 172
Kikkoman 177
Kirin 9, 28
Kissinger, Henry xi, 150

Kobe earthquake xxv
Komeito 184, 197, 199, 200
Konica 9
Korea xiii, 1, 46, 61, 80, 81–2, 99, 100–1, 102, 103, 108, 114–5, 125, 186
Kuroda, Makoto 148
*kuromaku* 24, 180, 182, 189, 197, 232
Kyocera 179

Lee Kuan Yew 5, 135–6, 222, 229
Lenin 66
Liberal Democratic Party (LDP) xvii, 18, 34, 60, 77, 78, 84, 98, 103, 114, 115, 117, 128, 137, 140, 141–2, 147, 158, 167–72, 180–1, 186, 189, 190, 193–4, 199, 205–6, 208–9, 225–6
Lion 177
List, Friedrich xv, xvi, xviii, 29, 40, 48, 50, 59, 146, 152, 159, 218
Long-Term Credit Bank (LTCB) 38, 39
Louvre Agreement 19, 20, 231

MacArthur, General 46, 109, 136, 150
Maekawa Mission xvi
Maine, Sir H. 11
Makita 177
'managed trade' xix, 215
Mansfield, Ambassador 49, 50
Manufactured Imports Promotion Org. xvi
Marubeni 196
Matsushita 9, 21, 32, 54, 91, 166, 178
Mazak 49
Mazda 20, 31–2, 217
Meiji Restoration 94–101, 106, 112, 144, 151, 213, 219
Ministry – of Agriculture (MAFF) 138, 158, 224
  Construction 159, 181
  Education 5, 75–8, 95, 98, 107, 110, 113, 115–8, 120–1, 127–8, 132–3, 138–9, 197, 201
  Finance (MOF) xii, xxiv, 2, 6, 10–4, 16, 20, 22, 23–4, 29, 35; 38–9, 137–8; 143, 151–2, 154, 156–9, 181, 184, 207, 217, 226
  Foreign 70, 81, 105, 107, 159, 172, 220, 221, 223

Health & Welfare (MHW) 8, 119, 138–9, 155
Home Affairs 159, 184, 190, 204
International Trade & Industry (MITI) xiii, xvi, xxii, xxiv, 16–7, 28, 35–6, 38, 47–8, 50, 58, 63, 138, 143, 145, 147–8, 150–3, 159, 168, 172, 174, 195, 212, 214, 228
Justice 125, 143, 153
Posts & Telecommunications xvii, 152–3, 197, 207–8
Transport 50, 129, 139, 141, 144, 159, 180, 195, 196
Mitsubishi 9, 20, 21, 29, 34, 36, 99, 155, 156, 163, 166, 171
Mitsui 9, 47, 92, 99, 104, 156, 163, 165, 166, 172, 196
Moorhouse, James MEP ix, 213
Morita, Akira 32, 37, 148, 151, 167, 192, 212
Motorola xvii–iii
Mussolini 41, 115, 129

NEC 167
*nemawashi* 191
Netherlands 91–2, 126
*Nihonjinron* 64–6, 68, 71, 75, 80, 219–20
Nikkeiren 162, 165, 167, 172, 174, 197
Nikko Securities 2, 22, 24
Nippon Credit Bank (NCB) 217, 226
Nippon Steel 166, 170, 174
Nissan 20, 31–2, 43, 151, 156, 166, 172–3, 175, 178, 217, 218, 227
Nomura Securities 2, 3, 6–7, 22–4, 25–7
NTT 198–9, 227

OECD 212, 220
Ohmae, Kenichi 56, 77, 155, 208–9, 210
oil crisis xxi, 31
Ojimi, Yoshihisa 212–3, 214, 220
Okinawa xiii, 61, 92, 113, 127–8
Okita, Saburo 48, 150
Omron 177
Ono, Bamboku 149
Orwell, George xxii, 28, 53, 65, 72, 75, 78, 91, 107, 113, 116, 133, 150, 220
Ozawa, Ichiro 171, 184, 189, 190, 205

# INDEX

pachinko 195
Pickens, T. Boone 30
Pioneer 177
Plaza Agreement xx, xxi, 19, 27, 36, 231
Portugal 86
Prime Minister – Ashida 195
   Fukuda 194, 195
   Hashimoto 23, 25, 36, 39, 115, 125, 128, 159, 186, 194, 205–6, 208
   Hata 190
   Hatoyama 169, 187
   Hosokawa 121, 135, 190, 218
   Ikeda 159, 169, 195
   Kaifu 123–4, 180, 191, 194, 200, 205–6
   Katayama 168, 191
   Kishi 47, 116, 123, 129, 130–1, 159, 169, 186, 195
   Miki 187, 191, 194, 197
   Miyazawa 18, 180, 190, 191, 198–9, 200, 201, 205
   Mori 225, 226
   Murayama 102, 128, 132, 168, 186, 191, 198, 205
   Nakasone 132–3, 145, 182, 189, 197, 198–9, 200, 201, 205, 213
   Obuchi xxi, 18, 225
   Ohira 197, 205
   Sato 85, 115, 159, 191, 195
   Suzuki 197
   Takeshita 24, 180, 182, 188–9, 191, 194, 198–9, 200, 201, 205
   Tanaka 3, 115, 182, 187–8, 190, 193–4, 196–7
   Uno 170, 199, 200, 205
   Yoshida x, 130, 159, 169, 170, 195, 222
   1945-2000 complete list 192
   murders of 103–4
privatization xi, xxi, 38, 39, 173

quality control xiv, 19, 43, 52–3, 133, 151, 227
Quayle, Vice-President 212

Reischauer, Ambassador 50, 76, 77, 80, 89–90, 133, 143, 219
Renault 217, 227

Sakakibara, Eisuke ('Mr.Yen') 151, 216, 220, 222

Sanwa 166
Sanyo 33, 166
Sanyo Special Steel 7
Sasakawa, Ryoichi 50, 115–6, 129–30, 195, 222
scandals – Daiwa Bank 12–3, 15, 33
   *jusen* xxi, 6, 20–1, 38, 156–7, 171
   Lockheed 3, 144, 187–8, 190, 195, 196–7, 205
   McDonnell Douglas 187–8, 196
   Minamata 204
   Nippon Shoji 8
   Recruit 8, 187, 194, 195, 197–200, 201, 205
   Sagawa Kyubin 139–40, 200. 205
   securities companies 22–7
   shipbuilding 168, 195
   Showa Denko 195
   Sumitomo copper 15–8, 33
SECOM 179
Second World War xi, xiv, 2, 15, 20, 35, 43, 76–7, 79, 107–14, 134–6, 168, 205, 222
Seibu 166
Seiko (Hattori) 177
Sharp 33
Shionogi 177
Shiseido 177
Showa bank crash (1927) 4, 104
Smith, Adam xv, xxiii, 37, 40, 47–8, 50, 64, 71, 96, 147, 152, 160
Social Darwinism 96
Social Democratic Party of Japan 171, 183, 193
*sokaiya* 6, 7, 29, 154, 191, 233
Sony 21, 32, 33, 36, 37; 179
Soviet Union, Russia ix, xxii, 40–1, 46, 53, 64, 67, 74, 100–1, 131, 151, 153, 168, 186, 215
Spain 86, 91
Spencer, Herbert 96
Stalin 10, 101
Sumitomo 8, 10, 11, 13–15, 24, 26, 28, 32–3, 78, 84, 123, 131, 141, 148, 152, 231
Suntory 204
Sun Tzu xii, 4, 24, 64–5, 70, 90, 218
Sunshine City 131
Suzuki 177
Switzerland xiii, 121, 187

Tadano 177
Takashimaya 177

Takeda 8, 177
Takenaka 177, 189
*tamamushi iro* 215, 233
*tanshin funin* 163
*tatemae* xiii, xv, xvii–iii, 3, 8, 10, 23,
    41, 45–6, 52–4, 61–3, 71–2,
    82–3, 87, 116–7, 123, 138, 145,
    154, 164, 167, 183, 190, 196,
    209, 211, 215, 226, 232
*tobashi* 7, 227, 233
Tokai 166
Tokyo Gas 177
Tokyu 25, 166, 177
Toshiba-IHI 166, 172
Toyota 9, 30, 36, 54, 151, 166, 171,
    172, 175, 177, 178, 227
trade frictions xiv–v, xviii–ix, xx–i,
    20, 34–5, 37, 39, 43, 49, 63,
    143, 147, 148, 150, 159, 166,
    172, 186, 189, 213–5, 216,
    223–4

UK xv, xxii, 17–8, 31, 43, 83, 91, 99,
    103, 121, 131, 161, 163, 174–5,
    178
United Nations 125, 135, 147, 222–3
USA x, xi, xvi, xxii, 3, 14, 16–7, 19,
    21, 28, 30, 32, 42, 46, 49, 52,
    67, 83, 97, 103, 112, 131–2,
    145, 148–50, 184, 192, 196,
    210, 214, 221, 224–5
US Commerce Secretary xi

US-Japan Security Treaty xi, 169,
    186–7, 209
US Presidents – Carter 115
    Eisenhower 169
    Fillmore 77, 83
    Jackson xv
    Madison xv
    Reagan 50, 194
    Roosevelt 111
US trade deficits xv, xxi, 20, 147
US Trade Representative (USTR)
    xviii, xx, 37, 49, 214, 216,
    223

Weber, Max 5, 11, 141

*yakuza* 10, 15, 20–1, 22, 38, 67, 115,
    182, 191, 203, 225, 233
Yamaichi Securities xvii, 1, 2, 4–5,
    10, 23, 27, 36, 44, 74
Yamato Kyubin 140
Yasuda 99, 166
Yasukuni Shrine 80, 84, 114, 131,
    132, 135
Yen-dollar exchange rate xx, xxv, 2,
    19, 20, 27, 59, 228, 231
YKK 44, 178

*zaibatsu* 7, 47, 99, 104, 163–5, 233
*zaikai* 163, 165, 169
*zaiteku* 33, 233
*zaito* (see also FILP) 206–7, 233